STRATEGIC SUPPLY MANAGEMENT

A Blueprint for Revitalizing the Manufacturer-Supplier Partnership

KEKI R. BHOTE

American Management Association

This book is available at a special
discount when ordered in bulk quantities.
For information, contact Special Sales Department,
AMACOM, a division of American Management Association,
135 West 50th Street, New York, NY 10020.

Library of Congress Cataloging-in-Publication Data

Bhote, Keki R., 1925–
    Strategic supply management : a blueprint for revitalizing the
manufacturer-supplier partnership / Keki R. Bhote.
        p.   cm.
    Includes index.
    ISBN 0-8144-5925-0
    1. Industrial procurement—Management.   2. Competition,
International.   I. American Management Association.   II. Title.
HD39.5.B488   1989
658.7'2—dc20
                                                                88-48029
                                                                    CIP

Printing number

10   9   8   7   6   5   4   3   2   1

To my wife,
Mehroo,
whose loyal support and absolute faith
have been a tower of strength during my
burning the midnight oil in the creation
of my books.

Contents

List of Figures and Tables

Foreword

The idea that the supplier and the professional customer are partners is one whose time has come. As each commercial organization marches to its objective of customer satisfaction, it is self-evident that the quality of our offerings will be the sum total of the excellence of each player in our supply stream.

In manufacturing, a common formula of product cost states that material procured from outside sources aggregates nearly 50 percent of that cost. Clearly, suppliers play a major role in the customer satisfaction objective. The achievement of that customer satisfaction is going to require virtual perfection on the part of the entire supply system within the next few years. Virtual perfection cannot be accomplished without cooperation. Cooperation is a synonym for partnership.

This book makes the case for the win-win relationship between supplier and customer. It details practical ways and means inside and between each shop.

But in so doing, it challenges the participants to reach out instead of handing off. That seems to be the hard part for designers, specifiers, and negotiators on the procurement side. They are used to "doing their job" and handing off an assignment to competing suppliers. The procurement side people are not used to bringing others into their deliberations early or entertaining others' detail suggestions. The buying party presumes that time will be unduly consumed and that objectivity will be lost in the negotiating process.

Simultaneously, many suppliers have not prepared themselves sufficiently with talent that is readily available nor do they have the compatible interfacing skills needed to work well during the early involvement period.

Indisputable case evidence shows that if each party reaches out effectively to the other, the effort and time employed by early mutual involvement in design and in specifying ultimately saves time and cost and enhances quality. The negotiating process may be modified but is not compromised.

This book *is* a blueprint aimed at those ends. Appropriately employed, it can help responsible professionals record bolder and blacker print on that proverbial line at the bottom.

Robert W. Galvin
Chairman of the Board
Motorola Inc.

Acknowledgments

When does the germ of an idea for writing a book get planted? For me, the start was the example of my mother—a famous author in India. She nurtured in me the love of writing. Her prescription was to research a subject so thoroughly and to examine it from all angles so completely that the urge to share one's findings with the public became the engine of authorship. To her, I owe everything.

The second great influence in my life has been Bob Galvin, Chairman of the Board of Motorola. His leadership, as one of the truly great captains of American industry, his vision, and his abiding faith in people have been a beacon light to guide and inspire me.

Perhaps, my greatest teacher and most revered "guru" has been Dorian Shainin, a giant in the world of quality. His admonition "Talk to the parts, they are smarter than the engineers" has been the foundation of the many designed experiments that I have conducted.

Another guiding light has been Don Bohl, the publisher of the Management Briefing series of the American Management Association (AMA). His encouragement and powerful support have not only made this book possible, but also my earlier books published by AMA. I am especially grateful to Adrienne Hickey, the Senior Editor for Planning and Acquisitions at AMA, for her pivotal role in creating this book and for her coaching at every turn. I also wish to thank Richard Gatjens for his patience and counsel as editor, as well as Bob McCarten and Harry Salant of AMA for their sponsorship of my seminars, on which this book is based.

At Motorola, many colleagues have made significant contributions to this book: Bill Schmidt, who led the way with the first supplier partnership process within the company; Ken Stork, who coined the phrase "Supply Management" and is the very center of gravity of Motorola's efforts to convert hands-off suppliers into productive partners; Tom Reardon, who established the most successful "Partnership for Growth" process within the Communications Sector; Bill Wiggenhorn and Carlton Braun for their brilliant insights from a training and education perspective; Jim Baum, Gary Cox, Kathy Sullivan, Bob Growney, Bob Becknell, Harry Woodworth, Norm Sanders, Bob Wasni, Tom Koch, Joe Archie, Sylvio Scatchell, Carl Cooper, Jane Smith, Lu Gustafson, Jean Seeley, Dick Wendt and Luke Salmon, for their help—by their practice, not precept.

I also gratefully acknowledge the contributions of scores of suppliers, customers and other benchmark companies who have been the crucibles for testing, honing, and polishing the principles and practices contained in this book.

Finally, my heartfelt thanks go out to my family: to my son, Adi, whose practice of many of these principles will soon overtake mine; to my daughters Safeena and Shenaya and my son Xerxes for their loyal support and absolute faith; and above all to my wife, Mehroo, who has sustained me in countless ways and has been a tower of strength at every step of the long journey from concept to completion.

Keki R. Bhote

Part I

SETTING THE STAGE

Chapter 1

The Deindustrialization and Reindustrialization of America

Why is there such a difference in productivity, quality, and cost between U.S. and Japanese companies? . . . Japanese manufacturers make a profit when they locate in the U.S., but American manufacturers have to move abroad to beat competition. The conclusion is inescapable: The problem lies in American management. I ask the well-meaning people of the United States to begin America's re-industrialization in earnest.

—Hajime Karatsu, Keizai Koho Center, Japan Institute for Social and Economic Affairs

The Parable of the Tank of Milk

There is an oft-quoted parable in India involving that country's greatest emperor, Akbar. The monarch wanted to give nourishment to the slum children in his capital. He directed each household to pour one jar of milk, overnight, into the mosque tank to build up a reservoir of milk. Hundreds of his affluent subjects responded that night. The next morning the tank was filled alright—but with clear water instead of milk! Perplexed, Akbar turned to his prime minister, the omniscient Birbal, for an explanation. "Your Majesty," Birbal responded, "you have just witnessed a classic case of individ-

3

ual gain and collective loss. Each household dumped a jar of water into the tank, hoping that it would go undetected among the hundreds of gallons of milk brought by others. But all households had the same idea. The result: a tank of useless water instead of nourishing milk!''

The Threat of Deindustrialization

This folktale has a parallel within the industrial United States. Confronted by stiff international competition, high manufacturing costs, and eroding profits, many U.S. companies have been scrambling to go offshore for their manufacturing and purchased materials. For the short term and on a company-by-company basis, this strategy for survival is understandable. For the long term, however, it can spell national suicide. The addition of each company's jar of water could leave the U.S. tank with no milk. Carried to its ultimate absurdity, the practice could produce a land without suppliers, without manufacturing, without an industrial base!

The Hemorrhaging of the U.S. Supplier Base

The statistics are grim. Until the dollar plunged to its lows in world currency levels, 20,000 to 30,000 manufacturing workers were losing their jobs each month, according to U.S. Bureau of Labor statistics. On the supplier front, there are already several commodities for which no viable U.S. suppliers exist. The steel supply base is decimated. Machine tools have lost their competitive edge. Even the much-vaunted, hi-tech semiconductor industry, as a supplier to the world of computers and other twenty-first-century types of products, is fighting to maintain its world-class leadership. Quite apart from the implications of these trends for national security, can the United States afford this economic hemorrhage? With the loss of manufacturing yesterday and of suppliers today, can customer companies—including our large (OEM's)—survive tomorrow? And can U.S. consumers, who up to now have carried the world's greatest market on their broad shoulders, continue to consume without jobs? The growing service sector cannot fill this manufacturing/supplier void: It can never be as large or as high-paying. It is unthinkable that the United States could be reduced to an ignominious hamburger-exchange economy.

"Emigrate, Automate, or Evaporate"

The typical U.S. response to this threat is captured in the slogan "emigrate, automate, or evaporate." The rationale for emigration is based on the no-madic search, in developing country after developing country, for the mirage of a reduction in direct labor costs. The chase continues, despite the fact that direct labor costs today constitute less than 5 percent of the sales dollar. Belatedly, there is a growing awareness that—given the hidden costs of poor quality, the need for increased technical support from home, and long cycle times—offshore production is not necessarily a bargain.

Hence the thirst for automation—programmable automation. If the goal of automation is to reduce direct labor, however, it is as much a will-o'-the-wisp as offshore production. Further, automation without simplification is a cure worse than the disease. Computerization, in the absence of an effective systems approach, can generate useless information at the speed of light! It is not surprising, then, that some suppliers, especially the smaller ones, are resigned to evaporation and extinction. They want to throw in the towel and sell out, before it is too late.

From Business-as-Usual to Protectionism

Several suppliers, who have neither gone offshore or automated, fall into a few unproductive classifications:

- *The "business as usual" types.* For them, the halcyon postwar years have not ended.
- *The "looking for the pony" types.* These are the optimists, buoyed by the plunge in the dollar vis-à-vis the yen.
- *The "whistling loudly past the graveyard" types.* They are the nervous Nellies who proclaim with more bravado than conviction a manifest U.S. destiny.
- *The "quick fix" types.* They move from fad to fad—quality circles, zero defects, suggestion systems, zero-base budgeting, organizational development, whatever top management dictates as the program of the month—without tangible improvements.
- *The "protectionist" types.* They camouflage their inability to compete internationally with appeals to Congress for trade barriers, couching them in "fair trade," "reciprocal trade," and "level playing field" slogans.

A Blueprint for Success

Is there hope? Can American suppliers slug it out with foreign competition and win? Can a blueprint be developed that will systematically improve the major parameters of suppliers' business performance? Can such a blueprint have universal scope: from food products to electronics, from metal stampings to high tech? Can it apply to small companies with limited resources as well as to large companies with "leverage"? Can the blueprint be used both by a company's customers and by its suppliers? The answer is a confident and unequivocal *yes!* The objective of this book is to set forth in detail just such a blueprint.

If you are a manager in a customer company, you will be able to greatly—and continually—improve the quality, cost, and cycle time of your purchased materials. You will learn about such powerful tools as commodity teams, design of experiments, multiple environment overstress tests, *poka-yoke,* cost targeting, value engineering, group technology, and drastic lead-time reduction.

If you are a manager in a supplier company, not only will you learn how these tools apply to you and to your supplier; you will also learn how to secure longer-term contracts, larger dollar volumes, and higher profits from your customers.

With the use of the techniques described in the following chapters, the resulting improvement levels could be as dramatic as those pictured here.

Improvements	*Levels*
1. Quality	100 times current levels and more
2. Material costs	Up to 10% overall cost reduction every year
3. Delivery	Near-instant customer delivery without a build-up of finished goods inventory
4. Inventory turns	From the current 3 to 6 turns up to 50 and more
5. Cycle time	10 times current levels and more
6. Profit on sales	Double current levels and more
7. Return on investment	Triple current levels and more
8. Meeting the Japanese challenge	Recapturing lost customers

The Reindustrialization of America

The improvements shown in the preceding table are not just theoretical possibilities. Scores of leading U.S. corporations are already implementing the techniques described in this book. Among the front runners are the automotive companies. They are coaching their suppliers in quality improvement, in general, and statistical process control, in particular. The methods of these companies are somewhat dictatorial and sometimes misguided, but they have clearly set the pace for the tiers of suppliers that largely depend on them for their business. The major aerospace companies are also mounting similar campaigns with their suppliers. Although there are many other companies on this honor roll, mention must be made here of the "perennial greats": IBM, Xerox, Hewlett Packard, Motorola, 3M, General Electric, Black & Decker, and Westinghouse. They are demonstrating to their suppliers, by example, not precept, that it is possible to achieve plateaus of competitiveness that were considered almost beyond reach even in the mid 1980s.

Reverse Traffic Across the Pacific

There is yet another unconventional source of encouragement. It is paradoxical that as the U.S. companies rush to East Asia, a reverse traffic across the Pacific simultaneously brings Japanese entrepreneurs intent upon establishing manufacturing companies in the United States. There are now more than 500 Japanese-owned, Japanese-managed companies here—almost all of them successful. These "transplants" operate under the same political, union, and industrial "handicaps" that old-time American companies now use as push-button excuses for their poor performance. The critical difference is *management!*

While the less competitive U.S.-owned companies are preoccupied or burdened with such extraneous concerns as stock prices, quarterly reports, the tyranny of the financial analysts, hostile takeovers, and short-term profits, the Japanese transplants in the United States march to a different drummer. They worship customers, not profit. They promote supplier partnerships, not supplier confrontations. They utilize the worker's brain, not just his brawn: They listen to him, encourage him, actually treat him as a resource, not just as a springboard for pious and empty slogans. And always, but always, they elevate quality to a superordinate value. Together with well-managed U.S.-owned companies, they are proving that there is nothing culturally ingrained about Japan's industrial success.

The Revolution in Industrial Assumptions

Before beginning the long journey toward full U.S. supplier competitiveness, let us first examine some of the old myths that have governed our industrial outlook since World War II and assess the new realities that we must confront for the 1990s. Table 1-1 compares the old, post-World War II model of industrial assumptions with the new model needed for the next decade and beyond.

In terms of product, whereas the old model projects long life cycles and design cycle times, the 1990s model adjusts to ever-shortening product life cycles and the urgent need for reduced design cycle times as one of the most important ways of beating competitors to the punch. Manufacturing here has been rescued from its subservient role in the old model to play a major corporate strategy in the new. Large factories producing unrelated products with long sustained runs are giving way to focused factories producing related products in small quantities with quick setup changes. The battles between functional and matrix organizations in the old model are made

Table 1-1.   The revolution in industrial assumptions.

Old, Post-World War II Model	*New Model for the 1990s*
1. Long product life cycle (10–20 years)	1. Short product life cycle (2–5 years)
2. Narrow product families	2. Proliferation of options
3. Long design cycle time (2–4 years)	3. Short design cycle time (6–18 months)
4. Manufacturing considered an appendage	4. Manufacturing considered a key strategy
5. Large factories producing everything	5. Focused factories producing product families
6. Long production runs	6. Economic build quantity (EBQ) $\rightarrow$ 1
7. Concentration on direct labor reduction	7. Focus on: • Materials cost reduction • White-collar cycle time reduction • Manufacturing cycle time reduction
8. Automation	8. Flexible manufacturing systems (FMS)
9. Fitting people into preconceived organizational charts	9. Tailoring organizational charts to fit worker talents
10. Functional and matrix organizations	10. Ad hoc team organizations
11. Use of worker's brawn	11. Use of worker's brain
12. Workers' ideas severely limited	12. Workers' ideas a fountain of creativity
13. Manager as boss	13. Manager as consultant/coach
14. Supplier an antagonist	14. Supplier a partner
15. Long supplier lead times (8–18 weeks)	15. Short supplier lead times (1–2 weeks)
16. Economic order quantity (EOQ): A formula approach	16. EOQ $\rightarrow$ 1
17. Quality is expensive	17. High quality, low cost synonymous
18. Acceptable quality level (AQL) dependency	18. AQL $\rightarrow$ 0
19. Traditional quality control	19. Design for experiments (DOE) and statistical process control (SPC) in product/process development
20. End customer as the only customer	20. Next operation as customer

Figure 1-1. Characteristics of the factory of the future.

The Seven "Ones"

- Economic build quantity (EBQ)[1] approaches 1.
- Inventory turns[2] approach 1 per day.
- Data integrity (count accuracy)[3] approaches 100%.
- Factory overall efficiency[4] approaches 100%.
- Product quality[5] approaches 100%.
- Management involvement[6] approaches 100%.
- Happy, creative, productive people[7] approach 100%.

---

[1] EBQ currently 100–1,000 units.
[2] Inventory turns currently 2 to 18 turns per year. Ideal cycle time should be 2 times direct labor time.
[3] Count accuracy currently at 50%.
[4] Factory overall effectiveness (FOE) = up time × machine efficiency × nondefect rate (FOE currently at 10% to 75%).
[5] Quality (composite yield) currently at 25%–85%.
[6] This means:
 • Management involvement with people.
 • Manager as consultant, not boss.
[7] Worker currently hired for brawn, not brain.

obsolete by the preeminence of interdisciplinary teams in the new model. And the team building block does not even show up in that expression of bureaucracy known as the organization chart!

The manager's approach to people is also changing radically as the role of boss or authority gives way to that of a consultant and coach responsible for sustaining workers' ideas and encouraging their enthusiastic participation. Finally, in the old model quality is viewed as a necessary evil; high quality and low cost are seen as incompatible; and brute-force inspection and test are accepted as the only means of achieving quality. The new model places quality at center stage as the most effective of all cost-reduction tools and achieves it through defect prevention at the design stage of a product or process, primarily through the powerful technique of "design of experiments."

The Seven "Ones"

Another perspective on the long-range goals for tomorrow's factory is shown in Figure 1-1 as the seven "ones" (or 100 percent).

Economic build quantity (EBQ). In the factory of the future, long production runs or even quantities based on EBQ formulas must give way to a figure approaching *one* for maximum responsiveness to the ever-increasing diversity of customer tastes and demands. Further, this must be done at even lower costs than long, sustained runs.

Inventory turns must move from the dreary, single-digit numbers per year characteristic of most U.S. industries to the ideal of *one* turn per day or 300 per year. (Some U.S. companies are matching Toyota's record of more than 100 turns per year.)

Data integrity must be elevated to a 100 percent correlation between recorded and actual data versus the current dismal achievement of 50 percent, despite manufacturing requirement planning (MRP) and computer networking.

Factory Overall Effectiveness is a new paramater that multiplies machine up time, machine efficiency—that is, cycle time/(cycle time + setup time)— and the nondefect rate. Ideal efficiencies should approach 100 percent as opposed to the current range of 10 to 75 percent.

Quality is measured in several ways. In manufacturing, the best measure is overall, or composite yield, from one end of the factory to the other. This yield should approach 100 percent as opposed to the yields 25 percent and 85 percent that are now widely prevalent. (Even an 85 percent yield means a defect rate of 15 percent, or 150,000 defective parts per million (ppm). This is the expanded scale that is increasingly used to express quality levels.)

Management Involvement. No management sin is as widespread or as corrosive as the autocratic style that instills fear among employees or, at the very least, turns off the spigot of worker creativity and participation. In the factory of the future, the manager must be visible to his people: he must listen to them and be 100 percent involved with them, in the best tradition of a sports coach.

Worker Creativity and Productivity: Given such management involvement, plus training, encouragement, and support, workers can achieve, with enthusiasm, the self-fulfilling prophecy of creativity and productivity.

Prerequisites for Success

To restore U.S. competitiveness and sustain it over long periods of time, American industry must keep the following essential points in mind.

1. Most important, American management must return to its roots and recapture the leadership qualities it once took such pride in. This involves the inculcation of superordinate values to bind the company into cohesive unity; the worship of the customer over the worship of profit; and a genuine concern for employees that brings out the best in them.

2. The customer company must be the role model for its suppliers; in short, it must be a practitioner of all the techniques described in this book, not a preacher. How can a customer company insist on one and two orders of magnitude in quality improvement from its suppliers if its own quality practices are antediluvian? How can a customer company demand adherence to effective supplier statistical process control if all it knows is control charts, an aging technique with limited usefulness! How can a customer company demand reduced costs from its suppliers when it has little knowledge—and even less implementation—of powerful cost-reduction tools such as value engineering, early supplier involvement, and group technology? How can a customer company pound a supplier for reduced lead times when its own cycle time, in terms of work in process, is from ten to twenty times a maximum theoretical cycle time? Nothing can erode credibility more in the minds of anxious suppliers, willing to do the right thing, than the hypocrisy of the customer company sending out telltale signals of "Do as I say, don't do as I do!"

3. The customer company's expertise in quality, cost, and cycle time tools must be transferred to the supplier company through frequent visits, training, and problem solving. Assistance by table pounding or remote control are about as effective in bringing about quality improvements as internal management exhortations and pious pronouncements generally are.

4. Finally, the momentum of a breakthrough in a supplier's quality, cost, and cycle time performance cannot be sustained if it is confined to just one pair of supplier-customer relationships. This is only one link in the long chain of supplier-customer pairs, ranging from raw materials to the consumer. A customer company should make certain that this blueprint of success is extended beyond its immediate suppliers to their suppliers, subsuppliers, and subsubsuppliers.

With these prerequisites in place, U.S. competitiveness will be on the launching pad, ready for lift-off.

Chapter 2

The Four Stages
of Supply Management

There are four stages in manufacturing, supply management, and quality—from Stage 1: Primitive, to Stage 4: World Class. Customer and supplier companies must first assess which stage they are in—and then mount a process to rapidly advance to Stage 4, if they are to be players in the major leagues of world class competition.

—Keki R. Bhote, American Productivity and Inventory Control Conference,
San Francisco, July 12, 1988

What Is Supply Management?

Since the late 1950s, there has been an uneven transition from the old concept of purchasing as a clerical appendage of management to a newer concept of materials management that embraces inventory control, materials logistics, and distribution in addition to the buying function. Since the mid-1980s, this role has been greatly enhanced—perhaps even revolutionized—and labeled supply management.

ited information is transmitted to them. But there is a greater tendency to let the supplier "do his thing" without interference.

Stage 3.   Suspicion begins to yield to limited trust; the advantages to be gained from reducing the vast pantheon of suppliers are recognized; the discipline of a preferred supplier list is forced upon Engineering and Purchasing alike; and supplier suggestions are sought—though, usually after the design is frozen.

Stage 4   is nirvana. Both sides have *earned* full trust through translating the goals of partnership into tangible results. Legal contracts have given way to a handshake. There is now only one supplier per part number (single sourcing) and no more than single digit suppliers for an entire commodity. The supplier, because he is already best-in-class, has been preselected. He is involved from day one of the design and works closely with the customer's engineers. The customer's professionals visit the supplier frequently to help solve problems and to train supplier personnel in needed disciplines.

Management

Stage 1.   Management is obsessed with reducing direct labor costs, while purchasing, which controls 10 to 20 times the dollar content of direct labor, suffers from benign neglect. Management-by-crisis is the norm as management belatedly tries reduce material costs that often exceed competitors' selling prices. Not only is there no commitment to supplier partnership; the term is not even understood. Finally, there is chronic inability to tap the mother lode of supplier creativity.

Stage 2.   Management's emphasis is still on direct labor, which is coupled with a childlike faith in automation as an alternative to an offshore exodus. With cost as a preoccupation, there is a nomadic search for any supplier that can dangle cost reductions. In this stage, customers and suppliers are circling each other, jockeying for a me-win, you-lose advantage. Supplier creativity, in the form of ideas, is not discouraged but neither is it encouraged.

Stage 3.   Management promotes techniques such as computer-aided engineering (CAE), computer-aided design (CAD), computer-aided manufacturing (CAM), and even flexible manufacturing systems (FMS) that go beyond the narrow horizon of production to include engineering, management information systems (MIS), and so forth. The enormous potential of materials for profitability, however, is still not fully recognized. Supplier quality is now elevated to a position of preeminence, and commitment to partnership is underlined by an "open kimono" policy, where there is a mutual sharing of strategies, plans, technologies, and costs. Supplier cost reduction ideas are encouraged, but the customer hogs the savings.

Stage 4. Management, recognizing supply management's enormous potential for profit, elevates it to a key corporate strategy. A concentration on quality is followed up by a similar emphasis on cycle time and effective cost reduction, there being a large area of congruence among all three disciplines. Management has traded in fire fighting for the enlightened prevention of problems. The supplier is included as a team member and is involved early-on in the design phase, and savings stemming from his ideas are shared on an equitable basis.

Organization

Stage 1. Functional barriers between departments minimize visibility and desynergize the organization. Decisions are made sequentially—from Marketing to Engineering to Finance to Purchasing to Manufacturing. Purchasing is held in low esteem as a glorified clerical function, its people chained to their desks, filling out requisitions and expediting orders. In large corporations, a decentralized purchasing department severely fragments the economic leverage of the corporation.

Stage 2. Functional organizations give way to matrix organizations. Although this succeeds in building teamwork within a business unit, the dilemma posed by serving two masters—a functional boss and a product manager—causes endless tensions and needless politicking. In some companies, there is a move to split the materials management into groups: sourcing, which evaluates and select suppliers; and purchasing, which handles the on-going transactions on a day-to-day basis once the supplier has been selected.

Stage 3. The merits of centralized supply management over decentralized purchasing are found to outweigh its drawbacks, even in large companies with global operations. In addition, supplier quality assurance (SQA) is detached from a large quality assurance bureaucracy and reports to Supply Management. This includes the incoming inspection function even as it is systematically reduced to near zero.

Stage 4. Here the ideal organization unit is the commodity *team*, with Engineering, Purchasing, SQA, *and the supplier* working together, preferably in close physical proximity, to achieve mutual and effective cost reduction. Management trades in fire fighting for the enlightened prevention of problems, and the supplier becomes virtually an extension of the customer company.

Measurement

Stage 1. Purchasing's performance at this point is measured solely in terms of the price reductions squeezed out of vulnerable suppliers. Clever buyers, however, can play games, with reductions from budgeted targets that make them look good even if there are no real gains in product costs.

Stage 2. The boss of Purchasing has a typical performance measurement: "Don't pay too much. Don't run out. And never, never shut a line down."

Stage 3. Purchasing is initiated into the mysteries of cycle time management and pursues lead time reduction with suppliers; but reducing inventories becomes such a preoccupation that sometimes this results in missed shipments to customers. Furthermore, the burden of lead time reduction is shifted to suppliers, who are ordered to build warehouses close to the customer's plant for early delivery. Suppliers, then, are forced to either absorb the costs of warehousing or pass them on to the customer in the form of higher prices—a lose-lose situation!

Stage 4. The measurement criteria, which must be mandated by management, is the total cost of procurement. This includes not only price but the cost of poor quality and the cost of poor delivery. Purchasing's contributions to cash flow improvement and to the return on investment of a strategic business unit are stressed. Cycle time itself is elevated from being merely a focus on manufacturing to its being adopted by the entire organization as the management wave of the future.

Quality

Stage 1. Quality here is in the Dark Ages. Specifications, the starting point for quality, are vague, arbitrary, capricious. Acceptable quality levels (AQLs) are boiler-plate numbers and, by tradition more than by logic, are never less than one percent defective. Heavy emphasis is placed on incoming inspection as a postmortem screening function. Control over supplier quality is exercised through ineffective surveys that stress quality assurance manuals, organization charts, and other trivia. The concept of C_{P_k}* is unknown, as is the world of statistical process control (SPC).

Stage 2. Specifications at this point have some "science" thrown in: Formulas and computers are used to translate product requirements into component values and tolerances. AQLs are expressed on an expanded scale of parts per million (ppm). A one percent, or 10,000 ppm, level for AQLs is reduced in this stage to 2,000–5,000 ppm. Modest C_{P_k}s of 1.33 and less are

---

* C_{P_k}, standing for Process Capability (with the K representing a correction factor), is a measure of variation in a product or process. The higher the C_{P_k} the less is the variation and the better the yield. C_{P_k}s below 1.33 represent poor quality; C_{P_k}s of 2 should become a minimum U.S. requirement; those above 5 are ideal for quality and cost excellence (see Chapter 14 for details).

introduced to suppliers, but cumbersome, costly, ineffective control charts are still thrust down their throats.

Stage 3. Classification of characteristics, in which important parameters are highlighted and separated from the unimportant ones, is introduced here and the supplier held fully accountable for such important parameters, with defect levels approaching absolute zero, that is, $^{C}P_{k}s$ of 2.0 and over. Incoming inspection is reduced to "skip lot" because supplier quality has improved sufficiently to permit the inspection of only a fraction of the lots submitted. Supplier quality training is started, and the supplier is encouraged to use statistical design of experiments (DOE) to solve chronic quality problems and then to maintain statistical control with precontrol, a simpler, more cost-effective and more statistically powerful tool than control charts.

Stage 4. Important specification parameters are determined not by guess or by gosh, or even by formulas, but by the design of experiments, which can easily separate important component parameters from unimportant ones. The supplier confidently uses design of experiments both for problem solving and at the design stages of his product and process. As a result he can easily achieve $^{C}P_{k}s$ of 5.0 and over, with important benefits such as zero defects, 100 percent yields, customer certification (that is, no incoming inspection), and drastically reduced inspection and test in his own shop.

Cost

Stage 1. Here, the practice of getting three quotes and then selecting the lowest bidder is the order of the day. With specifications frozen, the supplier is afraid to suggest cost reduction ideas lest his bid be thrown out as nonresponsive. Not only is there a proliferation of suppliers, but there is a mindless proliferation of part numbers, brought on by undisciplined and autonomous engineers. The part number system is randomly generated, except for the first couple of digits that may indicate a major part category.

Stage 2. Bidding and negotiations through bluff and bluster are the primary strategies for reducing costs. There is a move at this point toward parts standardization, and an attempt at the discipline of only using parts from a preferred parts list.

Stage 3 sees the shedding of ineffective cost reduction tools and the adoption of powerful ones, such as value engineering; a reduced part number base through the reduction of models; learning curves and experience curves and a description data base that attempts to curb the needless generation of new parts.

Stage 4 advances to the incorporation of cost targeting, in which estimated competitor costs are targeted for reduction by a joint engineering-supplier team. The reduction of part numbers starts at the origin, namely, with the shedding of unprofitable businesses and product lines. Group technology, a new discipline that defines parts with similar product characteristics and manufacturing methods, is used to further limit parts proliferation and reduce setup and inventory costs.

Cycle Time

Stage 1   is characterized by large safety stocks (as insurance against "just-in-case" bottlenecks) and long lead times. Inaccurate forecasts from customers are passed on with even more inaccurate forecasts to suppliers, and there are frequent changes in quantities and timing.

Stage 2   is characterized by the adoption of manufacturing requirement planning (MRP) systems and an overdependence on the computer to solve inventory problems. Production still uses the "push" system, in which units at a given work station are produced to a rigid schedule regardless of whether the next station needs such units or not. There is an abiding belief in the productivity of long production runs, and setup times are regarded as God-given. Flow patterns are process-oriented, with material crisscrossing the factory floor several times to accomodate large and inflexible processes.

Stage 3   begins to utilize the major attributes of cycle time reduction: focused factories, where similar products are produced by a dedicated, cross-functional team; "pull" systems, with the back end of the line pacing what is produced at earlier work stations; small lot sizes made economical by greatly reduced setup times; and shortened product flows to reduce waiting and transportation times.

Stage 4.   At this juncture, the linearity of a schedule is made sacred. This means that total output is held relatively constant over short periods of time. The focused factory team includes not only manufacturing in all its aspects but support functions like quality assurance, materials management, engineering, and partnership suppliers. The team has true "ownership," in a real application of people power. Finally, the philosophy and practice of cycle time management is extended to all indirect labor operations, so as to reduce design cycle time, customer-marketing cycle time, order entry cycle time—in fact, cycle time reductions in all white-collar operations. Delivery of product to the customer becomes almost instantaneous, giving a company a decided edge over its competition.

The remaining chapters of this book are devoted to the *implementation* of stage 4 in each of the seven areas.

PART II

THE SPIRIT AND PRACTICE OF PARTNERSHIP

Chapter 3

Forging a Customer-Supplier Partnership

We need to throw off the old shackles of adversarial confrontation and work together with our family of suppliers in an enlightened era of mutual trust and confidence. In pursuing these new relationships, we recognize the need to pursue such liaisons as long-term contracts, dedicated supplier concepts, joint ventures, equity participation, single sourcing and supplier participation in the design and development of forward product programs, corporate contracts and team buying of multi-GM-divisional requirements. Also, we need to provide to the supplier community appropriate advance information for their own future planning and development.

—Darrah C. Porter, executive director, Purchasing, General Motors

The Silent Revolution in Supplier Relations

There is a silent revolution going on in the United States. It concerns supplier relations. When a world-renowned company like General Motors, known for its conservatism and tendency to "make" rather than "buy," puts forth a policy statement such as the one quoted above, it becomes almost axiomatic that supplier relations in the United States are moving into an era of enlightenment.

Figure 3-1. A supplier's hypothetical response to a customer's corrective action request.

PRODUCTS INCORPORATED
P.O. Box 000 Avondale Estates, Georgia 30002
METROPOLITAN ATLANTA AREA
Phone: 404/000-0000

COMPONENT PARTS
AND ASSEMBLIES

COMMERCIAL & MILITARY
APPLICATIONS

DESIGNING & ENGINEERING
SERVICES

PROPRIETORY ITEMS

FABRICATION
of parts and/or
assemblies of metal,
rubber, plastics, glass
or combinations thereof
by all types of
fabricating machining
and processing
techniques

SURFACE FINISHING
of metals, plastics,
rubber, and glass parts
to all Federal and
Military Specifications

Attn: Mr. Stanley Dean,
Purchasing Agent

UNIVERSAL CORRECTION ACTION

In accordance with company policy, we wish to inform you that you received merchandise of the same quality that every other customer gets, and we think you are pretty chicken for sending this garbage back to us. We can't use it either. We ship whatever the hell comes off the production line, and whether or not it meets specifications, we are certain that it contains the right part number most of the time, which is what you ordered. Concerning your statement with regard to late delivery, which incidentally was only 3 months overdue, what the hell do you want? You did better than most of our customers. Next time, order a bigger dollar volume and we will give it our red carpet, extra-special-attention treatment. It might even be only two months late then! (Note the improvement.)

For corrective action per your chicken request, we will investigate future orders more carefully so that we will ship so late that you will be in such a helluva bind that you will accept whatever the hell we send you.

Oh, about that little note which says "Cancel this order" —too late! As you can see, we are doing everything in our power to be cooperative and force this garbage on you, and if you are too stupid to deviate and use as is, we want to remind you that we have your money and you're stuck with it.

Hoping for future orders,

Your Friendly Supplier

P.S. With regard to your statement that our part doesn't resemble your drawing, we wish to point out that you are in error. Your drawing does not resemble our part, which we hastened to point out to our salesman two weeks after we accepted your order. Don't blame us if you were negligent enough not to inquire about this minor detail, because everybody else knows about it.

This is a far cry from the mistrust and antagonism that characterized customer-supplier relations even as late as the early 1980s. Typical of that period is the letter from a supplier shown in Figure 3-1. It is written in response to a customer's corrective action request that had been made because of the poor quality of the supplier's material. Obviously, the letter is a spoof. Exaggerated though it may be, it nevertheless captures the hostility marking many real-life situations.

Contrasting the Old and the New Models

The dimensions of the revolution in customer-supplier practices are as profound as the revolution in industrial assumptions described earlier and highlighted in Table 1-1. Here again, we can compare an old, post-World-War-II model, with its comfortable myths, to the new verities of a model for the 1990s.

Weekend Fling vs. Long-Term Marriage

Table 3-1 contrasts the two models in a number of categories. The starting point is corporate strategy. In the old model, price was the primary strategy; in the new model, it is a stable partnership with the supplier based on a solid foundation of mutual trust and loyalty. The old model led to a weekend relationship. If the supplier had cost or quality problems, he was cast aside, and the customer began a nomadic search for the greener pastures of a supposedly low-cost supplier. "After all," Purchasing would argue, "we have ten others to take his place." In the new model, senior managers on both sides start with a cautious courtship, followed by a long-term, solid marriage. If the supplier has cost or quality problems, the customer finds it cheaper to help him solve those problems than to replace him. As a result, supplier turnover can be drastically cut from more than 100 percent in a ten-year period to less than 5 percent.

Safety in Quantity vs. Safety in Quality

In the old model, the customer utilized a vast army of suppliers in the belief that there was safety in numbers. The structure controlling these multitudinous suppliers was flat, resembling a reverse thumb-tack organizational chart. For the most part, each supplier would provide the lowest-level component that the customer did not want to make. In the new model, the customer carefully selects the best-in-class (or benchmark) suppliers—few in number—who offer high quality, low cost, dependability, and flexibility. The supplier structure is a pyramid, with "cottage industries" at the bot-

Table 3-1. The revolution in customer-supplier practices.

Category	Old Post-World War II Model	New Model for the 1990s
• Strategy	• Price, price, price	• Sound, stable partnership
• Foundation	• Little trust or loyalty	• Mutual trust, loyalty, responsibility
• Longevity	• Weekend fling	• Long-term marriage
• Supplier turnover	• More than 100% in 10 years	• Less than 5% in 10 years
• Number of suppliers	• Vast	• Very, very few
• Supplier structure	• Flat (reverse thumb tack)	• Pyramid
• Make vs. buy	• Bias for make	• Bias for buy
• Forward integration	• None: Piece parts only	• Suppliers make kits, black boxes
• Selection	• By purchasing/ sourcing	• By top management
• Contracts	• Formal, legal	• A handshake, honor system
• Reach-out to subsuppliers	• Little or none	• Direct influence 2 to 3 levels down
• Physical proximity	• Far-flung; price, the locus	• Close enough for frequent visits
• Training	• Nonexistent	• Ongoing
• Technical help	• Very little	• Quality, cost, engineering help

tom, followed in ascending order by tertiary, secondary, and primary suppliers. Customers have a greater appreciation of "buy" over "make," and suppliers are encouraged to adopt forward integration, that is, to expand from providing merely piece parts to producing kits, subassemblies, and even proprietary systems.

Timid Lawyers vs. a Handshake

In the old model, the two parties drew up formal contracts, couched instilted "legalese" and armed with a variety of loopholes in fine print to allow for escape from the fundamental obligations of the business. An executive of one reputable customer company, frustrated by all the loopholes in the printed requirements, suggested one further requirement: "Regardless of specifications, the part must work!" The new model involves a simple handshake that bypasses complex and costly legal procedures, while elevating business integrity to an honor system.

Remote Control vs. Co-Location

The old model had the customer chasing suppliers to the ends of the earth for price, regardless of the difficulty of communications, language barriers, cycle time, and a host of other ills endemic to remote control. Training the supplier was unheard of, and Heaven forbid that he should be given technical help to improve his performance. Reaching out to assist the supplier's suppliers was also a no-no. In the new model, physical proximity is a goal. There is a growing realization that the relationship between effective teamwork and distance is an inverse square law. The supplier must be close enough to permit frequent visits. Training is a customer obligation, and technical help to the supplier in quality, cost, cycle time, and technology is a matter of enlightened self-interest. Finally, the momentum of supply management is greatly accelerated when the customer company extends a helping hand not only to his immediate suppliers but to their suppliers as well. The customer-supplier bond is but one link in the long chain from raw materials to the consumer. For supply management to reach its full potential, each one of these links must be energized and strengthened.

From a Win-Lose Contest to a Win-Win Partnership

The new model for the 1990s makes the old win-lose contest between customer and supplier obsolete. The conversion to a win-win partnership results in benefits for both. Table 3-2 summarizes these benefits.

The customer expects and is entitled to excellent quality: zero defects, and no necessity for incoming inspection. He is entitled to receive lower prices each year. Surprising as this may seem, it is easily achievable. Through supplier cycle time reduction, he is the beneficiary of much shorter lead times and lower inventories. And by applying the concept of early supplier involvement, he can both reduce his product costs at the outset and his own design cycle time.

Table 3-2. Benefits of a customer-supplier partnership.

Customer Company Benefits	*Supplier Company Benefits*
• Excellent quality	• Larger volumes
• Lower prices each year	• Longer-term agreements
• Shorter lead time	• Quality, cost, cycle time assistance
• Lower inventory and cycle time	• Training, coaching
• Early supplier involvement	• Stable forecasts
•• Savings ideas	• Advance planning information
•• Reduced design cycle time	• Security and growth
	• Increased profits and ROI

As quid pro quo, the supplier is entitled to similar benefits. Many short-sighted buyers feel that just giving a supplier their business is enough of a reward and that if a partnership exists at all, it should lean 90 to 10 in the customer's favor. But to lift a phrase from the stock market, "a bull may make money, a bear may make money, but a hog never does." Through the drastic reduction of the supplier base, the supplier can be awarded larger volumes of business. He may expand it even further with other customers because of his increased effectiveness and competitiveness. He could receive longer-term agreements (rather than formal contracts) that extend beyond a single order or a single year to multiple years. Two- to three-year agreements are now common in companies where partnership has been installed. Some progressive companies have extended these agreements to five years.

One of the most important benefits to the supplier is the frequent, active, and powerful help that a customer company can provide, especially in the areas of quality, cost, and cycle time improvement. It is casting bread on the waters to have it returned buttered. It stands to reason, however, that the customer must have professional experts who are really capable of delivering concrete help, people whose assistance will not be limited to sidewalk supervision or the issuing of platitudinous directives. Similarly, supplier training (never even on the customer's screen in the old days) in areas where the supplier may be weak becomes a hallmark of partnership. In addition, if this training is to be implemented, the customer's professionals and effective problem solvers should coach supplier personnel. It is learning by doing, rather than learning by listening.

A frequent and justifiable appeal from suppliers is for forecasts that will be more stable in terms of both time and quantity. (Of course, in an advanced stage of cycle time management, quantities shipped become so small, so frequent, and so steady that forecasts then become superfluous). The supplier is also entitled to advance information on the customer's consolidated plans for products and quantities so that he can make his own plans for orderly growth. A casualty of unplanned partnership is the supplier who is suddenly deluged with more and more orders because of his excellent performance, but who then cannot cope with the unplanned increase either in terms of quality or delivery or both.

The bottom line for successful partnership, then, is not only a customer who receives continual cost reductions but a supplier who sees his profitability and return on investment increase. Both are simultaneously possible if partnership is managed well.

Chapter 4

From Management to Leadership

A revolution is brewing. . . . The concept of leaderhsip is crucial to the revolution—so crucial that we believe the words "managing" and "management" should be discarded. "Management," with its attendant images, connotes controlling and arranging and demeaning and reducing. "Leadership" connotes unleashing energy, building, freeing and growing. . . .

—Tom Peters and Nancy Austin in *A Passion for Excellence*

Management Is a Poor Substitute for Leadership

In Search of Excellence, by Tom Peters and Robert H. Waterman, Jr., was a landmark book. Published in 1984, it constituted a managerial continental divide for American industry between the old give-up-itis in the face of Japanese competition and the new resolve to see homegrown success stories replicated in America. In their brilliant sequel, *A Passion for Excellence*, Peters and Austin fairly explode with confidence, painting a picture of a can-do America in vivid anecdotal colors.

32

The Attributes of Leadership

In advancing the thesis that leadership transcends management, Peters and Austin advocate measures that are dynamite because they are simple. Superior performance, they claim, has a simple model: care of customers through superior quality and service, constant innovation, and turned-on people. Leadership, not management, is the key. And the brand of leadership they propose is management by wandering around (MBWA). "To wander, with customers and suppliers and our own people, is to be in touch with the first vibrations of the new. . . . The No. 1 managerial productivity problem in America is, quite simply, managers who are out of touch with their people and out of touch with their customers." And out of touch with their suppliers, we might add.

There are several attributes of leadership that successful CEO's have in common: vision; deeply held personal values that become corporate values and permeate the entire organization; an ability to inspire and fire up their people with enthusiasm; a willingness to listen and pay attention to employees and to give them a sense of worth and involvement; and the desire to encourage entrepreneurship as an antidote to bureaucracy.

These leadership characteristics are applicable to customer and supplier companies alike. In relations between the two, the starting point is vision. Top managers must face, even anticipate, change.

Elevating Supply Management to a Key Corporate Strategy

The relationship between direct labor costs and the cost of purchased materials represents a major change. Direct labor, today, has shrunk to an inconsequential 5 percent of sales and less, while purchased material has grown to a hefty 50 percent of sales and more. Yet in terms of management attention, more than 50 percent is expended on production, while less than 5 percent is spent on purchased material! Direct labor continues to be propped up with great organizational support: manufacturing engineering, industrial engineering, process engineering, test engineering, maintenance engineering (design support), production planning, inventory control, cost accounting, and so forth. Purchasing, by contrast, suffers from mindless, management neglect.

Figure 4-1 shows direct labor, overhead, and purchased material as percentages of the total sales pie. It also shows that in the factory of the future the direct labor portion will shrink even further, approaching zero, while purchased material will increase to 60 percent of sales. And in the "lights out" factories of the 1990s—peopleless and paperless—where computers will

Figure 4-1. The leverage of purchased materials.

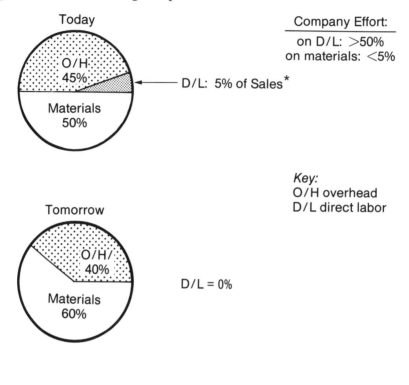

Today

O/H 45%

Materials 50%

D/L: 5% of Sales*

Company Effort:

on D/L: >50%
on materials: <5%

Key:
O/H overhead
D/L direct labor

Tomorrow

O/H/ 40%

Materials 60%

D/L = 0%

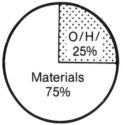

"Lights Out" Factory (peopleless, paperless)

O/H/ 25%

Materials 75%

---

*Traditionally, the cost accounting department spends 6% of sales in trying to monitor and control direct labor costs, which represent 5% of sales!

control computers that will run machines, direct labor will indeed be zero, while materials will soar to a staggering 75 percent of sales.

The impact of this change is profound. Even today, purchasing has a minimum of ten times the leverage on corporate profits as does direct labor. No other function—not engineering, not sales—can contribute in so direct a manner to profitability. Further, in many companies, supplier quality is the No. 2 cause of poor quality, next only to design. Top management therefore has both a golden opportunity and a compelling responsibility to elevate supply management to a key corporate strategy. This can spell the difference between winning and losing, between a distinct competitive edge and an insurmountable handicap.

Fighting Back via Supply Management

Xerox, American Samurai, by Gary Jacobson and John Hillkirk, is an excellent case study of a giant corporation that has fought back—to win. Faced with a precipitous decline in its market share, it developed a corporate strategy (of which supply management was a centerpiece) designed not only to stop that landslide but to reverse it.

The arduous task confronting Xerox is shown by these statistics: Over a five-year period, its market share had dropped from 60 percent (in 1975) to 40 percent (by 1980). Its manufacturing costs were twice that of the competition. Product lead times were 50 percent longer than competitive lead times, and, on a part-for-part basis, competitor quality was 85 percent better. It was estimated that to achieve parity, the company had to improve costs by 25 percent a year. The very survival of Xerox was at stake.

In its fight to overcome these odds, the company focused on supply management as the centerpiece of its strategy. To revolutionize this crucial aspect of its operations, Xerox:

- Reduced its supplier base over a five-year period from an unwieldy high of 5,000 to a more manageable 180
- Centralized supply management, incorporating supplier quality assurance (SQA) into that function
- Established the nation's first early supplier involvement (ESI) process, with value engineering (VE) as its centerpiece.
- Inaugurated supplier training, including ESI, VE, just-in-time (JIT), benchmarking, and quality improvement
- Created commodity teams
- Adopted cost targeting
- Reduced lead times from suppliers by 50 to 80 percent
- Cut inbound logistics costs to 50 percent of historic costs by consolidating volume and traffic flow
- Reduced job classifications and head counts by 60 percent

Table 4-1. Results of Xerox's corporate strategy, 1981 to 1986.

Parameter	Achievements
Cost reduction	• Product costs: Reduced to 52% in 5 years. • Design costs: ⅓ of historic costs. • Prototype costs: ½ of historic costs.
Quality	• Supplier quality: From 10,000 parts per million (ppm) to 610 ppm in 5 years. • In-plant failure rate: reduced to ¼ of old defects per unit (DPU).
Cycle time	• Work-in-process (WIP): From 3.5 months to 0.8 months in 3 years. • Design time: reduced to 50% of historic times. • Inbound logistics costs: ½ in 5 years.
Delivery	• Still 95%, with half the materials missing target date.
Procurement costs	• From 9% to 2.5% of purchased $ in 5 years.
Bottom line	Market share: From 40% to 50% in 5 years.

- Copied the secret Japanese technique of "lessons learned," whereby engineering meticulously logs all mistakes so that the same mistakes can be avoided by the next generation of engineers or on the next designs
- Used electronic communications for order releasing, invoicing, engineering drawings, accounts payable shipping notifications, and mail of all types

The dramatic results of Xerox's campaign are summarized in Table 4-1.

Another company, in the electronics business, assessed its strengths and weaknesses relative to the best of its competition in developing its long-range plans. It found that while it had several advantages in ther marketplace, cost was rated as the No. 1 weakness in all of its eight businesses. Because 70 to 80 percent of its product costs were in purchased materials, it formulated a corporate strategy that concentrated on supply management. After an intensive, three-year effort, it was able to reduce its overall purchase costs by 18.5 percent, with accompanying improvements in quality (already above par vis-à-vis its international competition) and cycle time reductions. The bottom line: This company was able to recapture several of its customers who had switched to Far East suppliers because of the lower prices they offered.

Do You Trust Your Suppliers . . . Have They Earned Your Trust?

In addition to vision, top management must possess character, an integration of personal beliefs and behavior that can be translated into firm, unshakable values that the corporation will make its own. Among those values that are held sacred is the commitment to customer-supplier partnership, as defined in Chapters 3, 5, and 6.

As the senior partner in that relationship, the customer—and specifically its top management—must make the first move toward that commitment. An indispensable attribute of commitment is trust. As Robert W. Galvin, chairman of Motorola and an industrial statesman par excellence, asked of his own people at a supplier partnership conference: "Do you really and truly trust our suppliers?" He then addressed the suppliers at the conference: "Have you suppliers earned our trust? Trust is the quintessence of our partnership." A statement of that caliber is not just rhetoric, not just management. It is leadership. It is inspirational. It demonstrates an abiding faith in the goodness of people and their corporate entities. Without trust, partnership is dead in its tracks. With it, everything else is achievable.

A Litmus Test

Trust, loyalty, fairness. That is the vocabulary of partnership. The following questions are a litmus test to determine the spirit and strength of partnership.

- Are both customer and supplier willing to share their strategies, plans, technologies, and costs with one another? (Xerox calls such sharing an open kimono policy)
- Is the customer willing to stay the course with a supplier, even though the latter may have had temporary setbacks in quality, cost, or delivery. Is he willing to help put the supplier back on his economic feet?
- Is the supplier willing to stay the course with a customer, who may be under intense competitive pressures and whose very survival* may be at stake?
- Is the customer willing and able to help the supplier, with frequent visits by his professionals, in quality, cost, and cycle time improvement?

---

*Harley-Davidson, the world-class motor cycle manufacturer whose market share had severely eroded under the onslaught of Kawasaki, Honda, and other new two-wheel giants, was greatly assisted in its comeback trail by a close, tight-knit group of partnership suppliers who rallied to its cause. The company credits these loyal suppliers for its born-again renown.

- Is the supplier willing and able to undertake a similar partnership with his key suppliers and encourage them in turn, to form partnerships with their core suppliers, in order to strengthen the entire supply chain?*
- Is the customer willing to allow a fair increase in profit to the supplier in return for yearly reductions in supplier prices?
- Is the supplier willing to pass on lower prices to the customer as a result of productivity and quality improvements, especially when the customer's professionals have rendered tangible help in effecting such improvements?
- Is the customer willing to have the supplier share in savings proposed by the latter, especially through the early supplier involvement (ESI) technique?
- Is the supplier willing to accept financial penalties if he is responsible for lapses in quality, delivery, or performance?

Many companies, both customer and supplier, would fail this litmus test in the early stages of partnership. But as the relationship ripens and matures, as the supplier becomes more and more an extension of the customer company, an upbeat upward spiral of trust and loyalty will develop.

The Rush to Offshore Suppliers: Losing Sight of the Forest for the Trees

Having changed the company focus from direct labor to purchased materials, elevated supply management to a key corporate strategy, established a climate of supplier trust, and determined the best types of supplier alliances for various products, top management must next turn its attention to setting policy with respect to onshore versus offshore suppliers.

A popular cartoon pictures a company's top management gathered around a table. The controller is addressing them: ". . . and we can save millions by making the 'made in U.S.A.' labels in Taiwan!" It is a biting commentary on the myopic vision and restricted analyzing capability of "bean counters." Sometimes accountants can become so obsessed with the minutiae of their calculations that they lose sight of the forest for the trees. Many of them, in comparing a U.S. site to an offshore location for a supplier, would carefully consider purchase prices and, perhaps, a few other factors; but there are many factors that accountants would find difficult and impossible to quantify. It is up to top management, then, to develop a calculus that takes in the larger realities in determining the true cost differentials between onshore and offshore purchases. Table 4-2 lists the hidden cost pen-

---

*Toyota, which has only 250 suppliers, in contrast to GM and Ford, each with a few thousand, extends its partnership reach four levels down in the supply chain. The benefits of its guidance and coaching in this pyramidal structure show up in the $400 to $1,000 cost differential between Toyota cars and those of the U.S. "Big Two," despite the yen revaluation.

Table 4-2.   The hidden cost penalties of offshore purchases.

Governmental/Political	*Strategic/Tactical*	*Tangible*
• Political instability	• Customer bonds weakened	• Inventory/cycle time increased • Poor tooling
• Currency exchange rate fluctuations	• Customer-marketing-engineering links poor	• Quality often a casualty • Extra source inspection costs
• U.S. trade barriers		• Freight costs higher
• Foreign/U.S. government regulations • Public Law 98-39 • EPA restrictions	• Early supplier involvement and value engineering much more difficult	• U.S. tariffs • Customs delays • Brokerage fees
• Product liability exposure		• Port entry fees
• Patent infringements	• Visits/technical help/training to suppliers ruled out	• Labor cost escalations • Cash flow problems
• Foreign content laws	• Longer product cycles • Design changes more difficult	• Cost of frozen cash • Premature payments with no guarantee of good, usable products
• Foreign tax structure	• Longer lead times	
• Foreign work rules	• Schedules must be frozen • Perils of long-range forecasting	
• Standards differences (e.g., Electronics Industry Association (EIA) vs. Japan Industry Standards (JIS))	• Danger of forward integration • Technology transfer drain • Travel/communication costs increased • Cultural/language barriers	

alties of offshore purchases. It is a formidable list, containing both tangible and intangible costs. The list forms the basis for the tough decisions for which only top management can develop a sixth sense.

Governmental and Political Minefields

Take the number one concern of political continuity. Other than Japan, whose yen revaluation has made it almost off limits for many commodities, there is not a single country in the Asian Pacific rim that can be considered politically stable. Add to this fact the vagaries of foreign currency exchange rate fluctuations; the protectionist sentiments in the U.S. Congress; Public Law 98-39, which assesses additional customs costs for assisting an offshore toolmaker; and a host of other political minefields and you have a catastrophe waiting to happen.

Strategic/Tactical Drawbacks

An emerging, global industrial theory has it that manufacturing is best performed close to where its market is located. Manufacturing for North American markets is best performed in North America, for West European markets in Western Europe, for Far Eastern markets in the Far East. The same law can be applied to suppliers as well. The reason is CUSTOMERS. That is what business is all about. Customers like to visit suppliers and kick the proverbial tires! They like to see and touch the product being made. They cannot do this across the span of oceans. The magic bond between the customer, marketing, and engineering, so very necessary in the early development of a product, is broken by miles of poor communication.

Cultural and language barriers add to the already disturbing "disconnects." Early supplier involvement and its powerful technological arm, value engineering, become casualties. The all-important technical and problem-solving help that the customer, as senior partner, can render is ruled out by distance. Design cycle times, which can be dramatically reduced by the customer and supplier working togther in close physical proximity, get longer and are frequently overtaken by product cycles that keep getting shorter and shorter! Schedules must be firmed up, even frozen, months in advance, negating the flexibility and the variety that rules the marketplace today. Add to all these woes the danger of an ambitious offshore supplier seeking an alliance today only to become a competitor tomorrow, and who siphons off the technology lent him. With all these drawbacks, one wonders why so many hardheaded American businessmen fall for the siren song of offshore suppliers.

Tangible Penalties

The political dangers and strategic/tactical drawbacks are hard to quantify. But what excuse is there for not quantifying the effects of the extra inventories and cycle times, the freight costs, the port entry charges, U.S. tariffs, and brokerage fees? One manufacturer, in attempting to juggle labor costs and value-added taxes, allowed a part to cross the ocean seven times before sale to a customer! There should be an economic jail for such cycle-time stupidity!

Some companies have developed a rule that an offshore purchase should be considered only if the price differential is a minimum of 25 to 30 percent below a U.S. source. As the following example from a company's offshore purchase analysis shows, a differential of 75 percent is a far more realistic figure. Even that figure may be too conservative if all the intangibles are reckoned into the final decision. The example lists the freight, duty, port entry charges, and brokerage fees for Far East parts brought into the United States.

Commodity	Percentage of Material Cost
Castings	96%
Grilles	107
Capacitors	69
Total range on all parts	7–107%

Additional costs	
Travel: Commodity teams	3.5%
Far East salaries	7.4
In-transit inventories	8.3
Scrap	2.1
Total	21.3%

Average differential	78.3%

Another company on the West Coast retooled a large die-cast part for a computer printer in Taiwan. The unit price quoted by the Taiwanese supplier was 50 percent under a U.S. supplier quotation. But problems soon developed with the die-casting die, and the initial castings were rejected. The Taiwanese tooling was finally approved, a year later, but by this time the new prices had increased by 42 percent over its previous quote—in effect, reducing the differential between this offshore supplier and the U.S. supplier to virtually zero.

It is small wonder that one buyer lamented, "Going offshore can take a company from the black into the red in one big hurry. The pitfalls are real, the savings often illusory!"

Monitoring the "Process," Not Just the Results

There is a favorite saying in the ranks of top management: "Never mind the elegance of your golf swing. It's where you land the ball that counts." This bias toward results over "process" characterizes much of top management's thinking. Yet it is patient practice, with the powerful help of a coach, that shapes style and eventually leads to even more spectacular results. Top management can no longer afford to monitor merely the two ends of a project such as supply management—the setting of goals in the beginning and the review of results at the end—while neglecting the all-important *process* by which goals are converted into results. This noninvolvement in the process, almost a callous laissez-faire approach, is one of its worst sins.

Top management's role in the process of supply management is, first, just to understand. The principles and practices described in this book can deepen that understanding. Second, it must gain knowledge, through benchmarking, of what the best companies do in this field. Third, it must provide guidance and encouragement in the implementation of a supply management plan. Fourth, it must lend a helping hand, especially to intimidated suppliers, in overcoming stumbling blocks. Fifth, it must know how to ask the right questions while following progress. Last, it must get involved, lead, and coach the people directly involved in the process to advance the cause of partnership beyond empty slogans and condescending tokenism.

Wee Willie, Not Babe Ruth!

Finally, only top management can provide the climate in which continual never-ending improvement will take place. There are two approaches. The first can be called the Babe Ruth style. As the Babe's true performance fades with the passage of time, only his dramatic home runs linger in memory. Yet he was noted for long periods of strikeouts, punctuated by the spectacular, but infrequent, home run. The second approach can be labeled the Wee Willie style, named after Wee Willie Keeler, a Hall of Fame player who hit very few home runs but who scored more singles—and more consistently—than the glamour stars.

Figure 4-2 shows the difference between the Babe Ruth and Wee Willie approaches to improvement and competitive effectiveness. The Babe Ruth approach on the left depicts improvement through a series of strategic leaps—dramatic, but infrequent. The Wee Willie approach shows improvements in small but steady steps, with cumulative gains well in excess of those produced by strategic leaps.

The Babe Ruth approach can leapfrog a competitor with a breakthrough in technology, corporate strategy, or location. But the disadvantages of this approach far outweigh the advantages because

Figure 4-2. Babe Ruth vs. Wee Willie approaches to improvement.

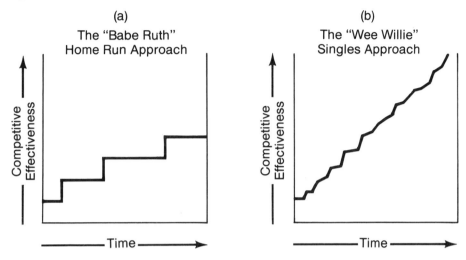

- It depends on breakthroughs, especially in technology, and these occur only a few times in a whole generation.
- It depends on timing, and most companies miss crucial opportunities because of profit squeezes, capacity/resource limitations, or lack of technology foresight.
- It requires major capital outlays.
- Its risk to reward ratio is very high, rather like a game of Russian roulette.
- It does not tap the creative potential of lower-level employees.

By contrast, the Wee Willie approach recruits loyal, trainable people whose capabilities can be improved through training, job rotation, and full participation. Its advantages are:

- Low capital requirements.
- Low risk and continual rewards.
- Less corporate staff and overhead.
- Enthusiastic workers, secure in their jobs, who use cooperation, suggestion systems, and quality circles to spot and solve problems without the need for management assistance.

How Many Industrial Engineers—Zero or 3,000?

The results almost always confirm that the fast but erratic hare loses out to the slow but steady tortoise. The story of New United Motor Manufacturing Inc. (NUMMI) in Fremont, California, is a case in point. NUMMI is the joint venture between Toyota and General Motors (GM). GM may be the name, but Toyota is the game.

Fremont was one of the worst GM plants and was shut down in 1982. When General Motors operated its old Fremont plant, it had seventy industrial engineers to support a work force of 5,000. When NUMMI reopened Fremont in 1984 with 3,000 selected from the same 5,000 workers, it had either zero industrial engineers or 3,000, depending on the definition of an industrial engineer! NUMMI had trained its entire work force in the rudimentary principles of industrial engineering: time and motion study, work simplification, and methods improvement. The workers did their own industrial engineering withcut the professionals. Yet they converted NUMMI into GM's showpiece plant with the lowest absentee rate, the lowest turnover, the highest quality, and the highest productivity!

The Wee Willie concept is infinitely superior to the Babe Ruth approach in customer-supplier relationships. Selecting loyal suppliers and training them does not require capital outlays. Their loyalty can be sealed with partnership. With these suppliers acting as extensions of the customer company, with their early involvement in design and with their ideas, the climate is established for hits at bat—for both sides—in a never-ending continuum of time.

Chapter 5

The Imperative of a Reduced Supplier Base

We need fewer suppliers . . . it's difficult enough to find one supplier who can supply the quality you need, much less two, three or half a dozen.

—W. Edwards Deming

Multiple Suppliers: The Illusion of Security

A common purchasing practice, even today, is to use multiple suppliers for the same part. Buyers defend this practice with the following arguments:

- It ensures continuity of supply in case of a strike or other unforeseen shutdown at any one supplier's plant.
- It strengthens the buyer giving him an economic advantage over a more fragmented group of dependent suppliers.
- It enhances competition among suppliers, who can be whipsawed into price reductions.
- It provides maneuvering room for swings in quantities, business conditions, or technology.

The buyer clings to these myths as his security blanket. They are not valid for the simple reason that they have failed to deliver what the buyer truly wants: improved quality, reduced prices, and reduced lead times—not on a one-shot basis but continually, year after year.

The Compelling Logic of a Reduced Supplier Base

If the objective of a customer company is to obtain substantial and continual improvements in these important parameters, it cannot do so by remote control, memos, table pounding, or threats. And if these crude measures fail, the answer does not lie in revolving-door suppliers. There is only one road to success. *The customer must establish close physical linkage with the supplier, including frequent visits to provide tangible help,* especially in the new disciplines of design of experiments, statistical process control, value engineering, and total cycle time. It is impossible to give this vital help to a large, scattered, undisciplined, and unreliable supplier base. Even the largest of customer companies find that there is just not enough time, money, or manpower to go around.

The first order of business for a customer, therefore, is to reduce his supplier base. It is the starting point on the road to partnership. It is a prerequisite to attaining all the advantages to both customer and supplier that were listed in Table 3-2.

A Comfortable Sequence

A customer company should establish a policy of phased reduction in the number of its suppliers. The exact counts depend on several factors, such as total volume, total dollars, technology, supplier capability, supplier availablity and tooling constraints with existing suppliers. A suggested sequence, however, can be considered:

1. A reduction from three or more suppliers per part number to two
2. A single supplier per part number
3. A maximum of fifteen to thirty suppliers for an entire commodity or part category
4. A maximum of two to ten suppliers for an entire commodity*

---

*The advantage of a drastic reduction in the number of suppliers for an entire commodity must be balanced against the disadvantages of remote location (see the section on location in this chapter).

Examples: One large company, with plants in several different locations all over the United States, started its supplier partnership program by reducing its supplier base on three priority commodities—sheet metal/stampings, plastics, and die castings. At the end of the first year, it achieved the following results. Long-term goals are also included.

Commodity	Number of Suppliers		
	At Start	One Year Later	Long-Term Goal
Sheet metal/ stampings	149	43	20
Plastic parts	175	32	10
Die castings	76	18	6

Another company adopted an extreme policy of no more than one supplier for an entire commodity, both for its U.S. and its worldwide operations. Not only has this policy not backfired, except for one major stock-out, but the company claims that this drastic reduction in its supplier base has been instrumental in price and quality gains year after year.

McDonald's, the renowned hamburger chain, has a long-standing policy of one supplier for an entire commodity in each regional center. As an example, it has only one meat supplier for its entire Midwest operations. In over two decades, there has not been one single interruption to any McDonald outlet. That is the quintessence of partnership!

An Achievable Time Table

In moving from the number of suppliers per part number and the number per commodity to the total supplier base, the following time table is recommended:

2:1 reduction in one year (50 percent reduction)
5:1 reduction in two to three years (80 percent reduction)
10:1 reduction in four to five years (90 percent reduction)

Again, the extent and timing of such overall reduction can vary from company to company depending on size, corporate policy, competitive factors, and threats to survival.

Examples: The following examples of supplier base reductions are based on published articles in trade journals.

Company	Percentage Reduction	Results
Allen Bradley:	20 percent in two years	Poor
Ford:	45 percent in three years	Modest
3M:	64 percent in three years	Acceptable
Motorola:	70 percent in three years	Acceptable
Hewlett Packard: (one division) months	47 percent in four months	Spectacular
Xerox:	90 percent in one year	Spectacular

Benefits of a Reduced Supplier Base

By advocating a reduced supplier base, I do not mean to imply that it is impossible to achieve improvements in quality or price with multiple suppliers scattered all over the globe. But improvements under these conditions will be small in percentages, long in time tables, intermittent in frequency, and grudging in nature from suppliers who see no other way of retaining the customer's business. A reduced supplier base, on the other hand, facilitates partnership, frequent visitations, and mutual efforts toward reaching common goals. That it can have spectacular results is demonstrated by the following case study.

Example: A division of a multinational company launched a supplier reduction drive. After fourteen months, it had registered a 30 percent reduction in its supplier base. Its documented savings are listed in Table 5-1. Relevant company statistics include the following: division sales: $300 million; materials purchased: $155 million; profit after tax: 4 percent; asset turns: 3.2 percent; return on investment: 12.8 percent.

What can we learn from this particular company's experience?

1. It was not the reduced supplier base per se, but the painstaking efforts of customer and suppliers in attacking quality defects and long lead times, coupled with higher supplier volumes, longer-term agreements, and, above all, active on-site assistance to these suppliers in reducing their costs (while increasing their profits), that were the underlying reasons for this company's success. But the reduced supplier base was essential in focusing the customer's limited quality and materials management resources on these improvements.
2. The 30 percent reduction in the supplier base in fourteen months was modest. The inertia in getting started wasted time up front.
3. Parts certification, a 50 percent certification (that is, no incoming inspection) was achieved on partnership parts. Another 30 percent of

Table 5-1. Results of a supplier reduction drive.

Improvement Category	$ Savings
1. Improved parts quality from suppliers	
• Incoming inspection reduction through certification: From 0.4% of sales to 0.1%	900,000
• Inspection/Test cost reduction (Precontrol vs. 100% checks) From 2.5% of sales to 2.1%	1,200,000
• Internal failure cost reduction (scrap/rework reduction) From 3.0% of sales to 2.5%	1,500,000
• Warranty costs: Improved parts reliability From 1.0% of sales to 0.4%	1,800,000
2. Material cost reduction 5% of total purchases	7,750,000
3. Reduced inventory costs	

Turns	Average Inventory	Inventory Cost (@ 20%)	
Before 5	$31,000,000	$6,200,000	
After 11	$14,100,000	$2,820,000	3,180,000

4. Materials management budget reduction	90,000
Total	16,420,000

	Bottom-Line Results			
	Profit After Tax	Asset Turns	ROI	Cash Flow
Before:	4.00%	3.2	12.8%	$X
After:	6.75%	4.0	27.0%	$X + 3,180,000

these parts was placed on "skip lot" (every fifth lot checked, on average).

4. Inspection and test costs could have been reduced further had more aggressive $^{C}P_k$ requirements been used (see Chapter 14).

5. Internal failure costs and warranty costs could have been reduced further with more effective supplier reliability stress tests.

6. Material cost reduction percentages could have approached 10 percent with early supplier involvement and value engineering.

7. Greater inventory turns could have been achieved if the customer company had given more active help to suppliers in cycle time management.

The Preferred Supplier List: A Brake on Proliferation

While attempting to reduce the total number of suppliers coming in through the front door, the customer company's management must make sure that there is no proliferation through the back door. One important contributor to such an escalation is an uncontrolled increase in the number of new parts generated. Measures to turn the clock back on such proliferation constitute a powerful method of reducing costs (see discussion of this topic in Chapter 19).

Another cause of escalation in the number of suppliers is the tendency of the engineering department to work with any supplier who is convenient—geographically, technologically, or cooperatively. Sometimes, this is done without the knowledge of Purchasing. As a result, when the part is ready to be ordered, the Engineering favorite gets the order, to the chagrin of the purchasing department.

An opposite scenario is also possible. Engineering may have worked diligently with an existing and helpful supplier in designing the part, only to find that purchasing, for reasons of cost or favoritism, has selected some other supplier at the start of production. The engineer and his supplier feel cheated, especially if a great deal of time has gone into the development of the design.

To prevent both abuses, the preferred supplier list has come into vogue as an element of the partnership process. Drawn up initially by each commodity team (see Chapter 7) and approved by a higher-level steering committee (see Chapter 6), the policy prescribes that no purchases can be made from suppliers not on the preferred supplier list. Such a policy has several advantages:

- The list provides a ready guide for supplier selection.
- It is a brake on supplier proliferation.
- It disciplines both engineering and purchasing to stay with an approved supplier list.
- It encourages early supplier involvement (see Chapter 19) without the supplier's having to fear being left high and dry at contract time.
- Target costs, target quality, and specifications can be established with the supplier almost at the conceptual stage of design (see Chapter 20).
- It is a stimulus to partnership, resulting in tangible benefits to both customer and supplier.

The criticism leveled at preferred supplier lists, usually by engineers, is that new and worthy suppliers, especially those strong in technological innovation, are likely to be locked out. However, this disadvantage does not even surface where there is a commodity team, on which engineering is strongly represented. The team has the responsibility to review and update the preferred supplier list periodically. It assesses the credentials of a new supplier to be placed on the list, an assessment based upon the latter's superiority in technology or materials, upon availability during emergency situations or disruptions, or upon overall potential. In such rare circumstances, the older preferred supplier should be adequately compensated for a potential loss of business.

Single Sourcing: A Potential for Blackmail?

A logical sequence is to go from three or four or more suppliers per part number to two and then to one—that is, to single sourcing. In this context, it is necessary to draw a sharp distinction between *single* sourcing, which is strongly recommended, and *sole* sourcing, which should be avoided. In single sourcing, there are several suppliers, from which the best is picked. In sole sourcing, there is only one source, selected mostly on the basis of technology. There is nowhere else to turn. Although sole sourcing makes a customer company very vulnerable, its risks can be substantially reduced with financial incentive plans (see Chapter 19).

Many purchasing professionals, however, revolt at the thought of single sourcing. They equate it with supplier blackmail. They have nightmares of a single supplier source, freed from the yoke of competition, raising his prices, allowing his quality to deteriorate, or lengthening his lead time. Such a supplier is obviously not worthy of partnership to begin with. The key words in partnership are trust and commitment. If there is no trust a priori, that is, before partnership is entered into, and if either party fails to accept the responsibility for achieving mutual advantage, there is no basis for partnership.

More charitable buyers accept the fact that blackmail is not a concern in true partnership. But what about discontinuities in supply if a single source is affected by strikes or natural calamities? Again, the answer lies in choosing a partnership supplier whose labor climate is nonconfrontational and, preferably, participative. On those occasions when a strike is imminent, the supplier can warn the customer well ahead of the event and recommend a temporary buildup of safety stock.

Having Multiple Suppliers Is Being Insurance Poor

Disruptions caused by natural calamities, such as a flood, lightning striking the supplier's plant, or his truck falling off a bridge, are legitimate concerns. But the small probability of such events must be balanced against the extra cost, on lot after lot received, of splitting an order among two, three, or more suppliers. There is no need for such a cost penalty 99 percent of the time for a disruption probability of less than 1 percent. The insurance premium is unaffordable! Further, for the most critical and complex parts, where costs are high, quality a question mark, and deliveries uncertain, exorbitant tooling costs often prohibit the use of more than one supplier per part. Examples include die-cast parts, injection-molded plastic parts, and integrated circuits (for masks). It makes no sense, therefore, to have several suppliers for garden-variety parts, where stock-out risks are much lower.

Example: A manufacturer of die castings purchased aluminum ingots, totalling $10 to 12 million each year, from five different suppliers. This total represented the largest purchases made by the company and amounted to almost 20 percent of its sales. The purchasing practice was to start with the known market price for the ingots (considered a commodity, with prices in the public domain) and then to have the different suppliers bid against one another so that it could obtain the best discounts from market figures. The net result was that one supplier would get an order one month, another the next, and so on, based on lowest price. In this way, the manufacturer's yearly purchases were split among five suppliers, each of which cornered $2 to 2.5 million per year.

The company launched a supplier partnership drive and finally bit the bullet by selecting the best of its five suppliers, based on product quality, price, delivery time, and the supplier's flexibility and cooperativeness. It entered into a long-term agreement. The supplier's volume increased almost five times. A blanket-order arrangement was drawn up to assure short lead time. As a result, the customer company obtained a reduction of 18 percent below market prices, that is, a reduction of 11 percent below previous low bids. With a single supplier, the customer was able to concentrate on quality and problem-solving assistance. Other fringe benefits were reduced bidding and negotiating costs, lower transportation costs, and a smaller amount of paperwork.

Location, Location, and Location

A prospective store owner asked a noted consultant in the retail business what the latter would consider as the three most important factors in opening his store. The answer came back quick as a shot: "Location, location, and location!" In the arena of customer-supplier partnerships, a supplier location close to the customer is far more important than is recognized even by most supply management experts. It is not enough to reduce the supplier base. An unwritten law states that the frequency of customer visits is in inverse proportion to the distance between customer and supplier. The generic principle of communication effectiveness versus distance is illustrated in Figure 5-1. And frequent visits are necessary, especially in the early stages of partnership when relationships have to be established, bonds forged, and

Figure 5-1. Communication effectiveness vs. distance.

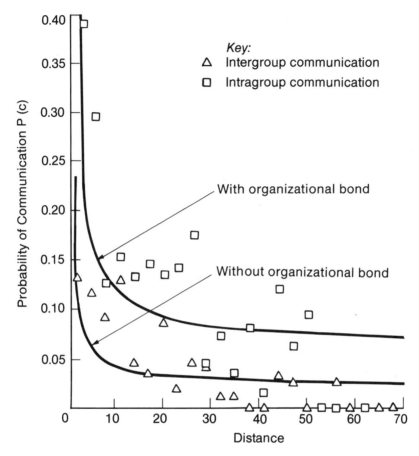

Source: Adapted from T. J. Allen and A. R. Fustfeld, "Research Laboratory Architecture and the Structuring of Communications," *R&D Management,* Vol. 5, No. 2 (1975).

trust nurtured. Frequent visits continue to be necessary, so that the customer can render active help to the supplier especially in technology, quality, and cycle time. They are an essential feature of early supplier involvement, which is discussed in Chapter 19.

Milking a Cow

You cannot milk a cow by remote control. You must sit down on the stool and go to work on it. Similarly, you cannot legislate supplier improvements by remote control, by sitting at a desk and pounding your fists, by writing memos, by barking over the telephone, or by exhortations. The best way to achieve desired customer goals is to sit down with the supplier at his site and milk the four "udders" of quality improvement, productivity improvement, cycle time improvement, and management improvement for the mutual benefit of both. No other way will give substantial or lasting results.

Needed: Problem Solvers, Not Table Pounders

But, ask the skeptics, how can a customer provide technical or quality help to a supplier when the latter is the expert on the technology of the product or part he is producing. The answer is that the customer company's visiting professionals need not be experts in a particular technology. But they must be problem solvers. They must be able to tackle the most important quality problems confronting the supplier using powerful tools such as design of experiments (Chapter 13) and multiple environment over stress tests (Chapter 15), and they must demonstrate that a complete and permanent solution is achieved. This is best done *with* the supplier's technical people rather than *for* them; in any case, success must be proved.

Turning a Sow's Ear Into a Silk Purse

The spirit of partnership requires that a supplier be treated as an extension of the customer's own company. This means that the number of supplier visits should be almost as frequent as the number of visits Engineering makes to help its own production operations. (A wag in production responded that such a rule would result in a supplier being as lonesome as the poor production department that never sees the face of an engineer!)

It has been my personal experience that it is easier to convert a local supplier in stage 1 of supply management to a stage 3 or 4 status than it is to transform a distant stage 2 supplier. The reason is physical proximity and what it makes possible: the ease of frequent meetings (generally, once a week) with the supplier's entire management team; the ease of designing, conducting, and interpreting statistical experiments; and a rapid buildup of mutual trust and responsibility.

Example: The New United Motor Manufacturing Co., Inc. (NUMMI) is a joint venture between General Motors and Toyota, located in Fremont, California. NUMMI is now the showcase within General Motors. In the space of two years it has risen to become the best quality plant within GM as well as its most productive. Its secret: management!

Early in its history, its purchasing department had to choose between two suppliers for a family of parts. The first, from Tennessee, offered a price of $109,000. The second, a local supplier in Fremont, quoted a figure of

$136,000. Purchasing had researched the two suppliers and determined that their quality, delivery, and other factors were comparable. There was no question in the minds of the buyers that the Tennessee supplier should be awarded the contract. But the pro forma approval of the general manager was required because of the size of the award. The Japanese general manager wanted to know: "Where is this Tennessee?" When the puzzled buyers pointed out Tennessee on a map, the general manager said that it was too far away. "No," replied the buyers, "it's only a few hours away by plane—at most, a two-day round trip." The general manager was patient, but firm. "I wish you would reconsider," he said (translation: the answer is no). "The Fremont supplier is a better choice. He is almost next door to us. You must visit such a supplier almost daily; and in very little time, the $27,000 cost differential will not only disappear but reverse itself!" The general manager turned out to be right. Even within the first few months, the cost gap had narrowed, along with several other parameters of supplier performance.

A similar example was related to me by the director of purchasing for Nissan-U.K. Here the Japanese general manager was even more demanding. He ordered that the higher-priced local supplier be selected over the lower-priced distant supplier and further directed that the cost differential be reduced to zero within six months. Result? The gap was reduced to zero in four-and-a-half months. In one year, the local source had a 3 percent lower price than the distant supplier.

Chapter 6

The Infrastructure of Partnership

Those companies making a conscious effort to improve the working relations with their suppliers are the ones that are successfully regaining parity with their foreign competition.

—Pierre Landry, Xerox

Once the advantages of a reduced supplier base are recognized, there are as many ways to move toward full partnership with suppliers as there are companies. But an infrastructure of support is a necessary prerequisite. Such an infrastructure includes:

1. A supply management steering committee
2. Annual corporate negotiations with suppliers
3. Supplier conferences
4. Supplier councils
5. Supplier suggestions and appeals

Each is discussed in the following sections.

56

Supply Management Steering Committee

As a first step, the customer company should form a supply management steering committee, drawn from its senior management ranks. Its responsibilities are to:

1. Draft a mission statement.
2. Establish partnership goals and a timetable for their achievement.
3. Benchmark other customer companies for the best in supply management.
4. Select commodities for prioritization.
5. Select commodity teams.
6. Monitor the partnership "process."
7. Evaluate the effectiveness of partnership (see Chapter 9).

Mission Statement

Supply management is eminently worthy of being elevated to a key corporate strategy. The starting point of this strategy is a mission statement. For example, here is a statement from a company that is a pioneer in launching supply management:

> Select the best suppliers who are capable of providing the highest product reliability, the highest performance reliability, the highest degree of innovation available, and the highest level of responsiveness, all at the lowest cost.

This may sound like motherhood and apple pie. Most companies are saddled with such seemingly empty rhetoric. The difference is that this company has translated its mission statement into a hard-hitting set of objectives, goals, timetables, detailed plans, and management involvement in the "process" of achieving these plans.

Setting a Timetable for Realizing Partnership Goals

Typical steering committee goals for supply management include a reduction in the part number base; a reduction of the supplier base; and improvements in quality, cost, and cycle time parameters. For example, one company, with more than $2 billion in sales, established the short- and long-term goals shown in Table 6-1 in its supplier partnership effort. The goals are ambitious, but in benchmarking terms, not quite best-in-class.

It is said that the normal gestation period in industry, that is, the time between the birth of an idea of a technique and its full implementation, is

Table 6-1. One company's short- and long-term goals in its supplier partnership effort.

		Goals	
Category	*Current Levels*	*Short-Term (1 Year)*	*Long-Term (3 + Years)*
Part number totals	96,000	54,000	10,000
Number of suppliers	4,000	2,000	500
Quality:			
(a) Incoming inspection (parts per million)	6,000	1,000	100
(b) Percentage of parts certified	10%	40%	80%
Overall cost reduction (%)	—	5%	8%
Cycle time			
(a) Long lead time average (weeks)	18	10	2
(b) Inventory turns	4	8	30

nine *years!* Such a pace may have been acceptable during the years when U.S. industry towered over its international competition, but today survival itself depends on the rapid adoption of techniques with proven track records. This is as valid for supply management as it is for other innovations.

Figure 6-1 depicts one company's timetable for supply mangement from concept to fruition. The pace is leisurely, considering that this company's dominant position in the marketplace was at that time threatened by Japanese competitors. It took three years just to get through the stages of inertia, disbelief, give-up-itis, and frustration! On the credit side, this company was not only an early entrant in the new field of supply mangement, with no blueprint to guide it, but it also established very ambitious goals.

In today's frenzied world of global competition, the timetable must be shortened to three years (perhaps five at most) whenever survival is at issue. The timetable is, generally, established by benchmarking the company's best competitor and the observed supply management gap.

Commodities for Prioritization

An important task of the steering committee is to decide which commodities (or part categories) require the most urgent attention. The priority decision may be based on one or more of the following:

Figure 6-1. Supply management timeline.

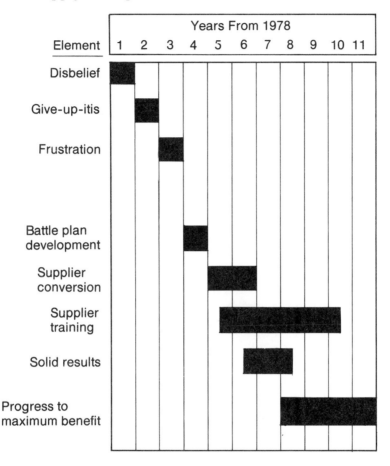

- Dollar volume
- Value added dollars
- Unit volume
- Current/potential suppliers
- Quality improvement
- Suppliers' performance, history
- Outsourcing policy
- Industry/economic outlook

Given its preeminence in recent years, many companies are pinpointing quality improvement as priority 1.

The steering committee also selects the members of each commodity team and its leader. The role of the commodity team is so vital to the success of supply management that Chapter 7 is entirely devoted to its mechanics.

At the very start, the steering committee must obtain an up-front budget allocation to cover the salaries and expenses of the commodity teams. The willingness of top management to commit such resources is a tangible measure of its true support for the partnership process.

As an example, one small company, with limited resources and hurting at the marketplace because of high material costs, took the bold step of budgeting $770,000 for its commodity teams, despite the objections of its product managers, who were concerned with short-term profits. The "gamble" paid off handsomely. The commodity teams turned in savings of over $9 million—with improved quality and cycle time as icing on the cake!

The New Discipline of Benchmarking

Sun Tzu, the renowned Chinese general in the ninth century A.D., wrote a treatise on *The Art of War*. He stated: "Know your enemy and know yourself. In a hundred battles you will never be in peril." Sun Tzu's dictum forms the basis of benchmarking, a term introduced into American industry only in the 1980s. We need only to substitute the word "competitor" for "enemy" to see that the advice is equally applicable today.

Since benchmarking is little known in U.S. industry, its general objective and practice need to be explained before discussing its use in supply management as a key steering committee responsibility.

Benchmarking can be defined as a continuous process of:

- Determining those factors that are critical to the long-term success of a company's business
- Comparing a company's own performance on those factors against the current or potentially best-in-class company (regardless of whether it is a competitor or not)
- Using that information to develop business strategies and functional action plans
- Closing the gap in those factors between the company and the best-in-class performer
- Continually recalibrating company performance against the best-in-class company to achieve continual, never-ending improvement

The aim is to make the company the very best in the market it serves. Without benchmarking, a company's strategies are blind guesses. Even if it pursues time-related improvement, the rate of such improvement may be inadequate. For example, one U.S. company improved its quality by a factor greater than ten-to-one over a five-year period. It felt smug about its performance until it discovered in the marketplace that its benchmark Japanese competitor had achieved even higher levels of quality by almost an order of magnitude. So the external view, which benchmarking provides, is absolutely essential.

Benchmarking also goes well beyond conventional competitive analysis, sometimes labeled reverse engineering (see Chapter 19), in which a competitor's product is dissected to gain insight into its costs, technology, materials, and manufacturing. Benchmarking considers not only the competitor's product, but also his strategies, markets, services and practices—in short, any factor that contributes to the competitor's success.

Benchmarking has been adopted as a corporate strategy among the more progressive companies in the United States. It is becoming an essential technique in the fiercely competitive milieu of the Japanese *Kaisha*—the large corporations in that country that seek growth and market share with the same fervor that their American counterparts seek profit.

Benchmarking Applied to Supply Management

Applied to supply management, benchmarking becomes a major task of the steering committee. The following roadmap has been used by companies with successful results in supply management.

1. Establish the standards and parameters by which supply management progress should be measured, such as material, quality, cost, cycle time improvement, and part number reduction and supplier base reduction.
2. Measure current performance against these standards in your own company. (Benchmarking measures the gap between your company and the best-in-class company. There is no point in the exercise if your own baseline is not known or is fuzzy.)
3. Prepare a questionnaire for use during visits to potential benchmark customer companies.
4. Conduct practice benchmarking exercises with other divisions of your own company or with nearby companies.
5. Figure 6-2 shows the variety of sources from which information can be gathered and the relative reliability of each type. These range from public sources—where information is the easiest to gather but less accurate—through company watchers and industry players to the targeted benchmark company itself—where information may be the hardest to obtain but where the quality of the intelligence gained can be the most accurate and most useful. (It has been my experience that benchmarking even a competitor target company, if ethically approached, is not as difficult as it may first appear. Companies are willing and its managers are proud to share their successes, especially when there is reciprocity of information.)
6. Visit a few of the leading companies. Be sure to get information not only from the management levels of these companies, but also from lower-level employees who may have a somewhat different or more realistic perspective of their achievements.

Figure 6-2. Benchmarking: Sources of information.

7. Record the gap between the benchmark company (there may be more than one company that is best-in-class on different techniques) and your own with respect to each important parameter and determine the reasons for that gap.
8. Act to close the gap by establishing goals, terms, and a timetable.
9. Repeat the process periodically to ensure that the gap remains closed.
10. Survey the industrial landscape, domestically and internationally, to be alert to a new and potentially threatening competitor who may be lurking in the shadows.

Annual Corporate Negotiations With Suppliers: Utilizing Corporate Clout

Decentralization in many large companies is carried to such an extent that the left hand does not know what the right hand is doing. There are examples—too numerous to be considered exceptions—of buyers in different locations purchasing the same part from the same supplier with different prices under the same or different part numbers. There is an actual horror story of four engineering departments of a customer company, located in the four corners of the same building, specifying four different part numbers from the same supplier for the same part. In another hair-raising story, a defense contractor's 30,000 parts had escalated to more than 700,000 part numbers, based on the minutest of differences, such as marking, burn-in, packaging, and other trivia. It seems that each design team would go out of its way to alter part requirements ever so slightly so that no other group could use those parts. What a parts proliferation nightmare!

The purpose of corporate negotiations is to retain the flexibility of decentralization while taking full advantage of the total volume that a large company can order from a few chosen suppliers at much reduced prices. This spells LEVERAGE. It spells cost reduction that can be easily and swiftly effected. Obviously, the technique is more applicable to large companies, which can muster corporate clout, than to small ones. It is also more appropriate as a preliminary step to full partnership than as an ongoing partnership tool. But even here, it can be used successfully to monitor the relative effectiveness of two or more partnership suppliers in a given commodity.

Methodology and Scope

Corporate negotiations do not mean a return to a centralized, dictatorial bureaucracy within a company. The corporate negotiations staff need not include more than two to ten people, depending upon the size of the large company. But it should be highly professional, it should be respected by the purchasing department's rank and file for its competence and integrity, and it must have the full support of top management.

The starting point is the selection of a commodity, or part category, where there can be the largest and quickest return on investment. Usually, this is the highest dollar commodity. Alternatively, having too many suppliers for a given commodity to begin with may provide an even better opportunity for savings and quality improvement. A team, consisting of a corporate staff member as the leader and purchasing representatives from the various divisons, reviews the history of the commodity in terms of prices, quality, and delivery. It reviews parts commonality and opportunities for consolidations. It determines strategies to be pursued with suppliers. Bid packages are next sent out to preferred suppliers chosen on the basis of past performance as well as to new suppliers with a reputation for capability. Meetings are then held with each supplier. Final selections are made on the basis of prices negotiated. It must be pointed out, however, that quality cannot ever be a sacrificial lamb. In fact, the opposite is true. Some companies specify a maximum defect level, such as 1,000 ppm (0.1% defect rate). The preferred specification is C_{p_k} (see Chapter 13), with a minimum C_{p_k} of 1.33, a target C_{p_k} of 2.0, and an ideal C_{p_k} of 5.0. A supplier's acceptance of C_{p_k} is one of the most eloquent testimonials to its quality capability.

Corporate negotiations apply not only to products but also to supplier services such as airlines, hotels, car rental companies, travel agents, airfreight carriers, and truckers. Individually, such services may represent only a small fraction of product costs. Collectively, they add up to a respectable total. Further, the percentage cost reduction can reach as high as 40 percent!

The relative advantages and disadvantages of corporate negotiations can be summarized. On the plus side, they

- Reduce costs across whole commodities because of larger volumes.
- Prevent duplicate part numbers and duplicate costs for the same part.
- Encourage standardization and group technology.
- Bring all Purchasing together for intense preparation in negotiations.
- Serve as a halfway house to a reduced supplier base and "best-in-class" suppliers.
- Bring customer-supplier personnel into a closer relationship.
- Have a large benefit-to-cost ratio, with quick payback.

On the minus side, corporate negotiations

- Become less needed as the supplier base thins out and partnership matures.
- Tend to become preoccupied with price while quality takes a back seat, if the negotiating team is not sensitized to quality.
- Diminish local purchasing autonomy.
- Make customizing local requirements more difficult.
- Lose the advantage of supplier proximity.

However, if the whole exercise is not looked upon as another burdensome "corporate mandate," and the local/regional personnel are drawn into the planning and conducting of such negotiations, the sense of ownership will be enhanced and "guerrilla warfare in the hinterland" will not take place.

Example: Motorola purchases approximately 40 percent of its total sales in piece parts and services. It is known for decentralization and an abhorrence of corporate overhead. Its several divisions have total autonomy to buy whatever they need from whomever they choose as suppliers. Some coordination and networking occurs through a corporate purchasing council that meets three or four times a year.

The CEO decided that materials management was too important to be left to laissez-faire practices. A corporate director with a national reputation, Ken Stork, was hired to establish a tiny but important corporate role: partnership with suppliers. The charter was to keep the group lean and effective. Stork assembled a very small staff of highly respected professionals and started the partnership process with corporate negotiations.

The team approach was used. For each prioritized commodity, a team was set up, with members drawn from each major division of the company. Participation and open communications were encouraged. The engineering and quality disciplines were also included in the teams. Internal meetings focused on standardization potential, specifications "scrub," quality requirements, volume projections, and negotiating positions. Bids to preferred suppliers, meetings with them, and final selections followed. The whole process was repeated and refined each year. The results were spectacular in terms of cost reductions, quality improvements, and a sharp reduction in the supplier base. Similar results were effected by his deputy, Kathy Sullivan, Corporate Manager of Transportation and Travel, among service suppliers such as travel agencies, hotels, car rental companies, and transport carriers.

In the intervening years, under Ken Stork's dynamic leadership, the corporation has graduated to leading strategies in supply management—such as the tearing down of "functional silos," the pursuit of total cost over the old emphasis on price, the crafting of commodity teams, and the establishment of early supplier involvement.

Supplier Conferences

Periodic conferences with suppliers are another step on the road leading to partnership. Once a customer company has decided to begin such a partnership, an opening conference with suppliers will serve to set the stage. Here, the customer company can communicate its new requirements and, in return, outline the benefits such partnership offers to the supplier community. An initial conference also serves as a warning to suppliers that there is a new ball game in town, where 50 percent and more will lose the opportunity to do business with the customer company. It makes clear that only those companies willing to revolutionize their management philosophies and to put their quality, cost, and cycle time houses in order will be chosen as partnership suppliers.

A deadline is usually set by which time suppliers must conform to the minimum goals established for quality, cost, and cycle time improvements. At such an opening meeting, the customer company offers help to suppliers, either directly or through consultants in the field who can accelerate supplier performance in these vital parameters.

The second conference concentrates on the suppliers chosen for potential partnership. Here the obligations of partnership, on both sides, are discussed in depth, and progress is reviewed. Subsequent conferences are directed to preferred suppliers and eventually confined to the narrow base of partnership suppliers. A chosen theme sets the tone of each meeting. The purpose of these subsequent conferences is to:

- Move partnership to stages 3 and 4 of supply management.
- Exchange plans with respect to business, product, and technology.
- Provide supplier guidance and training.
- Overcome roadblocks in partnership relationships.

Ordinarily, these all-day conferences are held either once or twice a year, with invitations going to both potential and actual partnership suppliers. (Here, Pareto's law applies, in that 20 percent or less of the total number of suppliers will generally account for 80 percent or more of the total dollars expended on material purchases). Senior managers on both sides attend.

The agenda at the plenary sessions will almost invariably include: (1) an overview of the customer company's business; (2) a rundown on product and technology developments combined with future projections; (3) a supplier panel discussion, in which supplier issues, concerns, and expectations are aired; and (4) recognition or awards given for superior supplier performance.

Smaller breakout training sessions concentrate on:

- Supplier management orientation
- Quality tools (especially SPC and DOE)
- Cycle time reduction
- Value engineering and other cost reduction tools
- Participative management
- Ratings of suppliers' strengths and weaknesses (done only in one-on-one sessions)

Supplier Show and Technical Symposium

Some customer companies supplement the conference with a supplier show and technical symposium. Its main purpose is to provide the customer's engineering, manufacturing, and purchasing personnel with a wider exposure to the products and technologies available from its key suppliers. Perhaps even more important than the show itself is the series of technical seminars that the experts from the suppliers' companies conduct on topics of interest to the customer's engineers. The papers presented at these sessions, which can last from one to three days, are state-of-the-art subjects, and serve as excellent bridges between the isolated islands of the customer's and suppliers' technical communities.

Example: In 1982, a company launched its supplier partnership process with a one-day conference for 250 of its top suppliers. The conference theme was "The Challenge," with emphasis on the global challenge, market erosion, and profit stagnation. The company stressed that survival was not a one-way street: The survival of the suppliers themselves depended on how their customers fared in the fierce arena of international competition; and the survival of the company depended on how suppliers responded to the requirements for quality, cost, and services it had to meet in order to stay ahead of its competition.

The second conference, a year later, had "Meeting the Challenge: Improving Quality" as its theme. The company shared its growth opportunities and new product developments with its suppliers and invited them to present their perception of what progress had been made by the infant partnership.

The third conference, two years later, selected "The Continuing Challenge: Quality, a Strategic Roadmap" as its theme. With quality issues at the forefront two years in a row, topics such as supplier certification and quality education were highlighted. Just-in-time, cycle time improvements, value engineering, capital improvements, and automation were introduced.

The fourth and fifth conferences focused on "The Continuing Challenge: Making our Best Better" and "Winning Through Partnership." Over the five years, there has been a notable transition from customer domination to a much more equitable customer-supplier partnership, and the results achieved on both sides are a testimonial to the success of that partnership.

Supplier Councils

The logical sequel to supplier conferences is the formation of a supplier council, where the "voice of the supplier" begins to carry greater weight as well as greater responsibility. Membership in the council is divided pretty evenly between major managers from the customer company and key executives from the supplier companies.

The councils' objectives are to:

- Advance partnership in concrete terms with "best-in-class" suppliers.
- Provide a forum for policy discussions, airing of expectations, planning and consultation.
- Resolve friction between customer and supplier, deal with supplier concerns, and evaluate recommendations.
- Measure partnership progress on both sides.

Supplier members are usually presidents or general managers of their respective companies, with a fourth of their membership rotating every two years. There is a maximum of twenty supplier companies represented, usually coincident with the top 10 or 20 percent of suppliers who account for 70 to 80 percent of total material dollars spent. In addition to dollar volume, supplier selection is based on technological contributions, "best-in-class" candidates, and ability to represent other suppliers. Customer company members are drawn from members of the supplier partnership steering committee; commodity team leaders and support staff are permitted to attend supplier councils as observers.

Meeting two to four times a year, usually for two days at a stretch, supplier councils feature plenary sessions, breakout sessions for committees and teams, and final reports back to the council at large.

A list of the topics that make up the agenda at supplier council meetings indicates the scope and usefulness of this body:

- Partnership policy formulations
- Management commitment to partnership (both sides)
- Review of customer-supplier expectations
- Measuring partnership progress
- Meshing of product/technical plans (both sides)
- Newsletter contents for all partnership suppliers
- Planning annual partnership supplier conferences/shows
- Furthering the effectiveness of early supplier involvement
- Supplier suggestions: encouragement, evaluation, rewards
- Financial incentives and penalties: based on exceeding or falling short of delivery, quality/reliability, or performance targets
- Supplier evaluation, qualification, certification
- Supplier training/direct assistance: in topics such as management, quality, cost, cycle time, employee participation
- Extension of partnership to subsuppliers
- Sensitivity to forward or backward integration
- Resolution of roadblocks in day-to-day dealings at lower levels

One of the most useful functions of a supplier council is to act as a collective supplier conscience for the customer company. In the practice of supply management, "there is many a slip 'twixt the cup and the lip," between policies carefully crafted by the customer company's top management and its implementation at the buyer levels. The supplier council, much better than any single supplier, could address these counterproductive discrepancies without fear of inciting a vendetta against an individual supplier.

Supplier Concerns

What suppliers are concerned about can be gleaned from the following statements made at a supplier council meeting:

"We [the suppliers] hear about the lofty goals of partnership, the importance of quality, etc., from you [the customer's steering committee], but when push comes to shove, the only thing your buyers hammer away at is price!"

"Our perception is that you have not communicated adequately, or in a timely fashion, the objectives and importance of supplier partnership to your purchasing, quality, engineering, and other departments."

"Partnership practices do not appear to be consistent across the various divisions of your corporation."

"After eighteen months of partnership, it appears to be more of a one-way street—in your favor. It may be unrealistic to expect a 50-50 benefit, but why in hell should it be 90-10!"

"We feel your supplier rating system is artificial, cumbersome, and of limited value."

"Why do your quality people insist on getting piles of control charts from us when they don't even look at them, when the charts are of little use to us, and when precontrol can so easily be substituted for them?"

"In the eighteen months of partnership, we have not seen real problem-solving help from your quality professionals—only exhortations that we must do better."

"In the spirit of partnership, why can't you give us more stable forecasts both in time and quantity? You keep jerking us up and down in schedules, just as you used to."

"While there is improvement, your print requirements are still unrealistic and your engineers are still mighty opinionated."

"The suggestion system you introduced for us is good, but the answers [to suggestions] take too long and acceptance is check mated by excuses."

These criticisms were formulated by the supplier side in a caucus held during the formal supplier council meetings. The suppliers did not pull their punches. They were not afraid to "tell it like it is." The customer company's steering committee did not take offense at the charges leveled. In fact, it thanked the suppliers for their candor and formed teams to investigate the legitimate issues raised. Since that time, the climate of cooperation at the lower levels has improved steadily.

Supplier Suggestions: A Prop to Partnership

In the realm of ideas, the supplier is a gold mine that has yet to be creatively tapped. This book outlines two specific ways in which supplier ideas can be encouraged and rewarded. Chapter 19 deals with early supplier involvement, when supplier ideas at the very outset of design can provide the customer company with a distinct competitive edge. It also suggests a system of financial rewards or royalties for the use of such supplier ideas.

In addition to ideas on a specific part pertaining to his order, a supplier can also be encouraged to contribute ideas of a more general nature that may further the cause of partnership. Some companies have established a suggestion system for this purpose, paralleling suggestion systems already instituted in their own organizations. This involves forms for the supplier to document his suggestions, provisions for evaluating them quickly and fairly at the customer company, and recognition (generally nonmonetary) of those suppliers whose ideas have been accepted. Unfortunately, the suggestion system has not taken root in the American industrial culture. Hence, its extension to supplier companies is not likely to meet with dazzling success unless the cause is championed and nurtured all the way.

Chapter 7

The Nuts and Bolts of Supply Management

Survival depends on winning . . . losing means extinction. . . . There is no alternative to partnership—but I submit that our expectation level of how that partnership must work, and the results it must yield, must be raised by an order of magnitude. Our involvement with each other—trust and respect for each other—must be magnified. Nothing else is acceptable—because nothing else will win the ball game.

—Bill Weisz, vice-chairman, Motorola, supplier conference, 1986.

The Commodity Teams: Workhorse of Supply Management

In Chapter 6, we outlined the functions of a top-level supply management steering committee and the role it plays in developing the infrastructure of partnership. One of its most important tasks is the selection and nurturing of commodity teams that are at the very center of supply management.

The core composition of a commodity team consists of representatives from purchasing, engineering, and supplier quality assurance. Depending on circumstances, this core membership may be augmented by representatives from manufacturing engineering, cost estimating, finance, and other specialty functions, as needed. The core members should be assigned *full-time* to the commodity team for the quickest and largest return on investment. Several companies that started supply mangement with just part-time core membership are discovering that their quality, cost, and cycle time results are less than spectacular.

Commodity team members should be selected with great care. They should have a proven track record in their respective disciplines and command the respect of their colleagues. They should have the ability to bring people together, to knock down departmental walls, and dismantle the vertical silos that are the root-cause of company turf wars. The team leader is usually chosen from engineering, purchasing, or supplier quality assurance, depending upon the degree of technological sophistication required for the commodity.

Large customer companies can generally afford one commodity team per commodity. Smaller companies with limited resources may have two or more commodities assigned to each team. It is not necessary at the start of the supply management process to tackle all commodities. The most important commodities—in terms of expected quality, cost, or cycle time improvements—are selected first. In some cases, a pilot run with just one commodity and one team can light the way for large-scale efforts later on.

As the organizational linchpin of supply management—as its quarterback—the commodity team has both initial tasks that continue until partnership suppliers are selected and ongoing tasks to sustain that partnership.

Initial Tasks of Commodity Teams

Among the most important of these initial tasks are to:

- Establish goals for quality, cost, cycle time, maximum part-number base, and maximum supplier base; the costs to achieve them; the expected benefits; and a timetable.
- Review the technology of the commodity (whether high tech, smoke-stack, or garden variety) and the potential for growth or obsolescence.
- Mount a drive for a significant part-number reduction in that commodity. A ten-to-one reduction is entirely feasible (see Chapter 19 for details).
- Assist in conducting make-versus-buy analyses (see next section).
- Systematically reduce the supplier base (as outlined later in this chapter), notify terminated suppliers, and benchmark potential new suppliers, including transplant suppliers.
- Design guidelines for engineers so that meaningful, cost-effective commodity specifications can be established.
- Promote design of experiments (DOE) within the engineering commu-

Table 7-1. Factors included in an accurate make-versus-buy analysis.

Make	*Buy*
• Direct labor and materials	• Supplier price
• Cost of incoming inspection of piece parts	• Cost of incoming inspection of product
• Costs of poor quality: scrap, analyzing, repair, line inspection, and test	• Freight, scrap, return
• Direct labor and administrative overhead	• Purchasing, supplier quality assurance, engineering costs: product
• Technical/managerial capability and plant capacity tied up	• Inventory costs: product
• Inventory costs: piece parts	
• Purchase transaction and handling costs: piece parts	
• Quality assurance and engineering costs: piece parts	

nity so that product specifications can be translated into component specifications with well-defined target values and realistic tolerances (see Chapter 13 for details).
• Train commodity members, and engineering, supplier quality assurance, and purchasing departments, in quality, cost, and cycle time improvement techniques.

Make vs. Buy: A Vital Consideration for Commodity Teams

An important consideration for any customer company is a "make" versus "buy" decision. Generally, such decisions are made by accounting or manufacturing, with little input from the purchasing function. In companies where manufacturing is dominant, the unwritten policy is: "Make what you want to make or what is easy to make; buy from suppliers what you don't want to make or what is too difficult to make—when in doubt, make." This preconceived rule of thumb is giving way to a more enlightened approach guided by commodity teams, which are more professional and more even-handed in their outlook than make-versus-buy committees.

In a traditional make-versus-buy decision, only superficial cost factors are taken into account: For example, direct labor and materials for "make" and supplier price for "buy." Even here, the supplier price is a true cost—a fixed cost—while the make cost is a rubber yardstick, with manufacturing manipulating cost figures, similar to "cost plus" arrangements in some defense contracts. An accurate analysis should include the factors shown in Table 7-1.

In general, unless a traditional make cost is at least 10 percent under the buy cost, the additional factors shown in Table 7-1 will swing the balance in favor of buy. Further, the customer company is not stuck with a "museum piece" production line in his own shop, if some technological or process breakthrough renders it obsolete.

Example: A defense contractor conducted a make-versus-buy analysis on an electronic timer, as shown in Table 7-2. The original, but superficial, analysis indicated that the make cost of $5.55 was less than the buy costs of $5.81 by 4.7 percent. However, when factors traditionally not included in either make or buy costs were taken into consideration, the differential swing was decidedly against the make decision by a comfortable 11.6 percent margin. And when the start-up costs of $1.51 was added, the differential of $2.22, or 36.2 percent, was even more convincing.

The Mechanics of Reducing a Supplier Base

Before beginning a process of supplier base reductions, the commodity team should gather pertinent data on current suppliers as well as on potential new suppliers. This involves:

- A review of the "hard" factors associated with current suppliers: their number, and the quality, price, and lead time performance of each
- A review of the "soft" factors associated with current suppliers: location—whether local, regional, national, or offshore; cooperativeness; responsiveness; flexibility; dependability; the longevity of the customer-supplier relationship; and especially, supplier loyalty during the relationship
- A review of the capabilities of current suppliers: their technical, financial, quality, and manufacturing abilities, as distinguished from their actual performance
- An assessment of new suppliers, using the same benchmark techniques described in Chapter 6. This should include suppliers established by transplant companies, that is, offshore companies with plants in the U.S. Transplant companies, to their credit, have not only brought manufacturing and suppliers back to the United States, but they have also done much to strengthen their suppliers' quality and cycle time.

Table 7-2.   Make-versus-buy analysis on an electronic timer.

	Make Unit Cost ($)		Buy Unit Cost ($)
Cost Element	*Initial Cost*	*Recurring Cost*	
Cost quote		5.55	5.81
Incoming inspection		0.10	0.02
Cost of poor quality: scrap, analyzing, repair, inspection, test		0.38	0.09
Direct labor overhead		0.33	0.04
Administrative overhead		0.11	0.03
Technical, managerial manpower invested	1.51	0.26	0.03
Freight, material handling		0.06	0.03
Inventory costs		0.04	0.07
Total cost	$1.51	$6.83	$6.12

An Alternative to Selecting Only Benchmark Suppliers

Benchmarking, however, can be a difficult road. Often there is no perfect supplier to be found or, if one is discovered, he may be in Japan or Korea, thousands of miles away. It is my conviction, based on benchmark searches, that there are few suppliers, domestic or international, who can instantly measure up to the high quality standards that are required to leapfrog American industry's Japanese competitiors.

Such a search is reminiscent of a mythical story of two young children determined to find the blue bird of happiness. They roamed all over the world, over land and sea, hill and dale, until they discovered it in their own backyard. The supplier in the customer company's backyard may not be that ideal benchmark supplier, but he can be developed into one. And the conversion of such a "prodigal" supplier can bring more joy than finding a benchmark supplier far, far away, with little mutual history, compatability of purpose, or common value systems.

Developing Suppliers Into "Best-in-Class"

Converting a small supplier with little sophistication, limited resources, and poor quality into a best-in-class supplier has several advantages over benchmarking:

- It is less expensive.
- It is less time-consuming.
- It rewards current suppliers for years of loyalty and cooperation.
- The resultant quality and cost performance is greater, less reversible, and more continuous in improvement.

This system is not just a hypothetical road map. It represents an accumulation of my experiences as I have coached several of my company's suppliers, transforming their quality levels from the dreary 1 to 5 percent defect rates down to 100 ppms, zero defects, and beyond zero defects toward zero variation. And the time span for such a transformation is ten to twenty weeks, not years.

But, as the mathematicians say, there are a few necessary and sufficient conditions for this metamorphosis.

1. The customer company itself must have an enviable track record on quality so that it can become a role model.
2. Its quality professionals must have hands-on experience in the design of experiments, multiple environment overstress tests, and the prevention of operator-controllable defects through the use of *poka-yoke*.
3. The supplier should be in close physical proximity to the customer to facilitate frequent visits by the customer's professionals.
4. The supplier, preferably, should be a small company. That does not mean that large companies are "beyond the pale." But with size comes bureaucracy, arrogance, and inertia. "Big" is no longer beautiful; "small" is now super.
5. The supplier management's attitudes are important. The supplier owner/CEO must be humble and willing to learn; he must be hungry; he must feel—to use a crude expression—in his gut the threat of extinction.
6. The supplier must be committed to continuous improvement no matter how far from world-class quality he is at the starting line.

Different Approaches to Supplier Base Reduction— Stage 1

The commodity team can choose from several methods for reducing the number of its suppliers, depending on the urgency for results and the number of existing suppliers.

The Pareto Approach

Pareto's law states that a few causes produce most of a given effect. Applied to supply management, a few suppliers—generally about 20 percent or less—

account for a very large share—generally 80 percent or more—of the total dollars purchased. Similarly, 20 percent or less of the suppliers account for 80 percent or more of the best quality track record. The commodity team can either identify the 80 percent of suppliers that have low dollar volumes or that have poor quality—or it can use a combination of both volume and quality criteria to identify candidates for elimination. This is both the easiest and the fairest method. Records of purchase volumes and quality history—through supplier rating systems—can be used for comparisons.

The Meat Ax Approach

A few large customer companies, enjoying volume leverage, tend to use rather brutal and dictatorial methods. The entire supplier population is invited to one or more supplier conferences. All are given an equal chance, regardless of past history, to meet new customer requirements, such as:

- Elimination of incoming inspection—with the supplier committing to zero defects in his shipments
- Maximum two-week lead times
- On-time shipments
- Cost reductions passed on to the customer

Suppliers are told that they have a specified number of months in which to conform to these requirements or they will "be on the outside, looking in." Some customer companies offer the names of consultants who can bring the suppliers "up to speed," especially with respect to quality. The Greeley division of Hewlett Packard is a classic example of a customer company using a meat ax approach.

The Competency Staircase Approach

A few companies use selected strategies as a step-by-step or competency staircase approach to supplier reductions. Figure 7-1 depicts this method. To begin with, quality is a "given." The first cut is made on the basis of technical competency, followed by cuts associated with manufacturing competency, commercial (financial) competency, responsiveness, size, and location. The final result of the weeding-out process is no more than one supplier per part number and single-digit numbers of suppliers for an entire commodity. Xerox used this staircase approach to reduce its supplier base from 5,000 to 300 in just one year!

The "Triage" Approach

Some companies practice a modified "triage" approach; the term and the practice are based on the medical approach to casualties that was adopted

Figure 7-1. The staircase approach to a reduced supplier base.

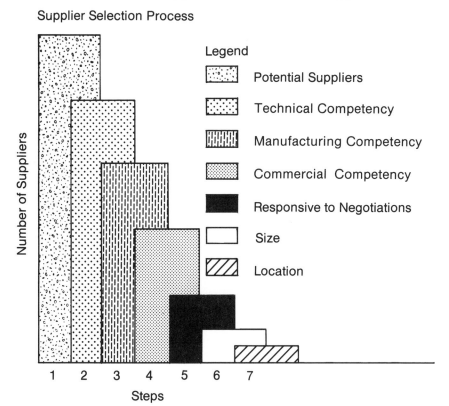

Supplier Selection Process

Legend

[:::::] Potential Suppliers

[:::::] Technical Competency

[IIIII] Manufacturing Competency

[:::::] Commercial Competency

[■■■■] Responsive to Negotiations

[ ] Size

[////] Location

in World War I. The wounded were divided into three groups: those who were so badly wounded that medical help would serve no useful purpose, those with superficial wounds needing little treatment, and those in the middle who could be saved if the full capacity of the medical team was utilized. Similarly, in the supplier selection process, suppliers are divided into three groups: the first, the great majority, those who have such poor track records that they become targets for extinction; the second, a very tiny corps of near-perfect suppliers who need no attention and are candidates for partnership; the third, suppliers who are not up to the new and high standards of the customer company but who are worthy of salvation. The resources of the customer company could then be devoted to this third group of suppliers.

Phasing Out Current Suppliers

After the first cut—regardless of which of the above four approaches to supplier reduction is used—terminating the rejected suppliers becomes one of the most difficult tasks faced by a commodity team. In economic terms, a customer company may have little choice; but emotionally, it is tantamount to a unilateral divorce proceeding. Many suppliers feel let down, even victimized, especially if they have rendered years of loyal service. Under these circumstances, it is best to explain the whole partnership process to all suppliers well in advance of actual reductions, so as to give them a grace period of at least six months in which to substantially improve and, perhaps, to give a few deserving suppliers a second chance. As stated in Chapter 5, it is easier, more effective, and more soul-satisfying to convert a local, but marginal, supplier into a partnership supplier than to go searching all over the globe for a new best-in-class supplier.

There are other reasons for caution in throwing existing suppliers overboard. One is fairness. A customer company may have a poor supplier-rating system. (Even though many companies believe they have a good rating system, there are inequities and arbitrariness in most systems.) In other cases, the rating system may not have been explained to the affected suppliers. Another reason involves existing tooling, which may be difficult or expensive to transfer to a new supplier. A fourth reason is the large engineering backlog that could build up in order to change drawings and print requirements that are both necessary and inevitable when switching suppliers. Finally, there are legal obligations that must be very carefully weighed when dealing with minority suppliers. The wrath of the government when translated into fines and cancelled contracts—if a minimum percentage of the procurement business is not directed to minority suppliers—is a far more important economic and political consideration than the merits of one supplier over another. I have been able to transform minority suppliers into partnership suppliers even in those cases where the starting point in quality and cycle time proficiency was low. What is needed is active, concrete *help* sustained over a few months, after which these suppliers reach a take-off stage with self-sustained progress.

Selection of Finalist Suppliers—Stage 2

Once the supplier base is appreciably reduced for a particular commodity—say, from 100 to 20—as described in Stage 1, the commodity team prepares a detailed survey questionnaire (which may differ from commodity to commodity) that is sent out to these semifinalist suppliers. It is similar to, although less comprehensive than the questionnaire detailed in Appendix 1 of this book. The purpose of the questionnaire is to evaluate the semifinalist suppliers' capabilities without an actual visit by the commodity team, in order to conserve time and resources. Since the supplier reponses are in writing, the commodity team also furnishes detailed guidelines so that the meaning of each question in the survey is clearly understood. The guidelines also permit each supplier to determine a quantitative score—supported, of course, with documentation to prevent the supplier bluffing his way to disproportionately high score.

The commodity team then evaluates the responses of the semifinalist suppliers. It may wish to communicate with a particular supplier if the responses are not quite clear or if the documentation in support of a particular question is inadequate. Based on these scores, the commodity team reduces the list: say, from 20 to a range of 5 to 10 finalist suppliers.

Selection of Partnership Suppliers—Stage 3

Next, the commodity team prepares a questionnaire—similar to but more detailed and thorough than the questionnaire in Stage 2—to serve as a survey instrument during in-depth visits to the finalist suppliers.

Appendix 1 is a hypothetical survey sent by the commodity team of the ABC company. Drawn from questionnaires of real customer companies, it is of benchmark quality and is intended to provide the reader with a standard of excellence that many customer companies—to say nothing of supplier companies—may not be able to meet. I feel, however, that unless we raise the height of the bar, American companies—both customer and supplier—will settle for mediocrity and lose out to international competition.

The Appendix 1 questionnaire has ten categories for assessing the capabilities of finalist suppliers. These include financial strength, management commitment, design expertise, quality proficiency, cost competitiveness, service flexibility and dependability, manufacturing capability, cycle time concentration, extension of partnership to sub-suppliers, and employee participative climate. Each category is assigned an importance weight and a rating scale. The weight multiplied by the rating establishes a score for each category. The category scores when added together provide an overall score of the supplier's capability. Each category has ten questions. The categories, weights, rating scales, and detailed questions can be modified depending on the nature of the commodity, the standard that the customer company wishes to establish, the degree of readiness among the finalist suppliers, their size and location, and offshore versus domestic suppliers. As a note of caution, however, a customer company should not develop a questionnaire for its finalist suppliers that *it* could not pass. (Despite this obvious conflict between precept and practice, a fair percentage of customer companies using questionnaires to assess their suppliers are incapable of passing their own surveys!)

Before the commodity team actually visits the finalist suppliers, its team members should be trained in the dynamics of team-visit evaluations. General Motors is a benchmark company in the use of this technique. It conducts comprehensive assessment seminars to not only train its own commodity teams in survey techniques, but it also opens these seminars to its suppliers so that they can better prepare for the surveys. The training should include: interviewing techniques; observing body language that may reveal more than the spoken word; how to recognize tell-tale signs of poor quality, for example, by peering into the scrap barrel; how to see, touch, and feel processes in operation; and how to talk in particular to manufacturing people who, as recipients of the deficiencies and delinquencies of other departments, are likely to be more forthright than their management.

The commodity team should also notify the finalist suppliers ahead of its visit, explain the purpose (to select the partnership suppliers), identify key departments to be interviewed, and state up-front that it expects to talk to people in the lower echelons in order to gain varying insights.

Team visits to finalist suppliers last from one to four days, depending upon the complexity of the technology and the process, the importance of the commodity, and whether the supplier is a new or an existing one. Various layers of the supplier's organization structure are interviewed, starting with top management and extending to internal "customers" of various functions, such as marketing, sales, engineering, quality assurance, and purchasing. The internal "customers" of such functions are likely to be more objective in the assessment of their "suppliers" than top management.

At the end of each day, commodity team members review their findings and the individual scores on each question among themselves. At the end of the interviews, the team computes the total score and has a final wrap-up meeting with the supplier's entire management team, where it highlights the supplier's strengths and weaknesses.

After the team returns to its home base, it compares the scores of all finalist suppliers and selects as many partnership suppliers that are targeted for the commodity. The team also transmits a written report on its survey to each finalist supplier.

The suppliers selected for partnership are then given information on the customer company's plans so that they can intelligently anticipate future requirements for capacity, tooling, raw materials, and electronic data transfers. The road to partnership is often littered with wrecks of suppliers when capacity planning is not transmitted by the customer company. As a result, the supplier in inundated with a flood of new orders, causing him to stumble over quality or delivery requirements, and a breakdown of the partnership process occurs.

Ongoing Tasks of Commodity Teams

The initial tasks of commodity teams come to an end when partnership suppliers are selected for the commodity. It is only then that the hard tasks of working with these partnership suppliers to achieve mutual goals begin. These tasks include:

- Orientation of supplier management
- Orientation of supplier's key personnel

- Detailed quality audit (Appendix 2) and detailed design of experiments (DOE) and statistical process control (SPC) audit (Appendix 3)
- Detailed cycle time audit
- Review of audit weaknesses and improvement plan
- Supplier training and workshops (discussed in this section)
- Facilitation of clear, firm, and mutually acceptable specifications (see Chapter 18)
- Classification of characteristics, "Bo Derek" scale cosmetic and visual criteria (see Chapter 18)
- Promotion of Early Supplier Involvement (ESI) and Value Engineering (VE) (see Chapter 19)
- DOE demonstrations
- Cycle time reduction demonstrations
- Raw-material blanket orders and sourcing for subsuppliers
- Reduction of offshore procurement
- Encouragement of forward integration

Supplier Training

There is an old saying that if you feed a man a fish, you've fed him once. If you teach him how to fish, you've fed him forever! Giving only occasional assistance to a supplier is the equivalent of feeding him once. Training him is feeding him forever. Supplier training is one of the most important obligations of a customer company in the partnership process. There is an important caveat, however. The customer company's professionals who conduct the training must be recognized experts in their respective fields. For example, if a quality professional teaches a supplier control charts—that are both obsolete and futile—while ignoring design of experiments as the primary technique to get to zero defects, and beyond, to zero variation, his teaching may do little to really improve supplier quality. Unfortunately, 90 percent of so-called quality professionals have little or no knowledge of design of experiments.

The first requirement in training, therefore, is expressed in the old adage: "Doctor, cure thyself." The customer company should begin by training its own people in supply management. The affected populations are its engineering, purchasing, and quality communities. This will reduce the gap between the pious pronouncements of the customer company's top management on supplier partnership and the actual practice of poorly trained buyers who hammer away at suppliers for price, price, and nothing but price.

On the supplier side, training must begin with its management. There is little point in training the supplier's technical people when its top management shows little understanding or support and is reluctant to get involved. The training sequence, therefore, should be supplier management, followed by its technical population. The supplier can then become the trainer for his own line workers.

Table 7-3 presents a comprehensive training curriculum for suppliers. (It can also be used for training the customer's engineering, purchasing, and quality personnel as well as its commodity teams.) The first and most important topic is quality, since it is also the most prolific cost-reduction technique as well as the prerequisite to cycle time reduction. These two subjects also need special attention—cost reduction because the traditional ways of reducing costs are so ineffective and the new tools so little known; cycle time reduction because so many supplier companies are not even familiar with the technique, and the few that are have no road map for implementing it.

From Seminars to Workshops to Consultations

Across the country, there is an awakening to the necessity for training for recharging the batteries of the brain, for converting the pair-of-hands worker to the knowledge worker. However, training without implementation is even worse than no training. It only adds costs. It can also add to the frustration of trained employees, as they see their training go to waste. Training, in seminar form, can only be considered a first step, an appetizer. The main meal comes in implementing the techniques picked up in training.

Fortunately, there is a road map. In supply management, seminars are best followed up by workshops, where suppliers bring back to the classroom actual examples of work done on techniques such as the design of experiments, SPC, value engineering, and cycle time reduction. These case studies are reviewed by the instructors in terms of both methodologies and results. There is also a motivation component to workshops. Other suppliers, listening to what one supplier company has achieved, are then encouraged—or shamed—into replicating good results in their own companies. I have trained hundreds of Motorola's suppliers. Many of them have returned to workshop sessions, where they presented the achievements in design of experiments and SPC that have saved their companies hundreds of thousands of dollars. It is one of the most heart-warming experiences to see babes-in-the-woods suppliers with no knowledge of even an elementary quality symbol such as standard deviation (σ) become professional problem solvers almost overnight!

The last step in truly effective training is a one-on-one consultation. A particularly thorny quality, cost, or cycle time problem at the supplier's site may require the customer company to provide hands-on consultation. This is especially true if techniques such as the design of experiments are to solve long-standing quality problems. It is said that one picture is worth a thousand words. An addendum would be: A demonstration of shirt-sleeve, on-the-job help is worth a thousand customer admonitions!

Examples: Many U.S. companies have now established extensive training programs for their own personnel. Nell Eurich, an educational consultant

Table 7-3. Training curriculum in supply management for supplier personnel.

Topic	Management	Technical Personnel	Line Workers
Quality seminar	- Economics of Quality - Management "To Do's" - Quality System/Costs - Audits - Customer/Supplier Quality Assurance - Overview of DOE/SPC	- The Seven Basic Quality Control Tools - Specs Optimization - Process Capability: c_{p_k} - Design of Experiments - SPC	- The Seven Basic Quality Control Tools - Simple Problem Solving - Precontrol
Quality workshops		- Case Studies in DOE and SPC	- Case Studies in Simple Problem Solving
Cost reductions	- Overview of Value Engineering - Overview of Other Cost-Reduction Techniques	- Value Engineering Principles/Practices/Case Studies - Experience Curves - Group Technology/Standardization - Design for Manufacturability	- Suggestion Generation - Quality Control Circles
JIT seminars	- Overview of JIT in Manufacturing and White-Collar Work	- Cycle Time Reduction in Manufacturing and Design - Supplier Lead Time Reduction	- Elementary Principles/Practices in JIT
Participative management	- Motivation Theories - Management Involvement - Participation in Action	- Role of Technical Personnel in Participative Management	- Role of Line Workers in Participative Management

at the Carnegie Foundation for the Advancement of Teaching, states that these training programs in total may soon exceed the size of the nation's entire university system. She estimates that U.S. companies are spending more than $40 billion a year to deliver education to some 8 million workers. By contrast, U.S. universities spend $60 billion annually to educate about the same number of students.

There is as yet no critical mass buildup for extending such corporate training to suppliers. But there are notable exceptions—companies that visualize a payoff down the road. Two such examples are in the public domain.

Ford and the American Supplier Institute

In 1981, the Ford Motor Company started its Supplier Institute to train its key suppliers in quality topics. Its successor today is the American Supplier Institute (ASI), a nonprofit, tax-exempt corporation dedicated to improving the quality, productivity, and world market position of American manufacturers. It is patterned after the nonprofit Union of Japanese Scientists and Engineers (JUSE) and the Central Japan Quality Control Association (CJQCA). ASI's main thrust is quality, especially the design of experiments. Its main claim to fame is the use of Taguchi's orthogonal arrays as the principal road to achieving the design of experiments objectives of reduced variation. (As we shall see in Chapter 13, the Taguchi methodology is complex and costly, and can be, in certain cases, statistically weak.) It also plows new ground with the introduction of two Japanese quality techniques: quality function deployment and the quality loss function. Recently it has added Flexible Manufacturing Systems (FMS) and Just-in-Time (JIT) to its expanding curriculum. ASI has trained more than 25,000 engineers and executives from more than 150 major companies—mostly Ford suppliers—in extensive seminars and workshops.

General Motors and the General Physics Corporation

Not to be outdone in the field of supplier training, General Motors formed an alliance with the General Physics Corporation in 1986 to provide a new and broad-reaching "continuous improvement" process for its suppliers. The new process, called "Targets for Excellence," is designed to evaluate and assist suppliers in five key areas: management, quality, cost, delivery, and technology. (Targets for Excellence replaces GM's older Supplier Performance Evaluation and Rating System (SPEAR), which was widely used for assessing the performance of its suppliers.)

Targets for Excellence offers the following supplier training topics and programs:

- The "Supplier Quality Process" is designed to accelerate the rate of improvement both within GM and throughout its supplier organizations.
- "Technology and Training Group," as an arm of GM and the General Physics Corporation, has developed a new GM supplier standard and trains GM and supplier personnel in supplier part qualification and certification, problem reporting, and resolution and supplier performance reporting.
- The "Supplier Assessment Seminar" is designed to help supplier managers understand and prepare for GM's new supplier quality process and also to improve the supplier's competitive position and help him to comply with other customers' requirements.
- "The New GM Standard for Supplier Performance Evaluation and Reporting" is intended to help suppliers understand the new supplier standard and improve their competitive position.
- "Continuous Improvement and the GM Supplier" focuses on the importance of continuous improvement and the supplier's responsibilities for achieving such improvement as part of his long-term business "health plan."

The Targets for Excellence manual, a two-inch-thick document, unfortunately intimidates rather than helps GM suppliers. It is filled with bureaucratic language and almost totally devoid of practical, down-to-earth techniques to help suppliers achieve the continual improvement that General Motors is trying to promote. The expected verdict in the court of supplier opinion: "Fine objective. Poor execution!"

An Example of Commodity Team Actions and Results

The entire mechanics of commodity team actions and their results can be illustrated by an actual example. One Texas-based company, in developing its supplier partnership process, focused on commodity teams as the most effective way to achieve its supply management goals. By and large, it followed the game plan outlined earlier in the discussion of the commodity team game plan, with a few special strategies of its own added:

- It decided on a *full-time effort* for each of its commodity teams so that they would not be distracted by fire fighting within their normal functions.
- It started by installing special software capable of gathering and analyzing data in order to maintain a computerized supply management system.

- It reexamined several of its "make" items that had automatically gone to its production department in the past. It put Manufacturing on notice that, henceforth, it would have to be competitive with outside manufacturers in order to get the business.
- It reassessed its kit and subassembly practice and decided that it would be more economical to encourage its partnership suppliers to build entire kits and subassemblies than to continue administering all the details associated with the hundreds and thousands of piece parts that made up the kits and assemblies.
- Although it considered offshore sourcing, it adapted the policy of favoring its existing suppliers and working with them, especially those within a few hundred miles of the company, and of converting them into best-in-class suppliers.

Here are the results after one year:

- *Supplier base.* The number of suppliers in seven commodities alone was reduced from 241 to 109.
- *Part-number base.* Reduced from 7,430 to 5,571.
- *Quality.*
  —Lots rejected were reduced from 8 to 2 percent.
  —Certified suppliers (zero inspection) were increased from 10 to 22 percent.
- *On-time delivery.* Late lots were reduced from 30 to 9 percent.
- *Cost reduction.*
  —Sixteen suppliers reduced costs in excess of 10 percent each, for a total cost reduction of $761,000.
  —In twenty-one commodities, costs were reduced by $7,096,000, or 12.2 percent, against a goal of 10 percent.
  —Overall cost reduction reached 16.6 percent in two years.
- *Techniques used to achieve cost reduction.*
  —Larger volume to partnership suppliers
  —Longer-term agreements with partnership suppliers
  —Cost-reduction targets established with these suppliers
  —Early supplier involvement
  —Value engineering
  —Move from "make" to "buy"
  —Move from piece part purchases to kits and subassemblies

Chapter 8

Organizational Lift-off

We tried hard . . . but it seemed that every time we were beginning to form up into teams, we would be reorganized. . . . I was to learn later in life that we tend to meet any new situation by reorganizing; and a wonderful method it can be for creating the illusion of progress, while producing confusion, inefficiency, and demoralization. . . .

Organizational Musical Chairs

Where did the above quotation originate? In the writings of Peter F. Drucker, the guru of management? In a Harvard Business School case study? No. It is from a Petronius Arbiter, a Roman general in the year 210 B.C.! In more than two thousand years, it would seem, the world has not advanced much—at least in terms of organizational practices.

While there are legitimate uses for reorganization within a company, what is distressing is its use in attempting to solve *all* problems, regardless of their root cause. The problem music starts and management rearranges neat little boxes on the company's organizational chart. A new head is chosen. The problem does not go away. More musical chairs, and the dance goes on. Long-term employees in such companies say that if they received a dollar for each management reorganization, they could become millionaires!

Frequent reorganizations are especially dislocating in supply management. In its early stages, relations between suppliers and various members of the customer's organization are cautious and tentative, even fragile. A supplier's patient building of bridges with a customer's engineering, purchasing, and quality control departments is summarily sabotaged by mindless shifting of personnel in the name of problem solving. And so, the first principle of organization in supply management should be to allow the all-important team relationships between customer and supplier to mature, without the violence of organizational upheavals on either side.

The Flat Pyramid

One of the characteristics of successful companies is the relatively few layers of management between the worker and the C.E.O. They generally have five or six layers versus twelve to fifteen for traditional companies. The advantages of this "flat organizational pyramid" are increasingly being recognized by American companies for the following reasons:

- It decomposes a bureaucracy that, in recent years, has grown in layers and reduced in spans. Too often, a manager has only one or two people reporting to him. The result is overmanagement and overcomplicated matrices.
- It facilitates faster, more open communications—up and down.
- It reduces the filtering and shading of unpalatable news traveling to the top.
- It eliminates the necessity of layers of middle management, whose main function is to gather and analyze data. Much of this can now be done by the omnipresent, omniscient computer.
- It pares down central staffs.
- Above all, it releases the creative, innovative potential in people who are now closer to the top and can better align their interests with those of the company.

This organizational delamination is important for supply management as well. The Mason-Dixon line between the paper pushers and the decision makers can be blurred, if not erased. Entire lower-order functions, such as expediting, incoming inspection, storage and handling, that add little value can be drastically reduced, allowing for more challenging assignments all around. With the new organizational freedom and intrapreneurship, Purchasing and Quality people can unshackle themselves from the prisons of their desks and go out into the real world of the suppliers and add something of value to both sides.

Function vs. Matrix and Centralization vs. Decentralization

Over the past thirty years, personnel departments have come up with yet another new organizational idea, called organizational development (OD).

Table 8-1. Supply management: Advantages of centralization vs. decentralization.

Centralized Supply Management	*Decentralized Supply Management*
Lower purchase costs	"Ownership" preserved at each plant
Corporate leverage strengthened	
Duplication of suppliers and part numbers reduced	Local plant requirements best met by local personnel
Uniform supply management policies, uniformly administered	Offshore procurements reduced
	In tune with focused factory and strategic business units—both trends of the future
Greater professionalism and specialization facilitated	
Electronic communication enhanced	Local help to local suppliers made possible
Paperwork reduced	

This has provoked numerous debates within industry. For example, should functional management continue to rule the roost or should it be scrapped and replaced by matrix management? The proponents of functional management decry the matrix approach. How can a person have two bosses, they ask. The matrix adherents are quick to respond that almost every person born has been subjected to matrix management—a mother and a father!

Another debate that the OD people have sponsored concerns centralization versus decentralization. The buzzword of the centralists is "economies of scale." The decentralists have their own rallying cry: "Smaller is better." Not to be outdone, the recentralists compromise with "balance."

These battles spill over into supply management as well. The functionalists stoutly claim that a consolidated purchasing and a consolidated quality control organization are required to deal with suppliers and the many nuances of partnership. The matrixers counter that the project organization, under the leadership of a product manager and including representatives from Purchasing, Quality, and so on, is the best way to attain "ownership."

But nowhere, in supply management organizations, are the battle lines so sharply drawn as between centralization and decentralization. Table 8-1 lists the advantages claimed by each side. By inference, the advantages of one side reflect the disadvantages of the other.

The Sourcing Function: A Halfway House

A recent compromise in the supply management wars between centralization and decentralization has been the creation of the sourcing function. A central corporate or divisional group, called sourcing, is given total responsibility for seeking out the best-in-class suppliers, negotiating with them, entering into contracts or agreements with them, and determining acceptable quality, prices, and cycle times. All this is done before the start of production. From that point forward, local purchasing and quality organizations take over the day-to-day dealings with the chosen suppliers on items such as releases, schedules, and other maintenance activities. On a national scale, the votes are not in on the effectiveness of sourcing as an organizational unit. Like all halfway measures, however, it is unlikely to be the answer to the riddle of "big is beautiful" versus "small is super."

The Team: The Basic Building Block of Organization

The solution to these endless debates over functional versus matrix organizations and centralization versus decentralization is so simple that it is "off the screen" of most managers. In fact, it does not even register in any organization chart. It is the team concept. Dr. Joseph Juran, one of the leading lights of world class quality, states that "the approach in solving chronic quality problems is through projects and teams—*and in no other way.*" Teams or task forces are frequently lumped with committees. There is a fundamental difference, however. Committees have a NATO (no action, talk only) notoriety! Teams and task forces, by contrast, have specific, quantified goals and timetables and are monitored by higher levels for progress. Teams tend to have a good track record. Their members bring different disciplines to bear on a project and, in the process, break down departmental walls. There is almost always a synergy, with the whole being greater than the sum of the parts. The bonds that are created between team members frequently spill over into close relationships, even if the teams are of an ad hoc nature. Behavioral scientists have estimated that on a linear scale of 1 to 1,000 with 1,000 being the maximum in effectiveness, various techniques attain the following scores:

Technique	Effectiveness Score
Company policy	1
Company Appeals to action	10
Training	100
Team organization and focused factories	1,000

According to this yardstick, teams and focused factories (see Chapter 21) have 100 to 1,000 times the effectiveness of management exhortations! Industry has several examples of teams that overcome bureaucratic rigor mortis. Table 8-2 lists typical teams in successful companies, their composition (by department), and the enormous benefits that only team power can achieve.

Supply Management Team Synergy

The ideal supply management team consists of Purchasing, Engineering, Quality Assurance, and the partnership supplier working together from the inception of design through the life cycle of the part or product. The symbiotic relationships that are established are, generally, in reverse proportion to the square of the distance between groups. People work best together when they are in close proximity to one another. That is why we have repeatedly stressed co-location in this book.

Table 8-2 shows five areas where teams involve supply management; new process design, early supplier involvement; ongoing supply management maintenance activities; commodity teams; and value engineering. What a simple but powerful way to achieve the aims of supply management for both sides! These ideal teams become a reality when a company moves from a traditional large plant—making all things for all people—to a focused factory that concentrates on a narrower family of similar products. The focused factory is treated in detail in Chapter 19.

Table 8-2. Typical teams in successful companies and benefits of "team power."

Typical Teams	Team Members	Benefits
1. New product introduction	Customer, marketing, engineering	— Translate "voice of customer" into realistic product specs — Shorten time of product to market
2. New product design	Engineering, manufacturing engineering, quality assurance	— Design products at half the cost, at half the cycle time, with half the defects, and with half the manpower vis-à-vis older designs
3. New process design	Engineering, process engineering, quality assurance, supplier	— Move toward 100% factory overall efficiency

(continued)

Table 8-2. *Continued.*

Typical Teams	Team Members	Benefits
4. Early supplier involvement	Engineering, purchasing, quality assurance, supplier	– Achieve target cost and quality
5. Ongoing supply management	Engineering, purchasing, quality assurance, supplier	– Move to zero defects and zero variation – Move to 100% yields – Continuous cost reduction each year – Move to two × theoretical cycle time
6. Commodity teams	Engineering, purchasing, quality assurance, manufacturing engineering	– Select "best-in-class" suppliers, move to stage 4 supply management
7. Value engineering	Engineering, manufacturing engineering, purchasing, quality assurance, supplier	– Reduce product costs by 10–25%, along with quality/reliability improvements
8. Diagnostic problem-solving teams	Engineering, manufacturing engineering, quality assurance	– Reduce chronic quality problems by minimum 50% in one year
9. Quality circles	Mostly direct labor teams (horizontal)	– Reduce manufacturing quality problems
10. Participative management, improvement teams	Cross-functional teams (vertical)	– Improve white-collar quality, cost, and cycle time

Horizontal Management: Filling the White Spaces

But what if the ideal of an interdisciplinary team is too much for a company to launch right away? There are, fortunately, changes in the tradi-

Figure 8-1. Traditional organization: Vertical management with white spaces.

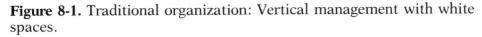
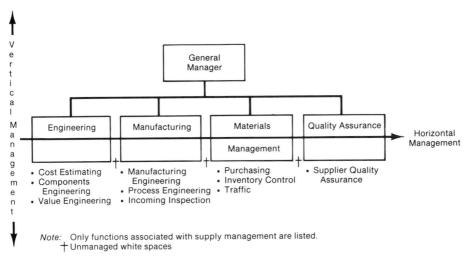

Note: Only functions associated with supply management are listed.
        + Unmanaged white spaces

tional organization that can be made as an interim step toward the ultimate. Figure 8-1 shows a traditional organization, with the primary functions of Engineering, Manufacturing, Materials Management, and Quality Assurance reporting to the general manager. This is called vertical management. Problems within each function are solved by that function, but problems between functions are frequently kicked upstairs to the top person or left unsolved. Yet products and processes flow across functions—across the white spaces of no-man's-land. These white spaces cause functional "disconnects." What is needed, therefore, is for associated functions that are part of the same product or process flow to be "wired together" in a horizontal management chain.

Focusing on functions that impact supply management alone, Figure 8-2 depicts this horizontal management, in which previously separate functions such as supplier quality assurance, incoming inspection, and components engineering that reported to Quality Assurance, Manufacturing, and Engineering, respectively, now all report into a single supply management umbrella.

At first glance, traditional managers are horrified by these radical changes. "What? Ask Purchasing to take care of supplier quality? That is like appointing the fox to be in charge of the chicken coop!" "Eliminate incoming inspection? The supplier now will get away with murder!" "Put components engineering under materials management? Why, that is the end to all engineering professionalism!" These are honest objections. Each deserves a rational response.

Figure 8-2. Horizontal management in supply management.

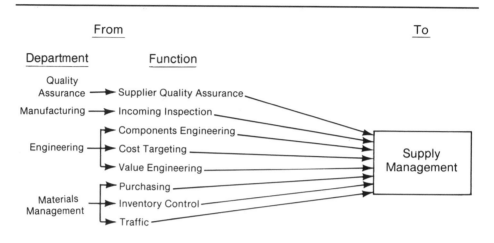

Supplier Quality Assurance: Purchasing's Quality Conscience

Responsibility for quality is often misunderstood and is misplaced if resident in a central quality organization. Who is responsible for design quality? The engineer, not Quality Control. Who is responsible for manufacturing quality? Production, not inspection or Quality Control. Who is responsible for supplier quality? The supplier, through Purchasing, not Quality Control. As long as Quality Control acts as an external policeman, departments such as Engineering, Manufacturing, and Purchasing will be the robbers, stealing from quality in the name of shipments. The answer lies in giving these departments full responsibility and accountability for quality. If Purchasing is measured on total costs of purchased materials instead of on purchase price, it will assume full responsibility for the quality of materials bought. With supplier quality assurance now in the same department, the two disciplines can work for a common cause instead of lobbing hand grenades over an organizational wall.

Incoming Inspection: An Anachronism

The same arguments on quality responsibility are applicable to incoming inspection. It is the supplier who produces quality, not incoming inspection, which, at best, is a postmortem operation. Every attempt should be made to eventually eliminate this anachronistic function through supplier certification, as outlined in Chapter 18. In the meantime, its logical home is with Purchasing and supplier Quality Assurance, not in a central manufacturing or quality control organization with built-in departmental walls and more organizational "disconnects."

Components Engineering: The Professional Arm

Traditionally, Components Engineering reports either to Engineering or to central Quality Control. Its major functions are to help in determining component specification, assist in parts reduction and standardization, qualify components submitted by suppliers for performance and reliability, analyze component failures to determine root causes, and work with suppliers to correct these causes and prevent recurrence. Because all or most of these functions belong in supply management, it stands to reason that the effectiveness of components engineering is greatly enhanced under the supply management umbrella. Such a move also frees the design engineer from the necessity of being the expert on component technology or from being involved in the many communications with suppliers. At the same time, Components Engineering brings needed professionalism to Purchasing, which until recently has been viewed as a mere clerical operation.

Supply Management Reduces—Not Adds to—the Head Count

Table 8-3 lists the various functions affected by organizing along supply management lines, states whether the manpower in that function is likely to go up or down, and gives the reasons for the change. It shows that in addition to improving product quality, cost, and cycle time, the overall head count is appreciably decreased.

As stated in Chapter 4, Xerox reduced the overhead associated with material purchases from 9 cents (for each dollar purchased) to a creditable 2.5 cents!

One Canadian manufacturer, in moving from traditional materials management to supply management, reduced its number of job classifications from twelve to five. It further reduced the associated head count from 125 to 45 in four years, while the total material dollars purchased increased from $90 million to $125 million.

Elevating the Purchasing Function: From a Clerical Image to Professional Respect

The final organizational uplift must be made within Purchasing—a key player in supply management. In the past, and even today, Purchasing has had a poor image. It is considered a nonprofession. It has been used as a dumping

Table 8-3. Manpower reductions under supply management.

Function	Manpower: Up/Down	Reasons for Change
Purchasing	Down	Fewer clerks, expediters; more professionals
Supplier quality assurance	Up	More visits, help to suppliers
Incoming inspection	Down	Supplier certification (90% reduction in 3 years)
Overall quality assurance	Down	Less inspection, fewer supplier quality problems
Components engineering	Down	More direct qualification by suppliers, fewer parts and suppliers, more standardization
Cost analysis	Up	Cost targeting—an important new discipline
Materials planning	Down	More JIT, less MRP
Inventory control	Down	Less inventory under JIT
Process engineering	Down	Problems reduced through design of experiments
Industrial engineering	Down	Line people do simpler industrial engineering tasks
Shop supervision	Down	Fewer line quality and material problems
Maintenance	Down	Concentration on preventive maintenance
Training	Up	A new activity for most companies
Overall	Down	20–50% reduction in head count

ground for has-beens and as an early retirement home on the job! The stereotype of the buyer, in the minds of his nonpurchasing colleagues, is one who gets three quotes and selects the lowest. "Any fool clerk can do that" is the perception.

Yet the role of supply management, as discussed earlier, is so important in its contribution to quality, cost, and cycle time management and profitability to the company that supply management deserves a place of honor on a par with Engineering and Sales; and its people deserve to gain recognition and professional respect. But wishing it or mandating it will not make this happen. Several measures are necessary to professionalize supply management in general and Purchasing in particular.

1. Injection of more technical, degreed, and management talent.
2. Encouragement of cross-functional rotation, especially from Engineering, Quality, and Manufacturing into Purchasing.
3. Plans for training, similar to a university curriculum from freshman to senior levels, which would include:
   General Proficiency
   - Technological familiarity with the products purchased.
   - Management/business perspective.
   - Knowledge of supplier's processes.
   - Sensitivity to people.
   - Motivation: from theory to practice.
   Special Skills
   - Working familiarity with world-class quality requirements.
   - Problem-solving techniques, using simple, but powerful design of experiments.
   - Value engineering.
   - Group technology/standardization.
   - Learning curve/experience curve: theory and practice.
   - Principles of contracting and purchasing law.
   - Cycle time reductions.
4. A materials resource data base (making use of national statistics).
5. Corporate purchasing councils to improve purchasing effectiveness and to promote professionalism.
6. Electronic communications with key suppliers to reduce cycle time in: establishing engineering drawings and specifications; order releases; shipping notifications; payments; and mail.
7. Promotion of white-collar cycle time reduction (where Purchasing can be a model for other parts of the company).
8. Recognition in terms of job grades, salaries, and other rewards based on supply management performance.

Example: General Electric (GE), the giant that is becoming more "general" than "electric," is a latecomer to supply management. But with its renowned thoroughness of purpose and follow-through, it tackled this new challenge by concentrating first on a weak link—purchasing professionalism. Its top management assessment, at the start, in 1983, was:

"Many of our people were doing their own thing . . . unknown to each other . . . with little or no interface with such functions as engineering and marketing."

"Many of them were 'good old Joes' . . . tucked away in a cubbyhole office out in manufacturing . . . filling out requisitions that had to be signed by 20 people before anything happened."*

The urgent need for professionalizing purchasing, as American industry struggles to regain its competitive edge, was put forthrightly by GE Chairman Jack Welch:

"It is insane the way we treat the purchasing function. Shame on you if you don't have the very best people buying those $13 billion worth of goods. Purchasing should be a home-run job. It's important! It's critical! We are going to be the most customer-focused, best purchasing outfit in Corporate America!"

In the first companywide purchasing conference in its corporate history in 1984, GE outlined the tasks for its purchasing people:

- "Start exchanging ideas on how to solve common problems so that we can do our jobs better and smarter."
- "We are going to computerize our data bases . . . undertake a major effort to consolidate our contracts with fewer but better suppliers . . . and most importantly, we will concentrate on professional development programs designed to change the image of the purchasing function . . . and sharpen our buying skills."
- "We will attract the best people we can find . . . more with technical degrees and cross-functional experience . . . more with sophisticated negotiating skills . . . and more who recognize the critical interface between purchasing, manufacturing, engineering, marketing and our suppliers."†

With characteristic vigor, GE went about its task of implementation:

- "All of our 2,400 purchasing professionals have been through the competency model evaluation . . . and the majority have taken positive action to upgrade their skills."
- "The number of fully degreed purchasing people has increased from 47% to 64%. The number of technically degreed people has gone up from 12% to 18%." [In one of GE's largest groups, 71% are college graduates, while 37% have engineering degrees. For new hires, the figure is 100% college graduates, and 88% have engineering degrees.]
- "We established the GEGS program [GE Goods and Services] as the most comprehensive commodity coding system in American history."
- "PDSS [Purchasing Decision Support System]—information on the company's purchases from various vendors, including dollar volume, prices, supplier quality etc.—was implemented. It facilitates real-time decision making."
- "44 Purchasing Councils—to coordinate purchases of common items—were established."
- "Quality Councils were also established to initiate quality policies and prac-

---

*From a G.E. presentation made during a customer-supplier conference, 1986.

†From a G.E. presentation made during a customer-supplier conference, 1986.

tices, such as a shift from AQLs [Acceptable Quality Levels] to PPMs [parts per million]."

- "A Purchasing Advisory Board—consisting of purchasing managers from top 17 major company divisions—was set up to consolidate and leverage buying clout and make professional development work."

- "A Material Resource Analysis System was established—to consolidate data on 375 corporate contracts; producer price index information; average hourly costs for selected industries; forecasts by commodity experts; and NAPM's [National Association of Purchasing Managers] diffusion index."

It is small wonder that General Electric remains a disciplined, well-oiled corporate machine, despite its vast size. It is destined to be one of the leaders in supply management, along with its many contributions to U.S. competitiveness.

Chapter 9

Measurement of Partnership Effectiveness

When you can measure what you're speaking about, and express it in numbers, you know something about it; but when you cannot measure it, when you cannot express it in numbers, your knowledge is of a meager and unsatisfactory kind: It may be the beginning of knowledge, but you have scarcely, in your thoughts, advanced to the stage of science.

—Lord Kelvin

The Pros and Cons of Supplier Rating Systems: Prepartnership

How the management of a customer company and its suppliers can mutually assess the effectiveness of their partnership is the subject of this chapter. Before introducing the parameters used to measure such effectiveness, however, it may be useful to discuss the older methods that have been used to gauge supplier performance in a prepartnership era.

Prepartnership Supplier Rating Systems

These methods are called supplier rating systems (or vendor* rating systems), and there are probably as many such systems as there are companies. A few generic types are worthy of review. Table 9-1 lists five typical supplier rating systems, the method used for each, and the advantages and disadvantages associated with each.

System 1: No Rating

Many customer company professionals are likely to condemn a no-rating system. Yet it is a rational alternative. The main purpose of a rating system is to select one supplier over another when reducing the supplier base. This should be a one-time activity, lasting for six months to a year, involving the gathering of data on selected suppliers for selected commodities. Even for this limited period, there is no need to gather data on all suppliers within a commodity. Generally, Purchasing and Quality people in the customer company know who the poor and marginal suppliers are, without the necessity of a formal rating system. Such suppliers can be eliminated automatically.

Many companies use rating systems to score their suppliers and to motivate them toward better performance. But keeping score as an end in itself is the classic case of doing something efficiently that does not need to be done at all! Scores, such as 72 or 85 out of 100, are far less meaningful to a supplier than his *own* actual quality, cost, and delivery performance. He wants to know specific details of where he did not perform so that he can focus on improvement measures. As for motivation, there are far more effective methods, such as encouragement, support, training, and hands-on help.

System 2: Quality Rating Only

Some companies use quality alone as a rating parameter. Their rationale is that quality is the most important measure of supplier performance and that other parameters are too subjective. The central difficulties with the quality yardstick are: (1) if incoming inspection data alone are used, the rating does not reflect the larger costs of poor supplier quality in terms of line and field defects; and (2) if the latter line and field failure costs are to

(text continues on page 104)

---

* Throughout this book, the term "vendor" has been scrupulously avoided. It frequently conjures up visions of a hot dog stand and is demeaning to the supplier community.

Table 9-1. Typical prepartnership supplier rating systems.

System	Method	Advantages	Disadvantages
1. No rating	—	• Zero cost • Numerical score for vastly different suppliers is meaningless • Suppliers want feedback on their own performance, rather than translation through a comparative score	• No comparisons for suppliers of like commodities • No yardstick to reduce supplier base • No basis for supplier recognition
2. Quality rating only	*Incoming inspection statistics* 1. Percentage defective in samples tested 2. Percentage of lots returned 3. Dollar value of lots returned as percentage of total material dollars *Total cost of poor supplier quality* 1. Cost of incoming inspection 2. Cost of line failures 3. Cost of field failures	• Quality is the single most important parameter of supplier performance • Other parameters, e.g., dependability, flexibility, and cycle time, difficult to measure • Price also difficult to measure if there are no suppliers for a particular part number	• Difficult to track line failure and field failure costs • Field failure costs gathered too late • Unfair to ignore other important parameters such as delivery, service • Does not provide a total guide in selecting suppliers
3. Quality and delivery rating; Graphic method	Quality rating: Lots accepted as percentage of lots received Delivery rating: Quantity on time as percentage of total quantity scheduled *(see graphic below)* A Suppliers: >95% rating on quality and delivery B Suppliers: 90–95% rating on either quality or delivery C Suppliers: <90% rating on either quality or delivery	• Two-dimensional (quality and delivery) • Pictorial comparison of several suppliers • Demarcation of A vs. B vs. C suppliers can be changed depending on company requirements • Simple to administer • Low cost	• Quality confined to incoming inspection data only; total cost of poor quality not considered • Delivery confined to incoming data only; total cost of poor delivery (line impact) not considered • Other factors, such as flexibility, dependability, not in rating
4. Quality and delivery rating; Cost index method	*(see formula and table below)*	• Two-dimensional (quality and delivery) • A big step toward total cost since it includes price and cost of poor quality and delivery in incoming • Systematically breaks down the average nonproductive costs so that actual costs need not be	• Quality and delivery confined primarily to incoming data. • Other factors, such as flexibility, dependability, not in rating. • Average costs per function may not reflect variations in such costs. • System expensive to

Graphic method — Rating Classification Map:

Delivery	Quality 85%	Quality 90%	Quality 95%	Quality 100%
100%	C	B	B	A
95%	C	C	B	B
90%	C	C	C	C

Quality Rating (%): 85% 90% 95% 100%
Rating (85%)

Cost index method:

$$\text{Cost index} = \frac{\text{Purchased cost} + \text{Nonproductive costs}}{\text{Purchased cost}}$$

Typical nonproductive costs: (cost at $50/man-hour)

Function	Man-hours per Occurrence	Return to Supplier	Accept with Repair	Accept Nonconforming Material	Material Late	Material Early	Excess Material	Short Material
Receiving Inspection	0.3	$15	$15	$15	$15	$15	—	—
MRB Review	0.9	45	45	45	—	—	—	—

Technical Analysis table (cost index calculation):

Rating Element	Weight								
Technical Analysis	1.0	50	50	50	50	—	—	$50	$50
MRB Disposition	0.6	30	30	30	—	—	—	—	
Production Reschedules	2.1	105	105	—	—	105	—	105	
Reinspection	0.3	—	15	—	—	—	—		
Packaging	0.4	20	—	—	—	—	—		
Shipping Documentation									
Inventory/Carrying Cost	0.2	10	—	20	60	—	20		
Nonproductive Cost/Occurrence		$275	$260	$140	$120	$75	$70	$155	
Number of Occurrences		2	—	4	6	1	—	—	
		$550	—	$560	$720	$75	—	—	

Total nonproductive cost: $ 1,905

Purchased cost: 152,320

$$\text{Cost index} = \frac{152{,}320 + 1{,}905}{152{,}320} = 1.0124$$

• Bonus points: Awarded for services beyond normal expectations—reduce nonproductive costs

Advantages:
- recalculated each time
- Cost comparisons with other suppliers are more meaningful and fair

Disadvantages:
- maintain for many part numbers and suppliers

	Rating Element	Basis of Score	Maximum Points
5. Comprehensive	Quality	C_{p_k} • *Total cost of poor supplier quality* • Cost of incoming inspection • Cost of line failures • Cost of field failures	35
	Cycle time/delivery	• *Total cost of poor supplier delivery* • Supplier cycle time/lead time • Supplier lead time • Cost of material delivered late (line stoppages) • Cost of material delivered early (inventory)	30
	Price	• Cost of wrong counts (+ or − from specified quantity) • Price vs. other suppliers in same commodity • Increase/decrease in last 12 months	25
	Service	• Responsiveness • Flexibility • Dependability • Technology	10

Advantages:
- Complete; all bases of performance touched
- Intangibles, such as flexibility, dependability, included
- Accurate
- Fair to all suppliers

Disadvantages:
- Extremely expensive
- Difficult to measure many of the listed parameters
- Benefit/cost ratio poor

be included, they are difficult to track, given the poor feedback system in most companies.

System 3: Quality and Delivery Rating: Graphic Method

A simple, ingenious, graphic system* has been used by the Joseph Pollak Corporation. This makes use of a quality rating (lots accepted as a percentage of lots received) as the x-axis on a graph, and a delivery rating (quantity on time as a percentage of quantity scheduled) as the y-axis. Suppliers are rated as A, B, or C or NR (*not r*ated and possible candidates for termination). As an example, A suppliers are those with a minimum of 95 percent quality and delivery rating, B suppliers are those with a minimum 90 percent quality and delivery rating, and so on. The boundaries of the A, B, and C classifications can be changed depending on a customer company's requirements (see Table 9-1). The performance of several suppliers within a commodity can be plotted and compared pictorially.

Although simple to administer and low in cost, this method looks at only the tip of the iceberg of total cost while ignoring the larger costs of poor line and field quality and the larger costs of line shutdowns, customer delays, and even customer cancellations because of poor delivery.

System 4: Quality and Delivery Rating: Cost Index Method

Several companies have devised rating systems that add a fixed dollar penalty to the part cost for supplier nonconformance such as incoming inspection rejections, late/early delivery, and over/under shipments. One company uses the dollar penalties shown in Table 9-2. The number of occurrences of such nonproductive costs are then multiplied by the penalties. These are totaled and added to the purchase price. The cost index for each supplier is this addition divided by the purchase price. If there are several suppliers providing the same part or family of parts, the one with the lowest product or purchase price times the cost index gets the business or is given the inside track.

Table 9-1 shows how another company, Rockwell International, uses a similar cost index system. It has time-studied various activity elements such as the Materials Review Board (MRB), packaging, and shipping, and arrived at average costs for these elements to determine the penalties to be levied. This appears to be a fairer way of assessing penalties than is the use of arbitrary figures, especially where the suppliers have no input into the methods of measurement.

---

*Published in the *Technical Supplement of the Electronics Division of the American Society for Quality Control* (Milwaukee, Wisc.: American Society for Quality Control) Spring 1987.

Table 9-2. Quality and delivery rating system for suppliers.

Nonproductive Cost Category	Penalty	No. of Occurrences	Nonproductive Cost
1. Incoming inspection lot rejection	$500	3	$1,500
2. Material delivered early	25	2	100
3. Material delivered late	200	5	1,000
4. Quantity in excess of order	100	1	100
5. Quantity short of order	150	2	300
	Total nonproductive cost		$3,000

Total $ purchased: $100,000. Cost index = $100,000 + $3,000/$100,000 = 1.03

Like the graphic method, the cost index system measures only a small fraction of the total cost of poor quality and delivery. Further, the average cost for each element of work may not reflect the considerable variations in such costs from one case to the next. The system is also expensive to administer, even if computerized. Nevertheless, the quantification of the costs of poor quality and delivery makes this a more meaningful and fairer method of comparing suppliers. In addition, bonus points, awarded for exceptional service rendered, are a way of reducing nonproductive costs.

System 5: Comprehensive Method

This system pulls out all the stops. It measures every facet of a supplier's performance—quality, delivery, price, and service—with weights assigned to each. Generally, quality is assigned the most weight (as shown in Table 9-1), followed by delivery. Both these parameters are measured in terms of cost impact. In addition, $^{C}p_k$ is added for quality and cycle time/lead time added for delivery. Price is measured in two ways: by comparisons with other suppliers of the same commodity, and by price increases/decreases provided by the supplier. Service has four subcategories: (1) Responsiveness refers to the degree of cooperation shown by the supplier; (2) flexibility is the supplier's ability to support changes in schedule; (3) dependability is the supplier's overall ability to make constant improvements in quality, cost, and delivery, as well as his loyalty during difficult times; (4) technology is the supplier's ability to push the state of the art in his product.

The comprehensive method is the most complete and accurate way of measuring supplier performance. It is also the most expensive approach and can produce less bang for the buck than other methods. It is recommended only for the most important suppliers or where a few contenders for selection as partnership suppliers are so close, in terms of preference, that a comprehensive rating system can serve as a true decision matrix.

General Weaknesses of Supplier Rating Systems

There are structural and administrative weaknesses associated with all these rating systems:

1. Frequently the same supplier, for the same part, is subjected to different rating systems in different divisions of the same company!
2. There are differences between the Purchasing, Quality, and Engineering departments in interpreting the same rating system, and when this happens the supplier is caught in the cross fire.
3. Unilateral and arbitrary decisions may be patently unfair to suppliers. There are several examples of suppliers who have taken exception to a particular specification and have received assurances from Purchasing and Engineering for a waiver, only to be "dinged" with a poor rating by a go-by-the-print incoming inspector. The same scenario can be repeated for a rush order, where the supplier goes out of his way to accommodate the customer, only to discover that he has been penalized for missing a delivery by one or two days.
4. These inconsistencies lead to numerous arguments and tiresome negotiations between customer and supplier personnel, with both sides more concerned about an artificial rating than they are about improvement.
5. There is an inherent conflict between simplicity and accuracy in these rating systems. The simpler the system, the more questionable is its accuracy. The more accurate the system, the more difficult and expensive it is to gather supporting data.
6. Finally, there is a fundamental difference between effectiveness and efficiency. It makes little sense to efficiently gather rating data on thousands of part numbers and hundreds of suppliers, when little is done with such data beyond rating for the sake of rating. Such systems should be reserved, Pareto fashion, for the truly important suppliers or when a few suppliers are in such a close race for partnership inclusion that the establishment of a six-month to one-year temporary rating system would serve a useful purpose.

Measuring Partnership Effectiveness Between a Customer and a Single Supplier

Supplier rating systems, comparing several suppliers, should only be used in a prepartnership era—and, then, only selectively and temporarily. Once

Table 9-3. Supplier-customer partnership one-on-one measurement of effectiveness.

For Customer	For Supplier
Quality • Number of certified parts as percentage of total • $^{C}P_{k}s$ on key parameters more than 2.0 • Prices vs. cost • Lots/$ rejected in incoming inspection as percent of total lots/$	Contracts/agreements • Increase in dollar volume/year • Increase in contract time Quality • Percentage yield improvement • Outgoing quality (percentage ppm improvement) • Classification of characteristics • Number of SPC/DOE projects
Cost • Percent reduction in bill of materials on all parts • $ saved through ideas/specs challenge	Cost • Percentage reduction from base line • Financial incentives for ideas, delivery, etc.
Delivery • Delinquency (lots/$) as percent of total	Cycle time • Manufacturing cycle time reduction (weeks/%) • Subsupplier cycle time reduction (weeks/%)
Cycle time • Supplier cycle time reduction (weeks/%) • Supplier lead time • Number of blanket orders	Forecast • Accuracy (actual vs. forecast) • Number of changes in forecasts
	Technical assistance • Design and spec consultations (No.) • Problem solving (No.) • Quality/SPC consultations (No.) • Cycle time consultations
	Training • Management orientation • SPC/JIT seminars/workshops • Worker participation

Table 9-4. Parameters measuring customer benefits from all partnership suppliers.

General

- Overall reduction in supplier base (%)
- Supplier reductions per commodity (%)
- Number of single source suppliers (% of total)

Quality

- Impact on quality/cost through supplier improvements
- Reductions in incoming inspection, head counts, and costs through supplier certification
- Reductions in line and field failure costs
- Reductions in inspection/test costs

Cost

- Reduction in overall bill of materials costs (%)
- Cost avoidance through early supplier involvement and value engineering
- Overall reduction in part-number base (%)
- Savings through corporate negotiations

Cycle Time

- Average supplier cycle time reduction
- Average supplier lead time reduction
- Increase in inventory turns
- Positive cash flow increases

Note: Select the fewest parameters needed to meet supplier partnership objectives. Too many measurements = too little action!

a supplier partner has been selected, on the basis of benchmarking, supplier rating systems become an anachronism, just as competitive bidding and negotiations with several suppliers become ancient history! The focus shifts to a one-on-one measurement system between a customer and a single supplier. *The objective is to strengthen the partnership bonds and to promote continual, never-ending improvement.*

Table 9-3 lists various measures by which a customer company can measure and monitor the supplier's contribution to partnership, and also shows how the supplier can measure the extent to which the partnership is benefiting him.

The customer can measure the supplier's quality, cost, delivery, and cycle time, in a number of different ways, in order to monitor the benefits he is receiving from partnership. The supplier, in turn, can measure his own quality, cost, and cycle time to see if they have benefited from the partnership relationship. In addition, the supplier can measure: increases in his dollar volume; longer-term contracts/agreements; improvements in the customer's forecasts in terms of accuracy and change reductions (so that he is not "jerked" up and down as in prepartnership days); direct and active help from the customer in terms of design, quality, and cycle time; and training, in subjects ranging from management to SPC and worker participation.

In establishing these parameters of performance, however, a few principles of measurement should be followed:

1. Both sides must be involved in the development of the measurements from the outset and agree on the yardsticks.
2. The measurements should be meaningful, fair, easy, and nonsubjective, with little calibration error.
3. The cost of each measurement should be at least an order of magnitude lower than the tangible benefits to be derived.
4. The fewest possible number of parameters should be selected to meet the objectives of measurement. Too many measurements translate into too little action.

It is also helpful for customer companies to track benefits derived from its entire roster of partnership suppliers along lines similar to one-on-one measurements. Table 9-4 lists the most typical parameters.

Part III

IMPROVING SUPPLIER QUALITY: THE CENTERPIECE OF SUPPLY MANAGEMENT

Chapter 10

The Quality Greening of Supplier Management

We believe quality improvement will reduce quality costs by 50% over the coming years. For us, this translates into billions of dollars of added potential profit and quality, leadership in our industry, ...

—John Akers, president, IBM

The Economic Imperative of Quality

There is a story about a man who has lost a valuable coin. His friend asks him why he is looking in one area when he had said he was sure he had lost it in another. "Because the light is better here," the man answers!

This tale has an analogy in industry's frantic search for a way to reduce costs. It looks in the wrong places because it is easier than looking in the right places. Mindless layoffs, arbitrary cuts in head counts, and the flight offshore to reduce insignificant direct labor costs are readily mandated, but their effectiveness in reducing costs remains a mirage.

Quality Used as a 2″ by 4″

The key to this magic kingdom of cost reduction, quality, is seldom considered. True, there has been a growing recognition of the importance of quality over the past ten years. But quality is dished out to a nervous management in portions of fear and blackmail: "Embrace quality or you lose your business"; "improve reliability lest the Damocles sword of product liability kill you"; "strengthen customer satisfaction or the ghost of Ralph Nader will stalk you"; and—the ultimate insult—"worship quality or the Japanese will eat your lunch!" The need for quality is much more positive.

Quality: The Engine That Drives a Company to the Bank

Figure 10-1 shows the relationship between quality and return on investment (ROI); profit, productivity, and market share. The data is adapted from the famous PIMS (Profit Impact of Market Strategy) studies conducted by the Strategic Planning Institute. It researched several thousand businesses, seeking correlations between various business parameters. Product quality is measured entirely on the basis of customer perceptions of both the product and the services associated with it, not as an absolute but relative to competitors. The quality index used is expressed as a percentage of sales, where customers perceive the company's products to be superior to the best of its competitors, minus the percentage of sales, where they perceive it to be inferior to the best of its competitors. As an example, if 70 percent of the company's products, in sales dollars, is superior to the products of its competitors, and 30 percent inferior, then the quality index will be 40 percent.

As we can see from the figure, comparing companies with high quality with those with low quality shows that:

- Return on investment increases from 16 percent for low quality companies to 31 percent for high quality companies.
- Profit increases from 6 percent for low quality companies to 14 percent for high quality companies.
- Similarly, as both quality and productivity go from low to high, the return on investment goes from 10 to 35 percent.
- As both quality and market share go from low to high, the return on investment goes from 11 to 35 percent.

In this remarkable correlation, profit, return on investment, market share, and productivity can be viewed as the outputs or results, while quality is the input or cause. Quality is the engine that can drive a company smiling all the way to the bank! It can be categorically stated that:

- There is no more powerful cost reduction tool than quality improvement.
- Quality is an absolute prerequisite to cycle time reduction.
- Quality is an essential step in reducing design cycle time, which is becoming one of the distinctive competencies of a company in the global

Figure 10-1. Relationship between quality and ROI, profit, productivity, and market share.

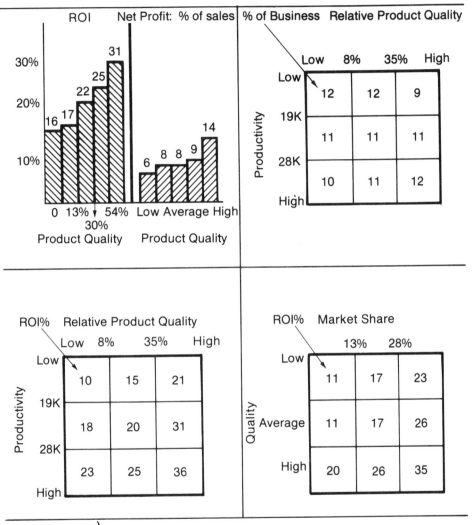

*Source of data:}200 participating companies: over 2,000 businesses in data base
PIMS program }

Note: Quality is defined as (1) customer's judgment, (2) product and service, and (3) not absolute but relative to competitors. Quality is measured by the quality index: percent of sales from superior products minus percent of sales from inferior products. Productivity is measured by value added per employee (expressed in constant 1973 dollars).

Figure 10-2. Influence of quality on business parameters.

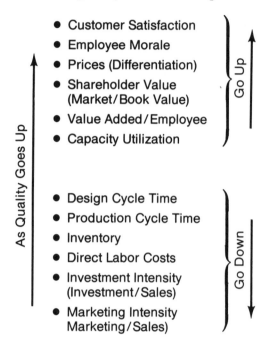

wars between corporations. (Even today, there is little realization that entire product life cycles are getting shorter than entire design cycle times.)

▪ Quality is one of the most important elements of—indeed a short cut to—customer satisfaction.

Further Spin-off Benefits From Quality Improvement

But that is not all. There is more frosting on the cake of quality. Figure 10-2 condenses further PIMS research data, pinpointing other important business parameters that directly benefit from quality improvement. Especially noteworthy is the fact that a company can command higher prices in the marketplace for outstanding quality. This is differentiation at its best.

The tragedy is that many CEOs, especially in the supplier community, have not yet seen the light of quality on the proverbial road to Damascus! They resist being converted. They still believe that the equation "high quality = low cost" is an oxymoron, a contradiction in terms. One survey conducted as late as 1986 among more than 500 corporate CEOs asked them to state their most important objective. The following results show that improving product/service quality came in last:

Objective	Percentage of CEOs Responding
Improve profts/earnings	36.7%
Growth	21.9
Improve returns to shareholders	11.1
Employee development	8.8
Long-term planning and strategy	6.4
Control costs, improve productivity	4.5
Restructure company	3.9
Improve product/service quality	3.9

The opening gun, therefore, in the war on poor supplier quality must be an earnest presentation by the customer company's senior management to the supplier's top management on the economic imperative of quality. Figures 11-1 and 11-2 should supply part of the ammunition. It should be clearly stated that it is in the supplier's own economic self-interest to embrace improved quality with the fervor of a dedicated convert to a new religion.

The Staggering Cost of Poor Quality

Why is quality improvement such a powerful cost reduction tool? Why is there such a huge cost reduction bang for a modest quality buck? The answer lies in the exorbitant cost of poor quality. There are three categories:

- External failure costs—including warranty, customer return recall, and product liability costs.
- Internal failure costs—scrap, repair, and analyzing.
- Appraisal costs—inspection and test.

These three categories, along with a desirable fourth category—prevention costs (the only desirable category of quality costs), which include quality engineering, reliability studies, and design of experiments—constitute the four elements of total quality costs first developed by Al Feigenbaum thirty years ago. In the intervening years, every annual Congress of the American Society for Quality Control has devoted sessions and papers to the cost of quality. Yet, thirty years later, nine out of ten U.S. companies do not gather or even know the costs of poor quality, which range from 10 percent to 20 percent of the sales dollar. I have made a study of companies that have not begun to reduce their costs of poor quality. This cost amounts to $100 to $200 per employee per day! What an incredible waste! What an enormous profit leak! If, somehow, these quality costs could be made to evaporate, a

Figure 10-3. The hidden costs of poor quality.

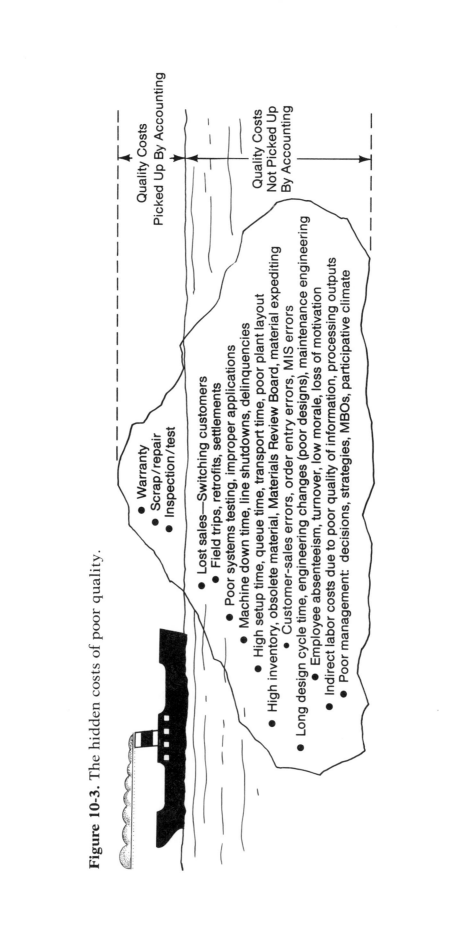

Quality Costs
Picked Up By Accounting

Quality Costs
Not Picked Up
By Accounting

- Warranty
- Scrap/repair
- Inspection/test

- Lost sales—Switching customers
- Field trips, retrofits, settlements
- Poor systems testing, improper applications
- Machine down time, line shutdowns, delinquencies
- High setup time, queue time, transport time, poor plant layout
- High inventory, obsolete material, Materials Review Board, material expediting
- Customer-sales errors, order entry errors, MIS errors
- Long design cycle time, engineering changes (poor designs), maintenance engineering
- Employee absenteeism, turnover, low morale, loss of motivation
- Indirect labor costs due to poor quality of information, processing outputs
- Poor management: decisions, strategies, MBOs, participative climate

traditional company, with a typical 5 percent profit on sales, could witness a profit jump to 15 to 25 percent of its sales. Even if the cost of poor quality is only halved, an easily achievable goal with the techniques described in Part III of this book, profits would double and triple!

Traditional Quality Costs: Only the Tip of the Iceberg

These four categories of quality costs, however, are all that nineteenth-century accounting methods can pick up. And they are but the tip of a huge iceberg. Figure 10-3 depicts the hidden costs of poor quality that are almost never calculated. Take, for instance, the loss of customer satisfaction. The U.S. Department of Consumer Affairs reports:

> Only one out of fifty unhappy customers bother to complain. The rest will simply switch to a competitor. In addition, the average unhappy customer will tell his or her story to at least nine others and 13 percent will tell more than twenty others.

What a tragic loss! But how do you measure it? Figure 10-3 lists many such unfathomable elements of the costs of poor quality: equipment down time, long manufacturing and design cycle times, indirect labor quality errors, and, worst of all, the costs of poor management strategies and decisions and the nonparticipative climate it creates of bossism, noninvolvement, and fear. It has been estimated that all these costs of poor quality, both those picked up and not picked up by accounting, amount to an astronomical 50 percent of the sales dollar! It is only since 1985 that quality research has begun to attack these hidden costs of quality through techniques such as the next operation as customer (NOAC), value engineering, and systems mapping.

In the area of traditional quality costs, Table 10-1 presents a summary of a survey I conducted in 1984 to determine what leading U.S. companies were doing to gather and reduce such costs. It shows that even some of these outstanding companies had only recently attacked quality costs and that the results—30 percent to 50 percent reduction in three to five years— are modest. We have a long way to go!

The second round in the war on poor supplier quality must be to convince the supplier's top management to start gathering the costs of poor quality. It need not be an accounting nightmare, with the bean counters calculating these costs to the fourth decimal place. It can be an estimate, even a very rough estimate, of just six elements: warranty, scrap, analyzing, rework, inspection, and test. But it is imperative that the supplier's management get a handle on these debilitating profit leaks.

Table 10-1. Survey of quality cost reduction programs introduced by leading U.S. companies.

Company	How Long—Years	Who Initiated	Initial Problems	Who Gathers Cost	Included in Preventive Cost	Allocated or Actual Cost	How Costs Break Down	Results (% Improvement)	Areas With Most Reduction	Areas With Least Reduction	Who Monitors/Evaluates
General Dynamics	1/2	Q.A.	CONVINCE MANAGEMENT AND UNCOVER HIDDEN COSTS	ACCOUNTING WITH QUALITY ASSURANCE GUIDANCE	QUALITY CONTROL MANAGEMENT/TRAINING/RELIABILITY/ENGINEERING	ACTUAL	Product		REWORK ---- WARRANTY ---- SCRAP	APPRAISAL COSTS	UPPER MANAGEMENT—VICE-PRESIDENT AND DIVISION STAFF
Mostek	1	Q.A.					Product	Good			
General Electric	24	Q.A.					Product	Excellent			
General Motors	10	Q.A.					Product	Excellent			
Hewlett Packard	4	Q.A.					Product	50			
GTE Automatic Electric	4	Q.A.					Plant	30			
Otis Engineering	5	Q.A.					Corporate	50			
Texas Instruments Science Service Division	Just start	Q.A.					Division				
Texas Instruments Corp.	1	Q.A.					Product				
Canon Business Machine	Just start	Q.A.					Plant				
Memorex	4	Q.A.					Division	27			
Whirlpool	6	Q.A.					Plant/product	Good			
Allis Chalmers	8	Q.A.						Excellent			
IBM	21	Q.A.					Plant/Product	Excellent			
Fairchild Republic	5	U.S. Govt.					Program	33			

Prescriptions for a Quality Breakthrough

The vast literature on quality is filled with a variety of nostrums, potions, and remedies, much of it with a nugget or two of substance along with the trivia. In a class by themselves are three towering personalities in the field who have formulated potent prescriptions for a quality breakthrough. The three are: Dr. W. Edwards Deming, who put Japan on the world quality map; Dr. Joseph Juran, one of the leading authorities on quality for the last forty-five years; Dorian Shainin, a renowned consultant on quality to more than 600 American companies.

Each brings a different perspective to quality improvement. Their contributions can be summarized: "Without Deming, management would not have been sold on quality; without Juran, the quality problems would not have been found; and without Shainin, the quality problems would not be solved!" Their prescriptions apply with equal force both to a customer company and to its partnership suppliers. But assuming that most customer companies are ahead of their key suppliers in quality improvement, the third round in the war on poor supplier quality must be the customer company assuring that its partnership suppliers understand, support, and implement these principles.

Deming's Castigation of Top Management

In Figure 10-4, Deming lists fourteen obligations top management has in achieving quality excellence. A first reading may give the impression of motherhood and apple pie. But each repeat reading reinforces the power of his admonitions. Of special note are his warnings against short-term profits, inspection, and multiple source supplies. Deming is unmerciful in his castigation of America's top managers. (Strangely, they take his tongue-lashings meekly.) He tells them that they, not their people, are responsible for 85 percent of quality problems and he urges them to dispel the corrosion of fear among their employees, which accounts for untold economic loss.

Juran's Breakthrough for Quality

Figure 10-5 lists Juran's seven-point sequence for achieving a breakthrough in quality. It is a systematic method of improving any supplier's quality. Juran's greatest contribution lies in his concentration on attacking chronic problems, as opposed to sporadic problems. Chronic problems, because they are almost perpetual, are the most insidious of all in terms of total costs that add no value to the product. They are taken for granted in the course of business and get baked into the accounting system as "allowable" costs.

Figure 10-4. Deming's 14 obligations of top management.

1. Innovate and allocate resources to fulfill the long-range needs of the Company and customer rather than short-term profitability.
2. Discard the old philosophy of accepting defective products.
3. Eliminate dependence on mass inspection for quality control; instead, depend on process control, through statistical techniques.
4. Reduce the number of multiple source suppliers. Price has no meaning without an integral consideration for quality. Encourage suppliers to use statistical process control.
5. Use statistical techniques to identify the two sources of waste—system (85%) and local faults (15%); strive to constantly reduce this waste.
6. Institute more thorough, better job-related training.
7. Provide supervision with knowledge of statistical methods; encourage use of these methods to identify which defects should be investigated for solution.
8. Reduce fear throughout the organization by encouraging open, two-way, non-punitive communication. The economic loss resulting from fear of asking questions or reporting trouble is appalling.
9. Help reduce wate by encouraging design, research, and sales peole to learn more about the problems of production.
10. Eliminate the use of goals and slogans to encourage productivity, unless training and management support is also provided.
11. Closely examine the impact of work standards. Do they consider quality or help anyone do a better job? They often act as an impediment to productivity improvement.
12. Institute rudimentary statistical training on a broad scale.
13. Institute a vigorous program for retraining people in new skills, to keep up with changes in materials, methods, product designs, and machinery.
14. Make maximum use of statistical knowledge and talent in your company.

Figure 10-5. Juran's seven point sequence for a quality breakthrough.

1. Breakthrough in attitude, away from control and fire fighting
2. Project identification, using the pareto principle for identifying the vital few (20% or less) causes accounting for the largest portion (80% or more) of the economic impact.
3. Project priorities, based on ROI, savings, urgency, ease of solution, or permanence of benefits
4. Steering committees to guide projects and diagnostic teams to tackle projects
5. Diagnosis: from symptom, to cause, to solution
6. Breakthrough in cultural resistance to change: Identifying cultural patterns threatened and extending ownership to members of the culture in planning and executing the change
7. Breakthrough in results: reduced inspection and reduced costs of quality

Figure 10-6. The systematic reduction of chronic problems.

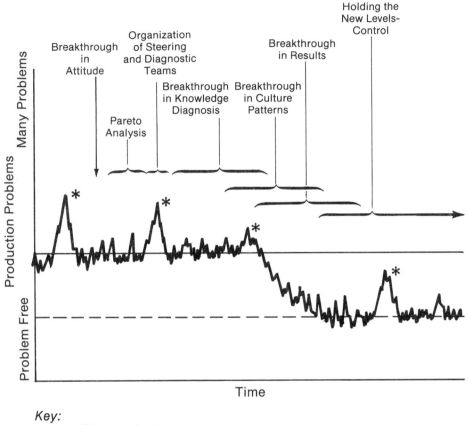

Key:
——— Old standard
– – – New standard
 * Sporadic deviations
   from standard

The difference between the old standard and the new standard is
regarded as a chronic ailment that can be cured economically.

Juran strongly asserts that these chronic costs can be dealt with only by
"establishing projects, with interdisciplinary diagnostic teams—and in no
other way." Figure 10-6 distinguishes between sporadic problems, which
are large in magnitude but short in duration because they are attacked by
conventional methods, and chronic problems, which are normally allowed
to fester. It also shows an implementation timetable for Juran's seven-point

sequence by which chronic problems can be reduced by factors of 2:1 in one year and 10:1 in three to four years.

Shainin: The Problem Solver par excellence

Deming, while strong on management, emphasizes control charts as his main statistical approach. As we shall see later, control charts are not a problem-solving tool; nor are they an effective maintenance tool. Juran is superb in leading to the problem in his diagnostic journey. But he offers only simple methods, marginally effective in solving problems, such as Pareto charts, cause and effect diagrams, histograms, and process capability studies.

Shainin, the least known of the Big Three, is the consummate problem solver. His techniques are particularly useful in solving problems that have been resistant to solutions based on engineering judgment. Some of these problems have had one, two, and three birthday candles lit on them! Shainin's message: "Don't let the engineers do the guessing, let the parts do the talking. They are smarter than the engineers!" What he means is that the parts contain all the information on causes of problems and on variation. Their secrets can be unlocked by the use of appropriate statistically designed experiments. Once these causes are reduced—preferably at the design stage of a product or process, before they become problems in production—they can be controlled in ongoing production with simple tools like precontrol that are far more effective than control charts.

Because of the vital importance of the Shainin tools and their superiority over the Taguchi methods that are gaining currency in the United States, a whole chapter (13) will be devoted to them. I feel strongly that if quality is the centerpiece for supply management, then the design of experiments is the pièce de résistance that every customer company and its partnership suppliers must implement if there is to be any hope of a break away from marginal quality improvements and a breakthrough to zero defects.

The contributions of each of the three quality "gurus" can be integrated into a set of unified prescriptions as depicted in Figure 10-7. Juran's quality management, Deming's quality philosophy, and Shainin's quality tools interact with and reinforce one another in a synergy that can be captured if management provides a quality system "umbrella," utilizing full worker participation, education and training, support and encouragement in an environment free from employee fear.

Quality Axioms: A Set of Management Beliefs

Once the supplier's management is converted to the new quality religion through the economic imperative of quality, the power of quality costs, and the principles of the three quality experts he must learn the catechism of

Figure 10-7. A set of unified quality prescriptions.

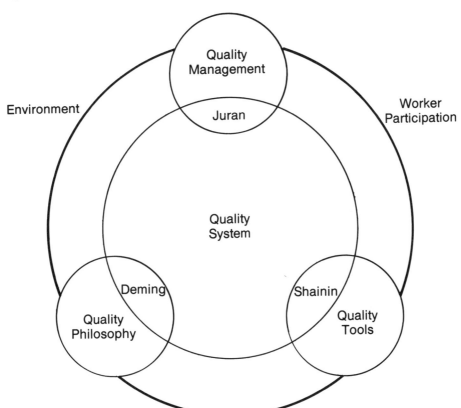

the new religion, as listed in Figure 10-8. Some of these are beliefs that quality professionals for a generation or more tried to get their general managers to accept, with a signal lack of success, until the Japanese competition heated up. Today they are axioms, requiring no proof.

From Beliefs to Support to Involvement

It is frequently said that "a product looks like its management." By extension, it can also be said that "a supplier's quality looks like its management." The quality improvement process starts with top management, progresses at a rate proportional to its commitment, and will stop soon after top management loses interest in the process. To assure that commit-

Figure 10-8. Quality axioms: A set of management beliefs.

---

1. The customer must be satisfied in every way, at all times.
2. High quality = Low cost = High profitability = High market share = Low absenteeism = Low employee turnover = High motivation.
3. The team is the best form of organization for quality progress, for supply management, for any improvement.
4. Improvement must be never-ending. There is no finish line to quality.
5. The "customer is the next operation" is a conversion from vertical management to horizontal management.
6. *All* employees are responsible for quality, not just quality assurance cast in the role of a policeman.
7. SPC is too little, too late. Design of experiments at the design stage of product and process is the key to prevention.
8. Reliability is best attained through multiple environment overstress tests.
9. Inspection and test add no value and can be drastically reduced with $^c\mathrm{P_k}>5.0$.
10. High quality is a prerequisite to JIT.

11. | *Measurements* | *Yesterday* | *Today* | *Tomorrow* |
|---|---|---|---|
| Quality | AQLs | ppms | Zero defects → Zero variation |
| Overall yields | 50–75% | 75–85% | 99 + % |
| Total defects/unit | 1–8 | 0.1–2 | <0.01 |
| Failure rates/year | 1–10% | 0.1–2% | → Zero failures |

12. Every employee is a manager in his/her area of operation.
13. Managers must be coaches, not bosses.
14. Training/workshops/consulting are keys to quality implementation.

---

ment, the supplier's management must translate the beliefs of Figure 10-8 into action, beyond support to involvement. There is a story about a hen and a pig wanting to do something for their master, the farmer, for having cared for them. The hen brightly suggests ham and eggs. "Oh no," cries the pig. "Yours is support, mine is involvement!"

Top management cannot support quality just by pious pronouncements—it must get involved. When management talks quality, but pounds and thumps for shipments, the body language is easily interpreted by lower levels in terms of management's real priorities. Slogans and words just will not do. President Eisenhower once said that "war is too important to be left to the generals." Similarly, quality is too important to be left to the quality manager! It cannot be delegated to the quality assurance manager, who, if he is lucky, gets to see the chief executive or the general manager no more than fifteen minutes each week. One measure of true involvement is the amount of actual time—clock time—that top management spends on quality. It had better be more time than is spent on profits!

The Infrastructure of Quality: The Quality System

Notwithstanding top management's goodwill toward quality, nothing much can be accomplished unless there is a "best-in-class" quality system in place. Table 10-2 presents a capsule summary of a quality system, developed by me, that is world class. It is divided into ten subsystems, with a total of one hundred essential subelements. It is not necessary that every partnership supplier be proficient in all one hundred subelements. In fact, there are very few customer companies that can claim such a distinction. But, depending on size, technology, and the level of quality to be achieved, a customer company can gauge the quality proficiency of a supplier by the percentage of the number of subelements in place and being practiced. It is a litmus test.

Table 10-2. Capsule summary of a world-class quality system.

Subsystem	Subsystem Elements
Quality Management	• Superordinate value; mission; scope; strategic intent; 5-year plans • Organization; quality costs; quality system audit; reviews • Quality pervasiveness; "process" focus; continuous improvement
Customer Quality	• Elements of customer satisfaction; determining customer needs: value research, sensitivity analysis, multi-attribute analysis, quality function deployment • Measuring customer satisfaction; maintaining customer enthusiasm
Design Quality	• Reliability: targets, prediction, de-rating, FMEA, FTA, PLA, MEOST • Design of experiments: multi-vari, components search, variables search, full factorials, B vs. C, scatter plot optimization, $C_{p_k} > 5.0$ • Group technology; value engineering; parts reduction; design reviews; field tests; sign-offs
Supplier Quality	• Partnership: reduced supplier base, organization, measurement, ESI • Classification of characteristics; $C_{p_k} > 2.0$; stress tests; DPA; certification • Cost reduction; JIT; training; financial incentives/penalties

(continued)

Table 10-2. *Continued.*

Subsystem	Subsystem Elements
Process Control	• Positrol; process certification; operator certification; precontrol • Total preventive maintenance; simple SPC tools
Production Control	• Supplier feedback/feedforward; lot-plot; yield/cycle time measurements • Field escape control: reliability stress tests; quality control: targets and shutdown criteria
Field Reliability	• Packaging; transportation; installation/instructions • Stress tests; initial customer quality; failure analysis • Fault diagnosis; maintainability; availability • Product liability
Support Services Quality	• Total quality of performance; next operation as customer • Flow charting, systems mapping, "is" and "should" matrix analysis
Quality Awareness/ Training	• Employee surveys; error cause removal • Training, testing, workshops, consultation
Quality Motivation	• Fear-free climate: MBWA; manager involvement; motivation factors • Improvement teams; job redesign; job excitement • Holistic concern for employees

Although it would be difficult to describe each subelement of the quality system in a few pages, we have outlined the major subelements in this and subsequent chapters. The following are the important subelements in the quality management subsystem. (The quality system should not be confused with the quality manual, which is mostly a boiler-plate collection of trivia!)

Quality as a Superordinate Value

A corporation has a personality that goes beyond the southeast corner of the profits and loss statement. There are important values that it holds sacred. As an example, for IBM, the preeminent value is service to the customer; for 3M, it is innovation; for Motorola, it is employees; for Maytag, it is reliability. Today, quality has climbed to a position among the top three or five sacred values of progressive American companies. Given the economic imperative of quality, it should become a superordinate value for partnership suppliers as well.

It is not enough for top management levels alone to embrace a superordinate value. It must become the warp and woof of the whole organizational fabric, of importance to every employee in the company. As an example, Ford began advertising under the slogan "Quality is Job 1" as long ago as 1979. But it was not until the employees embraced that value themselves and applied it to their daily work that Ford started to make the spectacular splash in the marketplace that characterized the company's fortunes after 1985. How quality can be made pervasive at all levels of a supplier company is discussed later in this chapter.

The Quality Mission

A corporate mission statement on quality provides the policy directive and the framework within which quality improvement is pursued. As an example, one company's mission statement reads as follows:

> It is our objective to produce products and services of the highest quality. In all of our activities, we will pursue goals aimed at the achievement of quality excellence. These results will be derived from the dedicated efforts of each employee in conjunction with supportive participation from management at all levels of the Corporation.

Many would consider such statements platitudinous. Nevertheless, a mission statement is a starting point. It sets the tone. It represents a firm management commitment to quality.

Scope

Quality has become an ever-expanding universe. In the 1940s, its scope was limited to inspection! In the 1950s, it focused on sampling plans. In the 1960s, it spanned all of manufacturing, from incoming inspection to shipping. In the 1970s, it covered total product, from design inception to field reliability. In the 1980s, it brackets product and all support services, from marketing to order processing, from accounting to personnel. In the 1990s, its scope will involve customers as well as suppliers and their suppliers and subsuppliers in a never-ending spiral of continual improvement fueled by the pursuit of excellence.

Strategic Intent

The difference between strategic intent and the more familiar strategic plans that corporations develop is the all-important time dimension. Strategic plans are short-term and dynamic. They change with various market forces, including competition. Strategic intent is long-term and stable. It is what a corporation wants to be ten to fifteen years down the road. It takes into account the strategic intent of its competitors, both present and future, and attempts to leapfrog such competition by setting its sights on a steady course.

In the quality arena, the strategic plan may be to improve quality by a factor of 10:1 or more over the next five years. But this goal may prove to be inadequate in the face of competition that has had a running start in achieving even higher levels of quality. The strategic intent of a corporation, by contrast, could be the achievement of zero defects, 100 percent yields, theoretical cycle time, and even zero field failures that would assure a strategic advantage regardless of competitive strategic plans that could change from year to year.

Five-Year Plans

Moving from strategic intent to strategic plans, it has become common practice to develop five-year plans for the company as a whole as well as for its divisions and for its different businesses. The quality plan should be a major element of such overall plans. It should include:

- An assessment of where the company stands versus its best (benchmark) competitors in terms of the quality of management, design, manufacturing, and suppliers.
- A list of major quality strengths and weaknesses.
- A statement of objectives to overcome such weaknesses.
- A list of specific goals and a timetable for reaching each goal.
- Detailed strategies to accomplish each goal.

Such five-year plans should not be put on a shelf and dusted off at the time the next five-year plan emerges, as is the usual practice in well-meaning but ineffective companies. It should be a living document, well-thumbed and eminently useful as a road map by which progress can be measured.

Organization

Many companies have large quality assurance organizations—serving as a security blanket—to check, reject, sort, and audit product. In some corporations the ratio of quality personnel to direct labor workers is as high as 1:10

or even 1:5. That is a brute-force method of achieving quality. It also suggests a "policeman" syndrome, in which there is little trust that line operations, be they in design, production, or purchasing, can shoulder their own quality responsibilities.

The quality organization should be microscopic in head count, macroscopic in knowledge. The ratio of quality personnel to direct labor workers should be a maximum of 1:200 (and 1:500 for the total employee population). One quick way of gauging the effectiveness of a supplier's quality system is to determine such a ratio. The quality department should be highly professional; it should command the respect of the entire organization and be the internal consultant on everything to do with quality, in short, the teacher, coach, cheerleader, and champion of quality. Its main task should be to help all departments in achieving "reach-out" quality goals, not to check on them or sit in judgment over them. It should be part of top management. Its independent power—to stop a shipment, shut down a line, or disqualify a supplier—should be assured.

There are two other organizational building blocks devoted to quality improvement. The first is a steering committee or council, consisting of the company president (or general manager, in a division) as the chairman and key top management personnel as members. Its purpose is to:

- Provide a climate under which quality, as a superordinate value, becomes accepted by rank-and-file members of the whole company.
- Prepare the groundwork for a quality breakthrough.
- Serve as the owner of the quality improvement process.
- Identify the most important "chronic" quality problems, prioritize them, and establish ad hoc diagnostic teams to solve them.

The second building block is the diagnostic team. It is the workhorse of quality, just as the commodity team is the workhorse of supply management. Its task is to analyze and solve chronic quality problems. Each diagnostic team is interdisciplinary in composition, with members drawn from Engineering, Manufacturing/Process engineering, and Quality Assurance as a minimum, and other functions added as needed. An important prerequisite for the diagnostic teams is training in problem-solving methods, especially the design of experiments as the best way to get to the root causes of the problem. It must also be pointed out that chronic problems are by no means the exclusive province of products. They exist in white-collar work and in all support services, where they are often even more insidious. Chapter 17 describes a road map for use in tackling such problems.

Quality Costs

As discussed in the section on the staggering cost of poor quality earlier in this chapter, no company—customer or supplier—can afford to be ignorant of the costs of poor quality. Small supplier companies need not establish elaborate accounting systems to assess the cost of poor quality. But they must develop the ability to estimate, with an accuracy of plus or minus 10 percent, the six important elements of costs of poor quality: warranty, scrap, analyzing, rework, inspection, and test, listed in descending order of importance. The steering committee can then prioritize areas where such costs should be tackled, and the diagnostic teams can systematically solve the chronic problems causing these cost and profit leaks. Progress milestones should be established. Once a month, the steering committee should conduct a review of the quality progress so far, focusing on remaining problems and the removal of organizational and technical stumbling blocks. With the right approach, diagnostic teams should be able to reduce the cost of poor quality by 50 percent in three years at a very minimum.

Quality System Audit

Once the quality system has been designed and is in place, management must make sure that the system is really working and is being adhered to by all functions. This is best ascertained by an audit similar to a financial audit. Appendix 2 shows a detailed questionnaire that can be used both as an initial commodity team audit of an already established partnership supplier and as an ongoing self-audit by the supplier or as an ongoing external audit by the customer.

This quality survey, like its counterpart for overall supplier evaluation detailed in Appendix 1, is hypothetical. It is based on questionnaires used by many large customer companies to audit the quality system capabilities of their major suppliers. But this survey surpasses any of them in its standard of requirements. In fact, it surpasses the standards set by Japanese committees that evaluate companies in Japan for the much coveted Deming Prize. It also surpasses the standards required by the committee that evaluates the quality of U.S. companies to select winners for the Malcolm Baldrige Award for outstanding quality.* This award, established by the U.S. Congress in 1987, rivals the Deming Prize in prestige.

Appendix 2 has ten categories or subsystems for assessing the adequacy of the quality system of partnership suppliers. These include: management

---

*Two quality awards in each of three categories (large corporations, small companies, and service companies) are given each year by the Malcolm Baldrige Award Committee. My company (Motorola) was honored in 1988 with the first award ever presented. It is refreshing to note, however, that Mr. Robert W. Galvin, chairman of the board at Motorola, cautioned all employees—his associates, as he calls them—not to rest on their laurels, but to continue to strive for never-ending improvement. The award should only be viewed as a passport to world class quality. In global competition, quality has no finish line!

of the quality system, customer satisfaction, design quality, supplier quality, process planning and control, production quality control, field reliability, support services quality, quality awareness/training, and quality motivation. Each subsystem is assigned a rating scale. When added together, the ratings provide an overall score of the supplier's quality system adequacy. Each subsystem has ten searching questions. Again, as in Appendix 1, the subsystems, rating scales, and questions can be modified depending on: the nature of the commodity, the level of the standard that the customer company wishes to establish, the general standards of the partnership suppliers, their location, and whether they are offshore or domestic suppliers. The mechanics of this quality system audit are similar to those of the finalist supplier surveys detailed in Chapter 7.

Within a supplier's organization, the audit can be conducted either by Quality Assurance or by top management. The best results are achieved by top management audits, as is the practice in Japan. The reason is a universal principle: People will do what management inspects, not what management expects. Further, conducting such an audit is the fastest way for top management to "get up to speed" on quality; to get to know the problems firsthand rather than through the filter of middle management; to get to know the people and mingle with them; and to demonstrate that it is willing to invest its personal time in "Quality as Job 1."

Evaluating The Supplier's DOE/SPC/Reliability: An Avant-Garde Survey

Just as an evaluation of the supplier's quality system is an extension of the evaluation of a supplier's overall capability, so too is an evaluation of the avant-garde tools of design of experiments (DOE), SPC, and reliability an extension of the general quality survey/audit.

Appendix 3 is a futuristic sample of such a survey. It has not been put into effect yet because there are hardly any supplier companies that would even be familiar with the terminology contained in the survey, much less achieve a passing score. For that matter, there are very, very few customer companies that would achieve a respectable score on such a survey. Nevertheless, the objective of the survey is to raise the consciousness of both customer and supplier companies to the new standard of excellence that is required if the United States is to recapture world quality leadership.

Some of the more "progressive" customer companies have devised questionnaires that survey the supplier's SPC capabilities. A majority of them, however, do not include design of experiments, and what passes for SPC practices, for the most part, are the worn-out techniques of control charts and such elementary tools as cause-and-effect diagrams.

Quality Pervasiveness

The acid test in any organization, supplier or customer, is how well management's lofty quality values and goals permeate down to the lowest-level workers, how well they truly "buy into" quality. The key is total *management participation*, starting with the president and filtering down to every supervisor. This is sometimes referred to as the "waterfall effect." James McDonald, president of General Motors, sums up the necessity for all levels of management to be personally involved when he says: "If management thinks people don't care, it's likely that people won't care. But, far more important, if people think that management doesn't care—then, it's almost certain that no one else will, either."

The Dimensions of Management Involvement

What does management involvement with employees mean? There are several facets to such involvement, but as a start:

- Managers must mingle with their people daily and not remain closeted in their comfortable castles, immersed in meetings and paperwork. An oft-quoted truism states that the success of a company is inversely proportional to the number of meetings it holds. As for paperwork, the weight of paper required to produce a single unit often exceeds the weight of the unit, even for heavy products such as aircraft and space hardware! A high percentage of paperwork is wasted effort. The time could be better utilized in problem-solving and in team-building.
- They must drive out fear among their people and encourage them to speak their minds.
- They must listen to their people, especially to suggestions for improvement, act on the recommendations, and implement them, even if the projected return on investment is only marginal. The encouragement and nurturing of employee ideas pays off a thousandfold in the long run.
- They must be cheerleaders, coaches, team builders.

Only then will workers give their all willingly, constructively, enthusiastically. A good way for management to feel the quality pulse of its people is to run a periodic quality perception survey. An example of a survey I designed and its results is given in Appendix 4. The negative/undesired responses, then become management's responsibility to correct.

Other measures to enhance quality pervasiveness in the entire organization include:

- Permitting workers to shut down a line for unacceptable quality, even if this means missing a shipment. That is the kind of body language that will communicate to workers that management's heart truly belongs to quality, not to end-of-month shipments.
- Quality bulletins and newsletters that report on quality progress to the whole organization.
- Quality charts and graphs, preferably maintained by the operators themselves, visible at each work station for all to see.
- "Quality traffic lights"—green, yellow, and red—at each work station to highlight quality levels, along with diagnostic indicators to pinpoint the source of quality problems.
- Quality training, utilizing simple design of experiments—that even direct labor personnel can learn and implement—to reduce variation; and SPC to maintain high quality levels.
- Recognition and rewards for individuals, teams, and groups in achieving quality goals. Recognition is considered one of the most powerful motivators.
- Vertical job enrichment and job redesign so that every employee can become a manager in his or her own area of responsibility.

Continual Improvement

The last element in the quality management subsystem is continual, never-ending improvement. Quality has no finish line. When a company and its employees are content with a given level of quality, they stop improving. When they stop improving, they slip backwards. What is needed is a constructive dissatisfaction with the status quo. Every person in the company from the president to the janitor should ask, each day: "What can I do better today than I did yesterday? What can I do better tomorrow than I'm doing today?" Yet, as noted in Chapter 6, these improvements need not be sensational, on the order of a Babe Ruth home run; the Wee Willie practice of a hit almost every time at bat is more effective in the long run. Small improvements, by a whole army of people, that are continual produce better results than spectacular technological or equipment breakthroughs that occur only once in a blue moon.

Successfully Utilizing the Quality System

Both successes and failures abound in the implementation of the quality system. Failures can primarily be laid at the door of management whenever management did not understand the quality system or misused it; did not get involved with the people but blamed workers for quality problems; did not make a long-term commitment to quality or bring quality into the mainstream of its businesses.

By contrast, successful companies that have mastered the quality system attribute most gains to one or more of the following:

- Management's leadership and promotion of a quality milieu.
- Statistical design of experiments.
- Statistical process control.
- Improved communications throughout the company.
- Capital improvements.

As an example of a quality improvement process, the Stacswitch Corporation of Costa Mesa, California, in three years registered the following improvements:

- Costs of poor quality were reduced by 44 percent.
- Gross profits increased by 124 percent.
- Total units produced increased by 8 percent and sales increased by 36 percent.
- Productivity increased by 27 percent as measured in sales dollars per employee.
- Scrap reduced to near zero; yields increased to 96 percent.
- A personnel reduction of 30 percent achieved without layoffs.
- Additional benefits: reduced employee absenteeism and turnover; better equipment utilization; improved supplier relations; fewer parts shortages; reduced part costs; reduced lead times to customers; lower maintenance engineering in production; and much higher customer satisfaction.

Chapter 11

Worship of the Customer

Customers are:

- *The most important people in any business.*
- *Not dependent on us. We are dependent on them.*
- *Not an interruption of our work. They are the purpose of it.*
- *Doing us a favor when they come in. We are not doing them a favor by serving them.*
- *A part of our business, not outsiders.*
- *Not just a statistic. They are flesh-and-blood human beings with feelings and emotions, like ourselves.*
- *People who come to us with their needs and wants. It is our job to fill them.*
- *Deserving of the most courteous and attentive treatment we can give them.*
- *The life-blood of this and every other business. Without them, we would have to close our doors."*

—Employee card at IBM, Austin.

137

The Main Purpose of a Business: Customer Satisfaction, Not Profit

If a survey were taken of American executives asking what the main purpose of a business was, the overwhelming response would be *profit*. Anyone who even dared to suggest customer satisfaction would be looked upon as a flat earth believer. Yet all management theory—from the Introductory Course 101 to the Harvard Business School, from Henry Ford in 1926 to Peter F. Drucker in recent times—states categorically that customer satisfaction is what business is all about. Profit is very important, but it is an output, not an input, a result, not a cause. There are instances where companies don't make profits, but no single company can exist without customers, not even in the Soviet Union!

The Japanese recognized the difference as far back as the 1950s. Worship of the customer has taken the place of emperor worship. In Japan, engineering graduates are not put on the bench, but sent to the field for six months to a year to learn all about customers. "The voice of the customer" forms the foundation of the latest Japanese technique—quality function deployment, which combines many disciplines, ranging from competitive analysis to value engineering. Even their final measure of success, market share, is a direct reflection of customer satisfaction. They firmly believe that if the customer is truly satisfied, profits will follow. In the United States, management tends to be so mesmerized by profits that the customer is not intensely served. This is true of customer companies and supplier companies alike.

The Role of Quality in Customer Satisfaction

If customer satisfaction, then, is the name of the game, where does quality fit into the picture? In times past, the definition of quality was narrow and confined to meeting specifications at the time of shipment to a customer, with zero field time and zero field stress. Today, in its larger and more strategic sense, quality has become all-encompassing, embracing all elements of customer satisfaction. Its scope has mushroomed, not unlike the expansion of our universe following its "big bang" creation.

Figure 11-1 shows a schematic network of the various elements of customer satisfaction that combine to form total customer satisfaction, which goes by such varying names as value, strategic quality, and customer enthusiasm. Figure 11-1 can also be considered a road map of the evolution of strategic quality from its humble beginnings following World War II.

Before the war, quality simply meant meeting specifications. The dimension of reliability was added to quality in the 1950s, maintainability in the 1960s, availability (the percentage of time the product was available to the

Figure 11-1. The elements of customer satisfaction.

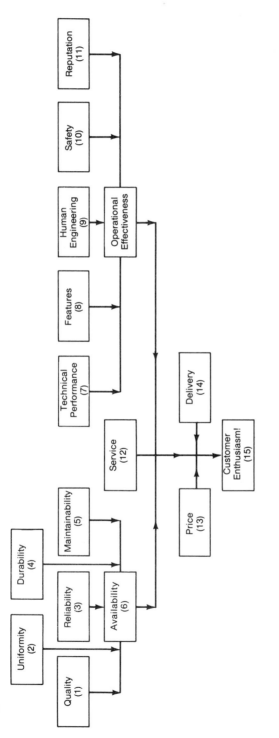

Notes:
1. Quality: Meeting specifications at time = O; Stress = 0
2. Uniformity: Design to target value not to wide specs
3. Reliability: Quality at time T and combined stresses
4. Durability: Total life before replacement
5. Maintainability: Accurate, timely, low cost repair
6. Availability: Percentage up-time during product life
7. Technical performance: Primary operating characteristics, proprietary position
8. Features: Support functions that make the product sell
9. Human engineering: Styling; color; ease of installation, use, diagnostics, etc.—"user friendly"
10. Safety: To user, to society (includes product liability)
11. Reputation: Image, perceived quality
12. Service: Before-sale cooperativeness, flexible schedules in production, full support after sale
13. Low price: Cost reductions based on technology, automation, learning curves
14. Fast delivery: Short cycle time, flexible deliveries, minimum inventory
15. Synonyms for customer enthusiasm: Total customer satisfaction; value; strategic quality

user) in the 1970s, and uniformity (design to target values) in the 1980s. Durability (or a product's total life before final breakdown and replacement) may be the next dimension to be added to quality.

On the operational side, the idea of "quality" started with technical performance (to primary operating characteristics). The first expansion was the addition of product features, the distinction being that technical performance makes the product *work*, while features make the product *sell*. Features are the bells and whistles that often overshadow the question of "Where's the beef!" With the growth of the consumer movement, human engineering was added to the quality portfolio. Human engineering spans styling, attractiveness, ease of installation, ease of controls, built-in diagnostics, and so on. With Ralph Naderism and litigation came safety as yet another dimension of "quality." Safety can be described as a catchall term that embraces user protection, product liability, and even usefulness to society. Finally, reputation must always be linked with quality. Reputation is perceived quality, the image that consumers conjure up of a company and its products. (To reverse a popular advertisement which claimed "The quality goes in before the name goes on," a new slogan of perceived quality could be: "The image lingers on after the quality goes out!") These elements can be added together to form operational effectiveness.

The combination of all of these elements, along with service, price, and delivery, results in "strategic quality," or customer enthusiasm, where the customer is so excited about the product that he performs free, word-of-mouth advertising. That is total customer satisfaction. That is world-class strategic quality.

"Bhote's Law"

But which element of customer satisfaction should a supplier pursue? It may be much too expensive or technically very difficult for a supplier to excel in all fifteen elements of strategic quality simultaneously. Sometimes trade-offs are inescapable. For instance, Cray Research, the supercomputer manufacturer, had to lower reliability in exchange for speed, the hallmark of its products. Further, no one element of customer satisfaction is more important than any other to all customers, in all places, at all times. A company entering a market, where its competition is well-entrenched, may have to select one or two elements of customer satisfaction as its quality niche. But again, which one? Fortunately there is a strategy, dubbed "Bhote's Law" by my students at the Illinois Institute of Technology, which states: "It is that element of customer satisfaction *missing from your product* which, if *important to your customer*, requires top management attention."

As an example, when the Japanese attempted, after a shaky start, to gain a toehold in the lush U.S. automobile market, they could not hope to compete against the Big Three on their own turf. However, their market surveys indicated that the Achilles heel of the Big Three was poor quality. It was also important to the U.S. customer, who felt that U.S. car manufacturers had turned off their hearing aids on quality. Quality, then, along with its twins—reliability and maintainability—became their niche strategy. Japan's 25 percent share of the U.S. automobile market, despite the "voluntary" quotas imposed by the United States, is a testimonial to the astuteness of that strategy.

On the other hand, it is well known that Japanese cars, in terms of safety and crash worthiness, are far inferior to U.S. cars. But domestic car manufacturers have not been able to capitalize on this element of customer satisfaction missing from their Japanese competition. For some perverse reason, the rank and file of American consumers do not consider safety to be important—attesting to the second half of "Bhote's Law."

Taking the Customer's Temperature

In order to truly determine which elements of customer satisfaction are both important and not being met by a supplier, it is necessary to have constant contact, and a close rapport, with the customer. This is captured in the famous saying of Konosuke Matsushita, the venerable founder of the Matsushita Corporation, to his staff: "You must take the customer's skin temperature every day." To a supplier company, this means a continuous process of:

- Determining the needs and requirements of the customer company.
- Separating the customer's "must" requirements from his "merely desirable" wish list.
- Translating customer requirements into correct factor order entries. (One major manufacturer discovered more errors in his order entry system than in his near-perfect product quality.)
- Catering to the customer company's need for product understanding, applications, training, installation, service, and so on. Figure 11-2 shows

Figure 11-2. Reasons why customers failed to return to the original auto dealer.

Percentage of Sample Surveyed	Reason Given
1%	Dealer died
3%	Moved to another location
5%	Obtained a better price elsewhere
9%	Switched to another car manufacturer
14%	Dissatisfied with service
68%	Dealer "didn't give a damn!"

the several reasons why customers do not go back to the car dealer from whom they purchased their last car. A whopping 68 percent did not return to the dealer because "he didn't give a damn" after the sale was consummated! After-sales attention to the customer is a cardinal rule in customer relations that must never, never be violated.

- Continually assessing a customer's future requirements and changing expectations, and working closely with him to formulate such requirements.

Determining the Customer's "Must" Requirements

It is amazing, three generations after Julius Rosenwald and Robert Wood laid the foundations of marketing and built Sears, Roebuck into a giant merchandiser, that the general U.S. concept of marketing is still "selling"—shoving a product down a reluctant customer's throat. Even today, there is a tendency for companies to design a product, without benefit of customer input, and peddle it to customers through slick advertising and other sales gimmickry. True marketing starts with an assessment of customer needs that come directly from the customer (except in the case of major technological breakthroughs) rather than with an engineering or sales or management interpretation of those needs. Under no circumstances should the cart of engineering design be placed before the horse of customer need.

Nor can market research be an accurate barometer of real customer needs. The two most celebrated monuments to market research's failures are Ford's Edsel and Coca-Cola's New Coke. Conversely, market research has also dismissed such eventual winners as the film *Star Wars* and Dove Bar, the deluxe ice cream bar, as flops! With that kind of track record, it is small wonder that market research malpractice suits may be the next hot topic in business litigation. Testifying before the Joint Economic Committee of Congress, Professor Edwin Mansfield of the University of Pennsylvania indicated that market research costs in U.S. companies were double those of Japanese companies. "We need to spend much less on market research and marketing studies and more on making products well," was his conclusion. Fortunately, there are better methods of determining true customer needs than market research.

Value Research

Value research is a technique in which customers are requested to separate the supplier's product features into three categories: those they like very strongly, those they dislike most strongly, and those features about which they are neutral. The strong "likes" can be capitalized on in promotion and advertising. The strong "dislikes"—the discovery of which is the major benefit of value research—are then removed through redesign, thus converting customer dissatisfaction into positive satisfaction. Finally, the neutral features are value engineered so as to lower the product's costs with no loss of customer satisfaction. An example, albeit from the consumer world, illustrates the power of value research.

Example: Sunbeam Electric made a fine electric steam iron, but always found itself in second place to GE, which dominated that market. Sunbeam tried a number of strategies—sales promotions, dealer discounts, and even price reductions—to no avail. Finally, a value research task force was established to get direct feedback from young housewives, who constituted the center of gravity of the customer population.

The strong dislikes category revealed four Sunbeam weaknesses. The housewives surveyed reported: (1) The iron was too heavy; (2) the hole to pour water into the iron was beautifully styled, but too small; (3) the iron was unstable when set on its end, in between ironing operations; (4) the steam came out with little force; "it has all the power of a wet noodle," they complained.

Sunbeam rapidly redesigned its iron. It found that there was a halfpound difference between its iron and GE's. All along, Sunbeam engineers had been convinced that the heavier iron was better for ironing. They had not reckoned with the modern housewife whose perceptions differed from those of an older generation. Sunbeam removed weight from the iron and simultaneously lowered costs. It opened up the hole for water entry. It broadened the iron base to increase stability. Most important, it developed a steam chamber, where pressure would build up and steam would come gushing out, at the press of a button, from a much larger number of ports. This gave the iron "go power," as the engineers termed it. The result: Sunbeam climbed easily into first place, ending years of GE domination.

Sensitivity Analysis

Sensitivity analysis is an iterative process between customer and supplier. Assume that a desired feature has an agreed-upon specification with an associated cost, as shown in point A of Figure 11-3 (a). If, now, the customer desires an increase in that specification and the cost of the increase is low, the change to the higher specification should be made. If, instead, even a small increase in the specification results in a much higher cost, the marginal increase in the specification becomes uneconomic to both the customer and the supplier. Figure 11-3 (b) shows an opposite set of conditions. If lowering a specification slightly results in a substantial cost reduction, the change should be made. But if there is a great and undesirable decrease in specifications for only a slight cost reduction, it is not in the interest of customer and supplier to make the change.

Figure 11-3. Sensitivity analysis: Incremental specifications vs. incremental costs.

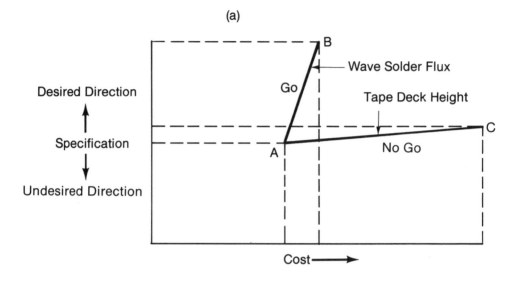

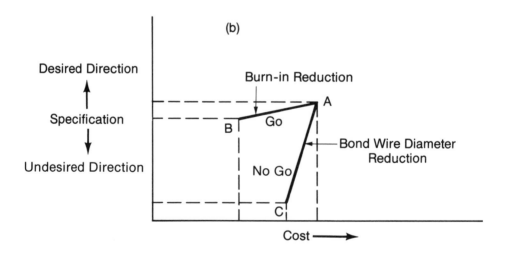

Example: A few examples can be cited to illustrate each of these four conditions. A supplier, providing a flux (cleaning agent) to a customer company for its wave solder operations, offered two choices—a 325 flux and an 880 flux, the latter costing 7 percent more. The customer ran solderability tests and determined that there would be more than a 10:1 improvement in solder quality, using the 880 flux. The savings, in far fewer touch-up operators, paid for the slight increase in flux cost several times over.

We see an opposite scenario in connection with a tape deck for a car radio, where the deck height of 27mm was considered to be a very desirable feature for the customer because it would assure him of the world's thinnest tape deck. However, the cost to the supplier of producing such a state-of-the-art deck was estimated to be so high that the sales feature was deemed uneconomical by both parties.

In another sensitivity analysis determination, a customer wanted a seventy-two-hour burn-in of his product to reduce latent field failures. The supplier made a study showing that 97 percent of the latent failures were apprehended in the first twenty-four hours of burn-in, at much reduced cost and a forty-eight-hour reduction in cycle time. The customer accepted the reduced burn-in requirement. (Later, the 100 percent burn-in requirement was eliminated altogether in favor of a sample thermal cycling and a vigorous follow-up and correction of every failure in the sample.)

The fourth example concerns a customer's suggestion to reduce the diameter of the gold wire in the wire bonding of a semiconductor device. Tests run on the wire bonds, however, indicated a sharp reduction in pull strength, with very little cost savings. The idea was abandoned.

Multi-Attribute Evaluation Technique*

This simple but powerful technique enables a supplier to determine which features are most important to a customer; how a customer rates him on each feature, and in total, vis-à-vis his prime competitors; and the worth to cost ratio of each feature vis-à-vis his prime competitors. Armed with such vital information, a supplier knows where to apply his redesign efforts so as to leapfrog his competition.

Table 11-1 shows the application of a multi-attribute evaluation technique to an automatic washing machine. Value research applied to the features of the washing machine revealed that customers felt that speed (number of combinations), temperature (number of combinations), water (amount used), lint (ability to remove it), and sand (ability to dispose of it), in that order, were considered to be most important. An importance (or weight)

---

*I am indebted to Dr. Frank Gryna, vice-president of the Juran Institute, for the development of this technique.

Table 11-1. Multi-attribute evaluation technique applied to an automatic washing machine.

A: The Decision Matrix

	Attributes					Total Score
	Speeds	Temperatures	Water	Lint	Sand	
Weight (Total = 10)	3	2.5	2.0	1.5	1.0	
Choices (1–10)						
Our Company	5 15	7 17.5	6 12	7 10.5	8 8	63
Competitor A	6 18	5 12.5	6 12	5 7.5	4 4	54
Competitor B	8 24	8 20	9 18	8 12	7 7	81*

* Best

B: Weight (Importance) to Cost Ratio

Attribute	Our Company			Competitor A			Competitor B		
	Weighted Rating	Cost	Rating/ Cost	Weighted Rating	Cost	Rating/ Cost	Weighted Rating	Cost	Rating/ Cost
Speeds	15	7.20	2.08	18	8.30	2.17	24	8.50	2.82
Temperature	17.5	7.50	2.33	12.5	5.50	2.27	20	8.25	2.42
Water	12	5.75	2.09	12	8.75	1.37	18	8.10	2.22
Lint	10.5	2.80	3.75	7.5	2.10	3.57	12	2.30	5.22
Sand	8	1.20	6.67	4	1.50	2.67	7	1.25	5.60
Total Score	63	24.45	2.58	54	26.15	2.07	81	28.40	2.85*

* Best

scale was developed. Speed was given a weight of 3.0, temperature 2.5, water 2.0, lint 1.5, and sand 1.0, adding up to a total weight of 10. Selected customers were then asked to rate each feature on washing machines of the supplier company and on those of its two principal competitors.

A rating scale from 1 (worst) to 10 (best) was used. Table 11-1 (a), the decision matrix, shows the results of the customer evaluations. On speed, the supplier company rated only 5, whereas competitor B rated 8. The rating, multiplied by the weight, gave the score for each company for each feature. As an example, competitor B rated 8 for speed, which had an importance weight of 3. Hence the rating score for B for speed was $8 \times 3 = 24$. Adding these scores horizontally, across all five features, gave the supplier company a score of 63 versus 54 and 81 for competitors A and B respectively. The decision matrix clearly pointed to speed and water as the weak features of the supplier company's machine.

Table 11-1 (b) takes the multi-attribute analysis one step further. It computes the worth to cost (or rating to cost) ratio for each feature for each company. The cost of each feature for the supplier company is known. The cost of each feature for the competitors can be estimated using highly professional cost estimators. For instance, the worth to cost ratio for speed for the supplier company was 2.08 versus 2.82 for competitor B. In fact, competitor B outperformed the supplier company in all features, with the exception of sand elimination. Obviously, the supplier company had its work cut out for it if it wanted to survive in the marketplace.

Quality Function Deployment

Since the 1970s, a movement called Quality Function Deployment (QFD) has gained currency in Japan. Many companies there are using it. Its proponents claim that it enables companies to achieve a "half-half-half-half" improvement on new designs, that is, an improvement of half the design cycle time, at half the cost, with half the manpower, and with half the defects (engineering changes), compared to older methods. Toyota, for example, has reduced its start-up costs by 61 percent since introducing QFD in 1975 and its product development cycle time by one-third, and has had a corresponding improvement in new product quality. Further, all Toyota suppliers are now using QFD.

The objective of QFD is to translate "the voice of the customer," who may only be able to specify requirements in subjective terms, like "smooth, comfortable ride" or "roomy interior," into the appropriate technical, quantitative requirements for each stage of product development and production. These include marketing strategies, planning, product design and engineering, prototype evaluation, production process development, component specifications, and test requirements, among others. QFD is an umbrella technique that spans disciplines such as the Design of Experiments, Benchmarking, Value Engineering, Failure Mode Effects Analysis, and Poka-Yoke that are covered in various chapters of this book.

Space does not permit a detailed treatment of this comprehensive but difficult discipline or of an equivalent American development called Conjoint Analysis, using revealed preference techniques. For the reader who wishes more enlightenment on the subject, the American Supplier Institute in Dearborn, Michigan, offers three-day courses on QFD.*

---

*Other excellent references include the first authoritative text on the subject published in the U.S.: *Better Designs in Half the Time: Implementing Quality Function Deployment in America*, Bob King (Methuen, Mass.: Goal/QPC, 1987); and "The House of Quality," by John R. Hauser and Don Clausing, *Harvard Business Review* (May-June 1988).

Figure 11-4. Customer satisfaction survey.

The XYZ Corporation solicits your help in filling out this Customer Satisfaction Survey form. It will enable us to gauge how well we are satisfying you, our valued customer.

Please ask your engineer, purchasing, manufacturing, and quality managers to rate us on the elements of customer satisfaction listed below, using the following rating system.

A = Substantially better than most of your suppliers
B = On par with your better suppliers
C = Needs improvement
D = Unsatisfactory

	Engineering	Purchasing	Manufacturing	Quality
Customer service: responsiveness				
Delivery on time				
Sales representative: attitude/responsiveness				
Product quality: on arrival				
Product reliability				
Field service support				
Pricing				
Other				
XYZ Corporation as a supplier— overall				

Comments:

Form completed by: _____ Date: _____

Please return in stamped, self-addressed envelope. Thank you for your help.

The Measurement of Customer Satisfaction

Many suppliers not only do an inadequate job of determining customer needs but also do not follow through to assess how well their customers are satisfied with the products they ship. Some companies use outgoing quality data, but their tests may miss the major concerns of customers. Others use field reliability data, in terms of failure rates per year or mean time between failures (MTBF). But, again, customer perceptions may differ vastly from such reliability figures, which measure only one element of customer satisfaction. There are, however, proven ways of measuring customer satisfaction.

Customer Satisfaction Surveys

Salesmens' opinions, field replacement parts traffic and inputs from distributors, dealers or services are no substitute for asking customers directly. A customer's image of a supplier's performance is more important than hard, objective data.

Figure 11-4 is an example of a typical survey form used by a supplier to establish an ongoing score of customer satisfaction. The elements of customer satisfaction range from responsiveness and on-time delivery to quality/reliability and price. Comparisons are with the best of competition as a benchmark. In this particular case, the supplier company's customers are original equipment manufacturers, where the customer has a multiple identity in terms of the various departments, such as engineering, purchasing, manufacturing, and quality, that interface with the supplier, each with a different perspective on supplier performance.

This kind of "image" survey is generally conducted twice a year, and progress in customer satisfaction is quantified. Perceived weaknesses in any of the elements of customer satisfaction should receive the attention of top management and be corrected immediately.

The "PIMS" Method of Assessing Customer Satisfaction

In Chapter 10, we highlighted the Profit Impact of Market Strategy (PIMS) data, published by the Strategic Planning Institute (SPI). PIMS has also developed a unique approach to determining customer satisfaction. It is labeled "quality," but actually covers several elements of customer satisfaction.

Figure 11-5 is an example of the PIMS method of gauging customer satisfaction. Several elements of customer concerns are grouped under two broad headings—product-related factors and service-related factors. An importance scale is assigned to each factor, with a total of 100 points. The

Figure 11-5. Quantifying customer satisfaction: The "PIMS" method.

Business _____ Year _____

Customer Concerns (Key Purchase Criteria)	Relative Importance to Customers (%)	Customer Rating							
		Competitor A 1-10	Competitor B 1-10	Competitor C 1-10	Average for Competitors	Your Business 1-10	Your Business Superior	Your Business Equivalent	Your Business Inferior
Product-related factors	60%								
1. Flexibility	15	3	4	4	3 2/3	6	15		
2. Reliability	25	8	5	7	6 2/3	7		25	
3. Serviceability	15	4	6	7	5 2/3	9	15		
4. Packaging	5	7	9	8	8	3			5
5.									
6.									
7.									
Service-related factors	40%								
1. Quotation response	10	6	8	7	7	4			10
2. Delivery time	22	8	5	8	7	9	22		
3. Warranty service	5	9	8	8	8 1/3	9		5	
4. Financing	3	5	4	6	5	5		3	
5.									
6.									
7.									
Totals	100%					Data Form 3 Input	52	33	15

% Superior = 1 point above average for competitors
% Equivalent = within 1 point of average for competitors
% Inferior = 1 point below average for competitors

Line 316 ⟶
Line 317 ⟶
Line 318 ⟶

Relative product quality = Superior minus inferior = | 37 |

customer is asked to rate the supplier on each factor on a scale of 1 to 10 and to do the same for the supplier's competitors. The average rating for all the competitors is then computed and compared against the supplier's rating. If the supplier's rating exceeds the average competitor rating by one point or more, the full weight (importance) of the given factor is assigned

Table 11-2. The quantitative measurement of customer satisfaction.

Element	Records	Parameters
Quality	Customer incoming inspiration	1. $ of rejected material as % of total material $ received 2. Rejected material (units) as % of total material (units)
Reliability	Warranty returns	1. Warranty $ as % of sales 2. Unit failures as % of units sold
	Customer surveys	1. % of customers satisfied for dependability 2. List of five highest complaints
	Service surveys	1. Reliability ranking vis-à-vis competition 2. List of five highest complaints
Service	Customer surveys	% of customers satisfied with services
	Service surveys	Service ranking vis-à-vis competition
	Analyzing time	Average time to analyze five most repetitive failures
	Repair time	Average time to repair five most repetitive failures
Technical performance	Independent testing agencies Customer surveys Service surveys	Performance ranking vis-à-vis competition
Human engineering	Independent testing agencies Customer surveys Service surveys	Ranking vis-à-vis competition of the following parameters: styling, convenience, installation, and instructions Ease of controls, safety
Cost	Published prices Trade-in value	Price ranking vis-à-vis competition
Delivery	Order inputs vs. ship dates Freight bills	Average delay between promise and ship date $ of premium freight as % of total sales $

to the superior column on the right. If the supplier's rating scale is within one point of the average competitor rating, the full weight of the given factor is assigned to the equivalent column on the right. If the supplier's rating scale is below that of the average competitor by one point or more, the full weight of the given factor is assigned to the inferior column on the right. The scores in each of these three columns, for all factors, are then totaled. The customer satisfaction, or quality, rating for the supplier is the superior column minus the inferior column. In the example shown, the score is 52-15 or 37, out of a possible maximum of 100. Those suppliers who score above 50 are considered excellent. (This was the method used to calculate the quality of the several thousand businesses in the PIMS data of Figure 10-1.)

A Detailed Method of Quantifying Customer Satisfaction

Both the survey method and the PIMS approach use an arbitrary comparative scale to assess customer satisfaction. If a more quantitative measurement is desired, Table 11-2 shows an example of one in which each element of customer satisfaction is measured separately on the basis of detailed records, ranging from customer incoming inspection to warranty returns, from service surveys to reports from independent testing agencies. The actual measurement parameters can be negotiated between customer and supplier. This method does not attempt to determine a single score for the supplier as the PIMS method does, nor does it compare the supplier against competitors as the other two methods do. Rather, it is a longitudinal comparison—over time—of the supplier's progress in every element of customer satisfaction. It is a comprehensive method, but because of the considerable record keeping involved, its use is recommended only for the most important of the supplier's customers.

Chapter 12

Quality in Design: The Volley

Product life cycles today are getting shorter than design cycle times of yesterday. In this environment, the company with the shortest design cycle time will have the greatest competitive advantage. One of the most important factors in reducing this design cycle time is first-time quality success.

—Jim Swartz, manager of benchmarking, Delco Electronics

Design Quality—The Root of All Evil

Among the many causes of poor quality, design engineering must be considered the number one contributor, the root cause of the evil. The corrosive influence of poor design quality is universal. Customers see it, not on just a few units, but across the board. Suppliers get blamed, even though specifications and applications are often beyond their control. Manufacturing is the "stuckee" that must clean up the engineering mess, sometimes at breakneck speed. Service receives the storm of complaints that, ironically, it probably warned about earlier in the design cycle. Line workers become the scapegoats, as Engineering stands by hypocritically bemoaning the workers for having "lost their pride of workmanship." And hovering over all these effects caused by poor engineering is the danger of product liabil-

Figure 12-1. Japanese/U.S. engineering change comparison.

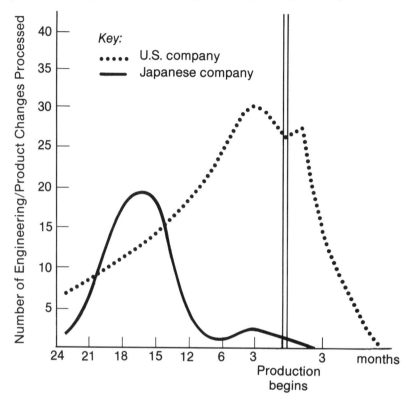

90% of Japanese changes are complete 18 months before production.

Source: Larry Sullivan, "Quality Function Development," *American Society for Quality Control Journal.*

ity suits. Prosecution lawyers wax especially ecstatic whenever they discover a design flaw that can affect every unit in the field.

There is another reason why design quality is of paramount importance today. Not only are product life cycles shortening from the comfortable range of ten to twenty years in the 1950s and 1960s down to two to five years in the 1980s, but customers' demands for product variety are also accelerating. Take the tennis shoe as a classic example. In the old days, there was fundamentally one design, with variations confined to size and, perhaps, color. Today there are jogging shoes and walking shoes that are customized to fit every human podiatric contour, along with built-in microprocessor controls to register miles traveled, pulse, and blood pressure. Shoes have become a veritable mobile medical laboratory! This exploding product variety requires not only shortened design cycle times but a continuous stream of product innovations calculated to leave the competition behind and off balance. The best way to achieve these challenging goals is to make sure that designs are quality effective the first time around, with a minimum of engineering changes required.

Measures of Design Quality Effectiveness

Figure 12-1 compares the number of engineering changes in Japan's automotive industry versus those in the United States. It plots the number of engineering changes before and after the start of production (Job 1). Engineering changes in Japanese companies are not only far fewer than comparable changes in U.S. companies; they are also terminated, in general, before the start of production, whereas they continue for several months after the start of production in U.S. companies, where the production factory is used as an extension of the engineering laboratory. In fact, design quality effectiveness can be measured by production—the next operation as customer—using the following parameters:

- Number of engineering changes after the start of production.
- Overall yield end to end, or total defects per unit at the start of production.
- Design cycle time, from program kickoff to the start of production.

Quality Steps in the Product Development Cycle

The two most important tasks in assuring quality of design are:

1. The systematic reduction of variation—beyond zero defects.
2. The achievement of high reliability—the march to zero failures.

Each of these major tasks will be addressed in future chapters—the first in Chapter 13, the second in Chapter 15. The groundwork in preparation for these objectives will be dealt with in this chapter. There are seven steps in a product development cycle, in each of which quality and reliability considerations must be weighed.

1. Product Mission

In defining a product mission, the customer and supplier should address the following quality/reliability issues:

- Mission purpose.
- Environments encountered.

- Reliability goal and warranty policy.
- Maintenance and logistics philosophy.
- Unique safety and product liability considerations.

2. Product Specifications

This is where the foundation for design quality is laid. The following specifications, dealing with product, environment and service, must be considered.

- Performance requirements.
- Ranges for each environment (see Chapter 15).
- Reliability as a specification: mean-time-between failures (MTBF) or failure rates per year.
- Diagnostics: built-in versus external; self-diagnostics versus professional; mean-time-to-fault location.
- Repair: mean-time-to-repair.
- Field Service: repair centers; exchange units; parts availability; starter kits; support equipment; instruction manuals; training of customer and field personnel.

3. Product Feasibility Study

In this conceptual phase, the following bases are touched:

- Computer-aided design analysis (simulation).
- Software architecture review for data handling, fail/safe conditions, and self-test architecture.
- Reliability block diagram and reliability budgets (see Chapter 15).

4. Preliminary Design

In this step, alternative design concepts and design trade-offs are examined. The analytical tools to optimize design approaches are:

- Thermal analysis and critical component selection/qualification.
- Parts de-rating.
- Structural analysis.
- Reliability analysis: Failure Mode Effects Analysis (FMEA), Fault Tree Analysis (FTA), Product Liability Analysis (PLA) (see Chapter 15).
- Maintainability analysis.
- Manufacturability analysis.
- Software analysis; mission software and self-test diagnostics (verification).

- Circuit analysis, electromagnetic compatibility (EMC), etc.
- Computer models and Monte Carlo simulation.
- First design review.

5. Prototype Design

This is the fine-tuning process of evaluation.

- Use of design of experiments (DOE) to separate important variables from unimportant ones, both for the product itself and for the process used to produce the product (see Chapter 13).
- Multiple environment overstress tests to "smoke out" the weak links in design (see Chapter 15).
- Test plan, including software.
- A second design review.

6. Engineering Pilot Run

This serves to validate previous design of experiments with B versus C tests and to optimize the values of key product and process parameters and their tolerances with scatter plot techniques (see Chapter 13). It is also used to determine process capability and minimum $^{c}P_{k}$ requirements (see Chapter 13). There is, generally, a third design review at the end of the engineering pilot run.

7. Production Pilot Run

Production pilot runs are performed with all hard tooling in place and the use of qualified components. Yields are evaluated, as are truncated multiple environment overstress tests and other special requirements such as burn-in, protection against electrostatic dangers, radio frequency interference, approval by agencies such as Underwriters Laboratory (UL) or the equivalent national organizations of other countries. Even a single failure is rigorously analyzed to prevent repetition within the company or at the supplier's facility.

General Guidelines for Achieving Quality/Reliability in Design

Among the general guidelines that should never be ignored if quality and reliability goals are to be achieved in design are the following:

▪ State-of-the-art advance should be an evolution, not a revolution. Engineers, tempted by the glamour of a new innovation or product or part, tend to overlook whether it is actually manufacturable and whether its reliability is proven.

▪ A new design should attempt to build on the old design, with no more than 25 percent change at any given time. This speeds up design cycle time and also assures a much greater probability of reliability success.

▪ At some point in the design cycle, generally no later than the completion of the engineering pilot run, the design should be frozen, with engineering changes saved for the next generation of designs that follow on the heels of the current design. In this manner, a stream of new product innovations can be launched, each with short design cycle times that can keep competitors off balance.

▪ Reliability should be a firm specification along with performance parameters. This is often overlooked by customers and refused by suppliers.*

▪ To the greatest extent possible, standard building block modules, circuits, and components (preferably mass produced) of known field reliability should be used. The injection of components with an unknown field history into products is tantamount to playing Russian roulette with field reliability.

▪ Designs should be adaptable to rules for manufacturability, manual and automated assembly, built-in diagnostics, serviceability, and computer-integrated manufacturing (CIM).

More specifically, there are several disciplines (over and above those detailed in Chapters 13 and 15) that should be part of the design regimen in order to ensure quality/reliability success in design:

Design Reviews

The purpose of design reviews is to make sure that performance, quality/reliability, cost, schedule, and service goals are met. There are two approaches. The first involves the use of an "alternate engineering team" that

---

*In a survey that I conducted in 1983, requesting that suppliers consider establishing reliability as a target (not a contractual specification), fully 100 percent of U.S. suppliers refused to consider any requirement beyond normal incoming inspection quality levels. Of offshore suppliers surveyed, 50 percent readily agreed to reliability targets. In a similar survey that I conducted in 1988, only 10 percent of U.S. suppliers agreed to reliability as a target, whereas 90 percent of offshore suppliers agreed. The message is clear: U.S. suppliers must "belly up" to the reliability bar if they are to meet future requirements for reliability—not only as a target, but as a contractual requirement, with financial implications.

is not directly associated with the design. The members of such a team should be highly experienced and objective. Their role in evaluating the design should not be that of a devil's advocate, but constructive and helpful. Generally, the first of such design reviews is conducted at the product feasibility or preliminary design stage.

The second approach makes use of an interdisciplinary team, consisting of the program manager of the project as chairman, together with members drawn from Manufacturing Engineering, Process Engineering, Quality/Reliability Assurance, and Service as a minimum, with members from Supply Management, Sales, and Finance as needed. This ensures that manufacturability, reliability, and serviceability issues will not be overlooked.

It is preferable to have three design reviews during the development of a new product—at the preliminary design stage, at the prototype stage, and at the engineering pilot run stage.

Table 12-1 is an example of a comprehensive checklist used during each

Table 12-1. Design review checklist.

Check	*Concept*	*Proto-type*	*Product Pilot Run*
1. Specs: Excessive or inadequate? Lack of customer definition?	X		
2. Features: Multi-attribute evaluation (importance, competitive rank, cost)?	X		
3. Reliability: Goal vs. prediction?	X	X	
4. Yield: Composite target?	X		
5. FMEA: Major concerns? Risk reduction after correction? Practical FMEA?		X	
6. Fault tree analysis: Service problems?		X	X
7. Liability analysis: Major concerns and prevention?		X	X
8. Thermal analysis: Fallout and correction?		X	
9. Component de-rating: Marginal areas?		X	
10. Model commonality? Circuit standardization? Software standardization? Preferred parts?	X	X	
11. Value engineering: Pareto analysis: Cost vs. function? Material/labor reductions? ESI?		X	X
12. Cost effectiveness: Product cost targets met? Equipment/tooline costs?		X	X
13. Design of experiments to reduce variability?		X	X

(continued)

Table 12-1. *Continued.*

Check	Concept	Proto-type	Product Pilot Run
14. Load dump/transient protection? Shorted loads? Floating grounds?	X		
15. Packaging? Encapsulation?		X	X
16. Critical component control: Proper suppliers selected? Qualification status? Supplier FMEA, SPC, reliability tests?		X	X
17. Field environment measurements? Specs vs. actuals?	X		
18. Multiple environment overstress tests? Weak links?	X	X	X
19. Ongoing reliability stress tests in production?		X	X
20. Electromagnetic compatibility: Susceptibility/emission fallout?		X	
21. Software requirements: Software handshaking? Microprocessor watchdog timer?		X	X
22. Test requirements: Test equipment designed/purchased? Proper testing at board/assembly level prescribed?		X	X
23. Producibility constraints? Critical process identified? New manufacturing technologies?		X	X
24. Serviceability? Constraints in diagnostic time, repair time?		X	X
25. Self-diagnostics?	X		
26. Competitive analysis?		X	
27. Field tests? Customer evaluation?			X
28. "Lessons Learned" log consulted?	X	X	

of three design reviews. Designed by me, its purpose is to serve as a memory-jogger for the team, to ensure that all bases have been touched, and that weaknesses are identified and corrected before materials are ordered and production begins. Most of these disciplines are covered in later chapters.

System Testing/Customer Evaluation

During the engineering pilot run or the production pilot run, it is advisable to conduct tests of the product in the customer's system. The preferred method is not just an ordinary "firing up" of the system, but a design of experiments, as described in Chapter 13, where various components of the customer's system are evaluated in terms of importance and contribution to variance. Unless this is done, the supplier of the component can be wrongly blamed for failures elsewhere in the customer's system.

Field Tests

In the development of a new product, a finite time of no less than three months should be allocated to gain valuable field experience in a test market before full production is started. This is the best way to get end-user feedback; to verify the relative importance of features to the users; and to confirm reliability predictions.

Japanese companies not only use this technique with designated customers and test markets within Japan; they also delay product introduction in the United States by a whole year, utilizing that time interval to get rapid feedback from Japanese customers. As a result, Japanese products entering the U.S. market are "scrubbed" for quality and cost.

Classification of Characteristics

In the development of component specifications for suppliers, many parameters are listed in the drawings or prints. The supplier is theoretically responsible for meeting every single specification. But the universal Pareto principle tells us that not all specifications are equal in importance. Generally, two to five parameters contribute more to the quality of the part than all the other parameters put together. These important parameters, mutually determined by the customer's commodity teams and the partnership supplier, are then flagged on the drawing. The supplier now has a clear understanding that these important parameters are tightly controlled—to a c_{p_k} of 2.0 and more, and that no defects will be allowed on them at any time. The remaining parameters are less important. They can be produced to a 1 percent or 2 percent acceptable quality level (AQL), without tight controls and with only cursory inspection by the customer. This differentiation between the important and unimportant parameters is called the classification of characteristics. It provides a powerful means of concentrating on quality while reducing costs and cycle time on the less important parameters.

Lessons Learned

One of the most closely guarded secrets in Japanese companies is a black book called "lessons learned." In it, the design team meticulously records all the failures and pitfalls it has encountered during the development cycle. The purpose is to avoid similar mistakes during the next design by a different group of engineers. The black book also records the successes and the reasons for such success. The next group of engineers, working on a similar project, combs the "lessons learned" book, end to end, before the start of its project. This is one of the techniques that American companies, except for a few enlightened ones like Xerox, have not yet picked up on.

Product Liability

No aspect of manufacturing has raised so much controversy as product liability and the lawsuits it has spawned. Consumers say they are fed up with shoddy, unsafe products from unscrupulous and uncaring manufacturers. Manufacturers claim that court judgments handed down on lawsuits filed by plaintiffs are capricious, punitive, unfair, and often so damaging that companies are driven out of business as a result. There is much to be said on both sides.

The brief on behalf of plaintiffs would certainly take into consideration that

- 20 million nonwork-related injuries each year are caused by U.S.-made consumer products.
- 110,000 of these products injuries result in permanent disability.
- 30,000 of these result in fatalities.

These are appalling statistics! American industry desperately needs to clean up its liability act.

For their part, manufacturers claim that the courts have simply run away from common sense:

- Court rulings have changed from a bias toward the principle of *caveat emptor*, "let the buyer beware," to that of *caveat vendor* "let the seller beware." This is contrary to the basic premise of Anglo-Saxon law, where the defendant is innocent until proven guilty.
- Courts pass out judgments not on the basis of merit but on the basis of the ability to pay—against big General Motors, for example, versus "the little old lady in tennis shoes," who has been injured.
- Contributory negligence on the part of the plaintiff is not accepted by the courts. The plaintiff need only show that he did not know that the product was defective.
- Liability extends beyond the manufacturer to the supplier, to his sub-suppliers, and to his sub-subsuppliers down the entire supply chain. It also extends to the distributor and retailer—in short, to anyone engaged in making or selling the product.
- A manufacturer in one state has instant liability in all fifty states.

- The proximate cause ruling states that a plaintiff need not show that the product defect was the sole cause of injury. A product's being a contributing cause is sufficient for a ruling against the manufacturer.

Examples: There are scores of "horror stories" that bring to the surface the incompetencies of juries, ambiguities in the law, antiquated court procedures, and inefficiencies of the court system. One such horror story involves a collision between two cars. The claim of the injured driver was amicably settled between the two parties' insurance companies. However, a bystander who had witnessed the collision and saw blood on the injured driver, sued the insurance company of the driver responsible for the accident, claiming that she had been traumatized, suffered loss of sleep, loss of appetite, and so forth. She was awarded $77,000 as compensation!

In another case, a car was stalled on a bridge. The driver was trying to start the car up again, when, through his rear-view mirror, he saw another car approaching his car at great speed. He jumped out of the disabled vehicle just in time. The car in the rear crashed into it. Two women in that car, one of them the driver, had been busy chatting with one another and did not see the stalled car in time. The women not only sued the car company of the first driver but its suppliers and their suppliers as well. To avoid lengthy litigation, which would have cost the defendant companies several hundred thousand dollars, they collectively decided to settle out of court, even though there was little basis for a legitimate case.

How to Deal With the Threat of Product Liability

It is unfortunate that unscrupulous lawyers—ambulance chasers, as they are known—make a mockery of the legal system. As stated earlier, some of these lawsuits can wipe out an entire company. Further, the cost of product liability insurance premiums has been climbing steadily, increasing by a dramatic 200 percent in the years 1983 to 1987 alone. Even more threatening, the corrosive fear of liability is inhibiting innovation in America. In a 1986 survey sponsored by Egon Zehnder International, 62 percent of senior-level executives at large companies agreed that "innovation and experimentation had been constrained in the last few years." Of this group, 92 percent blamed "fear of liability suits" as the leading impediment to innovation. A character in Shakespeare's *King Henry VI, Part II*, offers a solution: "The first thing we do, let's kill all the lawyers."

In a more serious vein, however, the fear of liability need not be a permanent block to innovation. Customer and supplier companies must strengthen their designs. Courts and juries come down much harder on design deficiencies in connection with personal injuries and damages than they do on deficiencies in all other disciplines combined. Figure 12-2 provides general product liability guidelines for engineers. Figure 12-3 gives the rea-

Figure 12-2. Product liability guidelines for engineers.

1. Key Definitions:
   - Hazard: a condition with potential for causing injury.
   - Risk: the percentage probability of the injury actually taking place.
   - Danger: the combination of hazard and risk. To reduce danger, either hazard or risk must be reduced.
2. The engineer should assume the design *will* go to trial.
3. The engineer should assume that every design decision will be scrutinized in court.
4. The following duties are imposed on engineers for product liability.
   - The duty to design for all foreseeable hazards, including guarding against foreseeable misuses of product and minimizing risks to users (and non-users) if accidents occur.
   - The duty to investigate and test to discover risks, including investigation and correction of field problems.
   - The duty to minimize risk by having an alternate design, safety device on the product, or a warning attached.
     — The designer may reject a safer alternate design if it is not feasible, unduly expensive, or involves other dangers. (Courts do not insist on completely fail-safe designs, "reasonably safe" is adequate.)
     — Warnings must be prominent enough to attract user attention and clear enough for the user to understand the nature of the risk. (Because warnings are inexpensive and practical, courts have even greater expectations for the effectiveness of warnings than courts have for alternate designs and safety devices.)
   - The duty to meet government/industry safety standards.
     — If a government standard is not met, the manufacturer is liable per se, without an opportunity to defend the design.
     — If an industry standard is not met or is less safe than competitive products, the manufacturer is not liable per se, but will be found liable by a jury.
   - The duty to report field defects. Under the Consumer Products Safety Act, a manufacture of consumer products must report a defect that can create substantial risk of injury to the product. Penalties for non-reporting are severe.
5. The following are successive lines of defense to product liability.
   - Avoid the accident.
   - If a hazard cannot be eliminated for functional reasons, provide protection against the hazard occurring.
   - Design so that an accident would cause only minimal damage.
   - Predict or warn against an impending accident.
   - Warn against a possible (as opposed to an impending) accident.
   - Provide protection for the user in case of an accident.
6. The following guidelines apply to trade-offs between safety and cost and between safety and function or utility:
   - The objective should not be safety at the expense of other parameters, but an optimization and elevation of all.

- Safety must be a specification along with cost, performance, and reliability.
7. Start with Product Liability Prevention Analysis. It is similar to a fault free analysis, but confined to safety hazards.
   - Assign probabilities and severities of failure to each branch down to the root cause. Probability × Severity = Risk Priority.
   - Determine the critical path (highest products of risk priorities).
   - Conduct FMEA.
   - Conduct a simulated physical FMEA, including two or more simultaneous failures.
   - Take corrective/preventive action to drastically reduce risk priorities.
   - Recalculate risk priority number and critical path.
8. Conduct a liability design review with a multidiscipline team drawn from engineering, test engineers, Q.A., production, materials management, and legal personnel.

Figure 12-3. Product liability prevention.

I. Reasons for documentation in product liability prevention
   A. *Preamble:* Scrupulously avoid the temptation for nondocumentation of the design or to dispose of such documentation with a period of time, even if it means violating company policy regarding documentation disposition. Design documentation must be retained at least as long as the product is in the field—up to 25 years and more.
   B. Missing, incomplete, or misleading documentation of design can be a potent tactical weapon in the hands of a plaintiff's lawyer.
      1. Missing records, no matter how innocent or routine, can be made to appear intentional and deceptive by a skillful attorney.
      2. Misleading or poorly written documents are used by attorneys to impeach the credibility of the manufacturer's engineers and management.
   C. The documentary record of design is the critical factor in affecting the success or failure of a product liability suit.
   D. Good and complete documentation can provide a record of the design process years after those involved in the design have left the company.
   E. A record will corroborate the testimony of a defendant about what occurred in the design process.

II. Actions needed for product liability prevention.
   A. Design phase.
      1. Chronological documentation should be made of *all* design work.
         a. Every drawing, sketch, and note should be signed, dated, preserved in the design project file, and entered into a project log book. A long and consistent retention policy is essential. Custodianship must be delegated to a specific individual or group.

(continued)

Figure 12-3. *Continued.*

---

   b. Notes should be kept of meetings, constructive comments, and other oral communications.

   c. All design changes should be documented (every letter revision).

   d. The reason for each design decision affecting safety should be recorded, including alternate designs considered and why they were rejected, as well as the advantages of the approach selected.

   e. All lab and field testing should be documented, including proof that industry/government standards were met.

  2. All documentation must be in plain English, so that a jury can esily interpret it.

  3. Remember that there is no statute of limitations on the time lapse between the design and the failure of a product. Designers can be deemed responsible even 25 years (or more) after their work on a project.

 B. Manufacturing Engineering Phase

  1. Documentation must be kept of all changes (configuration control).

   a. Original drawings, specifications, and engineering samples should be preserved. The master copies should always be kept by the chief engineer.

   b. Test data, reasons for changes, and letter revisions should be dated and recorded in the log book.

 C. Warning labels must be permanently attached to the product and clearly displayed.

 D. Instruction sheets should contain clear do's and dont's (any changes must be logged) and should be in great detail. (The longer, the better—the fact that consumers do not read instructions does not matter.)

 E. Warranties must be prepared in consultation with the corporate attorney.

---

sons for preventing product liability and provides a list of actions that must be taken, especially by engineers, to do so. Both figures are an excellent road map for avoiding litigation or, should it take place, for minimizing financial losses.

Chapter 13

Design of Experiments: Preeminent Problem- Solving Tool

Our new quality thinking should be reduced process variability around the nominal, as an operating philosophy, for never-ending quality improvement.

William Scollard, vice-president of engineering and manufacturing,
Ford Motor Company

A 100:1 Quality Improvement in Six Months

Chapter 10 described a synergy that occurred when the philosophy of Deming, the management of Juran, and the statistical engineering tools and techniques of Shainin were brought together in a quality system to achieve a quality breakthrough. A key element—in fact, an indispensable element—of that quality system is a family of techniques called the design of experiments (DOE). Without DOE, quality improvement would be in the bush leagues, each step small, erratic, and painfully slow. With DOE, product quality can be improved not by a meager 10 percent, 20 percent, 50 percent, or even 100 percent but by factors of 10:1—even 100:1. And the time frame is not the usual snail's pace of five years and more, but six months or less. If quality is the centerpiece for a company's resurgence, the design of experiments is the *pièce de résistance* within quality.

A Rubber Hammer

A story that is making the rounds among converts to the new religion of DOE illustrates this route to world-class quality. Bill Conway, the former chairman of the Nashua Corporation, and an early champion and beneficiary of statistical methods, was host to a high-level delegation from Ford. The delegation wanted to probe the reasons for Nashua's quality success. Conway started the meeting with a challenge. "Suppose I ask two of you successful vice-presidents at Ford to enter a contest. The winner will win a trip around the world for his whole family. I know that both of you are totally motivated and dedicated, by virtue of your exalted position at Ford. The contest is to see who can drive a nail into this wall. One of you will get a hammer, the other nothing but management encouragement! Who do you think will win!" The answer was obvious. Motivation is important, management encouragement is important. But employees, at all levels, must have tools. And they must be the *right* tools. DOE is that tool. It is a sledgehammer. Unfortunately, U.S. companies, by embracing just statistical process control (SPC), have only a rubber hammer, a tool that is weak, cumbersome, and obsolete except as a maintenance technique.

A Comparison of Three Approaches to Quality: Japan versus the United States

Figure 13-1 illustrates a comparison of a quality progress, as a percentage of a hypothetical ideal, with time both for Japan and the United States. It shows the considerable lead the United States had after World War II dissipating by the mid-1960s, with Japan widening the gap in the years thereafter. This is distressful in itself; but when the three major quality tools used by the two countries are examined, the gap becomes even more alarming.

The Traditional, Ineffective Tools

Traditional tools consist of such brute-force methods as inspection and sorting; detection and correction; fire fighting and management by exhortation. With these methods, quality control acts as the policeman, so that all other departments can continue as robbers! As seen in Figure 13-1, Japan abandoned these infantile practices as early as the 1960s, while the United States persevered with them well into the early 1980s. Even more tragic, at least 70 percent of U.S. suppliers, especially the small ones, are still operating in this dark age of quality.

Figure 13-1. Contributions of traditional, SPC, and design of experiments tools to quality progress.

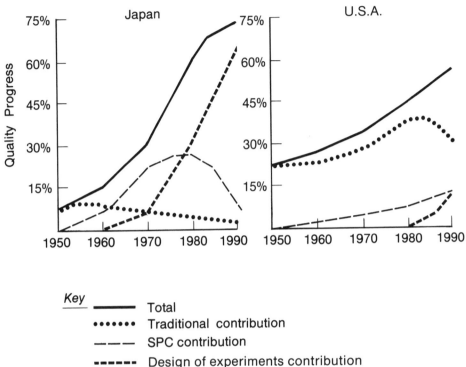

Key
— Total
•••••• Traditional contribution
— — SPC contribution
■-■-■ Design of experiments contribution

SPC Tools—Too Little, Too Late

With the help of Deming, Juran, and other U.S. trainers,* Japan launched SPC in the 1950s and rode its crest till the mid-1970s, when it concluded that SPC in production was "too little and too late." A major tool within SPC is presumed to be control charts. The Japanese, for all practical purposes, have abandoned the use of control charts as being weak and ineffective.

SPC had been used in the United States, especially during World War II, but in the optimistic era of the 1950s and 1960s, when U.S. industry reigned supreme, the baby was thrown out with the bath water. It was a revolt against the mysteries of the world of statistics. What reushered in the SPC

---

*I have played a role in the quality training of Motorola's Japanese joint venture as well as in the training of Japanese suppliers. Some of my publications have been translated into Japanese and circulated by the Japanese Union of Scientists and Engineers.

age was the 1980 telecast of the NBC White Paper "If Japan Can, Why Can't We?" This program became a continental divide between traditional quality practices and those of SPC. It gave the American public at large its first glimpse of the reasons behind Japan's success: quality in general, and SPC in particular. Deming was rescued from the U.S. industrial wilderness and elevated to the status of prophet within his own country. SPC became the new buzzword, the new quality theology. But, as we shall see later, the results of eight years of SPC in the United States have been modest at best, and furthermore, distract industry from the main tasks of problem solving and variation reduction.

Design of Experiments: Japan's Secret Weapon

The secret weapon of Japan's quality is the Japanese industry's widespread use of design of experiments. The objective here is to discover key variables in product and process design well ahead of production; to drastically reduce the variations they cause (and only then keep the reduced variation under control with SPC); and to open up the tolerances on the large number of unimportant variables so as to reduce costs. DOE can also be used as a problem-solving tool (the very best problem-solving tool) on old products that were not subjected to the preventive disciplines of DOE before production. Figure 13-1 shows the spectacular rise in the use of DOE in Japan since the 1970s. Hundreds of Japanese companies conduct thousands of these designed experiments each year to make product and process designs "more robust." As an example, Nippon Denso, the main electronics supplier to Toyota, conducts 3,000 DOE experiments each year, a figure well in excess of the total number of DOE experiments conducted by all U.S. companies put together! The discipline is a variant of the classical design of experiments founded by Sir Ronald Fisher of Great Britain in the 1930s. The principal DOE architect in Japan is Dr. Genichi Taguchi, who adapted the classical methods into a system called the "Orthogonal Array."

Taguchi: Good News and Bad News

By contrast, DOE was practically unknown in the United States until the 1980s—except by a small, forlorn group of academics and missionary statisticians. However, a belated movement is now under way. Mesmerized by the Taguchi name, it has imported his methods wholesale. The irrational logic is: "If it is Japanese, it has to be good!" There are both positive and negative aspects to this blind copying. The good news is that Taguchi has put DOE on the quality map of America. More and more U.S. companies are being weaned away from SPC and have introduced DOE for problem solving and variation reduction in the place of such ineffective methods as engineering judgment and varying one cause at a time. *The bad news is that Taguchi's methods are complex, expensive, time-consuming, and statistically weak if interactions are present.*

The Measurement of Process Capability

Just as in cycle time management, inventory is evil, so also in quality assurance, variation is evil. Why is this so? Why has the brand-new discipline of variation reduction become one of the most important tasks of development engineering, manufacturing engineering, and quality assurance? There are two reasons.

The first is the economic loss resulting from customer dissatisfaction. Figure 13-2 illustrates a comparison of the U.S. and Japanese views of spec-

Figure 13-2. U.S. and Japanese specification limits vs. target values compared.

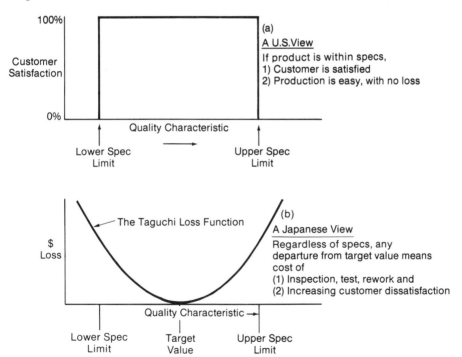

Taguchi Interpretation of a Specification Limit

That value where external costs at customer (including loss of sales, warranty, etc.) equal internal costs (inspection, test, analyzing, rework)

ifications. In the U.S. view, if a unit is barely within one specification limit, it is assumed that the customer is 100 percent satisfied, and if a limit is barely outside that limit, it is assumed that the customer is 100 percent dissatisfied. In actual practice, there is nothing that digital about customer satisfaction. Figure 13-2(b) depicts the more realistic Japanese view that customer dissatisfaction is at zero when a product value is at, or very close to, a design center or target value and increases exponentially as the parameter moves away from the target value toward either specification limit. Taguchi has developed a "quality loss function", using a quadratic equation to quantify this loss in monetary terms. Customers want product uniformity and consistency, not units that vary all over the map, even if they fall within specifications. This uniformity is a feature of Japanese products that is seldom recognized by American manufacturers. For instance, on U.S. car assembly lines, doors are made to fit into the car frame with sledgehammers. On the Japanese car assembly lines, the doors fit naturally—like a Lego block—with little effort.

A second reason why variation is evil is that it perpetuates and institutionalizes the deplorable practice of scrap, repair, and analyze and rework in order to get a unit within its specification limits. This is total waste, amounting to 10 percent and more of the sales dollar, or twice the typical profit percentage of a company! If a product and its process have variation so reduced that a parameter is brought close to the design center, not only are these costs reduced to zero, not only are 100 percent yields and zero defects possible, but inspection and test costs, which add no value, can be drastically reduced and production thereby turned into a breeze.

c_p: **A Measure of Process Spread**

Before variation in a parameter can be reduced, it is useful to measure the variation. For this purpose, two yardsticks, c_p and c_{p_k}, have become standard terminologies. c_p is defined as specification width (S) divided by process width (P). Figure 13-3 shows six frequency distributions in which the specification width (always $40 - 20 = 20$) is compared to the process width (or process variation). From this we learn:

1. Process A in Figure 13-3 has a process width of 30 (as defined by traditional ± 3 sigma limits), to give a c_p of 0.67. It is a process that is out of control with 2½ percent reject tails at both ends. This used to be the norm for U.S. processes before the SPC age. Today, at least 50 percent of customer companies and 80 percent of supplier companies are still at this stage, if inspection and correction are not included. They compensate for such an out-of-control condition by brute-force sorting, scrap, and rework.
2. In process B, the process width equals the specification width, to give

Figure 13-3. c_p: A measure of variation.

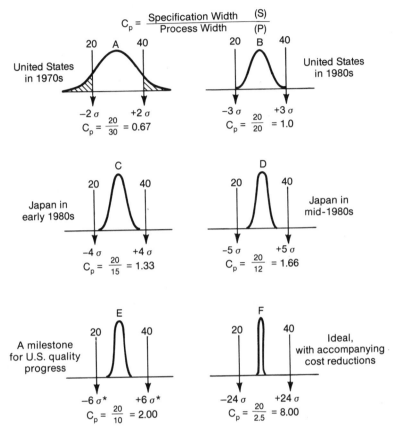

*An alternative way to describe variation is in terms of standard deviation, sigma (σ).
In Process B, the specification limits are at $\pm 3\sigma$. In Process E, the specification limits are at $\pm 6\,\sigma$—
virtually a 100% yield process.

a c_p of 1.0. Although somewhat better than process A, it too is almost out of control because any slight shift will cause defects. At least 75 percent of U.S. processes have not advanced beyond a c_p of 1.0. So much for our much-vaunted SPC!

3. Process C has a c_p of 1.33. It has a margin of safety between the narrower process limits and the specification limits. The Japanese used a c_p of 1.33 as a standard for their important parameters in the early 1980s.
4. Process D, with a c_p of 1.67, has an even wider safety margin.
5. Process E, with a c_p of 2.0, is an important milestone in the march to variation reduction. Here the process width is only half the specification width. Some of the more progressive U.S. companies, including Motorola and the automotive companies, have established a c_p of 2.0 as a minimum standard for their own as well as their suppliers' important quality characteristics.
6. Process F, with a c_p of 8.0, is an ideal. It is not only attainable, but can be achieved generally, at lower overall cost than the A through E processes.

In fact, there is no limit to higher and higher c_ps—of 10, 15, and more—so long as recurring costs are not added, and only the cost of DOE, to reduce variation, is incurred. These experimental costs should be viewed as investments rather than as costs in the best tradition of quality cost prevention. It has been my experience that with the use of the design of experiment tools discussed in this chapter, higher c_ps are obtained "for free." Costs are actually reduced because the unimportant variables associated with process spread can have their tolerances opened up at lower costs. Further, it does not take years to go from c_ps of 1.0 or less to c_ps of 5.0 and more. This can be accomplished in weeks, generally after no more than one, two, or three well designed experiments.

I have encountered suppliers who, when asked to achieve c_ps of 2.0, immediately demand a price increase. When I insist that we simultaneously want a c_p of 2.0 as well as a *price decrease*, it "blows their minds!" However, after explaining to them that c_ps of 2.0 and more will drastically improve yields, they fall in line.

c_{p_k}: A Better Measure of Variation and Process Capability

c_p is only an introduction to the concept of process capability. Because it measures spread only, it does not take into account any noncentering of the process relative to the specification limits of a parameter. Such noncentering reduces the margin of safety and, therefore, has a penalty imposed, called a *K* or correction factor. The formulas are:

$$c_p = S/P$$
$$K = \frac{D-\overline{X}}{S/2} \text{ or } \frac{\overline{X}-D}{S/2} \text{(whichever makes K positive)}$$
$$c_{p_k} = (1-K)\, c_p$$

where:

S = specification width; P = process width ($+3$ sigma limits)
D = design center or target value (D need not be at the midpoint of the specification width)
$\overline{X}$ = process average

When the process average, $\overline{X}$ and the design center, D, (also called target value) coincide, K is reduced to zero, making c_p and c_{p_k} equal. If, however, the process average is skewed toward either end of a specification limit, away from D, the value of K increases, causing c_{p_k} to be lower than c_p.

The equation is illustrated by the four examples in Figure 13-4. Here, A has a wide spread, with a c_p of 0.71. Because its design center, D, and its average $\overline{X}$ coincide, the c_p and c_{p_k} values are the same at 0.71. B has a narrower spread, with a respectable c_p of 2.5, but because it is away from the target value, the K factor penalizes the c_p to give a poor c_{p_k} of 1.0. C has a broader spread than B, with a lower c_p of 1.67; but it is closer to the target value D than is B and, so, the K factor penalizes c_p less, to give a c_{p_k} of 1.33— better than B's. D is ideal, with both a very narrow spread and a centered process, which give a c_p and c_{p_k} of 5.0.

Because it takes into account both spread and noncentering, c_{p_k} is an excellent measure of variability and process capability. In process control, centering a process is much easier than reducing spread. Centering requires only a simple adjustment. Spread reduction requires design of experiments. As in c_p, the objective should be to attain a higher and higher c_{p_k}, with a c_{p_k} of 2.0 only a passing milestone in the march past zero defects to near-zero variation. c_{p_k} is also a convenient and effective method of specifying supplier quality on important quality characteristics, way beyond the old 1 percent or 2 percent acceptable quality levels (AQLs) or even the newer and lower defect levels, expressed in parts per million (ppm).

Three Approaches to DOE: Classical Vs. Taguchi Vs. Shainin

Measuring variation by means of c_p and c_{p_k} is not enough. We must reduce variation. An analogy from the world of dieting is apropros. Thousands mount their weighing scales each day in an attempt to win the battle of the bulge. If measurement alone could reduce weight, Americans would be the thinnest people on earth! What is needed is an attack on the underlying causes

Figure 13-4. C_{P_k}: A better measure of variation.

$$C_P = \frac{\text{Specification width (S)}}{\text{Process width (P)}}; \quad C_{P_K} = (1-K)C_P \quad ; K = \frac{\text{Design center (D)-X}}{S/2} \text{ or } \frac{\overline{X}-D}{S/2}$$
(whichever makes K positive)

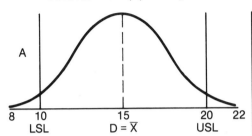

A

$C_P = C_{P_K} = 0.71$

Typical process capability
till early 1980s

| 8 | 10 | | 15 | | 20 | 22 |
| | LSL | | D = $\overline{X}$ | | USL | |

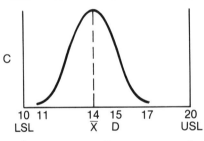

B

$C_P = 2.5; C_{P_K} = 1.0$

Despite narrow distribution, poor C_{P_K}
because $\overline{X}$ far from design center

| | 10 | 12 | 14 | 15 | | 20 |
| | LSL | $\overline{X}$ | | D | | USL |

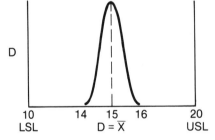

C

$C_P = 1.67; C_{P_K} = 1.33$

Wider distribution than B, but
also closer to design center, so
acceptable C_{P_K}.

| | 10 11 | | 14 | 15 | 17 | 20 |
| | LSL | | $\overline{X}$ | D | | USL |

D

$C_P = C_{P_K} = 5$
Ideal distribution

| | 10 | | 14 | 15 | 16 | | 20 |
| | LSL | | | D = $\overline{X}$ | | | USL |

For critical parameters: Minimum $C_{P_K} = 1.33$
Desirable $C_{P_K} = 2.00$
Ideal $C_{P_K} \geq 5.00$

of overweight—and, where quality is concerned, on the underyling causes of variation or spread. This is best done through the design of experiments.

There are three approaches to DOE:—the classical, the Taguchi, and those taught by Dorian Shainin. The classical tools start with fraction factorials and end with evolutionary optimization (EVOP). Taguchi's methods use orthogonal arrays (inner and outer), analysis of variance, and signal-to-noise. The Shainin DOE tools start with multi-vari charts, followed by variables search or full factorials, are verified with a "B vs C," and end with scatterplot optimization. Table 13-1 compares each of these DOE approaches in terms of its effectiveness, cost, complexity, statistical validity, applicability, and ease of implementation.

Although all three approaches are far, far superior to conventional SPC techniques, engineering judgments/hunches, computer-aided techniques, and varying one cause (or factor) at a time and keeping everything else constant, the Shainin tools are far more cost-effective in almost every category of comparison. They can help the United States leapfrog the Japanese in their own game of concentrating on design quality over production quality. The tragedy is that most U.S. companies are not even aware of their existence, much less their power!

The Trouble With Taguchi

Because a few prominent American companies such as Ford, Xerox, AT&T, and ITT have adopted the Taguchi methods and are thrusting them on their unknowing and unwary suppliers, it is important to know just what the Taguchi weaknesses are. The main blessing that Taguchi has conferred on industry is that he has taken DOE out of the rarefied realm of universities and into the design laboratories and production floors of industry. The motto implicit in his methods can be summed up: "Don't just sit there, do something." Nevertheless his orthogonal array technique has several fundamental flaws:

- It is complicated. Engineers are uncomfortable with even such simple statistical concepts as standard deviation, let alone analysis of variance, F-tests, and signal-to-noise ratios.

- It is expensive. With inner arrays multiplied by outer arrays, the number of experiments gets unwieldy. Any attempt to reduce the number of experiments results in loss of accuracy and repeatability. Often, the entire series of experiments has to be repeated.

- There is no replication to gauge the magnitude of experimental error.

- It does not make use of randomiziation. This is a cardinal sin in statistics. Variables not included in the experiments should be given equal

Table 13-1. Three approaches to design of experiments compared.

Characteristic	Classical	Taguchi	Shainin
Technique Used	▪ Fractional factorials, EVOP, etc.	▪ Orthogonal arrays	▪ Multi-vari, variables search, full factorials, etc. (Seven simple tools in all)
Effectiveness	▪ Moderate (20% to 200% improvement) ▪ Retrogression possible	▪ Low to moderate (20% to 100% improvement) ▪ Retrogression likely	▪ Extremely powerful (100% to 1,000% improvement) ▪ No retrogression
Cost	▪ Moderate ▪ Average of 50 experiments	▪ High ▪ Average of 20 to 100 experiments	▪ Low ▪ Average of 20 experiments
Complexity	▪ Moderate ▪ Full ANOVA required	▪ High ▪ Inner and outer array multiplication, S/N, ANOVA	▪ Low ▪ Experiments can be understood by line operators
Statistical Validity	▪ Low ▪ Higher order interaction effects confounded with main effects ▪ To a lesser extent, even second-order interaction effects confounded	▪ Poor ▪ No randomization ▪ Even second-order interaction effects confounded with main effects ▪ S/N concept good	▪ High ▪ Every variable tested with all levels of every other variable ▪ Excellent separation and quantification of main and interaction effects
Applicability	▪ Requires hardware ▪ Main use in production	▪ Primary use as a substitute for Monte Carlo analysis	▪ Requires hardware ▪ Can be used as early as prototype and engineering run stage
Ease of Implementation	▪ Moderate ▪ Engineering and statistical knowledge required	▪ Difficult ▪ Engineers not likely to use technique	▪ Easy ▪ Even line workers can conduct experiments

opportunities to enter or leave the experiments through the use of randomization.

- It selects factors to be included in the experiment through brainstorming. This is a highly subjective method. It introduces too many irrelevant variables and wastes time and money. (The Shainin approach of zeroing in on the family of the important variables, through techniques such as multi-vari charts and components search, greatly reduces the number of suspect variables and, hence, the number of experiments required.)

- It does not consider interactions unless, on the basis of engineering judgment, a severe interaction is "suspected." This is a grave structural flaw. Engineers are hard put to guess at even the main variables, let alone interactions between them.

- The orthogonal array* belongs in the family of fraction factorials and suffers from the same statistical weaknesses that characterize that generic family of saturated designs, namely, the confounding of interaction effects (especially the higher-order interaction effects) with main effects. In fact, the orthogonal array is far more saturated than is the fraction factorial in classical DOE, making its results even more suspect.

- Beyond the orthogonal array, it has no other tools to fall back on if the problem is not solved.

- The bottom line is that its results are marginal to poor, with benefits that can and do evaporate.

The Shainin Diagnostic Tools

Fortunately for the United States, Dorian Shainin, whose weighty contributions to American industry include the Shainin lot plot plan, multiple environment overstress tests, and precontrol, has also contributed DOE tools that can diagnose and greatly reduce variation, leading us beyond zero defects, beyond $^{C}p_{k}$s of 2.0, to near-zero variability. These tools are:

---

*Recently, a published Taguchi case study was used to compare the Taguchi orthogonal array with Shainin's variables search. The data from the case study were replaced by totally meaningless random numbers. The results should have been insignificant, that is, with no one factor outranking another. The procedure was followed for three trials. One trial out of three failed the test because one or more factors outranked the others! The same random data were then used in variables search. In each case, the results were insignificant, as they should be. In short, the Taguchi method is not sensitive enough to distinguish between important and unimportant variables under all conditions. Thus its use could lead to erroneous decisions connected with changing a product or process. Variables search, by contrast, is completely rigorous and does have the sensitivity to distinguish between levels of significance and insignificance among the variables.

- *Simple* - understood by engineers and line workers alike. Ths mathematics involved is unbelievably, almost embarrassingly, elementary!
- *Logical* - based on common sense.
- *Practical* - easy to implement, in design, in production, by suppliers.
- *Universal in scope* - applicable to a wide range of industries from electronics to chemicals to food; from mass production to job shop; from big to small companies; and from process-intensive to assembly-intensive production.
- *Statistically powerful* - in terms of accuracy, with no violations of statistical principles.
- *Excellent in terms of results* - with quality gains, not in the inconsequential range of 10 to 50 percent improvement, but in the dramatic range of 500 to 5,000 percent improvement!

Variation Reduction: A Detective Journey to the Red X

Figure 13-5 represents a surefire road map to variation reduction. It consists of seven DOE tools invented or perfected by Dorian Shainin. They are based on his philosophy: "Don't let the engineers do the guessing; let the parts do the talking." What he means by this is that parts contain valuable information on the causes of variation and that their secrets can be unlocked through the use of appropriate, statistically designed experiments. The analogy of a detective story is helpful in this diagnostic journey. With these DOE tools, clues can be gathered, each progressively more positive, until the culprit cause or variable—the Red X, in the Shainin lexicon—is captured, reduced, and controlled. The second most important cause is called the Pink X, the third most important the Pale Pink X. Generally, by the time the top one, two, and three causes—the Red X, Pink X, and Pale Pink X—are captured and imprisoned, 75 to 95 percent of the variation allowed within the specification limits will have been eliminated. In short, C_{p_k}s of 4 to 20 are achieved, not in five years, not in four, three, two, or even one year, not even in months, but with just one, two, or three DOE experiments in a matter of weeks.

The Road Map

The first line of defense shock troops among the seven DOE tools are multi-vari charts, components search, and paired comparisons, of which the multi-vari is the most important and widely used technique. Through a process of systematic elimination, they can reduce the number of variables from an unwieldy twenty (and even up to a thousand) to a much lower number of suspect variables. The next step is either a variables search or a full facto-

Figure 13-5. Variation reduction: A road map.

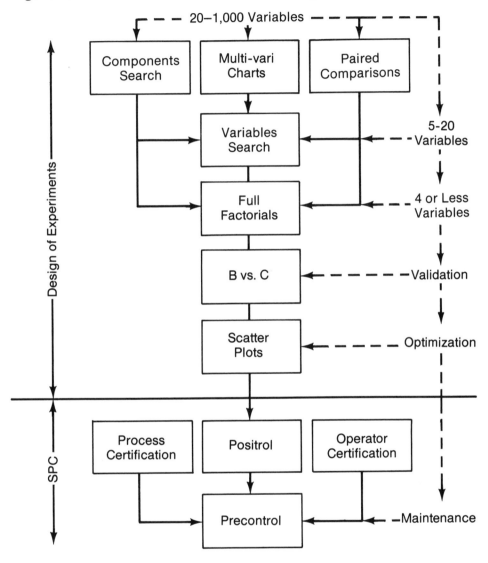

rial experiment. Variables search is used if there are five or more suspect variables left to be investigated. A full factorial is used if there are four or less suspect variables. At the end of either technique, the Red X, Pink X, and Pale Pink X are pinpointed. B versus C provides confirmation, verification, and validation that the Red X, Pink X, and Pale Pink X are truly captured. Finally, the scatter plot is a graphic tool that determines the optimum

(text continues on p. 184)

Table 13-2. The seven DOE tools.

Technique	Objective	Where Applicable	When Applicable	Sample Size
Multi-vari Chart	1. Discover family of red X-position, cycle, or time 2. Detect nonrandom patterns	Wherever stratified samples of consecutive units, at different times, can be measured	1. At engineering pilot run; at production pilot run; 2. During production problem solving	≥9
Components Search	Home in on a few key variables from a wide variety of variables to capture family of Red X or Red X itself	Where there are good and bad assemblies, capable of being disassembled and reassembled	1. When only a few units are available (prototype stage or in pilot runs) 2. During production problem solving	2
Paired Comparisons	Same as components search	Wherever there are good and bad assemblies or components that cannot be disassembled	Mainly in production, field returns, or failure analysis	≥12
Variables Search	1. Pinpoint Red X, Pink X, etc. 2. Separate and quantify the main effects and interaction effects of variables	In homing in on the culprit variables following multi-vari, components search, or paired comparison experiments	1. When more than 4 variables are investigated 2. At prototype, pilot run stages 3. In production problem solving	▪ 6 to 16 tests for 5 variables ▪ 2 more tests for each additional variable

Full Factorials	Same as variables search	Same as variables search	1. When 4 or less variables are investigated 2. Same as variables search 3. Same as variables search	• Maximum 16 or 32 tests
B vs. C	1. Evaluate a minimum amount of superiority of method B over method C or vice versa 2. Select B or C if there is no performance difference, but there is a definite cost difference	1. As a validation of Red X, Pink X factors selected in variables search or full factorial experiments 2. When problem is easy to solve, use as the only experiment, bypassing other techniques	1. In prototype or pilot run stages 2. In production, as a capping run 3. In nontechnical fields—sales, advertising, human relations, etc.—a universal tool	Usually 3 Bs and 3 Cs
Scatter Plots	1. Determine optimum values of important variables 2. Cost reduction of unimportant variables	Following previous 6 techniques	In pilot run of production stage	30

values and the optimum tolerances to use for the Red X and Pink X, so that rejects are banished for ever.

Table 13-2, a capsule summary of each of the seven DOE tools, shows the objective of each; where and when each tool is applicable; and the sample size needed—which in itself indicates the unbelievable economy of experimentation.

SPC Tools: The Tail That Has Been Wagging the DOE Dog

It is only when the diagnostic journey using the seven DOE tools shown in Figure 13-5 has ended with a substantial reduction in variation that the SPC tools at the bottom of the figure come into play. The true role of SPC (detailed in Chapter 15) is only the *maintenance* of reduced variation. These SPC tools, shown in Figure 13-5, are detailed in Chapter 14. Yet if a poll were taken among companies that have attempted variation reduction, 90 percent would be found to have started with SPC—a clear case of the SPC tail wagging the DOE dog. And 90 percent of them would equate SPC with little more than the weak control chart.

A few remarks on specifications and computer techniques will serve as a preamble to the discussion of DOE tools.

Arbitrary, Overbearing, and Wrong Specifications

A principal cause of poor quality is poor specifications. In my estimation, 50 percent of the poor quality attributed to a supplier can be traced to poor customer specifications. Most product and component specifications are either vague, arbitrary, tyrannical, or wrong. And process/equipment specifications are even worse. There are several reasons for poor product and process specifications:

- The customer company's customers are not consulted (the difference, between marketing and selling, discussed in Chapter 11).
- The importance of a product feature to a customer company's customer versus the cost of that feature is not assessed (see Chapter 11).
- The engineer's ego in creating a "state-of-the-art design" with his name etched into it in perpetuity.
- Specification limits and tolerances are used in the design of products and processes rather than the design center or target value being concentrated on.
- Reliability, in terms of mean time between failures (MTBF) or failure rates per year, is seldom included as a specification.
- Systems testing, in the customer's application, is almost never conducted with a design of experiments approach to identify important,

interacting variables in the customer's overall system, within which the supplier's black box is only one component.

All of these weaknesses must be overcome before product specifications can become meaningful and attainable.

The conversion from product specifications to component specifications for suppliers is even more pathetic. This can be attributed to:

- Engineering's fascination with technology regardless of need, lack of field experience, or ignorance of the match between the new technology and the supplier's capability.
- Engineering proclivity for indiscriminate and tight tolerances.
- Engineering's reliance on previous component drawings, "boiler-plate" requirements, supplier's published specifications, or just plain guesses and hunches pulled out of the air!
- Engineering's overreliance on the computer.

Overreliance on the Computer

With the growth of computer-aided engineering (CAE), computer-aided designs (CAD), and computer-aided manufacturing (CAM), today's designer has come to rely on the computer to solve all the world's problems. Component tolerances are frequently calculated using Monte Carlo simulation. This can only be done if the designer knows the formula for governing the relationship between output, or dependent, variables and the input, or independent, component variables. In many complex designs and processes, involving scores of components, even an Einstein could not develop such a formula. Further, even if there is a mathematical formula for the relationships between variables, the computer may not be able to separate the effects of interaction—either second-order or higher-order—between component variables. Finally, some engineers use a "worst case" computer analysis. But these worst cases have such an extremely low probability of occurrence in actual practice that they can add significantly to cost without adding any value.

These weaknesses connected with specifications and use of the computer can be overcome at the prototype, engineering pilot run, and production pilot run stages by well-designed Shainin experiments. A full treatment of all seven of the DOE tools is covered in my American Management Association briefing *World Class Quality: Design of Experiments Made Easier, More Cost Effective Than SPC* (1988).* In this book, only the most important tools— multi-vari charts, components search, variables search, and full factorials will be discussed in detail.

---

*Mr. Bhote is also the author of another AMA Briefing: Supply Management (1987).

The Multi-Vari Chart: Homing in on the Red X

Objective

The diagnostic journey to apprehend the cause producing the largest variation, the Rex X, generally should start with a multi-vari chart. Its main purpose is to reduce a large number of possible causes (or factors or variables—these are all synonymous terms) of variation, say twenty to one hundred variables, to a more pinpointed and more probable set of variables, say one to twenty. These prime suspects can then be further narrowed down to the Red X and Pink X with the use of variables search or full factorials. In some cases, the clues from a multi-vari chart are strong enoguh to identify the Red X without further experiments.

Methodology

The multi-vari chart is an experiment, where the potential causes can be grouped into one or another of several stratified families. The most typical stratification is to determine whether the major cause of variation is within-unit, unit-to-unit, or time-to-time. If the largest variation is time-to-time, the causes associated with unit-to-unit and within-unit variations can be eliminated. The more general classifications of within-unit, unit-to-unit, and time-to-time variations are called positional, cyclical, and temporal, respectively. Examples of each pattern of variation follow:

Positional

- Variation within a single unit (for example, porosity in a metal casting, pins in an integrated circuit [IC], or specific locations on a printed circuit board).
- Variation by location in a batch-loading process (for example, cavity-to-cavity variations in a mold press).
- Variations from machine-to-machine; test position-to-test position; operator-to-operator; or plant-to-plant.

Cyclical

- Variation in consecutive units drawn from a process.
- Variation among groups of units.
- Batch-to-batch variations.
- Lot-to-lot variations.

Temporal (Time-Related)

- Variation from hour-to-hour; shift-to-shift; day-to-day; week-to-week.

Figure 13-6 shows three possible scenarios of the largest variation. Here, a few units, generally three, four, or five, are produced consecutively. Then some time is allowed to elapse before another few units are produced and checked. The process is repeated, that is, consecutive units are separated by time intervals *until at least 80 percent of the out-of-control variation in the process being investigated is captured*. Generally, a multi-vari chart requires a total of nine units as a minimum (3-3-3) and forty to fifty units as a maximum.

By plotting the results of the multi-vari run, the largest variation can be determined to be positional (within unit) as in A, or cyclical (unit-to-unit) as in B, or temporal (time-to-time) as in C.

The multi-vari chart should not be confused with a control chart. (That would be an insult to the multi-vari chart's problem-solving abilities!) It is a snapshot in time of how variation in a process is "breathing." It is a stethoscope of variation. For this reason, the multi-vari chart is the only one of the DOE tools where the production sequence or checking sequence should not be randomized.

Multi-Vari Case Study: The Rotor Shaft

A manufacturer, producing cylindrical rotor shafts with a diameter requirement of 0.250″ ± 0.001″, was experiencing excessive scrap. A process capability study indicated a spread of 0.0025″, against the specification width of 0.002″—that is, a $^{C}P_k$ of only 0.8. The foreman was ready to junk the old turret lathe producing the shaft and buy a new one for $70,000 that could hold a tolerance of ± 0.0008″—that is, a $^{C}P_k$ of 1.25. However, a consultant suggested trying a multi-vari study first.

Figure 13-7 shows the dimensional spread of just fifteen shafts, run three at a time, one hour apart, from 8 A.M. to 12 noon. There are four readings on each shaft, two on the left and two on the right side. The two readings on each side record maximum and minimum diameter, that is, an out-of-round condition, while the readings from left to right account for taper. These four readings represent within-shaft, or positional, variations. The thin connecting lines between the four readings on each shaft are the unit-to-unit, or cyclical variations, while the readings from one time period to the next show the time-to-time, or temporal, variations.

A quick eye scan reveals, even to the novice unfamiliar with multi-vari charts, that the largest variation is time-to-time, especially between 10 A.M. and 11 A.M. This provided the foreman with a strong clue. What generally happens around 10 A.M.? A coffee break! When the next sample of three shafts was taken at 11 A.M., the readings appeared similar to those at the start of production at 8 A.M., when the lathe was still cold. The time clue led to a temperature clue as a possible Red X. The foreman discovered a low level of coolant in the lathe tank. When the coolant was added to the

Figure 13-6. Three types of possible variations in multi-vari charts.

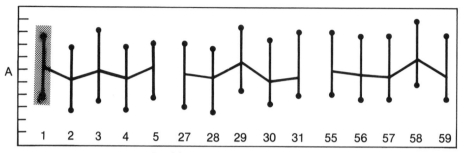

Positional Variation (within unit)

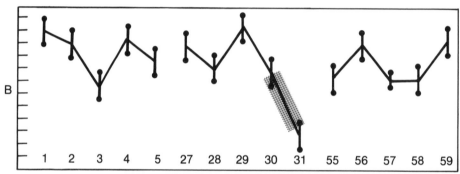

Cyclical Variation (unit-to-unit)

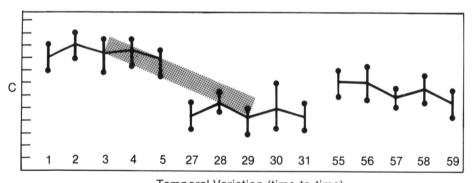

Temporal Variation (time-to-time)

Figure 13-7. Multi-vari case study: The rotor shaft.

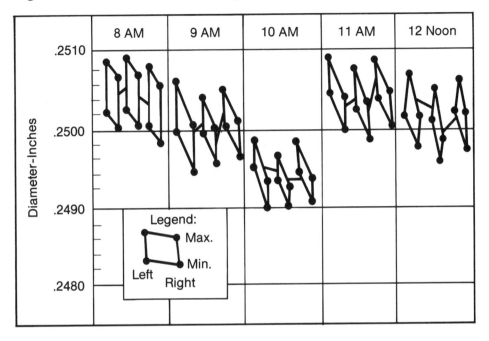

prescribed level, the time-to-time variation, which accounted for more than 50 percent of the allowed variation, was practically eliminated!

The next highest variation was within unit. The large out-of-round condition in each shaft was traced to a worn bearing guiding the chuck axis. New bearings, installed for a total cost, including labor, of $200, reduced another 30 percent of the allowed variation.

The variation in taper was next investigated. It showed a significant non-random pattern, with the left side always higher than the right side in all fifteen shafts. (It is essential that every multi-vari chart be scanned for such nonrandom trends that can provide strong clues.) This led to the conclusion that the cutting tool, as it traversed the rotor shaft from left to right, was not parallel to the axis of the shaft. A slight adjustment in the setting reduced another 10 percent of the allowed variation. In all, 50 percent + 30 percent + 10 percent of the allowed variation was eliminated.

The total variation, in follow-on production, was reduced from 0.0025″ to 0.0004″—twice as good as what the new lathe costing $70,000 could have accomplished! And the new c_{p_k} was $0.002/0.0004 = 5.0$. Scrap was now reduced to zero.

There is a moral in this case study. Too often, American industry is apt to throw out an old machine or process before investigating the underlying causes of variation, which can be eliminated with simple design of experiments, like the multi-vari chart. Ninety percent of the time, there is no need to incur the crushing burden of capital investment. The Japanese painstakingly search out the causes of variation in the old machines and optimize yields. However, the techniques they tend to use in production are brute force methods such as cause and effect diagrams. It may take them months, even years, to solve such problems, whereas the Shainin tools can achieve the same results in a few days with one to three designed experiments.

Components Search: Easy Sure-Fire Clues

Objective

Components search is another simple but powerful technique whose object is to reduce a very large number of possible causes of variation (even more than 1,000) down to the family of the Red X or the Red X itself.

Prerequisites

It is applicable in assembly operations as well as in process-oriented operations, where there are several similar processes or machines. There are a few prerequisites for its use:

- There must be good and bad units (that is, within specifications and outside specifications).
- The performance (output) must be measurable and repeatable.
- The units must be capable of dissassembly and reassembly without a significant change in the original output.

Procedure

Components search requires the following steps:

1. Select a good unit and a bad unit (drawn at random from a sufficient number of good and bad units, if quantities permit).
2. Determine the quantitative parameter by which good and bad units are to be measured. Measure both units and note the readings.
3. Dissassemble the good unit (at least by selecting the suspect components for dissassembly), reassemble and remeasure it. Do the same for the bad unit. If the difference, D, between the good and bad units ex-

ceeds the repeatability difference, d, within each unit by a minimum ratio of 5:1, a significant and repeatable difference between the good and bad units is established.

4. Based upon engineering judgment, rank the components most likely to have caused the problem, in descending order of perceived importance.

5. Switch the top-ranked component from the good unit or assembly with the corresponding component in the bad assembly. Measure the two assemblies.

   a. *If there is no change,* that is, if the good assembly stays good and the bad stays bad, the top component, A, is unimportant. Go to the next ranked component, B.

   b. *If there is a partial change* in the two assembly outputs, A is not the only important variable. It may be a Pink X family. Component A plus some other component(s) is causing the problem. Go to component B.

   c. *If there is a complete reversal* in the outputs of the two assemblies, that is, if the good unit reaches the level of the bad unit completely and vice versa, component A could be the Red X family. Stop the components search.

6. In each of the three alternatives in step 5, restore A to the original good and bad units to assure that the original conditions are repeated.

7. Repeat steps 5 and 6 with the next ranked component, B, then with C, D, E, and so on, if the result in each component swap is 5(a) or 5(b)—that is, no change, or a partial change.

8. Ultimately, the Red X family will be pinpointed if there is a complete reversal, either with a single component or with two or more components that had partial reversals (Pink X) swapped together.

9. With the important variables identified, a capping run (verification) of these important variables, banded together in the good and bad assemblies, must be conducted to verify their importance.

Components Search Case Study: The Hourmeter

A. PROBLEM DESCRIPTION

Components search is best illustrated by a real-life example. An hourmeter, designed for an off-the-road vehicle, had a 20–25 percent defect rate. The customer's requirement was perfect operation at −40°C. The defective units, however, could only work down to 0°C. The hourmeter consists of a solenoid cell, which pulses to trigger a solenoid pin, which in turn causes a bell crank to trip the counter, advancing it by one unit. The counter is attached to a numeral shaft containing numeral wheels, separated from each other by idler gears that rotate on an idler gear shaft. Both the idler gear shaft and the numeral shaft are attached to a mainframe of hard, white plastic. The pulsing rhythm is provided by an electronics board.

B. *ESTABLISHING SIGNIFICANT, REPEATABLE DIFFERENCES*

To start with, the good and the bad units were disassembled and reassembled in order to verify the consistency of the outputs and to quantify the difference between the good and the bad units.

	High *(Good Assembly)*	*Low* *(Bad Assembly)*
Initial results	OK at (H1): $-40°C$	L1: $0°C$
Results after disassembly and reassembly	OK at (H2): $-35°C$	L2: $-5°C$

The test for a significant and repeatable difference between good and bad units is determined by the formula:

$$D:d > 5:1.$$

That is, the ratio of D to d should be a minimum of 5:1, where:

$$D = \text{difference between good and bad assembly averages}$$

and:

$$d = \text{the average difference in repeatability within the good and bad assemblies.}$$

Therefore:

$$D = \frac{H_1 + H_2}{2} - \frac{L_1 + L_2}{2}$$

and

$$d = \frac{H_1 - H_2}{2} + \frac{L_1 - L_2}{2}.$$

So:

$$D = \frac{-40° + (-35°)}{2} - \frac{(0° + (-5°)}{2} = (-37.5°) - (-2.5°) = -35°$$

and

$$d = \frac{-40° + (-35°)}{2} + \frac{(0° + (-5°)}{2} = (-2.5°) + (-2.5°) = -5°$$

Therefore:

$$D:d = 35°:5° = 7:1,$$

which exceeds the required 5:1 ratio

C. RANKING OF COMPONENTS BY IMPORTANCE (ENGINEERING JUDGMENT)

The next step is to list the suspect components and rank them in descending order of importance, using the best available engineering judgment. Eight components were selected as shown below.

Rank	Components	Label
1	Solenoid, pin and shield	A
2	Idler gear shaft	B
3	Numeral shaft	C
4	Mainframe	D
5	Bell crank	E
6	Idler gears	F
7	Numeral wheels	G
8	Circuit board	H
9	Remainder of components	R (Remainder)

D. THE EXPERIMENT

Each was swapped from the good assembly to the bad and vice-versa. When component A, the solenoid, pin and shield, was swapped, the good unit remained good and the bad unit remained bad. Therefore, the suspect component A was not important. Similarly, component B was not important. The swap of component C showed a small partial change (perhaps a pale pink x). Components D and G, on the other hand, had large (but still partial) changes. Components E and F were unimportant.

E. TEST RESULTS

The results are shown in Table 13-3.

Testing Symbols

$A_L R_H = A$ from low (bad) unit, with remainder of components R, from high (good) unit.

Table 13-3. Components search case study: The hourmeter.

Test No.	Component Switched	"High" Assembly	Results	"Low" Assembly	Results
Initial	—	All components high	−40°	All components low	−0°
Disassembly and reassembly	—	All components high	−35°	All components low	−5°
1	A	$A_L R_H$	−40°	$A_H R_L$	−5°
2	B	$B_L R_H$	−35°	$B_H R_L$	0°
3	C	$C_L R_H$	−35°	$C_H R_L$	−5°
4	D	$D_L R_H$	−20°	$D_H R_L$	−5°
5	E	$E_L R_H$	−40°	$E_H R_L$	0
6	F	$F_L R_H$	−40°	$F_H R_L$	−5°
7	G	$G_L R_H$	−20°	$G_H R_L$	−5°
8	H	$H_L R_H$	−35°	$H_H R_L$	0°
Capping run	D & G	$D_L G_L R_H$	0°	$D_H G_H R_L$	−40°

Testing Symbols

$A_L R_H$ = A from low (bad) unit, with remainder of components R, from high (good) unit.
$A_H R_L$ = A from high (good) unit, with remainder of components (R), from low (bad) unit.

$A_H R_L$ = A from high (good) unit, with remainder of components (R), from low (bad) unit.

The same results are better portrayed graphically in Figure 13-8, which shows a clear separation between the original high (good) and low (bad) assemblies, as well as their replicated tests (disassembled and reassembled). The graph shows—more clearly than the table—a partial convergence between the high and low assemblies when components D (mainframe) and G (numeral wheels) were switched. These can be called Pink X components; possibly they interacted with one another, but they may also have interacted with some yet untested component. The contribution of the remaining components was found to be minor or zero.

In the capping run, when D and G were combined at low levels, with all other components at high levels, the results were bad. When D and G were combined at high levels, with all other components at low levels, the results were good. The graph shows a complete reversal of high and low, indicating that the family of the Red X has been narrowed down to D and G; that all other components are relatively unimportant and therefore their tolerances can be opened up; and that further components search can be discontinued.

Figure 13-8. Components search: Hourmeter case study.

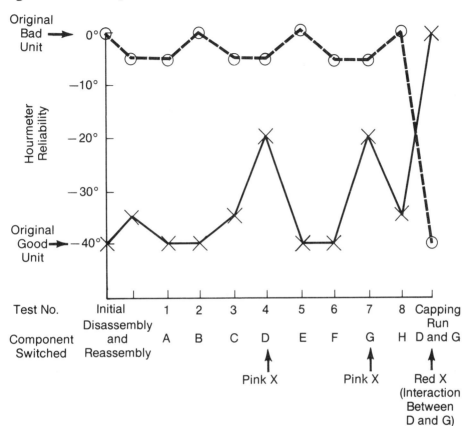

F. THE FINAL SOLUTION

Figure 13-9 is a summary of the final solution to which Components Search provided strong clues and pointed the way. *As a result, the defect rate went from the 20–25 percent range down to zero!*

Variables Search: The Rolls Royce of Variation Reduction

Multi-vari charts and components search are useful for homing in on the Red X. The next step is variables search, the Rolls Royce of DOE techniques

Figure 13-9. Final solution to hourmeter case study.

ANALYSIS OF EXPERIMENT

- Main frame and numeral wheels causing drop in performance

ENGINEERING ANALYSIS

- 60 x life-size model built
- Isolated *first* numeral wheel and main frame as problem
- Made measurements at critical points at different temperatures

RESULTS

- Main frame shrunk by up to 0.002″ bringing numeral wheel and idler shaft too close
- First numeral wheel off center by 0.005″
- Counter jammed when shrinkage coincided with eccentricity

SOLUTION

- Redesign mainframe (cost: $50,000)
- *Or* change numeral wheel specification and tolerance (low cost)
- Second alternative selected

POSTSCRIPT

- Yields rose from 75–80% to 100%

The reliability engineer, who conducted the components search study, wrote the following postscript to his report.

The problem had been with us for 18 months. We had talked to suppliers; we had talked to engineers and designers; we had talked to engineering managers; *But we never talked to the parts.* With the Components Search technique, we identified the problem in just three days!

and the most direct American answer to the Taguchi orthogonal array. Properly applied, it can:

- Solve complex technical problems with many variables whose relationships to the output (or dependent variable) cannot be captured by a mathematical formula.
- Take the guesswork out of any process control where previous engineering judgments have determined the levels of some process parameters, neglected others, and been ignorant of even the presence of still others. Such situations lead to chasing one's tail all over the map. Variables search, by contrast, defines the whole process precisely and permanently.
- Prevent problems to begin with, when it is used at the design stage of the product or process.

Objectives

- Pinpoint the Red X and Pink X (or interacting Pink X's resulting in a Red X).
- Separate these important variables from the unimportant ones.
- Tightly control the important variables (through Positrol and precontrol, to be discussed in Chapter 14).
- Open up the tolerances on the unimportant variables so as to reduce costs.

Principle

One of the important principles in DOE is to so design an experiment that every variable can be tested with each level of every other variable. As an example, if eight variables are the possible causes in the variation of a given output, and two levels of each variable are used—a high level and a low level—there are 2^8 or 256 combinations of possible tests. Only the full factorial technique can test all these combinations. But a full factorial making use of 256 experiments would be very complex, costly, and time-consuming. Hence various shortcuts have been devised, such as fractional factorial designs in the classical approach and the orthogonal array in the Taguchi approach. However, as stated earlier, both these approaches use a hit-and-miss method of selecting only a few combinations, such as sixteen or thirty-two, out of a possible total of 256. Which sixteen or thirty-two combinations should one use? No one knows! The results of these shortcuts, therefore, tend to be modest, inaccurate, and transitory, especially if there are interaction effects, which get confounded or commingled with main effects.

Variables search overcomes this selection difficulty by using a homing-in binary technique that is essentially a process of elimination. A game analogy can be used to illustrate the binary approach. The game involves asking a person to select any word in the dictionary. The object is for the "problem solver" or questioner to locate the selected word in no more than seventeen simple questions, with only "yes" or "no" responses from the person who has selected the word being permitted. The questioner starts with the middle page number in the dictionary and asks if the word is located after the middle page. A yes or no answer eliminates half the pages of the dictionary. The next question of a similar nature eliminates three-fourths of the dictionary pages and so on, until by the eleventh yes or no answer, the exact page location is determined. With another six tries, the exact location of the word on the page, and thus, the word itself, is pinpointed.

The same principle of binary questions is at work in variables search, where the culprit variables and their levels can be pinpointed from 256 or even 2,096 combinations and more by the use of only sixteen to thirty-six experiments, respectively! It is no wonder that variables search is far superior to fractional factorials and Taguchi's orthogonal array technique, which often depend on wild guesses when interactions are encountered. In fact, it can be proven that variables search can neatly separate all two-factor and three-factor interactions, as well as half of all four-factor interactions.

Application

Variables search is most applicable when there are five or more variables to investigate. While there is no theoretical upper limit, practical considerations limit the number of variables to fifteen. Further, the output must be measurable—a variable, preferably, though attributes can also be used. Finally, in the choice of "best" and "worst" levels, it is advisable to know and to quantify "best" and "worst" in advance, as will be explained in the following procedures.

Procedure

There are thirteen steps in two distinct stages to be taken. In stage 1,

1. List the most important input variables, or factors—A, B, C, D, E, F, G, H, . . . in descending order of each factor's ability to influence the output. This will be based on engineering judgment. However, such judgment can be—and often is—wrong.

2. Assign two levels to each factor, a best (B) that is most likely to contribute to good results and a "worst" (W) that is likely to give marginal results.

3. Run two experiments, one with all factors at their best levels, the other with all factors at their worst levels. Run two more experiments at the best and worst levels to assess residual and experimental error.

A newer rule suggests yet another two experiments, with best and worst levels. Then rank the "best" and "worst" levels in the six experiments in descending order of desired output. If the three "best" levels outrank the three "worst" levels, there is 95 percent confidence that the best levels are significantly better than the worst levels and that the Red X is captured.

4. Apply the D:$d > 5$:1 rule, as seen in the components search case study, where D is the difference between the average of the "best" readings and "worst" readings; and d is the average of the differences in repeatability within each "best" and "worst" pair of readings added together. So,

$$D = (B_1 + B_2)/2 - (W_1 + W_2)/2$$
$$d = (B_1 - B_2)/2 + (W_1 - W_2)/2$$

5. If the difference in outputs (*D*) between levels is greater than the difference in outputs within each level (*d*) by a minimum of a 5:1 ratio, the Red X is captured as being one or more of the factors considered in step 1. Go to stage 2.

6. If the ratio is less than 5:1, either the right factors were not chosen in step 1 or the levels used for one or more factors may have been reversed between "best" and "worst." The experimental team conducting the variables search should not be discouraged if this happens, since engineering judgment is frequently wrong. In such an event, there are three alternatives that can be considered:

(a) If the team feeling is that the wrong factors were selected in step 1, decide on new factors and rerun Stage 1.

(b) If the team feeling is that the right factors were selected, but the levels of some of these factors were mistakenly reversed between "best" and "worst," run B versus C tests on each suspicious factor to see whether the best and worst levels are reversed or not. (B versus C tests are explained in brief in Table 14-2.)

(c) A third method might be to try the selected factors, four at a time, using full factorial experiments to determine important and unimportant factors.

Stage 2 is begun only when the *D* to *d* ratio exceeds 5 to 1 (see Step 5 in the Stage 1 Procedure).

1. Run an experiment with the worst level of the most important factor, A, that is, A_W, along with the best levels of the remaining factors, labeled R_B. Measure the result of the $A_W R_B$ combination.

(a) If there is no change from the *best* results obtained by step 3 of Stage 1, the top factor A is unimportant.

(b) If there is a partial change from the worst results in step 3 of Stage 1, in the direction of the best results, then A is not the only important factor or variable. A could be a Pink X along with another factor.

(c) If there is a complete reversal, where the *worst* results given by step 3 of Stage 1 are approximated, A is the Red X.

2. Run a second experiment with the best level of A, that is, A_B, along with the worst levels of the remaining factors, labeled R_W. Measure the result of the $A_B R_W$ combination.

(a) If there is no change from the *worst* results in step 3 of Stage 1, the top factor A is further confirmed as unimportant.

(b) If there is a partial change from the best results in step 3 of Stage 1, in the direction of the worst results, A is further confirmed as not the only important factor or variable.

(c) If there is a complete reversal, where the *best* results in step 3 of Stage 1 are approximated, A is further confirmed as the Red X and no further experimentation need be conducted.

3. Perform the same components search swap of steps 1 & 2, sequentially, on factors B, C, D, E, F, G, H, and so on, and separate the important factors from the unimportant ones.

4. If there is not a single Red X factor, but two or three Pink X factors that display a partial change, as in 1 (b), perform a capping run, or validation experiment, with these Pink X factors at their best levels and the remaining unimportant factors at their worst levels. The results should approximate the best results of step 3, Stage 1.

5. Next run another capping run with these Pink X factors at their worst levels and the remaining unimportant factors at their best levels. The results should approximate the worst results of step 3, Stage 1.

6. Make every attempt to maintain the important factors at their best levels when production starts (or for subsequent production runs) by:
- reducing and controlling supplier variability of the important components (and simultaneously getting a price decrease from the supplier, based on his higher yields).
- redesign of the important components, if necessary.
- reducing and controlling process variability of the important components.
- maintaining reduced process variability through Positrol (see Chapter 14).

7. Conduct scatter plot experiments (explained in brief in Table 13-2) to determine how far the tolerances of the unimportant components can be opened—especially if there is an appreciable cost reduction benefit—and the optimum value of the Red X factor and its tolerances to ensure a minimum $^{c}P_k$ of 2.0.

Use of Variables Search When Variation or Defects Exist Only in a Small Percentage of Units

In such cases a single unit each for "best" and "worst" is not enough. A sufficient number of units must be tested, both for best and worst combinations, to obtain a significant difference in the percentages between best and worst. This holds true both for Stage 1 and Stage 2.

Use of Variables Search Where Disassembly Is Not Possible

Here, the Stage 1 procedure is not changed. But in Stage 2, the sample size may have to be increased and brand-new units used for the $A_W R_B$, $A_B R_W$ combinations. While this may not give as accurate a result as a direct interchange, the main and interaction effects will still show up in a very pronounced manner.

Variables Search Case Study: The Press Brake

Description of Problem: In a metal stamping/forming operation, parts produced on press brakes could not be held to a $\pm$ 0.005″ tolerance (or process width of 0.010″). Tolerances as high as $\pm$ 0.010″ were being measured some of the time in production. The press brake was perceived to be a temperamental operation—in the "black magic" category—requiring the use of highly skilled operators to get consistent results. The causes of the large variation (^{Cp}ks down to 0.5) were hotly debated, with explanations ranging from faulty supplier material (inconsistent thickness and/or inconsistent hardness) to

Table 13-4. Variables search: The press brake case study.

Factor	Best	Worst
A. Punch and die alignment	Aligned	Not aligned
B. Metal thickness	Thick	Thin
C. Metal hardness	Hard	Soft
D. Metal bow	Flat	Bowed
E. Ram storage	Coin form	Air form
F. Holding material	Level	Air angle

Results: Numbers are expressed in process widths (i.e., two × the tolerance), in multiples of 0.001″, measured on five units in each experiment

	Process Widths (×0.001″)	
Stage 1	*All Best Levels*	*All Worst Levels*
Initial	4	47
Replication	4	61

D=50; d=7; so D:d=7:1 (more than required 5:1). So there is a significant, repeatable difference.

Conclusion: Red X (or Pink Xs) captured as one or more of the six factors.

(continued)

Table 13-4. *Continued.*

Stage 2

Test No.	Combination	Results	Conclusion
1	$A_W R_B$	3	A. Not important
2	$A_B R_W$	102	
3	$B_W R_B$	5	B. Not important
4	$B_B R_W$	47	
5	$C_W R_B$	7	C. Not important
6	$C_B R_W$	72	
7	$D_W R_B$	23	Pink X: Interaction
8	$D_C R_W$	30	with another factor
9	$E_W R_B$	7	?
10	$E_B R_W$	20	
11	$F_W R_B$	73	Probable Red X + interaction
12	$F_B R_W$	18	with another factor
Capping run	$D_W F_W R_B$	70	Complete reversal effected
	$D_B F_B R_W$	4	

press brake parameters that could not be controlled. Efforts to use newer press brakes, with much higher capital costs, had not resulted in any significant quality improvement.

Experiment: A variables search experiment was then tried. The objective was to get the process under control, consistently, to ± 0.005″ or closer. Six factors were selected, in descending order of perceived importance, and the best and worst levels for each factor determined. (In the interest of protecting confidential information, the precise, quantitative levels used are not mentioned. They are labeled only in general terms.)

The six factors chosen and the Stage 1 and Stage 2 results are shown in Table 13-4.

Conclusion: As a result of the variables search experiment:

1. The parts tolerances on the brake could be held to $\pm$ 0.002″ (process width of 0.004″), which was better than twice the original objective.
2. The $^{C}p_k$ was increased from an unacceptable 0.5 to a comfortable 2.5 (0.010/0.004) with just one experiment.
3. The material thickness and hardness were no longer important considerations and the tolerances on these parameters could be opened up. The bow in the material was the important parameter to control.
4. A fixture was devised to keep the holding material (Red X) always level, appreciably reducing operator-controllable variations.

Full Factorials: A Workhorse in Design of Experiments

Objective: In full factorial experiments, the objectives are to:

1. Pinpoint the most important variables—Red X, Pink X—following the homing-in techniques of multi-vari charts, components search, or paired comparisons.
2. Separate and quantify the main and interaction effects of the important variables.
3. Start the process of opening up tolerances on the unimportant variables.

These objectives, as we have seen, are similar to those for variables search. The main difference is that full factorials are used to investigate four or less variables, while in variables search, the number is five or more. In attempting to identify the causes of variation, engineers sometimes cannot think of more than four causes. Alternatively, previous homing-in techniques may have reduced the possible causes to four or less. As a result, the full factorials approach is a powerful workhorse in DOE and is used more frequently than other DOE tools, with the exception of variables search.

Principle: The power of full factorials is that every one of the four (or less) chosen variables is tested with all levels (generally two) of every other variable. Thus all possible combinations of factors and levels are tested, which allows for the systematic separation and quantification of all main effects as well as *all* interaction effects, including:

- Second-order interaction effects (that is, two main variables interacting with one another).
- Third-order interaction effects (or three main variables interacting with one another).
- Fourth-order interaction effects (or four main variables interacting with one another).

In full factorials:

- An investigation involving two factors and two levels is called a 2^2 factorial.
- An investigation involving three factors and two levels is called a 2^3 factorial.
- An investigation involving four factors and two levels is called a 2^4 factorial.

In this section, a 2^4 full factorial will be explained, because 2^2 and 2^3 factorials are simpler versions of the 2^4 factorial.

With four factors, each with two levels, there are 2^4 or sixteen combinations, and hence sixteen experiments are required. In order to overcome residual error inherent in all experimentation, these sixteen experiments should be repeated (or replicated), making a total of thirty-two experiments. (A technique using end counts and overlaps can reduce the number of experiments to sixteen, but this is not discussed here in the interests of brevity.)

The sample size in each combination of factors (called cells) need be no more than one to five for variables data, but must be large enough for attribute data to be able to distinguish one cell output from another. As an example, if the objective is to detect a 5 percent problem and reduce it, the sample size in each cell would have to be increased to one hundred units in order to differentiate between various percent defectives in each cell.

Finally, the sequence of testing should not be done in a methodical, predictable manner, but in a random order. This allows numerous causes not included in the experiment an equal opportunity of entering or leaving the experiment. The random order of testing can be determined through a random number table, described in most texts on statistics and quality control. For instance, if the sixteen combinations or cells are labeled sequentially, and a table of random numbers selects sixteen random numbers as shown below, the sequence of testing would follow the random numbers from low to high as follows:

Cell No.:	1	2	3	4	5	6	7	8	9	10	11	12	13	14	15	16
Random Nos.:	38	68	83	24	86	59	40	47	20	60	43	85	25	96	93	45
Testing Sequence:	4	11	12	2	14	9	5	8	1	10	6	13	3	16	15	7

Procedures

1. Select the four factors to be investigated, based on previous homing-in experiments and/or engineering judgment. Designate them A, B, C, and D.

2. Determine two levels for each factor. The first level, labeled (−), is usually, but not necessarily, the current level for that factor. The second level, labeled (+), is assumed to produce better results, but again this is not necessarily so.
3. Draw up a matrix (see Figure 13-10) showing the sixteen combinations by which each factor is tested with each level of every other factor.
4. Randomize the sequence of testing each combination (or cell).
5. Run an experiment with each combination in the sequence indicated by the random order table and record the output in each cell.
6. Repeat steps 4 and 5 using *another* random order for the test sequences.
7. Calculate the average of the two readings in each cell.
8. For the thirty-two sets of readings, add* all average readings in those cells where A is (−) and all the average cell readings where A is (+). The difference between A (−) and A (+) is due to factor A alone, because all other factors—B, C, and D—balance one another (or cancel one another). Similarly, add all the average cell readings where B is (−) and where B is (+). The difference is due to factor B alone. In like manner, calculate the difference between the C (−) and C (+) average readings and the D (−) and D (+) average readings.
9. Construct an analysis of variance (ANOVA) table. The procedure is explained in detail in the following case study.

Full Factorials: The Wave Solder Case Study

Description of Problem: The purpose of a wave solder process is to solder electronic components to a printed circuit (p.c.) board. Prior to this process, components are machine-inserted on to a p.c. board. The assembly is then put on a belt conveyor and passed, first, through a pre-heat chamber. Flux, a chemical cleaning agent that removes oxides from the component and p.c. board leads, is next applied. Finally, the assembly passes over a fountain (or wave) of molten solder at a given angle of incline at a predetermined temperature and at a predetermined speed to effect solder connections between the components and the board.

For many years, defect rates of 3 percent of the total number of connections had been tolerated as the best the process could achieve. In more modern measurements, this defect rate translates into 30,000 parts per million (ppm). A quality improvement team was able to reduce the defect rate

---

*The novice user of full factorials is tempted to select a single combination (cell) of factors that appears to produce the best output. This is a suboptimal solution. It ignores valuable data in the remaining fifteen cells. By looking at eight cells where a factor is (−) and eight where it is (+), we get a magnifying effect that allows a better determination of the appropriate level for each factor and the relationships between main effects and interaction effects.

Figure 13-10. Full factorials: Wave solder case study.

Product EEC IV - Model 2201
CAL No. New Machine Electrovert 337-12

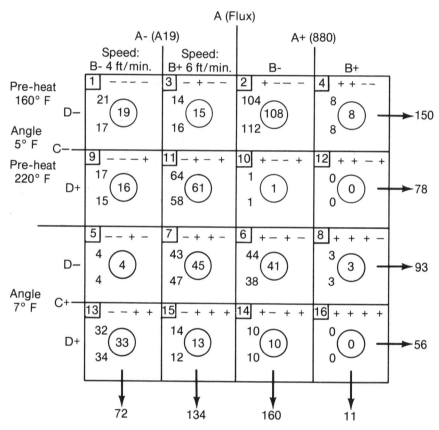

Four Factor Two–Level Matrix

A- = 72 + 134 = 206 } A- is worse than A + by   35 defects.   (-) A19 flux (+) (880)
A+ = 160 + 11 = 171 }   (-) 4'speed (+) 6'
B- = 72 + 160 = 232 } B- is worse than B + by   87 defects.   (-) 5° angle (+) 7°
B+ = 134 + 11 = 145 }   (-) 160° pre-heat (+) 220°
C- = 150 + 78 = 228 } C- is worse than C + by   79 defects.
C+ =   93 + 56 = 149 }
D- = 150 + 93 = 243 } D- is worse than D + by 109 defects.
D+ =   78 + 56 = 134 }

to 1 percent or 10,000 ppm by redesigning p.c. boards and improving sol-derability on the p.c. boards and component leads.

Objective: The team felt that the remaining improvements had to come from the wave solder process itself. Multi-vari studies indicated large variations within the board rather than board-to-board or time-to-time variations. Four possible causes were identified, requiring full factorial, 2^4 experiments. The target was to reduce the defect rate from 10,000 ppm to 200 ppm.

Four factors and two levels* for each factor were selected.

Letter	Factor	Levels	
		$(-)$	$(+)$
A	Flux	A 19	A880
B	Belt speed	4 ft./min.	8 ft./min.
C	Angle of incline	5°	7°
D	Pre-heat temperature	160°F	220°

The results of the experiments are shown in Figure 13-10.

An analysis of variance (ANOVA) table was constructed, as shown in Table 13-5. The procedure is as follows:

1. In the "cell group" column, enter the cell numbers from Figure 13-10.
2. In the "factors" column, enter the appropriate $(-)$ and $(+)$ signs for factors A, B, C, and D in cell 1. Here A, B, C, and D are all $(-)$. The $(-)$ and $(+)$ signs merely indicate the levels of the factors used. Similarly, enter the appropriate $(-)$ and $(+)$ signs for A, B, C, and D in the remaining fifteen cells.
3. In the "output" column, enter the average of the outputs recorded in each cell from Figure 13-10.
4. In the 2-factor interaction columns, multiply, *algebraically*, the signs of A and B in cell 1 and record the sign of the product in the AB column. Here, since A and B are both $(-)$, the product sign for AB is $(+)$. Similarly, determine the algebraic product of A and C, B and C, and so on, and record them in the appropriate 2-factor interaction column.
5. Repeat the algebraic multiplications of A, B, and C, A, B, and D, and so forth, up to A, B, C, and D, and record the signs in the appropriate 3-factor or 4-factor interaction column.
6. Repeat steps 4 and 5 for all remaining fifteen cells.
7. In column A, add all the outputs where A is $(-)$ and add all the outputs where A is $(+)$. Note the difference between these two sums in the last row labeled "main and interaction effects contribution." Place

---

*$(-)$ represents current levels.

Table 13-5. Full factorials: Wave solder: Anova table.

Cell Group	Factors				2 Factors Interactions						3 Factors Interactions				4 Factors Interaction	Output
	A	B	C	D	AB	AC	BC	AD	BD	CD	ABC	ABD	ACD	BCD	ABCD	
1	−	−	−	−	+	+	+	+	+	+	−	−	−	−	+	19
2	+	−	−	−	−	−	+	−	+	+	+	+	+	−	−	108
3	−	+	−	−	−	+	−	+	−	+	+	+	−	−	−	15
4	+	+	−	−	+	−	−	−	−	+	−	−	+	+	+	8
5	−	−	+	−	+	−	−	+	+	−	+	−	+	+	−	4
6	+	−	+	−	−	+	−	−	+	−	−	+	−	+	+	41
7	−	+	+	−	−	−	+	+	−	−	−	+	+	−	+	45
8	+	+	+	−	+	+	+	−	−	−	+	−	−	+	−	3
9	−	−	−	+	+	+	+	−	−	−	−	+	+	+	−	16
10	+	−	−	+	−	−	+	+	+	−	+	−	−	+	+	1
11	−	+	−	+	−	+	−	−	+	−	+	−	+	−	+	61
12	+	+	−	+	+	−	−	+	+	−	−	+	−	−	−	0
13	−	−	+	+	+	−	−	−	−	+	+	+	−	−	+	33
14	+	−	+	+	−	+	−	+	−	+	−	−	+	−	−	10
15	−	+	+	+	−	−	+	−	+	+	−	−	−	+	−	13
16	+	+	+	+	+	+	+	+	+	+	+	+	+	+	+	0
Main and Interaction Effects Contribution	−35	−87	−79	−109	−211	−47	+33	−189	+115	+35	+73	+139	+127	−181	+39	

↑ Red X
(Flux + Speed)

↑ Pink X
(Flux + Pre-heat)

The (−) sign in the factor A column in the last row indicates that A− is worse than A+ by 35 defects. Similar signs in the other main and interaction factors indicate whether the (−) level or (+) level is worse.

a (−) sign above this entry if the A (−) sum is worse than the A (+) sum; or a (+) sign if the reverse is the case.

8. Similarly, add all the (+) and (−) outputs for each column B, C, D, AB through CD, ABC through BCD and ABCD and note the difference in the last row, as in step 7.

9. The last row now displays, in precise quantified form, the contribution of each main factor as well as each two-factor, three-factor, and four-factor interaction to the total variation.

Table 13-5 can now be interpreted as follows:

- The Red X is the interaction effect between A and B, that is, between the flux and the belt speed.
- The Pink X is the interaction effect between A and D, that is, between the flux and pre-heat temperature.
- The main effects of A, B, C, and D are relatively small compared to the interaction effects.

Conclusion: The 2^4 factorial clearly showed that the best levels of the four factors were A (+), B (+), C (+), and D (+)—in other words, the use of the A 880 flux, a belt speed of 6 ft./minute, an incline angle of 7°, and a pre-heat temperature of 220°F. A capping run on seventeen boards produced three defects. With 800 connections per board, *the defect rate dropped to 220 ppm!* This represented a 45:1 quality improvement. These are the kinds of spectacular results needed to solve problems. We must be totally discontented with 10 percent, 50 percent, or even 100 percent improvements. (Incidentally, neither the classical DOE or Taguchi methods could even begin to give comparable results.)

Application of DOE to Suppliers

If the design of experiments is vital to the customer company in optimizing product and process designs, it is equally vital to suppliers. Quality from suppliers influences product quality more than any other aspect of quality, except design quality. It is well known that most supplier processes have not been defined in terms of the numerous process variables that affect their products. An uncertain recipe, formulated by earlier process engineers, is slavishly followed. Limited experiments were probably conducted years ago to determine process/machine settings. Most of them were done by varying one variable at a time. Experience and operator intuition may have modified such settings.

There is an urgent need to help the supplier start from scratch, especially where there are chronic quality problems with a process. Forget reams of data and history. It is contaminated information. Instead, start with a stratified multi-vari study, to isolate the family of the Red X, and follow the experiment with variables search or a full factorial to pinpoint the important variables. Finally, do not tolerate defects under any circumstances. If the supplier can make some good units and some bad units, help him to capture the recipe that can and should produce *all* good units!

Chapter 14

SPC: Just a Maintenance Tool

Around 1981, in response to the onslaught of offshore competition, improvement fever began to spread in the automotive industry. Statistical methods in particular became popular. Seven years and billions of dollars later, many users are still waiting for an appreciable return on their investment in SPC.

—Dr. Hans Bajaria, president, Multiface Inc.

Variation cannot be satisfactorily reduced by statistical process control (SPC) or its principal tool, control charts. Nor can technical or quality problems be solved by SPC or control charts. Engineering judgment, guesses, hunches, opinions, and biases may reduce these problems. But the probability of solutions emerging from such engineering approaches is a dismal 10 percent or less, as evidenced by the longevity of chronic quality problems. The only reliable approach is the design of experiments (DOE) detailed in Chapter 13. DOE does supreme detective work in apprehending the culprit variables.

What, then, is the true role of SPC? It is to ensure that variation, once captured and reduced with DOE, is incarcerated in a maximum security prison. In other words, the only use for control charts is as a maintenance

211

Table 14-1. Positrol plan for a wave solder process.

Parameter (What)	Specification	Who	Measurement		
			How	Where	When
A 880 flux	0.864 GM/CC ± 0.008	Lab technician	Specific gravity meter	Lab	Once a day
Belt speed	6 Ft./MIN ± 10%	Process technician	Counter	Board feed	With each model change
Angle of incline	7° ± 20%	Process technician	Angle scale	Tilt post	With each model change
Pre-heat temperature	220°F ± 5°	Automatic	Thermo-couple	Chamber entrance	Continuously

tool. But, as we shall see later in this chapter, precontrol is simpler, easier, less costly, and statistically far more powerful than control charts. However, between the end of DOE and the start of precontrol, there are three disciplines that must be put into effect: Positrol, process certification, and operator certification.

Positrol

A major weakness in most companies is the attempt to control a *process* by checking the *product* it produces. That is like steering a boat by looking at the wake it produces. By then it is too late. A process, like a product, has inherent variables that must be pinpointed and reduced with DOE tools. The multi-vari case study on the rotor shaft and the full factorials case study on the wave solder in Chapter 13 are examples of such process variation reduction.

The role of Positrol (a term meaning "Positive Control") is to ensure that these important process variables—"the what"—stay reduced with a "who," "how," "where," and "when" plan and the Positrol log.

Positrol Plan

The purpose of a Positrol plan is to determine the nuts and bolts of this measurement process—and, first of all, *what* parameters are to be measured. Table 14-1 presents such a Positrol plan. The wave solder case study in Chapter 13, it will be remembered, identified four process variables— flux, belt speed, angle of incline, and pre-heat temperature—as process parameters that needed careful monitoring to ensure a 50:1 reduction in solder defects. The Positrol plan determines *who* should measure these process parameters, *how* they should be measured, *where*, specifically, they should be measured, and *when* (how frequently) measurement should take place.

Positrol Log

Once a Positrol plan is prepared, its execution must be recorded in a log maintained at the process. It should be logged by the designated person and monitored periodically by the supervisor, process engineer, or Quality Control. Table 14-2 is an example of a Positrol log on a sputtering machine used to metallize glass with a layer of chrome, nickel, and gold on one side of the glass and a layer of chrome and gold on the other side. Previous history on the sputtering machine indicated continual "in and out" rejects for metal adhesion on the glass. The process engineer would "twiddle" one knob after another in an effort to control adhesion, but end up "chasing his own tail"

Table 14-2. Positrol log on a sputtering machine.

Process: Metallization Machine: 903 Week Ending: 6-20-87

Machine Parameters			Monday 6a	Monday 12p	Monday 6p	Monday 12a	Tuesday 6a	Tuesday 12p	Tuesday 6p	Tuesday 12a	Wednesday 6a	Wednesday 12p	Wednesday 6p	Wednesday 12a	Thursday 6a	Thursday 12p	Thursday 6p	Thursday 12a	Friday 6a	Friday 12p	Friday 6p	Friday 12a	Saturday 6a	Saturday 12p	Saturday 6p	Saturday 12a
Power (W)	800–900	Cr	820	800	820	820	820	832	865	820	820	820	820	820	800	882	861	861	861	861	861	861				
	4760–4900	Ni	4848	4830	4779.2	4779	4772	4772	4797	4779	4779	4779	4817.5	4817.5	4765	4772	4817	4770	4855	4855	4819.5	4819				
	2300–2400	Au	2400	2400	2400	2400	2370	2370	2370	2510	2370	2370	2370	2370	2370	2370	2370	2340	2340	2340	2340	2340				
	1050–1150	Cr	1066	1066	1066	1066	1066	1066	1066	1066	1111	1111	1127.5	1127.5	1127	114	1127	1127	1148	1148	1148	1148				
	2300–2400	Au	2400	2400	2400	2400	2370	2370	2370	2570	2370	2370	2570	2570	2370	2370	2370	2340	2340	2340	2340	2340				
Gas Pressure (μ)	3.0	Cr	3.0	3.0	3.0	3.0	3.0	3.0	3.0	3.0	3.0	3.0	3.0	3.0	3.0	3.0	3.0	3.0	3.0	3.0	3.0	3.0				
	3.0	Ni	3.0	3.0	3.0	3.0	3.0	3.0	3.0	3.0	3.0	3.0	3.0	3.0	3.0	3.0	3.0	3.0	3.0	3.0	3.0	3.0				
	9.5	Au	9.5	9.5	9.5	9.5	9.5	9.5	9.5	9.5	9.5	9.5	9.5	9.5	9.5	9.5	9.5	9.5	9.5	9.5	9.5	9.5				
	9.5	Cr	9.5	9.5	9.5	9.5	9.5	9.5	9.5	9.5	9.5	9.5	9.5	9.5	9.5	9.5	9.5	9.5	9.5	9.5	9.5	9.5				
	9.5	Au	9.5	9.5	9.5	9.5	9.5	9.5	9.5	9.5	9.5	9.5	9.5	9.5	9.5	9.5	9.5	9.5	9.5	9.5	9.5	9.5				
Speed (IPM)	4.0	Cr	4.0	4.0	4.0	4.0	4.0	4.0	4.0	4.0	4.0	4.0	4.0	4.0	4.0	4.0	4.0	4.0	4.0	4.0	4.0	4.0				
	7.5	Ni	7.5	7.5	7.5	7.5	7.5	7.5	7.5	7.5	7.5	7.5	7.5	7.5	7.5	7.5	7.5	7.5	7.5	7.5	7.5	7.5				
	7.0	Au	7.0	7.0	7.0	7.0	7.0	7.0	7.0	7.0	7.0	7.0	7.0	7.0	7.0	7.0	7.0	7.0	7.0	7.0	7.0	7.0				
	5.5	Cr	5.5	5.5	5.5	5.5	5.5	5.5	5.5	5.5	5.5	5.5	5.5	5.5	5.5	5.5	5.5	5.5	5.5	5.5	5.5	5.5				
	7.0	Au	7.0	7.0	7.0	7.0	7.0	7.0	7.0	7.0	7.0	7.0	7.0	7.0	7.0	7.0	7.0	7.0	7.0	7.0	7.0	7.0				
Vacuum			3×10^{-6}	3×10^{-6}	3×10^{-6}	3×10^{-6}	3×10^{-6}	3×10^{-6}	3×10^{-6}	3×10^{-6}	3×10^{-6}	3×10^{-6}	3×10^{-6}	3×10^{-6}	3×10^{-6}	3×10^{-6}	3×10^{-6}	3×10^{-6}	3×10^{-6}	3×10^{-6}	3×10^{-6}	3×10^{-6}				
			3×10^{-6}	3×10^{-6}	3×10^{-6}	3×10^{-6}	3×10^{-6}	3×10^{-6}	3×10^{-6}	3×10^{-6}	3×10^{-6}	3×10^{-6}	3×10^{-6}	3×10^{-6}	3×10^{-6}	3×10^{-6}	3×10^{-6}	3×10^{-6}	3×10^{-6}	3×10^{-6}	3×10^{-6}	3×10^{-6}				
3×10^{-6}																										
Checked By																										
No. of Runs at End of Each Shift				12	14		10			9	5			9	7		8		9		8					

Comments/Problem Cause

and becoming thoroughly confused as to what to do. DOE experiments identified four factors—power, gas pressure, speed, and vacuum—as important and established the maximum outer limits for each of these parameters. A log was then maintained by the operators four times a day on this three-shift operation.

In many cases, it is more economical to use precontrol, rather than a log, for process control. Precontrol has the advantage of being able to lengthen the period between checks on each process parameter if the time between corrections (two pairs of yellows) is comfortably long. In more modern processes, usually microprocessor-based, parameter tolerances can be designed into the process, such that Positrol becomes automatic, eliminating the necessity for either a positrol log or precontrol. However, DOE tools must be used first to separate important process parameters from unimportant ones and to determine the tolerances on each parameter, before microprocessor controls are designed.

Positrol is a simple, commonsense technique for maintaining a process under control. Yet it is amazing how infrequently it is used to monitor processes, even where SPC has been widely used to monitor the products produced by these processes.

Process Certification: Overcoming Murphy's Law

The humorous, but real, foundation of process certification is Murphy's Law, the universal adage which states: "If something *can* go wrong, it *will!*"

The major causes of variation—design, processes, materials—can be reduced with DOE, and successes can be maintained with SPC. But there are a number of peripheral causes for poor quality—scores of little Murphies lurking around the corner—that can negate and checkmate all these fine preventive measures. The quality peripherals can be divided into three broad categories: systems, environment, and supervision. Table 14-3 is a partial listing of various quality peripherals that must be investigated before a particular process can be certified to produce good quality.

Process certification starts with a checklist of various quality peripherals that must be evaluated. Not all the checkpoints listed in Table 14-3 are applicable in all situations; conversely, many quality peripherals that may be unique to individual processes or quality systems are not listed in it. The checklist is usually drawn up by a process engineer and verified by a quality control engineer. Finally, a team, consisting typically of the process engineer, development engineer, quality engineer, foreman, and others, physically examines a process or work station, and only when all the quality peripheral requirements are in place does the process get a "certification" clearance.

Periodically, the team must reaudit such a work station or process to make sure that variations from policy, or sloppy practices, have not crept

Table 14-3.   A quality peripherals checklist for process
certification.

Quality System	Environment	Supervision
• Effective configuration management	• Water/air purity	• Clear quality goals
• Engineering change control	• Dust/chemicals control	• Clear instructions
• Equipment/instrument calibration	• Temperature/humidity control	• Combining tasks
• Preventive maintenance	• Human/product safety	• Natural work units
• Built-in equipment diagnostics	• Lighting/cleanliness	• Client relationships
• Visible, audible alarm signals for poor quality	• Electrostatic discharge control	• "Ownership" through vertical job enrichment
• *Poka-yoke*—foolproof checks	• Storage/inventory control	• Feedback of results
• Neighbor and self-inspection over external inspection		• Encouragement of suggestions
• No partial-build policy		• Coach, not boss
• Worker authority to shut down poor quality line		

back to cause potentially poor quality. It is recommended that recertification checks be conducted at least once a year. *If such certifications and recertifications were conducted on processes and work stations in even progressive companies, 80 percent would fail the very minimum requirements!* How can a company build a superstructure of quality when these basic foundations are weak!

Operator Certification

Operators are frequently blamed for poor quality when the real culprit is management. How can a worker produce quality when he is hired off the street and then given fifteen minutes of supervisor instruction? Training is

Table 14-4. Operator training: U.S. vs. Japanese companies.

U.S.	Japanese
• Short, spasmodic, unfocused	• Long, continuous, geared to major strategies
• Little testing or certification	• Testing and certification a prerequisite for jobs and promotion
• No cross-training	• Cross-training for multiple skills
• Training more on the job	• Training more in classroom
• Poor or no implementation of training	• Implementation the key
• No formal career planning for line workers	• Every worker has a management-by-objectives (MBO) plan, with training as the means of achieving career goals

the key word. It includes long-term training, testing, certification, and recertification in ever enlarging circles so that the line worker of today can become the knowledge worker of tomorrow. In Japan, training is an essential ingredient in its quality success story. Table 14-4 lists the differences in operator training between U.S. and Japanese companies. In Japan, the line worker is trained so that he can do the work of the technician; the technician so that he can do the work of the process engineer; and the process engineer so that he can reach for the work of the design engineer.

Only when DOE has identified and reduced the important variables, Positrol has controlled them, process certification has reined in quality peripherals, and operators have been certified, can SPC be applied to the product. The question now becomes: Which SPC technique—control charts or precontrol—provides the most powerful maintenance tool?

Control Charts: A Critique

The purpose of a control chart is to monitor a product or process and distinguish between "assignable" and "random" causes of variation. The former are few and large, and need correction. The latter are many and small, and should not be corrected.

The Roller Coaster History of Control Charts

Developed by Dr. Walter Shewhart in the 1920s, the control chart quickly became a bridge between the academic world of the laboratory and the hardheaded world of production. In the post-World War II period, however, as walls got plastered with control charts, their usefulness began to be challenged. No tools had been developed to tackle out-of-control conditions—not even such simple tools as brainstorming or cause-and-effect diagrams. Disillusionment set in, and the control chart was banished.

By the late 1970s, however, the Japanese challenge evoked an intensive search for the key to quality. U.S. companies latched on to SPC as that key. The control chart was recalled from exile and a coronation was held. Its reign continues. It has been a tyrannical reign, with several original equipment manufacturing (OEM) customers—especially some of the automotive companies—demanding the use of the control chart as a passport to doing business with them. They force control charts down the throats of unknowing or unwilling suppliers, and they bludgeon into submission those knowledgeable suppliers who dare to point out that the control chart emperor wears no clothes! As often happens, the royal court is filled with camp followers, hangers-on, and charlatans who exploit the desperation of companies to gain a foothold on the SPC bandwagon by offering courses, tutorials, consultations, and ubiquitous computer software programs—all dealing with the power and glory of control charts. Yet quality progress, as measured by c_p & c_{p_k}, has barely inched forward in the majority of American companies despite the widespread use of control charts. Sooner or later, as statistical literacy increases, disillusionment will once again set in and control charts will become as obsolete as they already are in Japan.

The Mechanics of Control Charts for Variables ($\overline{X}$ and R Charts)

The following is a step-by-step procedure to generate control charts* for use with variables data (that is, where there are scalar measurements that are continually variable, such as dimensions, weights, voltages, temperatures, speeds, and so forth).

Procedure for Trial Control Charts for $\overline{X}$ and R

1. Select key product parameter(s) from the process to be controlled, based on importance/jeopardy.
2. Take periodic samples (say, every half hour or every hour) from the process with a subgroup size of, say, four or five units in each sample.

---

*A full treatment of control chart practices could fill an entire book of this size. Because there is already a huge volume of published material—texts, videotapes, and computer programs—on control charts, it is assumed that most readers have some familiarity with them. In this book, only a few highlights will be examined in order to compare control charts with precontrol.

3. Run the process to obtain a minimum of twenty-five to thirty such samples.
4. For each subgroup, calculate average, $\overline{X}$, and range, R.
5. Calculate grand average, $\overline{\overline{X}}$, of all subgroup averages and calculate average range $\overline{R}$ of all subgroup ranges.
6. Calculate upper control limit ($UCL_{\overline{X}}$) and lower control limit ($LCL_{\overline{X}}$) for $\overline{X}$ chart:

$$UCL_{\overline{X}} = \overline{\overline{X}} + A_2\overline{R}$$
$$LCL_{\overline{X}} = \overline{\overline{X}} - A_2\overline{R}$$

(See tables for A_2 values of appropriate subgroup sizes.)
7. Calculate upper control limit (UCL_R) and lower control limit (LCL_R) for R chart:

$$UCL_R = D_4\overline{R}$$
$$LCL_R = D_3\overline{R}$$

(See tables for D_4 and D_3 values of appropriate subgroup sizes.)
8. Plot $\overline{X}$ and R charts. Draw in the control limits for $\overline{X}$ and R. If all $\overline{X}$ and R points (for each subgroup) are within their respective control limits, the process is considered stable—a constant-cause system.
9. If one or more $\overline{X}$ or R points falls outside its respective control limits, use statistical problem-solving methods to find assignable causes.

Figure 14-1 lists the formulas for calculating both the upper and lower control limits for $\overline{X}$ and R charts, as well as for the most common of the attribute charts, called p and c charts. (Attributes, as contrasted with variables, are discrete numbers associated with accept/reject, pass/fail, go/no-go criteria.) The chart additionally provides important formulas for calculating the upper and lower limits of *individual* values likely from the process. This is an essential step that most control chart practitioners don't even know about, much less use.

Case Studies Highlighting the Weaknesses of Control Charts

The several weaknesses of control charts are best illustrated by two case studies. The first involves control charting a bushing parameter.

In a machine-shop operation, a bushing had to be made to a length of 0.500 inches ± 0.002 inches—a typical requirement. Figure 14-2 shows the data generated by subgroups of five units, drawn from the process every hour on the hour. From the recorded data, the average, $\overline{X}$, and the range, R, are calculated for each subgroup. From the several $\overline{X}$ and R values, the grand average, $\overline{\overline{X}}$, and the average range $\overline{R}$, are derived. The formulas for

Figure 14-1. Control chart formulas for calculating (a) $\overline{X}$ and R control limits, p and c control limits; (b) process limits of individual values; and (c) typical values used in formulas.

Chart	Central Line	Lower Control Limit	Upper Control Limit
$\overline{X}$	$\overline{\overline{X}}$	$\overline{\overline{X}} - A_2 \overline{R}$	$\overline{\overline{X}} + A_2 \overline{R}$
R	$\overline{R}$	$D_3 \overline{R}$	$D_4 \overline{R}$
% Defective: p	$\overline{p}$	$\overline{p} - 3\sqrt{\dfrac{\overline{p}(1-\overline{p})}{n}}$	$\overline{p} + 3\sqrt{\dfrac{\overline{p}(1-\overline{p})}{n}}$
No. of Defective: c	$\overline{\overline{c}}$	$\overline{c} - 3\sqrt{\dfrac{\overline{\overline{c}}}{n}}$	$\overline{c} + 3\sqrt{\dfrac{\overline{\overline{c}}}{n}}$

(a)

Upper process limit	$\overline{\overline{X}} + 3\,\overline{R}/d_2{}^*$
Lower process limit	$\overline{\overline{X}} - 3\,\overline{R}/d_2$

$^*\ \sigma$ Population $= \sigma^1 = \overline{R}/d_2$

(b)

Subgroup Size n	A_2	D_3	D_4	d_2
4	0.73	0	2.28	2.059
5	0.58	0	2.11	2.326

(c)

the upper and lower control limits, shown in Figures 14-1 and 14-2 are then used to compute these limits for both the $\overline{X}$ and R charts.

The results are drawn in Figure 14-3 which clearly shows that all subgroup averages, $\overline{X}$, are within the upper and lower control limits in the $\overline{X}$ chart. Similarly, all subgroup ranges, $\overline{R}$, are within the upper and lower control limits for the R chart. This indicates that the trial control chart, which, incidentally, took one-and-a-half shifts and many readings to complete, has established that the process is stable (otherwise called a constant-cause system in statistical parlance). Process capability is now assured and full production can go forward, supposedly to fabricate thousands and thousands of units.

Yet if specification limits* are drawn, as shown in Figure 14-3 it can be seen that the upper control limit for *averages* is dangerously close to the upper specification limit for *individual readings*. Even without much statistical sophistication, any layman can reason that if average values are close to a limit, the individual values that make up the average can go beyond that limit. More precisely, the projected spread of individual values can be calculated by reference to the formulas for the process limits† shown in Figure 14-1. Figure 14-3 depicts these process limits. The upper process limit is 0.007″ above the upper specification limit, indicating that 7 to 10 percent of the bushings are likely to be defective. So, here is a control chart indicating that all is well and that production should continue at full speed, when, in actuality, the process is likely to produce a totally unacceptable rate of defective parts! In quality control literature, the risk of accepting product that should be rejected is referred to as a beta (β) risk. In this case, the β risk is at least 7 percent.§

The second case study has to do with control charting a sensor capacitance. An electronic element for sensing atmospheric pressure in an automobile had a capacitance requirement in the range of 31 to 45 pico-farads (pf). Figure 14-4 shows $\overline{X}$ and R control charts for the process.

In contrast to the first case study, both $\overline{X}$ and R charts here show several average and range readings outside the upper and lower control limits. The *inference* is that the process is hopelessly out of control and must be stopped dead in its tracks until corrected. Yet Production claimed it had produced hundreds, even thousands, of units without a single reject! To some extent, this can be seen from the raw data in the subgroups, where no individual

---

*Many control chart purists do not allow specification limits to be shown on control charts because they believe that such a practice inhibits continual process improvement, which somehow, almost magically, they believe can be accomplished with control charts!

†Again, in most control chart work, process limits are not even known, much less calculated or used to gauge process capability.

§If c_p and c_{pk} are used to calculate process capability, this particular process has a poor c_p of 1.25 and a totally unacceptable c_{pk} of 0.58. This alone stands as a dramatic condemnation of control charts.

Figure 14-2. Typical control chart data.

Bushing Length
Specification .500" ± .002"

Sample #	8 AM	9	10	11	12 PM	1	2	3	4	5	6	7 PM
1	.501"	.501"	.502"	.501"	.501"	.500"	.500"	.500"	.501"	.502"	.501"	.500"
2	.501"	.501"	.501"	.502"	.501"	.500"	.501"	.501"	.501"	.502"	.502"	.500"
3	.500"	.501"	.502"	.501"	.501"	.502"	.501"	.501"	.501"	.501"	.501"	.501"
4	.501"	.501"	.501"	.500"	.501"	.502"	.501"	.501"	.501"	.502"	.501"	.502"
5	.502"	.502"	.501"	.500"	.501"	.502"	.500"	.500"	.501"	.501"	.501"	.501"
Sample of X	2.505"	2.506"	2.507"	2.504"	2.505"	2.506"	2.505"	2.503"	2.505"	2.508"	2.506"	2.504"
$\overline{X}_1$	.501"	.5012"	.5014"	.5000"	.5010"	.5012"	.5010"	.5006"	.5010"	.5012"	.5012"	.5008"
R_1	.002"	.001"	.001"	.002	.000"	.002"	.002"	.001"	.000"	.001"	.001"	.002"

Sum of $\overline{X}_1 = 6.0128$
Sum of $R_1 = .0115$

$$\overline{\overline{X}} = \frac{\Sigma\overline{X}}{N} = \frac{6.0128}{12} = .50107 \qquad \overline{R} = \frac{\Sigma R}{N} = \frac{.015}{12} = .00125$$

Control Limits:

For sample averages $\quad \overline{\overline{X}} \pm A_2\overline{R} = .50107 \pm (.58)(.00125) \qquad\qquad$ UCL = .50180
$\qquad\qquad\qquad\qquad\qquad\qquad\qquad\qquad\qquad\qquad\qquad\qquad\qquad\qquad\qquad$ LCL = .50034

For range $\qquad$ UCL = $D_4\overline{R}$ = (2.11)(.00125) = .00264
$\qquad\qquad\qquad$ LCL = $D_3\overline{R}$ = (0)(.00125) = 0

Figure 14-3. Bushing length: $\overline{X}$ and R charts.

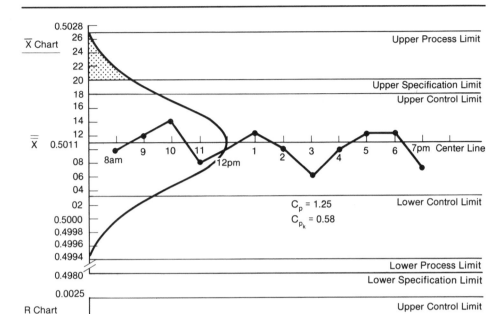

reading is even close to either the upper or lower specification limits of 45 and 31 pf. Further, the projected process limits for individual readings are 39.5 and 35 pf, well within the specification limit. (The projected process spread is slightly narrower than the spread of actual individual readings because the chosen subgroup size of 10 was unusually large.)

Here we have a condition the very reverse of that seen in the first case study, in other words, a control chart declaring that the process ought to be shut down when in fact production should continue.* On a long-term basis, the inherent variation depicted in the process can be reduced, but there is no need to shut down production, as indicated by the control chart. In quality control literature, this condition is called an alpha (α) risk, that is, the risk of rejecting a product that should be accepted.

---

*The process capability for this second case study is a respectable ^{C}p of 2.0 and a very acceptable $^{C}p_k$ of 1.92.

Figure 14-4.   Sensor $\overline{X}$ and R charts.

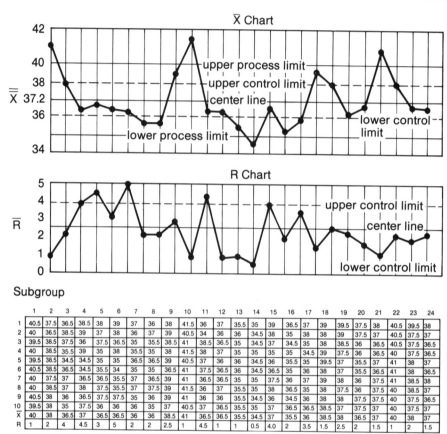

X Chart

R Chart

Subgroup

	1	2	3	4	5	6	7	8	9	10	11	12	13	14	15	16	17	18	19	20	21	22	23	24
1	40.5	37.5	36.5	38.5	38	39	37	36	38	41.5	36	37	35.5	35	39	36.5	37	39	39.5	37.5	38	40.5	39.5	38
2	40	36.5	38.5	39	37	38	36	37	39	40.5	34	36	36	34.5	38	35	38	38	39	37.5	37	40.5	37.5	37
3	39.5	38.5	37.5	36	37.5	36.5	35	35.5	38.5	41	38.5	36.5	35	34.5	37	34.5	35	38	38.5	36	36.5	40.5	37.5	36.5
4	40	38.5	35.5	39	35	38	35.5	35	38	41.5	38	37	35	35	35	34.5	39	37.5	37	36	36.5	40	37.5	36.5
5	39.5	38.5	34.5	34.5	35	35	36.5	36.5	39	40.5	37	36	36	34.5	36	35.5	35	39.5	37	35.5	37	41	38	37
6	40.5	38.5	36.5	34.5	35.5	34	35	35	36.5	41	37.5	36.5	36	34.5	36.5	35	36	38	37	35.5	36.5	41	38	36.5
7	40	37.5	37	36.5	36.5	35.5	37	36.5	39	41	36.5	36.5	35	37.5	36	37	39	38	36	37.5	41	38.5	38	
8	40	38.5	37	38	37.5	35.5	37	37.5	39	41.5	36	37	35.5	35	38	36.5	35	38	37.5	36	37.5	40	38.5	37
9	40.5	38	36	36.5	37.5	37.5	35	36	39	41	36	36	35.5	34.5	36	34.5	36	38	38	37.5	37.5	40	37.5	36.5
10	39.5	38	35	37.5	36	36	36	35	37	40.5	37	36.5	35.5	35	37	36.5	36.5	38.5	37	37.5	37	40	37.5	37
$\overline{X}$	40	38	36.5	37	36.5	36.5	36	36	38.5	41	36.5	36.5	35.5	34.5	37	35.5	36	38.5	38	36.5	37	40	38	37
R	1	2	4	4.5	3	5	2	2	2.5	1	4.5	1	1	0.5	4.0	2	3.5	1.5	2.5	2	1.5	1	2	1.5

Spec: 31 to 45 PF

$\overline{\overline{X}}$ = 37.2 PF ; $\overline{R}$ = 2.2; UCL $_{\overline{X}}$ = 37.88; LCL $_{\overline{X}}$ = 36.52; UCL $_R$ = 3.95; LCL $_R$ = 0
Upper process limit = 35.0; Lower process limit = 39.5

C_P = 2.0;   K = 0.04; C_{P_K} = 1.92

Precontrol: The Elegance of Simplicity

The Discovery of Precontrol

Precontrol was developed in the 1950s by the consulting company of Rath and Strong for a major Fortune 500 company that had become disenchanted with cumbersome and ineffective control charts. Precontrol's founder, Frank Satterthwaite, is a brilliant statistician who established the theoretical underpinnings of the technique in a comprehensive paper published in 1957. Unfortunately, just as precontrol was gaining recognition, U.S. industry, flushed with the glow of economic success in the post-World War II years, threw out all statistical methods, control charts and precontrol included. Then as SPC again became fashionable in the 1980s, with the control chart as its centerpiece, precontrol started to reappear on the statistical horizon. In 1986 the ratio of control chart users to precontrol practitioners was 99 to 1. Today the ratio is 90 to 10. In a few more years, as the simplicity and effectiveness of precontrol are better publicized, the control chart will be relegated to history, as it already has been in Japan, and precontrol will take its place as the principal maintenance tool in the SPC world.

The Mechanics of Precontrol in Four Easy Steps

The mechanics of precontrol can be taught to anybody in industry, including line operators, in less than ten minutes. There are four simple rules to follow:

Rule 1: Divide the specification width by 4. The boundaries of the middle half of the specification width then become the precontrol (P-C) lines. The area between these precontrol lines is called the green zone. The two areas between each precontrol line and each specification limit are called the yellow zones. The two areas beyond the specification limits are called the red zones.

Rule 2: To determine process capability, take a sample of five consecutive units from the process. If all five fall within the green zone, the process is in control. (In fact, with this simple rule, the usual samples of fifty to one hundred units to calculate c_p and c_{p_k} are not necessary. By applying the multiplication theorem of probabilities or the binomial distribution, it can be proven that a minimum c_{p_k} of 1.33 will automatically result.) Full production can now commence. If even one of the units falls outside the green zone, the process is not in control. Conduct an investigaton, using engineering judgment (which is not infallible—by a long shot) or, better still, the design of experiments to determine and reduce the cause of variation.

Rule 3: Once production starts, take two consecutive units from the process periodically. The following possibilities can occur:

(a) If both units fall in the green zone, continue production.

(b) If one unit is in the green zone and the other in one of the yellow zones, the process is still in control. Continue production.

(c) If both units fall in the yellow zones (with both in the same yellow zone or one in one yellow zone and the second in the other), stop production and conduct an investigation into the cause of variation.

(d) If even one unit falls in the red zone, there is a known reject and production must be stopped and the reject cause investigated.

When the process is stopped, as in (c) and (d), and the cause of variation identified and reduced (or eliminated), rule 2—that is, five units in a row in the green zone—must be reapplied before production can resume.

Rule 4: The frequency of sampling of two consecutive units is determined by dividing the time period between two stoppages (that is, between two pairs of yellows) by 6.* In other words, if there is a stoppage (two yellows), say, at 9 A.M., and the process is corrected and restarted soon after, and this is followed by another stoppage at 12 noon (2 yellows again), then the period of three hours between these stoppages is divided by 6, to give a frequency of sampling every half hour. If, on the other hand, the period between two stoppages is three days, the frequency of sampling is every half day.

Figure 14-5 is a graphic portrayal of precontrol, with a summary of the four simple rules. (The frequency distribution on the right is a special case, where the process width and the specification width are equal. It is only shown as an illustration.)

The Statistical Power of Precontrol

The theory behind the effectiveness of precontrol is based on the multiplication theorem of probabilities and the binomial distribution. While the

---

*When precontrol was first developed, the time period between two stoppages had to be divided by 24 to determine the frequency of sampling. This was later found to be much too conservative and the number was changed to 6. However, if much greater protection, against continuing a process that should be stopped, is desired, the frequency of sampling can be increased to 10, 12, 15, or even up to 24. In most industrial applications, such an increase is not at all necessary.

Figure 14-5. Simple precontrol rules.

1. Draw two precontrol (P-C) lines in the middle half of specification width.

2. To determine process capability, five units in a row must be within P-C lines (green zone). If not use diagnostic tools to reduce variation.

3. In production, sample two units consecutively and periodically.

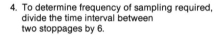

Condition	Action
1. Two units in green zone	Continue
2. One unit in green and one unit in yellow	Continue
3. Two units in yellow	Stop*
4. One unit in red	Stop*

*To resume production, five units in a row must be within the green zone.

4. To determine frequency of sampling required, divide the time interval between two stoppages by 6.

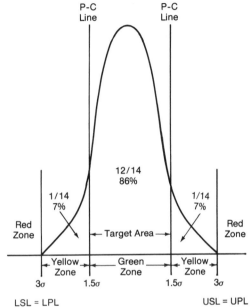

mathematical derivation of the alpha (α) and beta (β) risks for precontrol is beyond the scope of this book, the following is a summary:

- The worst α risk, the risk of overcorrection—that is, stopping a process when it should continue—is around 2 percent.
- The worst β risk, the risk of allowing a process to continue when it should be stopped, is close to 1.5 percent.
- When the process width is greater than the specification width—generally c_{P_k}'s of 0.8 or less—precontrol is so sensitive that it will stop the process at least ninety-nine times out of one hundred and force an improvement investigation.
- When the process width is 75 percent or less of the specification width—

$^{c}p_k$'s of 1.33 or more—the use of precontrol becomes most productive. The process is in control and precontrol will keep it there.
- When the process width is 50 percent of the specification width—$^{c}p_k$'s of 2.0—precontrol will allow hundreds and thousands of units to be produced without a single reject!

The beauty of precontrol, therefore, is that it is an ideal incentive/penalty tool. It penalizes poor quality by shutting down the process so often that problem solving with the use of design of experiments becomes imperative. It rewards good quality by sampling more and more infrequently. Control charts, on the other hand, have no sampling rule or built-in flexibility to deal with this important feature.

Charting Precontrol: Easing the Operator's Burden

With the use of control charts, keeping a graphic record with a chart is mandatory. With precontrol, by contrast, the machine or process operator has only to follow the simplest of rules—"two greens or one green and one yellow: continue; two yellows or one red: stop." There is no need to distract the operator with long and painful data entries or graph plots. However, if a precontrol chart is required for historic purposes or as proof of control from a supplier, the operator can just make easy slash-mark entries on pre-recorded forms having green, yellow, and red zones. Figure 14-6 is an example of a precontrol chart used in controlling the thickness of chrome nickel, and gold deposits on glass in a sputtering machine. The actual readings are recorded for each precontrol sample of two units. From these readings, ^{c}p and $^{c}p_k$ values are easily calculated and histograms plotted, if required. There is no need for manual calculations, handheld calculators, or expensive computer programs, and this is an important advantage for small suppliers who do not want to see money thrown at a process requiring expensive control charts.

Tackling Multiple Quality Characteristics

Precontrol is also a far more economical tool in controlling multiple quality characteristics on a product or process. As an example, if the variations in a thirty-six-cavity mold must be monitored in an injection molding machine, the number of readings required to establish even trial control limits in a control chart would average 3,600. By contrast, precontrol would determine process capability with five readings for each cavity, or a total of 180 readings. In monitoring the process, precontrol would require only 40 percent or 50 percent of the ongoing readings in control charts. Further, if the process is stable, the sampling rule in precontrol of six samplings be-

Figure 14-6. Typical precontrol chart.

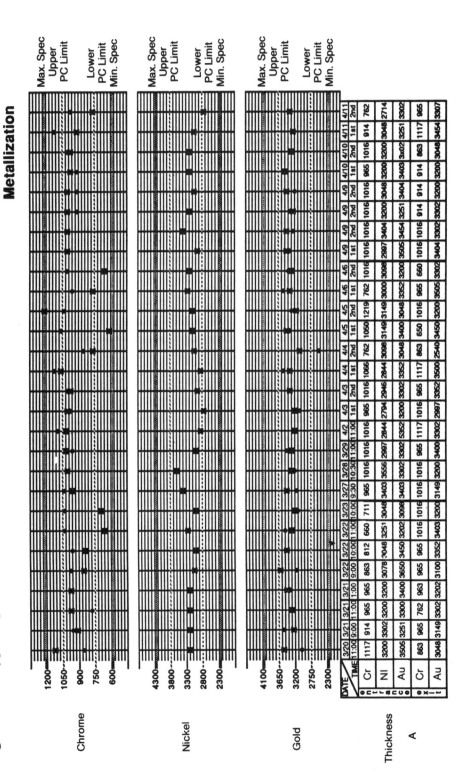

Metallization

tween two pairs of yellows would allow those percentages to be reduced to one to 10 percent of control chart samples.

It must also be pointed out that it is not necessary to monitor all parameters of a product or process continuously after initial process capability has been confirmed on each parameter. Only the most important or the most troublesome parameters need to be sampled. As an example, in the case of the thirty-six-cavity mold, there may be only three or four cavities with large variations that need ongoing surveillance. The rest can be monitored infrequently or not at all.

The Versatility of Precontrol

The rule of six samplings between two stoppages need not be associated with time alone. In a very fast operation, where several hundred units are produced in a minute, the quantity of units between two stoppages (two pairs of yellows) can be divided by 6 to determine sampling frequency.

Precontrol is also a versatile technique in determining when to adjust a process or change a tool, rather than at fixed or arbitrary time periods. The time to change is when the process drifts into one or the other yellow region. Two yellows give the signal. It is as simple as that.

Another feature of precontrol is its applicability to one-sided specification limits. As an example, consider a product with a minimum requirement of 10 volts, but no maximum. Instead of two precontrol lines drawn in the middle half of the distance between the lower and upper specification limit, there would now be only a single precontrol line. It would be located midway between a desired target or design center and the lower specification limit. Alternatively, it could be located between the product average and the lower specification limit. In the above example, if the design center is at 15 volts, the single precontrol line would be drawn at 12.5 volts. If the average of the product is 16 and the alternative method is used, the single precontrol line would be at 13.

Converting Attributes into Variables: The "Bo Derek" Scale

Because precontrol deals primarily with measurements of continuous values, called variables, it may appear to the uninitiated that it cannot be applied to attributes that deal in discrete numbers, such as accept or reject, pass or fail. They may argue that although precontrol is a good substitute for $\overline{X}$ and R control charts, the use of p and c control charts* is unavoid-

---

*These p and c charts suffer from the same fundamental weaknesses as $\overline{X}$ and R charts, and because they deal with attributes they lack the discriminating power of variables. They are even poorer than $\overline{X}$ and R control charts and, for this reason, will not be discussed in this book.

able. Attributes, however, need not be any limitation whatsoever on precontrol.

The trick is to convert an attribute into an "artificial" variable, using a numerical scale from 1 to 10. This is humorously called the Bo Derek scale in reference to the actress's movie *Ten*. Here the number 10 would correspond to perfection in the quality characteristic being measured while the number 1 would equate with the worst possible reject. There would be other grades of quality ranging between these two extremes. As an example, to convert attributes such as paint, color, scratches, gouges, dents, and pinholes to variables, a committee consisting of the customer, Sales Engineering, Manufacturing, and Quality would grade ten physical samples, with scores ranging from a totally unacceptable 1 to a perfect 10. These physical samples, then, would constitute a "variables scale" to determine the appropriate number for a similar defect in production. In case physical samples are too difficult or too inflexible to develop and maintain, color photographs can be substituted. (It may not be necessary to use a full 1 to 10 scale. A truncated 1 to 5 scale can sometimes suffice.) In a numerical scale of this kind, let us assume that the specification limits are from 4 (worst acceptable) to 10 (perfect). Because this is, in reality, a one-sided specification, a single precontrol line would be drawn at 7.

Weighting Attributes in Terms of Importance

Another weakness of p and c control charts is that they lump all types of defects into a single total for attributes. Such charts lack the sensitivity to grade defects by importance. In precontrol, every defect mode is assigned a weight in proportion to its importance. This weight, multiplied by the number of defects in that mode, gives the score for each defect type. These scores when added up result in a weighted total for a particular time, and a precontrol chart can then be plotted. Such charts have the effect of a magnified scale that is far more sensitive and pinpointed in terms of defect modes than a catchall p or c chart. Figure 14-7 is an example of such a precontrol chart. It expands solder defects, which used to be considered either "good" or "bad" into four categories of "over-solder" (top portion of chart) defects and four categories of "under-solder" (bottom portion of chart) defects, each with its own weight based on the importance of the defect in terms of potential field failure. The precontrol chart highlights the various types of defects found at a particular time; trends with time; and whether or not the weighted defect scores exceed the tight precontrol lines of fifty defects per million connections (that is, 50 ppm).

I. *A CAPSULE COMPARISON OF CONTROL CHARTS VS. PRECONTROL*
Table 14-5 compares control charts with precontrol. It clearly demonstrates the weaknesses of control charts versus the strengths of precontrol in terms

Figure 14-7. A precontrol chart converting attributes into variables on an expanded scale.

Wave Solder Operation

Over-Solder Code	Pts			
Solder Shorts	+20		X	XX
Near Shorts	+10			
Excess Solder	+5			
Capping	+5			
Total				

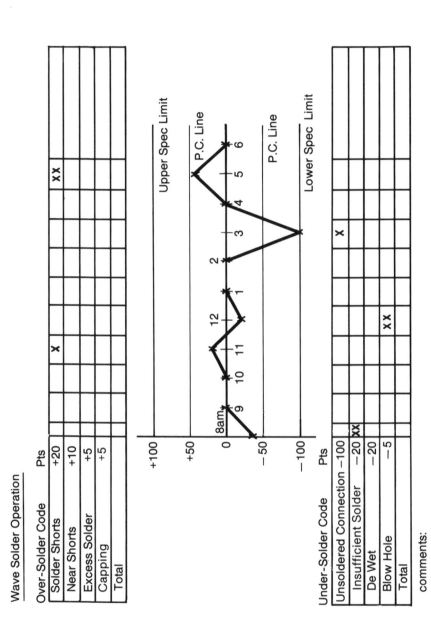

Under-Solder Code	Pts			
Unsoldered Connection	−100			
Insufficient Solder	−20	XX	X	
De Wet	−20			
Blow Hole	−5		XX	
Total				

comments:

Table 14-5. The advantages of precontrol over control charts.

Characteristic	Control Charts	Precontrol
1. Simplicity	• *Complex* calculations of control.	• *Simple:* Precontrol is middle half of spec width.
2. Use by operators	• *Difficult:* Charting mandatory, interpretation unclear.	• *Easy:* Green and yellow zones a practical approach for all workers.
3. Mathematics	• *Involved:* $\overline{X}$, R, control limits and process limits must be calculated.	• *Elementary:* User must know only how to divide by 4.
4. Small production runs	• Useless for production runs below 500 units; sampling of 80–150 units required before even trial limits can be established.	• Can be used for production runs above 20 units; precontrol lines predetermined by specs (which can be narrowed).
5. Recalibration of control limits	• *Frequent:* No such thing in industry as a constant-cause system.	• *None needed* unless specs "goal posts" are moved inward.
6. Machine adjustments	• *Time consuming:* Any adjustment requires another trial run of 80–150 units.	• *Instant,* based on two units.
7. Frequency of sampling	• *Vague, arbitrary.*	• *Simple rule:* Six samplings between two stoppages/ adjustments.
8. Discriminating power	• *Weak:* α risk of rejection by chart when there are no rejects is high. β risk of acceptance (in control), when there are rejects, is high; little relationship to specs.	• *Excellent:* α risk of rejection by precontrol is low; <2% under worst conditions, with c_{p_k} of 1.66. β risk <1.36% under worst conditions; 0% with c_{p_k} of 1.66.

(continued)

Table 14-5. *Continued.*

Characteristic	Control Charts	Precontrol
9. Attribute charts	P and C charts do not distinguish between defect mode types or importance.	Attribute charts can be converted to precontrol charts by weighting defect modes and devising an arbitrary rating scale.
10. Economy	*Expensive:* Calculations, paperwork, larger samples, more frequent sampling, long trial runs required.	*Inexpensive:* Calculations simple, minimum paperwork, small samples, infrequent sampling if quality is good, process capability determined by just five units.

of its simplicity; ease of use by operators; low degree of mathematical complexity; applicability to small production runs; recalibration of control limits; machine adjustments; frequency of sampling; discriminating power; conversion of attribute charts; and, most important of all, economy.

As a postscript, if precontrol had been used in Figure 14-2 to control the bushing length instead of control charts, the very first sample at 8 a.m. would have indicated that the 5 units checked would have fallen beyond the precontrol lines.

Precontrol Example: The Wire Bonder

An automatic wire bonder that bonds a wire the thickness of a human hair to the die and post of a transistor is put on precontrol to maintain statistical control. The integrity of the wire bond is checked with a destructive pull test on the wire. The specification for bond strength, before the bond is lifted on either side, is a minimum of 6 gm and a maximum of 14 gm. The initial sample of five units had the following readings: 8.7 gm, 9.0 gm, 9.4 gm, 8.9 gm, 10 gm. When full production began, the period between two stoppages (two pairs of yellows) averaged twelve hours. During subsequent production, the results of two sample units, drawn periodically from the process, were as follows:

Sample No.	Unit 1	Unit 2	Action
1	9.4	9.0	_____
2	9.0	8.8	_____
3	8.9	8.6	_____
4	8.5	8.1	_____
5	8.4	8.0	_____
6	8.0	8.0	_____
7	8.0	7.6	_____
8	7.5	7.3	_____
9	13.0	13.0	_____
10	12.0	12 .0	_____
11	11.6	11.4	_____
12	11.0	10.8	_____

The calculations and interpretation are as follows:

- *Precontrol lines:* Precontrol lines are at 8 and 12 gm.
- *Process in control?* Process is in control. All five units in the initial sample are within the precontrol lines (green zone).
- *Sampling frequency:* Sampling frequency should be 12/6 hours, that is, every 2 hours.
- *Action on continuous product:* Action on sample numbers 1 through 7 and 10 through 12: Continue product. Action on sample numbers 8 and 9: Stop production. (In actual practice, the process must be adjusted or corrected after sample number 8, and then five more units drawn and determined to be within the green zone before the sampling of two units is resumed. The same holds for sample number 9.)
- *Nonrandom trends:* There are three nonrandom trends in data associated with question 4:
  1. Bond strengths are getting lower and lower until a correction is made after sample number 8. Probable cause is bond contamination or loss of bond energy. In any case, the trend needs to be investigated, quite apart from whether production continues or stops.
  2. The second reading in each sample is almost always lower than the first. The probable cause may be in the measuring instrument or in the fixture.
  3. Sample number 9 indicates an overcorrection (pull strengths too high).

Elementary SPC Tools

The Japanese abandoned SPC tools for the more powerful DOE techniques with one major exception. They have trained their entire direct labor force in elementary SPC tools so that workers can tackle low-grade quality problems through their quality circles, *Kaizen* (improvement) teams, and employee suggestions.* The result? Instead of a few professionals to tackle problems, Japanese companies now have a whole host, albeit low-grade, of problem solvers.

Table 14-6 lists these elementary SPC techniques, often called the seven tools of quality control (the seventh tool, control charts, is discussed earlier in this chapter), that every Japanese line worker learns and uses. Several of these elementary tools are now being blindly copied by U.S. companies. Because they are both limited in value and fully explained in many texts on the subject of quality control, I shall only outline their objectives and methodologies in the following pages.

Uses of Simple SPC Techniques

PDCA (Plan, Do, Check, Act). Allegedly taught by Deming, the PDCA cycle has recently been claimed as a Japanese innovation. It is a variant of the traditional problem-solving approach of "observe, think, try, explain." As a technical problem-solving tool, it has the same poor effectiveness as brainstorming and Kepner-Tragoe detective techniques.

Data Collection and Analysis. This is the first step on the long road to variation identification and reduction. Sound planning is the key to effective data collection. The "why, what, when, where, who, and how" of data must be established "a priori" (that is, before the fact). This avoids drowning teams and plants in meaningless and useless data. Common pitfalls include: not defining the objective; not knowing what parameter to measure or how to measure it; not having sufficiently accurate equipment for the measurement; not randomizing (a fundamental statistical flaw in Taguchi's design of experiments); and poor stratification of data. Similarly, the analysis of data should only be undertaken with proven DOE methods rather than with hit-and-miss approaches such as PDCA, brainstorming, cause and effect diagrams, and so forth.

Graphs/Charts. These are tools for the organization, summarization, and statistical display of data. As in the case of data collection and analysis, the purpose of graphs and charts should be clearly established and their usefulness and longevity periodically reexamined.

Checksheets/Tally Sheets/Histograms/Frequency Distributions. Checksheets are used for process distribution; defective items, cause/defect locations

---

*The large number of suggestions turned in by Japanese workers is legendary. Whereas the average number of suggestions per employee per year in the United States is 0.1, the figure in Japan is more than 10. In those Japanese companies that compete directly with American firms, the number is closer to 50. Even more important, more than 80 percent of these worker suggestions are approved by Japanese management. The quality circles experiment with their own ideas, try pilot runs, and submit their suggestions to management only when they are sure of success. Management approval then becomes almost automatic.

Table 14-6. Elementary SPC tools.

Tool	Objective	Methodology	When to Use	Typical Users
1. PDCA (<u>P</u>lan, <u>D</u>o, <u>C</u>heck, <u>A</u>ct)	Problem-solve by trial and error	Plan the work; execute; check results; take action if there is a deviation between desired and actual results. Repeat the cycle time till deviation is reduced to zero.	When more powerful tools are unknown	Mostly line workers
2. Data collection and analysis	■ Assess quality ■ Control a product ■ Regulate a process ■ Accept/reject product ■ Interpret observations	Define specific reason for collecting data; decide on measurement criteria (attribute vs. variable vs. rank); assure accuracy of measuring equipment (minimum five) times greater than product requirement); randomize; stratify data collection (time, material, machine, operator, type, and location of defects); analyze data using several SPC, DOE tools.	At all times	Universal
3. Graphs/charts	■ Display trends ■ Condense data ■ Explain to others	Select two or more parameters to be displayed; determine method of display (bar, line, or circle graphs are the most common); select the most appropriate scales of the parameters for maximum visual impact.	At all times	Universal
4. ■ Checksheets	■ Transform raw data into categories	■ Determine categories into which data are subdivided (e.g., types of defects, location of defects, days in the week, etc.). Enter quantities in each category.	In preparation for a histogram or frequency distribution	Universal
■ Tally sheets	■ Arrange groups, cells in semipictorial fashion	■ Divide variable being recorded into ten levels or cells. Plot cell boundaries or mid-points. Make tally (with slash marks) of the number of observations in each cell.		

(continued)

Table 14-6. *Continued.*

Tool	Objective	Methodology	When to Use	Typical Users
• Histograms/ frequency distribution	• Translate data into a picture of the average and spread of a quality characteristic	• Convert tally sheet data into bar graphs (histograms) or line graphs (frequency distributions) showing the relationship between various values of a quality characteristic and the number of observations (or percentage of the total) in each value.	For process capability studies in preproduction or production	Engineers, technicians, line workers
5. Pareto's Law	Separate the vital few causes of a problem or effect from the trivial many; concentrate attention on former	Identify as many causes as possible of a problem and the contribution of each to a given effect ($, percentages, etc.); plot causes on X-axis, effects (cumulative) on Y-axis in ascending or descending order of magnitude. Prioritize action on those few causes that account for most of the effect (generally, 20% or less of causes contribute 80% or more of effect).	At all times	Universal— an excellent tool for prioritization in manufacturing or white-collar work
6. Brainstorming	• Generate as many ideas as possible to solve a problem or improve a process, utilizing synergistic power of a group	• Gather a group most concerned with problem; define problem precisely; ask each member to write down cause of problem or improvement ideas; then, open the floor for an outpouring of ideas, rational or irrational; no criticisms allowed; record ideas; narrow down the most worthwhile ideas.	• Initial problem solving • "Process" improvement	• Quality circles, • Improvement teams

• Cause and Effect Diagram	• Organize problem causes into main groups and sub-groups, in order to have total visibility of all causes, and determine where to start corrective action	• Define the problem; construct a "fishbone" diagram with the major causes (e.g., material, machine, method, and man) as the main "branches" and add detailed causes within each main cause as "twigs". Quantify the spec limits established for each cause where possible, the actual value measured for each cause and its effect upon the problem. If a relationship between cause and effect can be shown quantitatively, draw a box around the cause. If the relationship is difficult to quantify, underline the cause. If there is no proof that a cause is related to the effect, do not mark the cause. Prioritize the most important causes with a circle. Experiment with these in PDCA fashion until root cause is located.	Same as above	Same as above
• CEDAC Cause and Effect Diagram with the Addition of Cards	• Same as Cause and Effect Diagram, but earlier identification of causes and better worker participation	• Workers, at their individual work stations, identify causes on the spot as they occur. Cards used to identify such causes can then be readily changed by the workers.	Same as above	Same as above

(sometimes referred to as "measles charts"); and as memory joggers for inspectors and Quality Control in checking product. Their main function is to simplify data gathering and to arrange data for statistical interpretation and analysis.

Tally sheets are special forms of checksheets used to record data, keep score of a process in operation, and divide data into distinct groups to facilitate statistical interpretation.

Histograms and frequency distributions provide a graphic portrayal of variability. Their shape often gives clues about the process measured, for example, mixed lots (bimodal distribution); screened lots (truncated distribution); amount of spread relative to specifications (c_p), noncentered spread relative to specifications ($^{c_{p_k}}$).

There are two general characteristics of frequency distributions that can be quantified: central tendency and dispersion. Central tendency is the bunching up effect of observations of a particular quality characteristic near the center and can be measured by average ($\overline{X}$) of all the observations, mode (the value of a quality characteristic with the largest number of observations), and median (the value that divides the number of observations into two equal parts). Dispersion is the spread of the observations and can be measured by range (R), that is, the highest observation minus the lowest, and standard deviation, which is approximately one-sixth of range (but only for a normal distribution).

Pareto's Law. Vilfredo Federico Pareto was a nineteenth-century Italian economist who studied the distribution of income in Italy and concluded that a very limited number of people owned most of its wealth. The study produced the famous Pareto-Lorenz maldistribution law, which states that cause and effect are not linearly related; that a few causes produce most of a given effect; and, more specifically, that 20 percent or less of causes produce 80 percent or more of effects.

Dr. Joe Juran, however, is credited with converting Pareto's law into a versatile, universal industrial tool in such diverse disciplines as quality, manufacturing, suppliers, materials, inventory control, cycle time, value engineering, sales, and marketing—in fact, to any industrial situation, blue-collar or white-collar. By separating the few, important causes of industrial phenomenon from the trivial many, work on the few causes can be prioritized. Figure 14-8 is a typical example of the usefulness of a Pareto chart, the technique being applied here to reducing losses generated in a metal machining process. Three items, which alone accounted for $2,800 per month of loss (or more than 80 percent of the total loss) in (a), were prioritized for improvement and losses reduced to $1,400 per month in (b) before the remaining problems were tackled.

Brainstorming/Cause and Effect Diagrams/CEDAC. Brainstorming is a good example of a beautiful technique used for wrong applications. In the field of the social sciences and even in white-collar industrial work, it is a mar-

Figure 14-8. Pareto charts showing financial losses before and after improvement action was taken.

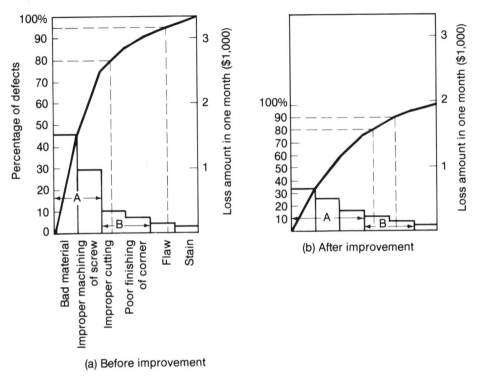

(a) Before improvement

(b) After improvement

velous tool for generating and stimulating the maximum number of ideas, uitilizing group synergy. In fact, in value engineering, it is an essential element of the VE job plan. However, its effectiveness in quality problem solving is highly overrated. Even though group ideas are generally better than individual ones, guessing at problems is a kindergarten approach to finding the root cause of variation.

Cause and effect diagrams were developed by Dr. Kaoru Ishikawa, one of the foremost authorities on quality control in Japan. As a result, it is often called the Ishikawa diagram or, by reason of its shape, a fishbone diagram. In Japan, it is probably the most widely used quality control tool for problem solving among blue-collar workers. However, its effectiveness is poor. At best, it is like playing Russian roulette. At worst, its success probabilities are not much better than the odds in Las Vegas. It is a hit-and-miss process in which the solution can take months, even years. Often, because only one cause is varied at a time, interaction effects are missed, resulting in partial

Figure 14-9. Cause and effect diagram of a wave solder experiment.

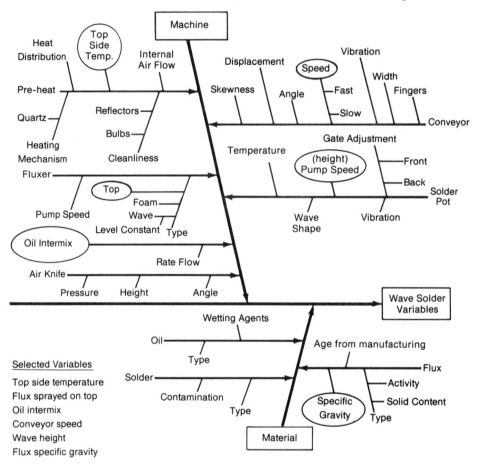

Source: Adi K. Bhote, Motorola, Inc.

solutions and marginal improvements in quality. But it has a few redeeming features.

Figure 14-9 is an example of a cause and effect diagram, listing all the possible causes that can produce solder defects in a wave solder process. (For the sake of simplicity, only two major branches—machine and machine materials—are shown. For a complete picture, board and electronic component branches should be added to the diagram). The figure is an excellent compilation of all the variables that can cause a solder defect. It also highlights, by means of circles, those variables judged to be important. In more complex charts, the specification limits and the observed variations from those limits are recorded for each cause. Such observations, if carefully recorded, can provide some leads in problem solving. In the final analysis, however, guesses, hunches, opinions, and engineering judgment are crude problem-solving tools in comparison to DOE techniques.

CEDAC is the acronym for *c*ause and *e*ffect *d*iagram with the *a*ddition of *c*ards. Developed by Ryuji Fukuda, another noted Japanese authority, the technique is explained in detail in his book *Managerial Engineering*, published by Productivity, Inc. CEDAC represents an improvement over the Ishikawa cause and effect diagram in that workers are free to change any "branch" or "twig" cause in the diagram as they observe new phenomena in a process and gain new insights. The use of cards, under their own control, facilitates such instant updating of causes. Worker participation is enhanced and raw, nonquantifiable information is captured before it "evaporates" in tedious data gathering. Yet CEDAC suffers from the same judgment weaknesses that cause and effect diagrams contain.

Chapter 15

Space Age Reliability at Commercial Prices

By use of well designed, higher-than-normal stress testing and good statistical analysis, it is possible and practical to reach unbelievably low failure rates and satisfy consumer demands for maximum reliability.

—Jack Reddy, President, Reddy, Rosen and Woods

The Lunar Module: A Textbook Example of the Ultimate in Reliability

It is dangerous to title a chapter using the phrase "space age reliability" after the Challenger disaster set back the ambitious U.S. space program. Even the milestones in the old Apollo flight to the moon were successfully crossed only after several failures and only after enormous sums of money had been thrown at the problems encountered. Yet there is one shining example of space age reliability that was achieved the very first time it was actually tested in space. This is the lunar module, which was subjected to rigorous multiple environment overstress tests under the guiding genius of Dorian Shainin. Of all the elements of space hardware used in the Apollo program, the lunar module was the only one that could not be tested "in the field." It had to work when landing on the moon and it had to work when taking off from the moon. There was no second chance. The objective

244

of this chapter is to capture lunar module reliability techniques that can be applied to commercial industry without the crushing financial burden of the kind of brute-force testing prescribed by military programs.

Reliability Goals, Targeting, and Prediction

Reliability Goals

Reliability, as distinguished from quality, has two extra dimensions in its definition—time and stress. More often than not, reliability is not quantified by a customer, or if it is, it is never in the form of a firm specification. The first line of defense, therefore, in the battle for reliability is a quantified reliability goal, mutually determined by customer and supplier. This is usually expressed in terms of a failure rate per year or mean time between failure (MTBF), or, in the case of automated equipment/processes, mean time between assists (MTBA). In addition, the environments to which the product is subjected must be carefully quantified. If there is a warranty agreement, the warranty period (or mileage or both) must also be specified. Automobile companies have now extended their warranties to customers from the old 12-12, that is, 12 months or 12,000 miles, to 7-70, that is, 7 years or 70,000 miles, which underscores the importance of reliability. Sometimes, a financial incentive or penalty is negotiated between customer and supplier—an incentive for exceeding the reliability goal or a penalty for failing to achieve such a goal.

Reliability Targeting or Budgeting

An overall product reliability goal is next subdivided by major subsystem or subassembly, based on such factors as parts count, complexity, and state-of-the-art components. This is known as reliability targeting or budgeting. As an example, a car company, with an overall reliability goal of 140 failures per 100 cars (usually designated R/100) during a two-year warranty period on one of its models, apportioned the following failure rates to its major subsystems:

	R/100
Engine	42
Power train	32
Electrical	26
Chassis	11
Other	29
Total	140

Each subsystem or subassembly can then be further broken down into sub-subassemblies and components, each with its apportioned failure rates.

Reliability Prediction Study

After reliability budgeting is performed, a reliability prediction study is conducted on the new product, and this can then be compared against the reliability goal. The failure rate of each part in the product is estimated, based on one or more of the following:

- Mil-Handbook 217D: Part Stress Analysis Method for electronic parts.
- RADC-TR-75-22: for nonelectronic parts.
- Government-Industry Data Exchange Program (GIDEP).
- Actual, accumulated field history on similar parts in similar products and similar environments.

Of the methods listed, the last is the most accurate and meaningful. Government publications such as Mil-H-217D tend to produce failure rates so high that they would be a disaster in the tough commercial world. However, Mil H-217D serves a useful purpose if its projected failure rates are used as comparison values—to determine stress effects—rather than as absolute values.

Table 15-1 is an example of both a reliability budgeting process and a prediction study on an electronic lean burn system developed by a supplier for an automobile company. It compares the predicted failure rates against targeted or budgeted failure rates for each component. It is obvious from the study that the overall predicted failure rate of 1.854 percent per year is inadequate to meet the lean burn system's targeted failure rate of 1.0 percent per year, as required by the car manufacturer. The Pareto principle of the "vital few" versus the "trivial many" is illustrated beautifully in this example, where five components out of a total of eighty-eight account for more than 80 percent of the total failure rate of 1.854 percent. To improve reliability to the targeted level, the failure rates of these five components must be drastically reduced.

Reducing High-Failure-Rate Parts Paper Studies

De-Rating

The object of de-rating is to reduce stress on parts sufficiently to almost make them "loaf." In civil engineering, designs are strengthened by factors

Table 15-1. Reliability prediction study on electronic lean burn system.

Part	Predicted Failure Rate %/year	Budgeted Failure Rate %/year	Quantity	Total Predicted Failure Rate %/year	Total Budgeted Failure Rate %/year
Microprocessor	0.500	0.300	1	0.500	0.300
ROM (1K)	0.180	0.100	1	0.180	0.100
RAM (64 Bit)	0.180	0.100	1	0.180	0.100
PROM	0.180	0.100	1	0.180	0.100
Custom I/O	0.300	0.200	1	0.300	0.200
Op-amp	0.035	0.020	1	0.035	0.020
To-3	0.100	0.005	1	0.100	0.005
To-220	0.040	0.020	3	0.120	0.060
To-92	0.002	0.002	5	0.010	0.010
Diodes (plastic)	0.005	0.003	8	0.040	0.024
Diodes (glass)	0.007	0.004	5	0.035	0.020
Power Zfner	0.010	0.005	1	0.010	0.005
Disc cap	0.001	0.001	7	0.007	0.007
Mylar cap	0.002	0.002	1	0.002	0.002
Electrolytic	0.003	0.002	3	0.009	0.006
Carbon film resis.	0.0001	0.0001	45	0.0045	0.0045
W/W resis.	0.0005	0.0005	3	0.0015	0.0015
P.C. board	0.010	0.006	1	0.010	0.006
Connectors	0.0025	0.002	2	0.005	0.004
Workmanship				0.025	0.025
Grand total				1.8540	1.000

of 6 to 1 and more as a measure of extreme protection. Similarly, in electronics, stresses, such as power, voltage, current, and temperature, are reduced on individual components to ensure the same reliability guard band. Computer-aided engineering and thermal scanning can detect overstressed mechanical configurations and "hot spots," respectively, and correct them at the prototype stage of design.

Failure Mode Effects Analysis

If the predicted failure rate is higher than the budgeted failure rate, as in Table 15-1, the few parts contributing the most to the total failure rate are then subjected to an intensive scrutiny. This is called a failure mode effects analysis (FMEA). Its objectives are to:

- Identify the weak links: (a) of product design; (b) of supplier parts; (c) of key processes. Each requires its own FMEA.

- Pinpoint failure modes and quantify their effects on customers.
- Correct potential failure modes "before the fact" to improve reliability.

Table 15-2 is an example of an FMEA. The first column identifies those parts with the highest projected failure rates in the reliability prediction study. The second column indicates the failure mode, that is, the way in which the part is most likely to fail. The third describes the effect of the failure on the end user. The fourth assigns the cause of failure, the probable root cause. The fifth, sixth, and seventh columns are a subjective rating (from 1 to 10; 1 being the best and 10 the worst) of (1) the probability of failure occurrence; (2) the severity of the failure (impact on the customer); and (3) the nondetectability of such a failure in the plant. The eighth column shows the results of multiplying columns 5, 6, and 7 to produce a risk priority number. A high score for risk priority would require more concentrated action than a low score.

Then comes the most important part of the FMEA discipline—the corrective action recommended (column 9). Typical actions would include redesigning the part; adding redundancy (through a parallel path); using stress screens to weed out infant mortality failures; changing suppliers; or changing materials. Another rating, reassessing the probability of occurrence, severity, and nondetectability (columns 10, 11, and 12) is estimated and the product of these three ratings calculated as a new risk priority (column 13). This new risk priority should be considerably lower than the old risk priority (column 8), reflecting a significant improvement in the projected reliability on the highest-failure-rate parts in the reliability prediction study.

FMEAs are most effective when conducted at three levels. The first is at the design preprototype stage, where the objective is to anticipate weak links of design of concern to the design engineer and to reduce or prevent these weaknesses. The second FMEA study is conducted by the supplier of the critical parts identified in the design FMEA study. The third is a process FMEA study, conducted by Process/Manufacturing Engineering on the key processes associated with the designated product. Unfortunately, if design FMEAs are rare, supplier FMEAs are almost nonexistent.

Practical FMEA

An interesting innovation in the FMEA technique is labeled "Practical FMEA." This is conducted at the prototype stage of design, where parts are deliberately made to fail in various predetermined ways in order to gauge the effect upon the outputs. It represents an improvement upon a paper study because it is an actual simulation that can take into account interactions between various parts. The results could go both ways, with certain effects upon monitored outputs magnified or found to be inconsequential.

Table 15-2. Failure mode effects analysis (FMEA).

Project Name: <u>Power Supply</u>   Prepared By: <u>D. Dengel</u>

1	*2*	*3*	*4*	*5*	*6*	*7*	*8*	*9*	*10*	*11*	*12*	*13*
Part Name/ Function	*Failure Mode*	*Effect of Failure*	*Cause(s) of Failure*	*Occurrence*	*Severity*	*Detectability*	*Priority*	*Recommended Corrective Action and Status*	*Occurrence*	*Severity*	*Detectability*	*Priority*
C3 660 uF/35V Electrolytic capacitor —	Open	Decreased noise filtering of battery line.	Defect in component manufacture. Excessive vibration.	1	2	10	20	Will be changed to 21MF by development engineering for improved filter action (Issue '0').	1	2	10	20
PI—Filter	Short	Catastrophic. Fuse F1 blows. ATC enters default defrost mode. DIS inoperative.	Excessive heat. Voltage transient defect in component manufacture.	5	9	1	45		5	9	1	45
L1 400 MH Toroidal inductor —	Open	Catastrophic. ATC enters default defrost mode. DIS inoperative.	Excessive vibration. Defect in component manufacture.	10	9	10	900	Epoxy toroid to circuit board to prevent vibration failure.	1	9	1	9
PI—Filter	Short	Decreased noise filtering of battery line.	Defect in component manufacture.	2	3	5	30	Corrected in pilot run (Issue '0').	2	3	5	30
C4 660 UF/35V Electrolytic capacitor —	Open	Decreased noise filtering of battery line.	Excessive stress in component manufacture.	1	2	10	20	Will be changed to 47MF by development engineering for improved filter action (Issue '0').	1	2	10	20
PI—Filter	Short	Catastrophic. Fuse F1 blows. ATC enters default defrost mode. DIS inoperative.	Excessive heat. Voltage transient defect in component manufacture.	5	9	1	45		5	9	1	45
C19 1 UF Monolithic capacitor	Open	Decreased stability of keep-alive circuit for clock microprocessor.	Defect in component manufacture.	5	9	10	450	Has been changed to 100MF for stability of keep-alive circuit at +85°C (Issue '0').	5	9	1	45
U27 Output filter	Short	Catastrophic. No keep-alive voltage for clock microprocessor. DIS inoperative. ATC enters default defrost.	Defect in component manufacture.	5	9	10	450		5	9	1	45

Figure 15-1. A typical fault tree analysis.

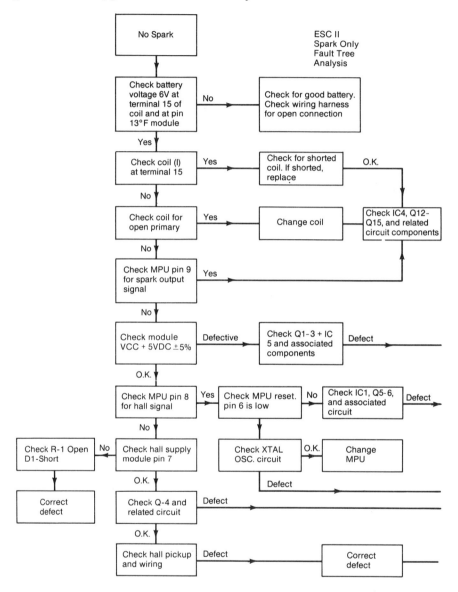

Fault Tree Analysis

Another discipline, closely allied to FMEA is the fault tree analysis (FTA). This is a mirror image of FMEA. In the latter, the study starts with a failed part and estimates its consequences to the customer. In FTA, the start is with a failure in the system that a customer is likely to see. Its several possible causes are then traced in an organized, decision-tree fashion. The objectives are to:

1. Identify various failure modes likely to be seen by the customer.
2. Diagnose these failures, using a systematic procedure.
3. Determine the root cause of these failures.
4. Correct and prevent such root causes "before the fact."

Figure 15-1 is an example of a fault tree analysis in which a "no spark" failure, leading to a "no start" condition in an automobile, can be traced to several possible causes, such as the battery, coil, microprocessor, or other electronic components in the engine.

Both FMEA and FTA are disciplines developed in the United States. Yet nearly twenty years after their introduction around 1970, most quality professionals do not know about them, much less use them. And for most design engineers, FMEA and FTA might as well be written in cuneiform. Japan, by contrast, imported these techniques in the late 1970s and uses them to such an extent that no reputable Japanese company would allow a product to go into production without an FMEA.

Incidentally, a major American tragedy—the Challenger disaster—could have been avoided if the failure of the notorious O-ring, which the supplier's FMEA had clearly identified as a major weakness, had been acted upon instead of being ignored or swept under the rug!

Product Liability Analysis

Product liability analysis (PLA) is the newest of the reliability disciplines. It has risen in importance because of the extreme danger and high costs of product liability suits. PLA provides one of the best exhibits in court by which a manufacturer or supplier can defend the integrity of his design. The PLA study is similar to FTA, but is limited to only those field failures likely to cause user injury.

Figure 15-2 is an example of a product liability analysis conducted on an ignition amplifier. The primary symptoms, "car dead" or "car intermittent," that could result from failure of the ignition amplifier are likely candidates for causing injury to the driver and therefore need a detailed PLA analysis. The relative probabilities of each potential failure mode are listed in brackets. Following such a PLA analysis, the design engineer or the sup-

Figure 15-2. Product liability prevention analysis: Ignition amplifier.

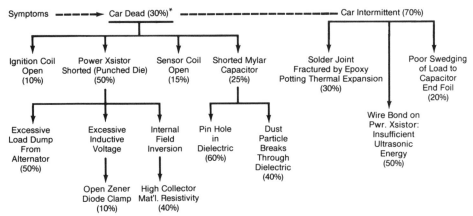

*Figures in brackets indicate *relative* probabilities of failure. Critical path is the highest numbers associated with multiplication of relative individual probabilities.

plier must decide on preventive actions to greatly reduce the likelihood of these dangerous failures.

Multiple Environment Overstress Tests: The Ultimate in Achieving Zero Failures

Just as the design of experiments is the ultimate tool in reducing and eventually eliminating variability, so multiple environment overstress testing is the ultimate tool in reducing and eventually eliminating field failures. Reliability prediction studies, FMEAs and FTAs are useful as reliability "appetizers" or starters. They are, however, only paper studies that need the follow-up of actual testing as the "main meal." There are four menus to choose from, ranging from "el cheapo" to "haute cuisine":

1. *Ordinary life tests.* In these the product is operated for hundreds of hours, or actuations, at benign room temperatures. Most life tests are a waste of time.

2. *Conventional stress tests that are "success oriented".* The objective here is to ensure that there are no failures when the product is subjected to stresses up to the design stress level. Success testing rarely uncovers potential failures that lurk just beneath the surface of the design.

3. *Single environment sequential testing.* Sometimes called accelerated life tests, the stresses in this method go beyond design stress levels, but are

performed one environment/stress at a time. Figure 15-3 is an example of such testing on a radio pager. The stresses—temperature, shock, dust, temperature cycling, mechanical actuations, humidity, and so on—are applied sequentially, with some stresses going beyond prescribed design stress levels.

The theory behind this method is that the acceleration of a particular stress, such as several hundred thermal cycles, will not only produce failures that can be corrected, but also allow a prediction to be made of the number of equivalent years of field life. But such correlation with actual field reliability is more hope than prediction. If any correlation with, say, five years of field history is achieved, it is an accident, a stroke of luck. Further, validation of such predicted reliability may not be known for years. In fact, repeated single environment sequential tests have resulted in such widely varying reliability projections that any meaningful prediction becomes a farce. The central weakness, however, in this method is that the all-important interaction effects between two or more stresses acting simultaneously on the product, as they do in the field, can be completely missed by testing the product one stress at a time.

4. *Multiple environment overstress testing.* The objective of multiple environment overstress testing (MEOST) is less to predict failure rates than to stamp out failures altogether. Its technique is to combine the most important environments/stresses and go beyond the design stress level of each environment to a maximum practical overstress level. The philosophy is not success testing but failure testing. It is only when failures (a minimum of four failures of the same failure mode and same failure mechanism) are generated before the fact that the weak links in the design can be smoked out.

Procedure

The following is a road map on the "how to" of MEOST. Experience has shown that when MEOST is first tried, as an alternative to conventional stress test, failures—similar to actual field failures on the product—are reproduced even before the combined stresses equal the prescribed design stress levels. In parallel tests with single environment sequential testing, MEOST has detected failure modes that the former did not uncover.

Multiple Environment Overstress Test: A Road Map

1. Prioritize customer specifications, including applications, environments, etc.
2. Test 40 units in the field under varying environment/stress conditions and monitor levels with appropriate instrumentation.
3. Plot a frequency distribution of levels for each environment/stress.

Figure 15-3. Example of single environment sequential testing on a radio pager.

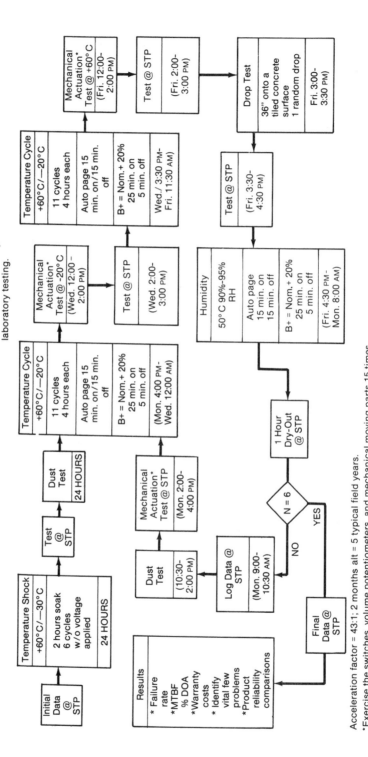

Goal: Simulate 5 years of typical field failures in 60 days of laboratory testing.

Acceleration factor = 43:1; 2 months alt = 5 typical field years.

*Exercise the switches, volume potentiometers, and mechanical moving parts 15 times.

4. Establish the limits for each level that include 39 out of 40 readings (2.5% tail). These limits become the design stress levels.
5. Combine all environments/stresses up to the maximum level determined in Step 4.
6. Select a sample of units (minimum 10, maximum 30), representative of the design being evaluated, and subject it to the combined stresses established in Step 4 for a fraction of the total service life of the product.
7. If failures occur within this limited "operating rectangle," discontinue testing, analyze figures, and strengthen the design.
8. If there are no failures, continue to time stress the units, beyond the design stress level, on a combined stress and time scale until a maximum practical overstress level is reached.
9. If failures occur, determine if the failure mode (or modes) is artificial (that is, not likely under actual field conditions) or realistic.
10. Ignore the failures, if the failure mode is artificial or, if realistic, there are three or less failures of a particular failure mechanism.
11. If four or more realistic failures of the same failure mode and same figure mechanism occur, plot the failure points (1% failures vs. stress time on Weibull paper). Connect the failure points and project down to a 1% failure point.
12. If this 1% failure point falls inside the operating rectangle, stop the testing, analyze the root cause of the failures, and change the design or materials.
13. If the 1% failure point falls outside the operating rectangle, continue testing with another set of units for a larger fraction of the total service life.
14. Repeat steps 7 through 12. If the 1% failure point falls outside the operating rectangle, the product is given qualified approval to go into production.
15. In cooperation with the customer, retrieve a few units from the field that have known operating times and test these units in the same manner. It would be desirable to repeat this test with increasing field times. If the 1% failure point clears the operating rectangle, the product can be considered to give the highest reliability that can be achieved.

Results

Figure 15-4 shows how four stresses/environments—temperature cycling, humidity, voltage, and transients—were combined, along with time, to stimulate field conditions. Table 15-3 shows the results of comparison tests on an automotive electronics subassembly, using both the old single environment sequential testing versus MEOST. There is clear evidence that while

Figure 15-4. Multiple environment overstress test plan.

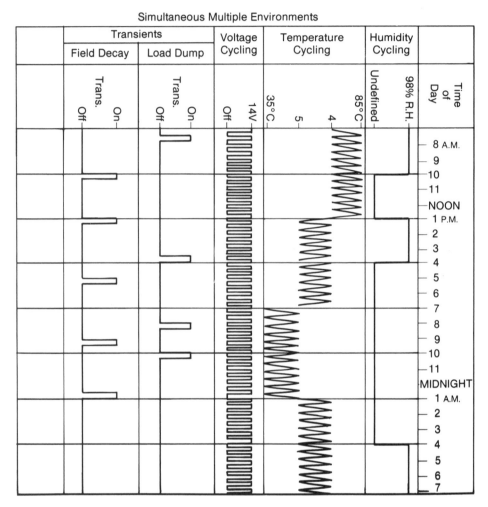

the former detected no failures, MEOST apprehended several important reliability failures both within the operating rectangle (no overstress) and beyond. It should also be noted that MEOST greatly reduces the quantity of units to be tested (between seven and fifteen for MEOST versus more than thirty for single environment sequential testing) as well as the time and costs required for such tests.

In another example, an electronic engine control module for a major engine manufacturer was put through the discipline of MEOST. The customer's requirement that the mean-time-between-failures (MTBF) on the module should exceed 200,000 miles in the hostile environments that engines are

Table 15-3. Multiple environment vs. single environment stress testing.

Product	Stress Level	Failure Rate	Problem	Found in Single Environment
Model A	*80 Hr.* Operating Rectangle	1/8	(Injection driver) Pk. I degraded	1/8 Yes
	Operating Rectangle	1/8	Darlington Shorted	No
	1.	1/8	Mylar cap open	No
	2.	1/8	ISC Darlington Shorted	No
	9.	1/8	(Injection driver) Shorted	No
	10.	1/8	(Injection driver) Shorted	No
Model A	*240 Hr.* Operating Rectangle	2/8	(Injection driver) Pk. I degraded	—
	3.	2/8	(Injection driver) Shorted	No
	6.	1/8	(Injection driver) Shorted	No
	7.	1/8	(Injection driver) Shorted	No
	8.	1/8	(Injection driver) Shorted	No
Model B	*240 Hr.* Operating Rectangle	1/8	Thick Film Resistor Chip	No
	4.	4/8	Lytic Broke Off	No
	5.	8/8	Loose Hybrid	No
Model B	*240 Hr.* 9.	1/8	Conformal Coat Peel	No
	9.	7/8	Power Dioded Shorted	No

subjected to was easily met. In fact, after two years of operation, the several thousand units in the field had not registered a single failure! That is world-class reliability.

MEOST vs. Computer Simulation

An interesting competition, reminiscent of the iron horse versus the old gray mare, has begun in twenty-first-century dimensions. A giant wind tunnel, capable of handling a huge aircraft "in a single gulp," has been built at NASA's Ames Research Center in California. It permits the realization of an old dream: testing planes on the ground rather than in the skies. The wind tunnel blows sixty-three tons of air each second through an intake port that is the size of a football field, thereby simulating flight conditions on the ground.

The competition to this actual simulation, which has been in the best tradition of MEOST, comes from the Numerial Aerodynamic Simulation Facility, also at Ames Research. This "digital wind tunnel" uses supercomputers from the Cray Corporation to simulate flight. The goal is "to fly airplanes" on a screen! Designers will be able to create a new aircraft and watch as the computer tests the airflow around it, just as if the drawing were really in a wind tunnel. Which system will win? The votes are not in yet. But until another Einstein comes along who can capture the numerous interaction effects between multiple stresses and environments in a formula, actual simulation will always have a competitive edge over computer simulation.

Chapter 16

Quality in Production and in the Field: Where It All Comes Together

Without feedback from the factory, improvements can't make the jump from factory floor to boardroom. U.S. executives would be well advised to pay as much attention to the assembly line as to the bottom line.

—Robert Chapman Wood, journalist

For some thirty years and more, U.S. industry, influenced by a new crop of MBAs, accountants, and legal beagles fixated on profits, relegated manufacturing to the status of a stepchild. It was looked upon as a necessary evil. Only the threat of foreign competition made American companies realize the vital role manufacturing has to play. The Japanese achieved a host of technological advances—in video recorders, semiconductors, ceramics, and laser printers—not by pouring money into research and development but by relentlessly pursuing manufacturing excellence. Cooperation between Matsushita's design teams and employees on the shop floor eliminated more than 75 percent of the cost of the videotape recorder while dramatically improving its quality.

259

The Resurgence of Manufacturing

These lessons hit home. In many U.S. companies, manufacturing has been restored to its honored place and is now considered a key component of corporate strategy. There is increasing emphasis on achieving 100 percent yields and theoretical cycle time (twice direct labor time). American industry now has the tools—the design of experiments and SPC—that permit manufacturing processes and equipment to be optimized so that they can produce thousands and thousands of units without a defect. These tools have proved to be far more effective than corresponding Japanese DOE tools. As an example, it took a reputable Japanese company two years to bring down defects in wave soldering to an acceptable level. It took an equally reputable U.S. company, using the specific DOE tools detailed in Chapter 13, less than a month to achieve defect levels 10 to 1 below the Japanese figures!

This chapter deals with the quality bases that must be covered as the product moves from design to production and on to the customer and the field.

Design for Manufacturability: "Make It Mistake Proof"

In the old industrial model of the 1950s, engineering and manufacturing were "sworn enemies." Engineering looked upon Production as incompetent and Production returned the compliment. In the new industrial model for the 1990s, the common enemy, competition, has forged an alliance between the two functions at the very start of design.

The most recent buzzwords in this alliance are "design for manufacturability" and "design for automated assembly." Two university professors, Jeffrey Boothroyd and Peter Dewhurst, have perfected these disciplines so that any assembly can be quantified in terms of a numerical score to measure ease of manufacturability. There are ten basic rules for achieving the best results in designing for manufacturability.

Design for Manufacturability Guidelines (Simplify Before You Automate)

1. Minimize number of parts.
2. Minimize assembly surfaces.
3. Design for Z-axis assembly.
4. Minimize part variations (DOE).
5. Design parts for multi-use and ease of fabrication.
6. Maximize part symmetry.
7. Optimize part handling.
8. Avoid separate fasteners wherever possible.
9. Provide parts with integral "self-locking" features.
10. Drive toward modular design.

This discipline*, along with many others, is equally applicable to both customer companies and supplier companies. A review of design for manufacturability is conducted during design reviews, first at the prototype stage and then at the pilot run stage.

Process Characterization and Optimization: A Base That Is Seldom Touched.

One of the main reasons for poor quality in manufacturing is that while much attention is paid to the design of the product, the process that produces the product is often treated as a stepchild. An autopsy of quality rigor mortis in production reveals that the process is selected as an afterthought to the product, often with little compatibility between the two. Development engineers do not feel responsible for the process. They relegate that to the process engineer, who in turn leans on the supplier of the equipment used in the process. All of them use arbitrary specifications, antiquated procedures, and uncertain experience in deciding process parameters. None of them have even heard of DOE.

World-class quality companies start their research on processes two to five years before commencing product development. With this lead time, process specifications and conformance to such specifications can be well established. When product development is started, compatibility between product and process is first examined, with the process engineer working in harness with the development engineer and the equipment supplier to assure yields as close as possible to 100 percent.

It is at this stage that the design of experiments should be conducted on the process as a whole, first by the equipment supplier and next, jointly, by a team consisting of the process engineeer, the development engineer, and the equipment supplier. The purpose is to completely define and characterize the process by separating the important process variables from the unimportant ones; by opening up tolerances on the latter; and by closely optimizing the levels and tolerances of the important variables and closely controlling them through Positrol (see Chapter 14), including the continual monitoring of key process variables through precontrol.

To assure process capability at the very start, before production begins, five units in a row must fall within the precontrol lines (see precontrol in Chapter 14), that is, in the green zone. This assures a minimum C_{p_k} of 1.33, and pilot production is allowed to begin. Eventually, through DOE, C_{p_k}'s of 5.0 and over are easily achievable.

---

* For more details on the use of this technique, the reader is referred to the text *Product Design for Manufacturing and Assembly* by Jeffrey Boothroyd and Peter Dewhurst, published by Boothroyd and Dewhurst, Inc., 1987.

Total Preventive Maintenance: A New Dimension in Process Quality

There is a saying among old production hands: "If it ain't broke, don't fix it!" It is precisely these outworn slogans masquerading as common sense that lead to equipment down time, equipment inefficiencies, and high product defect rates. Equipment breakdowns are as costly as product defects. They add to the costs of poor quality and lengthen cycle time.

In the 1970s, the Toyota group companies developed a system called total preventive maintenance (TPM)*. This system is total in scope, covering all machines, tools, instruments, computers, robots, and vehicles, as well as plant site equipment. It applies to all departments, from top management to operators. The objective is to improve factory overall effectiveness (FOE) for all equipment by reducing and eventually eliminating the six big losses: equipment failure; setup and adjustment; minor stops; reduced speed; product rework; and scrap.

Figure 16-1 depicts how factory overall effectiveness is measured. It is the product of availability (A), output effectiveness (O), and value-added time (V). Availability is the complement of down time, which in turn is composed of equipment failure time plus setup/adjustment time. Output effectiveness is the ratio of theoretical cycle time to actual cycle time, the latter consisting of time lost because of minor stops, reduced speed, and so forth. Value-added time is the ratio of the number of good parts produced to the total number of parts produced—in other words, yield. Many companies do not even have such measurements in place. The few that do generally have FOE's in the range of 10 to 75 percent, whereas the goal should be well over 95 percent, with up time and yields approaching 99.5 percent each.

Having measured FOE, the $64 question is how to achieve up times and yields approaching 99.5 percent or 100 percent. The answer for both is, first, with the design of experiments, followed by Positrol and precontrol of the truly important variables. Preventive maintenance goes into effect as soon as two units measured consecutively fall in the yellow zone (see precontrol in Chapter 14). This signals a gradual process shift, such as tool wear, before the product goes out of specifications. Records of such shifts can then be used to predetermine preventive maintenance in off hours. Process FMEA studies are also useful in preventive maintenance.

---

*For more insights into TPM, see an excellent article, "Total Productive Maintenance—Essential to Maintain Progress," by Dr. Robert W. Hall, professor of Industrial Management at Indiana University, in the fall 1987 issue of *Target*, a publication of the Association for Manufacturing Excellence.

Figure 16-1. Measurement of factory overall effectiveness.

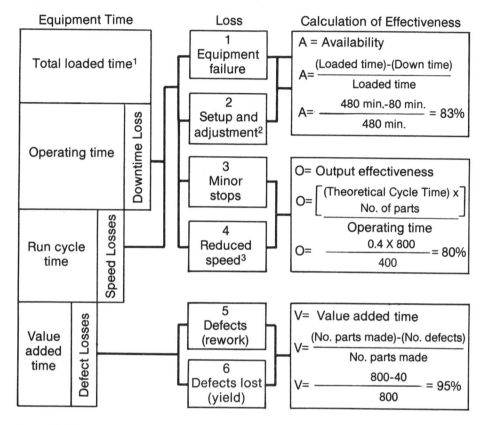

Overall Effectiveness = A x O x V = 83% x 80% x 95% = 63%

[1] Loaded time is not usually all working hours.

[2]Setups are necessary to make what the customer wants, so setup is value added activity. Unnecessary setup and adjustment time within each setup is a waste.

[3]A machine may not be desired to run at its theoretical cycle time. For instance, a machine in a cell may have idle time between cycles to balance with the cycle time of the cell. Others will be operated at speed, but only when parts are demanded.

Manufacturing Quality Control: Significant Elements of the Quality System

A comprehensive quality system was described in Chapter 10. Its major subelements for manufacturing include:

- Process certification (see Chapter 14).
- Yield prediction and cycle time prediction studies (similar to reliability prediction studies described in Chapter 15 but dealing specifically with yield targets and cycle time targets versus actuals).
- Gauge and test equipment calibration; reviews of calibration frequencies; pinpointing of out-of-calibration dates; and traceability to the Bureau of Standards.
- Quality "walk-through" of software.
- Conformance to plant safety guidelines.
- Electrostatic discharge protection.
- Conformance to Underwriters Laboratories (UL) and/or other international agency requirements.
- Storage, transportation, and packaging control within the factory.
- Engineering change control system.
- Nonconforming material control.
- Traceability requirements, including date codes, bar codes, and records.
- Failure analysis methods to determine root cause of a failure.
- Quality data control* to gather, analyze, and review quality data. Table 16-1 is a sample of the kinds of data and/or reports generated in a Fortune 500 company. Among these, quality costs provide a macroscopic view for management, but are not working tools on the shop floor for detailed analysis. Yield data are more meaningful for day-to-day tracking. Overall yields can be measured by:
    1. Internal failure costs: scrap, rework, and analyzing as a percentage of sales.
    2. First time yields: the number of units that pass without a single rejection from end to end as a percentage of the number of units started.
    3. Defects per unit (DPU): where the total number of defects at all work stations are added up and expressed as a multiple (or fraction) of each unit produced.
- Manufacturing flow chart identifying check/audit stations and shutdown criteria as to when and by whom a line producing defects can be stopped. (More and more companies are now granting line shutdown authority to their operators. After all, they know more of what is going on at a work station than higher levels of management.)
- Independent out-of-carton quality audits to determine initial customer quality.

Most of the subelements listed already exist in companies aspiring to world-class status. However, a few special quality subelements that are not found in such companies require emphasis:

---

*Looking at reams of data gathered over long periods of time is counterproductive. Only a multi-vari chart (see Chapter 13) offers stratified information in terms of time, cycle, position, and so forth.

Table 16-1. Quality data generated in a *Fortune* 500 company.

Data/Report	Purpose	Frequency	Gathered By	Analyzed By	Reviewed By
Self-inspection	Instant feedback to operator	Each operation	Operator	Operator	Supervisor, i.e., production engineer, quality control engineer
Neighbor inspection	Nonthreatening feedback to operator	At start of next operation	Next operator	Originating operator	Supervisor, i.e., production engineer, quality control engineer
Automated inspection (video recognition systems)	Foolproof checks (*Poka-yoke*)	Before next work station	Operator	Operator	Supervisor, i.e., production engineer, quality control engineer
Repetitive reject	Alert for three or more repetitive defects/day	Variable	Operator	Supervisor, quality control auditor	Problem-solving teams
Checklist/log	Gather process information	Hourly/short term	Operator, inspector, auditor	Supervisor, quality control auditor	Problem-solving team (if needed)
Precontrol	To control process to prevent defects for criterion parameters	Variable: from every 10 minutes to once/day	Operator	Supervisor, quality control auditor	Problem-solving team (for out-of-control condition)
Positrol log	To monitor key process parameters	Variable	Operator, setup, maintenance, etc.	Supervisor, quality control auditor	Maintenance, i.e., production engineer
Daily tally	To correct previous day's errors	Daily	Manual/computerized at each work station	Supervisor, quality control auditor	Problem-solving team (if needed)
Pareto charts	To provide trends and prioritize actions	Weekly	Production foreman, quality control engineer	Problem-solving teams, production manager, quality control manager	Plant manager
Yield reports	To determine composite yields (units) and $ losses	Weekly/monthly	Plant Cost Accounting	Production, quality control and plant managers	Business managers, director of quality control
Quality costs	To identify chronic problems and organize projects/teams for resolution; and to allocate and redistribute resources	Monthly	Accounting	Production, quality control and plant managers, business managers, quality control director	General manager

Field escape control. The factory can be considered the largest field service station in a company. It is also the earliest. Factory failures are a forerunner of field failures, especially if little is done to analyze and correct them. Field escape control scrutinizes all line failures with reliability implications and resolves them with special failure analysis techniques, including failure simulation. Its effectiveness is measured by the elimination of such failures in subsequent production.

Analyzing effectiveness. Despite the advent of computer techniques and fault tree analysis, analyzing line defects is still an art that only a few gifted technicians are able to master. The remainder need help in the form of training, service manuals, feedback from repair operators, and even artificial simulation of defects.

Elimination of 100 percent burn-in. Many electronic companies "cook" their products with power turned on for several hours, either at room temperature or at an elevated temperature, in order to weed out "infant mortality" types of failures that would otherwise be passed on to customers and end users. But burn-in is a tacit admission that the company does not know how to analyze and correct reliability-type failures. It is a band-aid, at best, and an expensive band-aid. Instead of burn-in, thermal cycling—and preferably power-interrupted thermal cycling—should be used. Instead of 100 percent of the production units being subjected to burn-in, thermal cycling should be confined to a small sample, say, eight or ten units per day. However, the small sample should be subjected to several thermal cycles, twelve as a minimum, and checked for important parameters both at the temperature extremes and at room ambient. Finally, the root cause of even a single failure in such tests should be relentlessly pursued and corrected.

Truncated, ongoing multiple environment overstress tests. The technique of multiple environment overstress tests (MEOST) was discussed in Chapter 15. The purpose of a truncated MEOST is to ensure that reliability achieved in design is maintained in production and in the field. The truncation may be achieved by limiting the multiple environments to just a few key ones, limiting the overstress, and limiting the time duration of the tests. Truncated MEOST is far more effective in terms of quality, cost, and cycle time than brute-force testing, demonstration, and even some field testing—practices prescribed by the military that have little value in terms of true hardware reliability, but are tremendously costly to the taxpayer.

Prevention of Operator-Controllable Errors: From Brute-force Methods to *Poka-Yoke*

Chapters 13 and 14 discuss in detail the prevention of product and process errors, both at the customer's and the supplier's plants, through the use of

DOE and SPC. Frequently, however, the lament goes up: "How can we prevent operator errors, the silly mistakes that, somehow, get through our own inspection and then get caught by our customer."

The Traditional, Ineffective Methods

Unfortunately, too much attention has been paid to brute-force methods that are only marginally effective, while the more elegant "mistake-proof" methods that are collectively called *poka-yoke* in Japan are hardly known, much less practiced. The variety of techniques in use can be classified according to their degree of effectiveness by giving them college grades.

Those that would flunk out, with *F grades*, include:

- Multiple inspections to eventually filter out defects. Because all visual inspections have only about a 40 percent effectiveness, this method piles up inspection upon inspection. It is the most costly as well as the most ineffective method. As an example, a printed circuit board manufacturer used five successive inspection checkpoints to assure the very low defect levels demanded by his customer!
- Cautioning, threatening, and berating operators and inspectors "to be more careful." Suppliers frequently cite this as an example of "corrective action" to their naive customers.
- P and C Control Charts, with all defects lumped together.

In the marginally effective *C grade* category would be:

- Off-the-job and on-the-job operator training.
- Written and audiovisual instructions to operators and inspectors.
- Pareto charts to separate the "vital few" defects from the "trivial many."
- "Measles charts" to pinpoint the locations of the most frequent defects.
- Cause and effect diagrams to attempt to trace the cause of defects.
- Highlighting the most frequent defects on cards or photographs hung above the operators' and inspectors' stations.

Methods warranting a more respectable *B grade* include:

- Clear, firm, meaningful specifications on operator-controllable parameters, as established between supplier and customer.
- Use of "Bo Derek" linear scales from 1 to 10 on each cosmetic/visual parameter, based on the agreement of the customer, Sales, Engineering, Quality Assurance, and Manufacturing. Perfect quality would rate a 10, poorest quality a 1. Such a scale, then, would be captured in physical samples or photographs, so that subjective inspection judgment,

which can vary from inspector to inspector and from time-to-time, is eliminated.

- Classification of characteristics, where important cosmetic/visual requirements are separated from the unimportant by the customer in agreement with the supplier.
- Quality circles, where line worker teams attempt to solve repetitive, operator-controllable defects.
- Design for manufacturability and foolproofing. As an example, a customer was endlessly plagued by plating defects from his suppliers. One enterprising supplier recommended a rule that wherever cosmetic considerations would be visible to the customer's customers, that is, the end users, plating would be eliminated in favor of painting, which is much more "forgiving" in terms of visual defects. Plating would be retained, for corrosion protection, only on those parts not seen by the end user. The customer adopted this supplier's suggestion across the board on all his product lines, with a savings of over $5 million!
- Video recognition systems to replace the faulty human eyesight of inspectors. The state of the art in video recognition systems, however, has not developed sufficiently to overcome the disadvantages of their high cost and slow speed.
- Overlays, masks, and templates to focus the inspector's attention on the specific location of a potential defect.
- Automated inspection instead of manual inspection. Its disadvantages are high cost and its being based on the concept of defect detection rather than defect prevention.

A Grade: Neighbor Inspection

In *neighbor inspections*, the next operator in a process flow becomes both an inspector and a controller who quietly, quickly, and nonthreateningly feeds back the defect to the previous operator who created it. This is much, much more effective than conventional inspection, where the inspector at the end of a long line of operators detects the defect. He or she then reports it to the inspection supervisor, who reports it to the inspection foreman, who feeds the information back to the production foreman, who notifies the production supervisor, who carries the defect back to the operator who caused the defect. In the meantime, many months may have passed.

As an example, in a large television plant, the overall defect rate was 15 percent. Control charts and quality circle activities were introduced, but the defect rate still never went below 6.5 percent. Neighbor inspection was then introduced and one month later the defect rate was reduced to 1.5 percent. Three months later, this was further reduced to 0.65 percent. The final figure for all interprocess defects was an incredible 0.06 percent.

It could be argued that making each successive operator an inspector for the previous operation would add considerably to direct labor time. However, visually eyeballing a few critical inspection points does not take much time. In fact, cycle time is greatly reduced because defect levels are driven down dramatically. In the example of the television plant, the direct labor time did increase initially from 30 seconds to 33 seconds, but returned to 30 seconds in less than a month.

A few caveats are in order, however, respecting the adoption of neighbor inspection.

1. There should not be too many checks imposed upon the neighbor operator. Only the most important defects, gathered from previous Pareto analyses, should be flagged.
2. Defects will not be reduced unless the operating methods that created the defects in the first place are changed. The line should be shut down so that managers can lead the improvement process, with the help of all the involved workers. The time lost because of a line shutdown will be more than made up by the dramatic reduction of future defects.
3. It is important to gain the acceptance of all line workers to the concept of neighbor inspection. They should view it not as a policing operation but as a help to the previous operator that can be rendered quickly and nonpunitively.

A Grade: Poka-Yoke (Mistake-Proof) Inspection

The principle of *poka-yoke* inspection* is to aid the operator with a checklist. But this is no ordinary checklist. It is based on sensors that light bulbs, ring buzzers, and even stop production if an error is made inadvertently by the operator. If he or she forgets something, the sensing device will signal the omission and prevent errors from occurring in the first place. There are two stages to *poka-yoke*. The first stage involves detecting an error that has taken place through sensing devices used by inspection. The second and more powerful stage involves preventing the operator from creating the error through the use of sensors that stop further processing.

An example illustrates the two stages. A manufacturer of a pocket calculator often received complaints from dealers and end-user customers about missing accessories, such as fillers, bubble-pack, instruction manuals, warranty cards, and pouches. He instituted a differential weighing system by which the weight of a production unit calculator could be compared against

---

*For a comprehensive treatment of this subject, *Zero Quality Control: Source Inspection and the Poka-Yoke System* by Shigeo Shingo, published by the Productivity Press, Cambridge, Mass., 1986, is *must reading*. Shingo illustrates the power of these techniques to get operator-controllable defects down to zero with numerous practical examples and case studies.

a correct unit containing all the accessories. The differential scale could detect, in grams, the absense of even the lightest accessory. This reduced the level of customer defects to near zero. However, the technique still relied on inspection after poor quality had been injected into the product. It continued to be a sorting function even though its effectiveness was near 100 percent—far better than the effectiveness of ordinary 100 percent visual inspections. This was Stage 1.

The manufacturer then went to Stage 2 *poka-yoke*. He installed bowed springs in front of the boxes containing each separate accessory. When the operator—not the inspector—reached for an accessory part from the box, the spring would be depressed, actuating a limit switch, which would turn on a green light bulb. These limit switches, in turn, were connected to a stepper switch, which in turn was connected to a go/no go gate. Only when all the accessories were accounted for would the gate open, permitting the unit to go into finished goods.

Poka-yoke, as described in Shigeo Shingo's landmark work, can be designed in two ways: (1) as a warning method, in which lights or buzzers are used to alert worker attention to a defect; and (2) as a control method, where the process is shut down automatically, thereby preventing further defects from occurring.

The sensors themselves can be of contact or noncontact types. With contact types, sensing devices detect nonconformance in product or shape. The sensors can be limit switches, microswitches, touch switches, differential transformers, relays, and so forth. Noncontact types include photocells, beam sensors, fiber sensors, area sensors, position sensors, dimension sensors, vibration sensors, and others.

The first reaction of the novice to *poka-yoke* may be that the sensing devices are too costly, too difficult, too time-consuming, and that they require 100 percent checks by the operator. However, these arguments are just pushbutton excuses for a lack of imagination. Sensing devices can be simple—in fact, the simpler, the better. Ideas for such sensors can come from tool and fixture designers, quality circles, industrial engineers, process engineers, or interdisciplinary teams. Cycle time increases in direct labor are minimal; and compared to the overall reduction in cycle time effected by 100 percent yields and no rework, they do not even merit discussion. Finally, there is no economic loss in 100 percent operator checks (as opposed to 100 percent external inspection) if the results are zero defects.

Field Quality Is What the Customer Says It Is

Many suppliers measure quality/reliability in the field in terms of conventional parameters, such as failure rates per year and mean time between failures. However, such measurements can provide a false sense of security. And when the customer complains, the supplier feels hurt and let down.

Pitfalls in Assessing Customer Feedback

There are a number of reasons why suppliers incorrectly assess customer dissatisfaction:

- A supplier's poor interpretation of a customer or end-user complaint. As an example, a car company received numerous customer complaints about the "poor fit of the car doors." It discovered, belatedly, that the complaints had nothing to do with "margin" or "flushness"; rather, customers were concerned about the amount of effort required to close the doors, and about the loose, mechanical sound they heard when slamming the doors shut!
- The supplier's application of a wrong cure for a quality complaint. For example, brute-force inspection or burn-in is applied when no trouble is found in the returned unit (that is, where the customer's complaint cannot be reproduced due to intermittencies, system glitches, wrong software instructions).
- No supporting customer quality research by the supplier. Because of an ostrich mentality, the supplier continues to claim that "our products are the best" without offering any supporting evidence.
- Price premium charged without a quality premium. The supplier makes no attempt to correlate whether the quality premium was real enough to justify the price premium.
- Supplier's disbelief in customer research methods (outlined in Chapter 11).
- The supplier's sales, marketing, engineering, and even management filtering out *negative feedback* from the customer in a sweep-under-the-rug mentality.
- Quality, per se, not being the customer's problem (see Bhote's Law in Chapter 11).
- Changing customer priorities and expectations.

Other Bases to Be Touched in Field Reliability

Besides direct feedback from the customer, other issues that must be addressed to assure maximum reliability and customer satisfaction are:

- *Packing* (as distinguished from packaging): What good does it do to have designed and built a perfect product, only to have it damaged in transit. Packing integrity can be verified by drop tests and random vibration tests that can simulate transportation stresses. One enterprising company regularly sends its product out, with the specified packing and using the specified carrier, to one of its remote plants and then has it shipped back with the same carrier in order to assess the reliability of the packing before the start of production. "Before" and "after" readings can then measure the degree of degradation.

- *Installation Instructions:* Fond fathers, assembling toys for their children at Christmas time, can attest to the frustrations felt in following unclear, complicated, and sometimes downright wrong instructions. It is best to enhance comprehension by the liberal use of illustrations and pictures and to test the adequacy of installation/inspection instructions by using relatively unskilled personnel in the supplier company who can act as guinea pigs before the product is shipped to the customer or end user. For more complex installations, service clinics should be conducted at the customer's site.

- *Operating Instructions:* Preferably, these should appear on the product itself. They should be kept clear and simple and be written up according to good human engineering principles. Remember, it is not necessary to have a pilot's license to operate the controls of a car! Experience shows that operating instructions and owner's manuals tend to be ignored by the customer except as a last recourse. He may "if all else fails, read the manual," but will look upon the necessity as a sign of defeat.

- *"Zero Time" Failures:* While every attempt should be made to prevent failures from reaching customers, through the use of the reliability improvement techniques discussed in Chapter 15, the next best move is to examine "zero time" failures that occur upon reaching the customer's site or in the field. These dead-on-arrival (DOA) failures are the "infant mortality" failures that have escaped reliability safety nets, such as burn-in, thermal cycling, and truncated multiple environment overstress tests. Every single DOA failure should be analyzed to determine how it escaped the safety net and how a similar failure can be prevented in the future.

- *Failure Analysis:* Failures can occur anywhere in the life cycle of a product—at the design/development stage, in pilot runs, in production, and in the field. Theoretically, every failure occurring anywhere should be analyzed. In the practical, real world, the following priorities, in descending order of urgency, are recommended:

1. Multiple environment overstress test (MEOST) failures—in design
2. Truncated MEOST—in production
3. Field escape failures
4. "Zero time" failures
5. Field failures
6. All other failures

The reason for such priorities is that field failures are after-the-fact-history, whereas before-the-fact failures are preventive in nature. Single failure modes may be given a lower priority; but two or more failures of the same failure mode should be attacked with the same sense of urgency as a full-blown crisis.

Failure analysis is an essential quality tool for both customer and supplier. Many customer companies do not have an independent, professional failure analysis capability, but instead depend on the supplier and his resources. In a partnership era, this is one of the important responsibilities of the supplier. In a prepartnership relationship, it is advisable for the customer to have a competent failure analysis capability, both for verifying the supplier's analysis and for determining the basis for warranty claims and financial compensation.

Failure analysis should be pursued until the root cause of the failure is isolated. Often the root cause is buried under several layers of effect-cause pairs. When this occurs, a few special techniques can be used:

- Components search, where disassembly and reassembly are feasible (see Chapter 13).
- Paired comparisons (listed in Table 13-2).
- Failure simulation, where the presumed cause of failure is deliberately introduced and removed to see if the observed failure mode can be artificially reproduced. This is known as switching the cause "on" and "off."
- "B" versus "C" experiment to determine the effectiveness of the corrective action. Here B represents the new design or process, while C represents the current design or process. The simplest rule in this experiment is to run three B units and three C units in *random order*. Then rank the six units in descending order from the best to the worst. If all three B units rank above the three C units, it can be statistically proved, with 95 percent confidence, that the B design/process is better than the C design/process. If there is no clear separation between the B and C units (that is, they overlap), do not make the change. (B versus C is listed in Table 13-2.)

After-Sales Service: The Black Sheep

Despite all the limitations and restrictions imposed upon it, Manufacturing—both for the supplier and the customer—is constantly improving its performance. The same cannot be said of after-sales service. Repair service, especially, enjoys the same notoriety that plagues the used car salesman. The economic landscape is strewn with shoddy maintenance, frequent breakdowns, overcharges, belated service calls, and indifferent attitudes. Further, the serviceman is always blamed, just as in manufacturing the line worker is blamed, for the sins of an antiquated and technologically backward service system. The quality of effective after-sales service begins with the interface between the supplier and his immediate customer and extends to the customer's customer (the end user), the customer's dealers, and the supplier's affiliated service stations. The experience of one supplier to a large original equipment manufacturer (OEM) who developed a comprehensive after-sales service system will illustrate what it takes to achieve world-class service quality. There are five categories in such a system:

1. *Supplier-OEM Customer Interface*
   - Mean time to diagnose faults and mean time to repair them established as firm specifications.
   - Supplier-customer reviews of "design for serviceability" held.
   - Warranty policies, including financial incentives and penalties for product reliability, determined.
   - Service manuals and installation instructions made available two months before product introduced into field.
   - Dealer exchange/float units in customer's pipeline one month before product introduced into field.
2. *Supplier Assistance to Customer's Dealerships*
   - Regional service representatives introduced to dealers.
   - Pamphlets to service writers provided to help diagnose end-user complaints.
   - Regional seminars/clinics conducted for dealers' service personnel.
   - Training videotapes produced for dealers' service personnel.
   - Exchange stations, where defective units can be quickly exchanged for good units, established in metropolitan areas, with a goal of one-day turn-around time.
3. *Supplier Assistance to Its Affiliated Service Stations*
   - Newsletter incorporating service tips published each month.
   - Feed-forward of production plant experiences (for example, MEOST data, field-escape problems, zero-time failures) instituted.
   - Assistance in design of service tools/equipment launched.
   - Networking among key service stations started.
4. *Supplier Parts Support to the Field**
   - Parts standardization program introduced, to facilitate parts interchangeability not only within the supplier's product lines but also for parts from its competitors. This program reduced the supplier's parts count by a factor of 6 to 1, dramatically reduced inventories, improved lead time for parts orders, and strengthened service quality.
   - Starter kits of unique and critical parts made available to service stations one month before product introduced into field.

---

* A world-class company in parts support in the field is Caterpillar. It gives a firm commitment to its customers and end-users that a part ordered from anywhere in the *world* will be delivered within forty-eight hours from the time it is ordered—or else the part is free.

5. *Supplier Assistance in Enhancing End-user Satisfaction*
   - Phone surveys and personal visits started, to determine and promote user satisfaction with product performance and reliability, service accuracy, timeliness, and completeness.
   - Detailed checks made of no-trouble-found phenomenon, where customers' original complaints could not be verified (each check sometimes took more than fifty hours to resolve).
   - Customers treated individually with every complaint dealt with on a one-on-one basis rather than by means of form letters.
   - Product evolutions focused on built-in diagnostics.

To sum up field quality and after-sales service, the admonition "Never forget the customer after the sale is consummated" should be etched across the forehead of all who, even indirectly, come in contact with customers. The suppliers and manufacturers who do not pay heed to this advice will in time wither away. The ones who do can overcome many initial deficiencies and go on to win!

Chapter 17

White-Collar Quality: The Achilles Heel

While blue collar productivity in manufacturing has been consistently above 80% and rising, white collar productivity in the offices has been below 40% and falling.

—From an internal report on productivity, Illinois Institute of Technology

Support Service Quality—Not Even Off the Launching Pad

Despite its uneven lurches along a bumpy road, manufacturing quality has been making encouraging progress in American industry. However, among the services that support manufacturing—from Marketing to Engineering, from Accounting to Personnel—quality is a deadbeat, almost a dropout. Service quality is at least twenty years behind product quality even in companies that are unfurling the banner of "companywide quality control."

One company, in beginning its drive for maximum customer satisfaction, assumed that product quality and reliability would be the largest source of customer complaints. Instead, its survey found the results listed in descending order of customer dissatisfaction in Table 17-1. Of nine categories of

276

Table 17-1.   Survey of types of customer dissatisfaction.

Nature of Customer Complaint	Rank Order
Billing and credit errors	1
Back orders	2
Late delivery	3
Difficulty in placing orders	4
Product quality/reliability defects	5
Follow-up	6
Packing/shipping errors	7
Poor technical explanations	8
Order errors	9

customer dissatisfaction, eight were related to support services, while product quality was in a somewhat respectable fifth place.

Another company compared the quality perceptions of its customers over a five-year period and observed a remarkable change.

Complaint Category	Total Customer Complaints	
	1982	1987
Product quality	60%	16%
All support services	40%	84%

Although the company had made overall gains in customer quality, with a tenfold improvement in product quality, the improvement in support services was minimal, its cut of the customer dissatisfaction pie actually doubling.

Service Quality: Passing the Buck

Why has support service quality remained untouched by the quality revolution? There are several reasons:

1. Quality is off the screen of consciousness of support service personnel:
   - The designer, who makes numerous engineering changes, is not even aware that the quality of his work can adversely affect the entire organization.
   - The accountant, who has no knowledge of the cost of poor quality, is blissfully ignorant that he has missed a golden opportunity to improve quality and profit.

- The personnel manager, who examines turnover among his professionals, feels no responsibility for making the corporate climate more hospitable to high achievers.
- The "legal beagle" who bemoans product liability suits, has no technical skills and little interest in liability prevention at the design stage.

2. Quality, although easy to define when applied to product, is difficult to visualize, let alone define, when applied to services.
3. Measurement of any type in indirect labor departments is a will-o'-the-wisp. Whereas two ends of the industrial spectrum—the general manager and the lowly direct labor worker—are measured (and measured very well), the vast majority of middle managers and white-collar workers are not pinned down by any performance measurement. In fact, they start rearguard actions to sabotage any attempts at concrete measurement for productivity, cycle time, or quality.
4. Without a base line for measurement, it is impossible to develop quality improvement tools.

Clearly, within the white-collar community, quality is passed off as someone else's responsibility, generally landing in the lap of the quality assurance department. But with its hands full in the battle for product quality, Quality Assurance is no better equipped to tackle service quality than are other professionals.

Companywide Quality Control (CWQC): The Pursuit of Excellence

There is a new movement afoot to elevate the concept of quality from just considerations of product quality to a concern for total quality of performance, covering all aspects of a business and all employees of a company. It is called companywide quality control (CWQC).* The conceptual framework for CWQC is still in the process of evolution. Nevertheless, a consensus definition includes the following:

- An elevation from *product quality* to the *quality of performance*, which encompasses profitability, productivity, delivery, safety, and many other aspects of a company's activities.
- *The quality of management*, such as the quality of its strategy, the qual-

---

*For an overview of CWQC, see Keki R. Bhote, "CWQC: A New Horizon for American Management," a paper presented before the annual Congress of the American Society for Quality Control, 1985.

ity of its organization, the quality of its decisions, and the quality of its core values.

- *The quality of satisfaction*—of the employee, of the stockholder, of the supplier, of the dealer and of society at large.

In short, CWQC can be described as the pursuit of excellence through constant, never-ending improvement by all employees in a company. CWQC is a process, not another program. It is a long-term development, not a short-term fix. It has no terminal life. It is continual, never-ending. It is evolutionary in implementation, yet borders on the revolutionary in terms of its scope, vision, and impact.

Pitfalls in Measuring White-Collar Quality

Given this broadened and comprehensive definition of quality, measuring it is the next logical step. The list of MBO principles in Chapter 21 cites important measurement principles, utilizing the discipline of management by objectives, by which any indirect labor department can be measured. The most meaningful measurements are a department's quality effectiveness, delivery effectiveness, and cost effectiveness. Table 17-2 presents a partial list of the parameters by which quality effectiveness can be measured in various support service departments. Cost effectiveness, in general, can be measured by the department cost expressed as a percentage of the total sales dollar, or by its head count expressed as a percentage of the total company head count. Delivery effectiveness can be measured in terms of cycle times (see Chapter 20) required for the processing of the most important functions within the department.

The quality measurements in Table 17-2 are logical, fair, meaningful, and capable of quantification. Yet, with a few exceptions, most companies have not even begun to introduce these parameters to gauge the quality health of their support services. A principal reason for this is the difficulty and expense of gathering such quality data in a consistent and repeatable manner. A cardinal rule in measurement is that the benefits derived from measurement should exceed the cost of the measurement by a minimum ratio of 10 to 1.

The few adventurous companies that have taken the first hesitant steps toward measurement have violated this fundamental rule by creating a mountain of cost to achieve a molehill of benefits. They count the many opportunities for errors in a given service operation and then measure quality as the actual errors, expressed as a percentage (or parts per million, ppm) of the total number of opportunities. Types of opportunity counts for various support services are shown in Table 17-3. In some cases, the unit of opportunity is weighted by complexity, such as the type and details of a

Table 17-2.   Expanded parameters for measuring quality in support services.

Department	Measures of Quality Effectiveness
Marketing	• Accuracy of market research • Gauging customer needs, expectations, changes
Sales	• Accuracy of sales forecasts • Accuracy in translating customer requirements to engineering • Accuracy of order forms—from customer to factory
Engineering	• Outgoing quality and field reliability: actual vs. target • Total yield at start of production: actual vs. target • Design changes: number of changes after production starts
Quality Assurance	• Cost of poor quality
Purchasing	• Cost of material purchases (price + cost of poor quality + cost of delinquency)
MIS Accounting	• Errors per line code • Accuracy of reports • Total quality costs
Personnel	• Voluntary personnel turnover • Number of unfilled requisitions
Law	• Cost of product liability lawsuits, cost of settlements • Cost of product recalls

sales order, or a page in a technical manual where text may have to be distinguished from drawings and schematics.

Consider a service manual of one hundred pages. The unit of opportunity for errors here can be counted as one page or expanded further into an average count of 300 words per page. Assume that the proofreader has discovered six errors. Using the page as a unit, the defect rate would be 6 percent, or 60,000 ppm. Using the word as a unit, the defect rate would be 0.02 percent, or 200 ppm.

There are several weaknesses in this type of artificial measurement:

1. Using an arbitrary unit, the quality level can be made to appear either very good or very poor. In the above example, the defect rate per page appears to be an unacceptable 6 percent. Yet when the word count becomes the unit of opportunity, the defect rate is reduced to an admirable 0.02

Table 17-3. Opportunities for quality errors in several support service areas.

Support Service Area	Type of Opportunity Counts
Secretarial/clerical	No. of transactions: Typed pages, filings, reservations, phone messages, etc.
Payroll	No. of transactions: Checks, line items, etc.
Medical insurance	No. of claims
Technical manuals	No. of pages; no. of words; no. of characters, etc.
Training	No. of student hours in seminars
Sales	No. of orders; no. of line items
MIS	No. of line codes
Purchasing	No. of purchase transactions
Stockroom	No. of picks
Accounting	No. of reports; no. of pages; no. of line items
Personnel	No. of requisitions

percent. Clever managers and white-collar workers can in this way manipulate the measuring process to make themselves "look good."

2. The cost of detecting errors, such as misspelled words in a secretarial report, may become exorbitant and oppressive. It may require a 100 percent check by an external person, or, when checked by the originator, may still involve a disproportionate expenditure of time (not to correct the errors, but to measure them).

Whether the measurement of failings is suitable to all situations can be judged by the following example: In the customer service department of Federal Express, surveys are conducted to determine the number of telephone rings before the phone is picked up. Tom Peters, the noted co-author of *In Search of Excellence* and *A Passion for Excellence*, conducted his own private survey of Federal Express. In twenty-three out of twenty-four calls placed by him, the telephone was picked up on the first or second ring. Such a quality achievement in a service industry premised on speed is both laudable and necessary. However, in a large plant with multiple phones, multiple callers, and multiple responders, the logistics, time, and cost of gathering such data may provide a cure worse than the disease. It is only when there is a potential for real customer dissatisfaction that a quality measurement should be introduced to reduce and eliminate the failing.

3. The customer may not be concerned with a particular quality measurement. As an example, a training department obsessed with typographical errors in its instruction manuals may introduce elaborate measures to reduce such errors at considerable cost. However, the customer—the trainee in this case—may be less concerned with the "typos" than with the overall

clarity, significance, and relevance of the test. This issue may not have been addressed in the search for a quality yardstick.

Next Operation as Customer (NOAC): Concept and Benefits

In support services, measuring artificial quality parameters—such as errors per hundred or per million opportunities—that may not even be relevant to customers can be costly and time-consuming. By contrast, the concept of the *next operation as customer* (NOAC) can be translated into a powerful tool to measure and improve support service quality in a very meaningful manner.

In most companies, there is a genuine desire to satisfy customers. But that spirit of service rarely exists within a company when the customer is redefined as the next operation—whether the operation relates to product, paper, or information. In fact, there is often mistrust between an internal operation and the next operation, that is, its internal "customer." (The epithet "enemy" is sometimes used, and only partly in jest.) Mutual frustrations, vague requirements, departmental barriers, and "turf" protection are the causes of such mistrust. Further complicating the picture, outside of production where the line flow is visible, there is no clear perception of who the customer is. The old Wendy's slogan "Where's the beef?" can be paraphrased here as "Where's the customer?"

The concept of NOAC is a relatively new phenomenon on the American industrial scene. It looks upon the external customer as the last link in a long chain of internal supplier-customer pairs. It visualizes every operation as having both an internal supplier and an internal customer. For example, Manufacturing becomes Engineering's customer. That is as traumatic to Engineering as a turnover is in football! No longer can Engineering slap a design together and throw it over the wall, like a ticking time bomb, for Manufacturing to catch. In the NOAC era, Manufacturing, as Engineering's customer, measures and grades Engineering's ability to deliver a product with a targeted quality, cost, and cycle time. Similarly, Supply Management becomes, in NOAC, Manufacturing's supplier. There can also be supplier-customer links within a department. For instance, within a publications department, the flow of information and paper would be from technical writing to drafting to layout to reproduction to printing, with each step having the previous operation as supplier and the next operation as customer.

NOAC's Rich Payback

There are amazing benefits to companies, both supplier and customer, when NOAC is installed as a discipline. For instance,

- There is better knowledge of internal customers and their needs and of internal suppliers and their constraints.
- Departmental walls (the new buzzword is "functional silos") are broken down. There is a refreshing change from "win-lose" contests to "win-win" teamwork.
- Customer requirements are clarified so that they resemble specifications from external customers.
- Customer and supplier can mutually determine requirements that are fair, unambiguous, and meaningful.
- Customer evaluation is a better form of performance appraisal than evaluation by a single boss.
- The customer has a right to go elsewhere within the corporation for services provided by the supplier if the latter fails to provide customer satisfaction. (In a few companies, there is even a move for the "customer" to go outside the company if a supplier department does not meet the former's requirements.)
- The external customer is better served if all links in the customer/supplier chain are strengthened.
- It is an excellent method for achieving continual improvement.

Applications of NOAC Principles

NOAC principles are particularly applicable to support services, where performance, historically, has defied measurement and improvement. Table 17-4 is an example of NOAC applied to supply management. Section A looks upon Manufacturing as the customer and Supply Management (materials management and supplier quality assurance) as the supplier. Manufacturing's requirements of the supply management function (the supplier) are compactly but clearly stated. Progression toward its "reach-out" goals can be measured and improved every quarter. In Section B, Supply Management becomes the customer, with Engineering as its supplier. In this role, it imposes an equally comprehensive set of requirements of "specifications" on Engineering.

The NOAC Road Map

It is now possible to construct a guide to the use of NOAC in all operations (including product), and especially in support services, both in customer companies and supplier companies. Table 17-5 outlines a ten-step process for implementing NOAC. Figure 17-1 is a form used in the eighth step to determine the variance. From these it can be seen that NOAC is the best way to:

- Assure total (external) customer satisfaction.
- Measure any indirect labor department's quality, cost, and cycle time

Table 17-4. Applications of NOAC to supply management and supplier quality assurance.

A. Major Customer:	Manufacturing
Supplier:	Materials Management/Supplier Quality Assurance
Function:	Provide materials to production lines
Requirements:	—Qualified parts —Certified parts (no incoming inspection) —No lost time waiting for purchased material —No line starts with partial build
Surveys of effectiveness:	—Once/quarter
B. Major Customer:	Materials Management/Sourcing
Supplier:	Engineering
Function:	Provide documentation and information to facilitate purchases
Requirements:	—On-time preliminary bill of materials —Preferred parts —Qualified parts —Realistic part specifications —Early supplier involvement in specs

progress, without getting bogged down in needlessly complicated and expensive methods such as counting errors versus opportunities.
- Develop the tools of constant improvement.

Table 17-6 is a more detailed version of Table 17-4 regarding the sourcing department. It lists the five major functions of a sourcing department. Each function has major customers and suppliers. As an example, selecting worldwide sources (or suppliers) is an important function of the sourcing department. The two most important "customers" of this function are the Program Manager and the plant manager. By providing useful inputs to the sourcing department, Design Engineering and Quality Control become its "suppliers" of needed information.

Figure 17-2 is an example of a scorecard of a department that administers a participative management program. The functions it performs and the services it provides are listed in priority order: information/assistance, feedback survey, training, and council/task force representation. More detailed services appear in bullet form to the right. The measurement criteria are timeliness, accuracy/completeness, cooperation, responsiveness, guidelines/options/alternatives, and overall effectiveness. A simple rating system,

Table 17-5. The NOAC road map.

Step	Comments
1. Determine final customer and his requirements	• This is, generally, the external customer. Internal customer requirements may be in conflict with the final, external customer's. The latter's requirements are paramount.
2. Flow chart the process	• Products, information, paper move horizontally across organizational charts. White spaces and "disconnects" need highlighting.
3. Determine the major internal customers in each process step	• For a white-collar process or department, there may be several customers. Only the most important customers should be considered a priority.
4. Determine the major functions/services in each process step	• A particular process or department may have several functions. Only the most important functions should be examined. These functions or services should be tangible, visible to a third party.
5. Select the process step with greatest improvement potential	• This is based on the step having the largest quality problem (from the external customer's viewpoint), the largest cost, or the longest cycle time.
6. Determine main customer requirements	• These are specifications, from internal customer to "process owner" of the process step and from process owner to supplier of the process.
7. Determine measures of effectiveness	• Measurement criteria and scores must be determined by the customer in agreement with the process owner or department head and must be fair and meaningful to both sides. Typical general criteria in support services would include timeliness, accuracy, completeness, cooperativeness.
8. Determine cause of variance from requirements	• Examples of causes are poor output specs, poor input specs, lack of consequences to organization and/or individual for not performing to requirements, lack of feedback, poor process itself, inadequate resources.
9. Improve process step	• See improvement tools section in this chapter.
10. Repeat steps 5–9 on next process step	• Select the next process step with the second greatest potential for quality, cost, cycle time improvement.

Figure 17-1. Interface analysis.

Issue/Desired Output:					
	Functions				
Desired Output of the Functions					
Actual Output of the Functions					
Reason for variance —Output specification —Input —Consequences —Feedback —Process —Resources					
Changes required if function is to produce desired output					

from 1 to 3 (best), is used to measure each customer requirement. Such a straightforward scorecard shows, at a glance, the strengths and weaknesses associated with a process or a department. For instance, the administration of the participative management program is perceived favorably by its major customers except for the categories of training in general and of problem solving in particular. The scorecard is monitored each quarter to gauge the progress toward maximum customer satisfaction.

Improvement Tools for Service Quality

Quality improvement tools for support services are different from those required for products, such as design of experiments. However, some elementary SPC tools discussed in Chapter 14 are applicable.

The Pareto Principle. The Pareto Principle, which separates the vital few causes of a problem from the trivial many, is a universal tool for all indus-

Table 17-6. Sourcing: Its functions, customers, and suppliers.

Functions (Products)	Customers	Suppliers
1. Select "worldwide" sources	Program Manager Plant Purchasing	Design Engineering Quality Control
2. Track new programs	Program Manager Plant Purchasing Quality Control	Design Engineering Component Engineering Program Manager
3. Assist Marketing Department quotes	Program Manager Cost Estimator	Program Manager Design Engineering
4. Forecast commodity/industry trends	Business Manager	Corporate Materials
5. Standardization (i.e., Preferred Parts List (PPL), Preferred Suppliers List (PSL))	Design Engineering Plant Purchasing Quality Control	Design Engineering Component Engineering Plant Purchasing Quality Control

try. It is especially useful in support service operations to isolate and correct the most repetitive problems. Figure 17-3 is an example of a Pareto chart, illustrating the most frequent types of errors associated with order processing, errors that cause considerable customer dissatisfaction. It shows that the top three errors account for 67 percent of all errors. This prioritizes and focuses the actions required to correct and prevent these leading problems.

Cause and Effect Diagrams. Cause and effect diagrams, as we have seen, are elementarty tools in solving technical product and process problems. Nevertheless, in support services, where the problems are generally non-technical, administrative, and human, the cause and effect diagram is a useful device. It groups all possible causes of an error or complaint, regardless of probability or severity, into major categories (branches) and into their subcauses (twigs). It is the logical step after a Pareto chart has prioritized an important error. The cause and effect diagram presents a total picture of all things that can go wrong, from which the most likely causes are selected for further action.*

---

*An amusing incident occurred in Kuala Lumpur, Malaysia, where I was conducting a management seminar at a conference center. Unable to regulate the room temperature, I tried to find the conference room coordinator. After several unsuccessful efforts, I finally located him. He and his associates were huddled over a cause-and-effect diagram, the object of which was to improve seminar services!

Figure 17-2. Measurement of the administration of participative management.

Service Provided in Priority Order by the Department Administering the Participative Management Program		Timeliness	Accuracy/ Completeness	Cooperation	Responsiveness	Guidelines Options Alternatives	Overall Effectiveness
INFORMATION/ASSISTANCE	• Group Staff Support						
	• Steering Committee Assistance	2.0	2.0	3.0	2.75	2.3	2.3
	• Goal Committee Assistance	3.0	2.5	2.9	2.9	2.9	2.9
	• Improvement Team Assistance	2.4	2.5	2.7	2.0	1.5	2.5
	• Assistance during PMP Implementation	2.6	2.6	2.9	2.8	2.6	2.8
	• Assistance in Culture Progression	2.5	2.3	2.5	2.5	2.3	2.5
FEEDBACK SURVEY	• Survey Results Preparation	2.9	2.6	2.8	2.7	2.4	2.7
	• Survey Analysis	2.8	2.7	2.9	2.8	2.4	2.8
	• Manager Briefing	2.8	2.6	2.8	2.8	2.7	2.9
	• Results Management Support	2.6	2.7	2.9	2.7	2.6	2.7
TRAINING	• Training Classes	2.2	2.6	2.6	2.6	2.2	2.7
	• Training Schedule	2.0	2.0	2.1	2.1	2.0	2.0
	• Training Status Report	1.6	1.4	2.0	2.4	2.0	2.0
	• Participative Problem Solving Training	N/A	N/A	N/A	N/A	N/A	N/A
COUNCIL/TASK FORCE REPRESENTATION	• Representation	2.5	2.0	2.5	3.0	2.5	2.8
	• Knowledge of Subject	N/A	3.0	N/A	2.0	3.0	3.0
	• Level of Participation	3.0	N/A	2.5	2.0	3.0	2.5
	• Pilot Program Support/ Follow-Up	3.0	2.5	3.0	3.0	2.5	3.0

Overall effectiveness of PMP department: _____

Comments: _____

RATING SCALE:
3-Exceeds Requirements
2-Satisfactory
1-Needs Improvement
N/A-Not Applicable

DEFINITIONS FOR MEASUREMENT CRITERIA

Timeliness: Ability to meet required service within agreed-upon time.

Accuracy/Completeness: Service rendered is within acceptable limits of user's needs and covers all requirements.

Cooperation: Willingness and ability to work well with others.

Responsiveness: Supportiveness; Availability; Approachability; Communicability

Guidelines/Options/ Alternatives: Service provider offers guidelines for user to follow, suggesting options or alternatives to complete a given task.

Overall Effectiveness: A summary and integration of the above parameters.

Figure 17-3. Total plant Pareto chart.

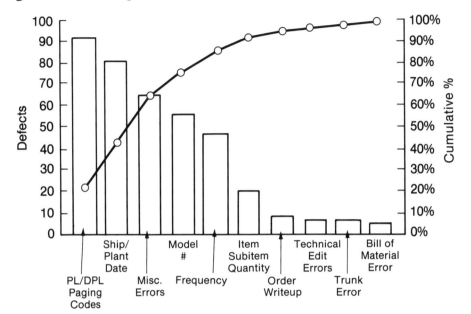

Brainstorming. Brainstorming, though not a productive tool for solving technical problems, is most appropriate for solving administrative and managerial problems in support services. It is a democratic and participative technique, it is synergistic, and it is effective. In fact, the worth of a final solution is proportional to the number of ideas generated in an initial brainstorming session.

Quality Circles. The pros and cons of quality circles in product work will be discussed more fully in Chapter 21. Their effectiveness in the United States has ranged from poor to mediocre. In support services, however, they can be an invaluable tool for solving nontechnical problems. Their chief value lies in the involvement of employees, in the power of their collective ideas, in the responsibility for results that quality circle members assume, and, finally, in the "ownership" feelings generated.

The Internal Audit. In some companies, a centralized function exists to audit financial aspects of departments and their systems and procedures. However, such an audit function rarely extends to measures of performance, especially quality. An internal quality audit of support services is best conducted by a team, consisting of a "customer" of the support service, a quality professional, and other knowledgeable people. It can use a survey instrument similar to that shown later in Appendix 2. The object is to determine the strengths and weaknesses of the particular support service and to counsel the department on ways of overcoming its weaknesses.

Technology Improvements. There is probably more general understanding of quality improvements in support services through technology break-throughs than there is of other methods already discussed. Computerization has revolutionized support services even more than it has manufacturing. Computers and associated software have been a boon to mankind and par-ticularly to office workers. Nevertheless, there are two caveats to bear in mind. First, in the headlong rush to computerize a process, the $64 question must be posed. Is the process or subprocess really necessary? There is no point in computerizing something and making it efficient when it does not need to be done at all! Second, the equipment must be reliable. How often have "customers" heard the lament "Our computers are down!" Perhaps improvement in equipment reliability is what support services need the most from their equipment suppliers.

"B" Versus "C" Tests. The technique of "B" vs. "C" comparisons is briefly described in Chapter 16 and in Table 13-2. "C" represents a *c*urrent method, "B" a *b*etter method. B vs. C is an extremely versatile tool, not only in product investigations, but also throughout a company's administrative and non-technical areas. It can be used to determine which of two personnel policies, two advertising campaigns, two sales promotions, two telephone systems, and so on is the better. The list of applications is endless.

As an example, a company was considering two types of gainsharing plans for its employees in order to reward performance over and above agreed-upon levels. Both plans were fairly equal in their financial implications. However, management wanted to know which plan the employees would favor. Three employees were selected at random and the two plans ex-plained to them. All three chose one plan over the other. This gave manage-ment a statistical confidence of 95 percent (based upon ranking theory and the law of permutations and combinations) that the plan chosen by the three employees would also be the preference of the rank-and-file employee in the company.

Value Engineering (VE). The use of this powerful discipline to reduce product costs and to improve product quality is treated in detail in Chap-ter 19. But its full potential for reducing costs and improving quality in support services has not been exploited. The value engineering methodology and the value engineering job plan (Table 19-1) are equally applicable to white-collar work.

The same questions that are asked in VE for a product should be asked when improving a white-collar "process" is at issue.

1. What does the process or activity or procedure do?
2. What does it cost?

3. What else will do the job?
4. What will that cost?

The creativity of a problem-solving team can then be applied to the following thought-provoking questions:

- Can the final (external) customer's requirements be simplified or made more quantifiable?
- Can conflicts between the final customer's requirements be reconciled?
- Can the process/procedure be eliminated or simplified?
- Can the process/procedure be computerized?
- Can the process/procedure be combined with another?/
- Can the process/procedure be performed by another group, department, or company?
- Can value be added to the process through greater customer satisfaction, greater quality/reliability, shorter cycle time?

Value engineering is as essential to NOAC as design of experiments is to product quality.

Conclusion. With NOAC as the centerpiece, the obfuscations and obstacles associated with the measurement and improvement of support service quality and productivity can, once and for all, be rendered obsolete.

Chapter 18

The March From AQLs
to Certification

There is more joy in Heaven upon the return of a prodigal son.

—Luke 15:7

A solid foundation for supplier quality having been laid in the previous chapters of Part III, the next step is to describe specific tools that can be used to convert even the poorest of suppliers into shining examples of quality success. This chapter presents a detailed road map showing how supplier quality can be transformed from the dismal quality levels of 1 percent and higher AQLs, through ppms of 100 and lower, through zero defects, and beyond to zero variation without adding cost—in fact, while reducing costs substantially. Two case studies will be used to further illuminate the journey.

What Will Not Work

The traditional road is a dreary, well-worn path that quality professionals travel in vain hope of supplier improvement. The road's blind alleys consist of:

- Switching from supplier to supplier in order to achieve even modest quality progress. For these travelers, hope is eternal!
- Not diminishing the supplier base in the process of this nomadic search for quality.
- Not shrinking the part number base with its ills of nonstandardization and duplication.
- Accepting blindly engineering specifications and tolerances.
- Automatically assuming that quality rejections are the supplier's fault
- Not classifying characteristics by importance.
- Little or no checking of form, fit, or function in the customer's application of the part.
- Not attempting to compare test equipment between incoming inspection and the supplier for correlation and accuracy.
- Seldom communicating with the supplier and *very* infrequently with the supplier's top management level.
- Relying heavily on corrective action requests (CARs), forms, procedures, manuals, and the written word with few visits to and almost no help to the supplier in solving problems.
- Gaining little knowledge of problem-solving as a unique and specialized discipline.

Fifty Percent of a Supplier's Quality Problems Are Caused by the Customer

Whenever a customer bemoans the poor quality of a supplier, the source of 50 percent of the trouble can be found when he looks into a mirror!

Before even involving the supplier, the customer should conduct design of experiments on key product parameters to separate the few important components from the unimportant; open up the tolerances on the latter to give the supplier reasonable leeway and to reduce costs; and determine the optimum values of the important components and their maximum allowable tolerances. Similarly, multiple environment overstress tests should be conducted on products to determine the weak-link components and strengthen their designs before establishing supplier requirements. Derating practices, described in Chapter 15, should also be used before finalizing specifications and transmitting it to a supplier.

As an illustration, one customer company specified a one-ampere diode. The diode was to be used in an under-the-hood application in a passenger car. The diode supplier built the part in compliance with the drawing. However, the part failed miserably in the field, causing embarassment all around. The customer imposed additional specifications. The part still failed at an unacceptably high rate.

Fingerpointing and recriminations did not help. The customer then at-

Table 18-1.   From AQLs to self-certification: Actions required.

Customer Actions	*Joint Actions*	*Supplier Actions*
• Translation of product specs. into component specs. with DOE	• Early supplier involvement (ESI) and cost targeting	• Continued design of experiments, SPC, *poka-yoke*
• MEOST, derating, thermal plots—to ensure reliability	• Clear, firm, meaningful, and mutually acceptable specs	• FMEA, DPA, failure analysis
• Internal education of engineers, quality assurance, purchasing, commodity teams	• Classification of characteristics	• Multiple environment overstress tests
• Feedback, communications at highest levels	• Correlation of equipment	• Total preventive maintenance (TPM) with process characterization
• Quality and JIT training	• Application reviews, systems test, field test	• Problem-solving teams
• Stable forecasts, linear schedules	• Product/process compatability	• Next operation as customer (NOAC)
	• Problem-solving demonstration projects using DOE, SPC, and *poka-yoke*	• "Field escape" review and failure analysis
		• Lessons learned log
		• Feed-forward information

tempted to monitor the supplier's processes, specifying in minute detail how the part should be fabricated, over and above the product requirements. The field failure rate hardly budged. Finally, the customer's engineers recalculated the design requirements and came to the conclusion that the rise in the diode's junction temperature in the car application warranted a substantial derating. A three-ampere diode was selected. The field failures on the new diode, produced by the same supplier, dropped to zero. The few pennies of additional cost were a drop in the ocean compared to the warranty costs and the hundreds of consumer complaints previously incurred.

Table 18-1 lists—under the headings of customer actions, joint actions, and supplier actions—the specific measures that are required to effect a rapid and dramatic improvement in supplier quality. Most of the items under customer actions have been covered in earlier chapters, but one item, feedback and communication at the highest levels, needs emphasis. At supplier conferences, top managers of customer companies frequently ask, "What do you suggest we do to be better customers for you?" More often than not, the answer is "Improve your communications with us. Let us hear from you more often." Communications with suppliers is as important as communicating with a company's employees.

A Demonstration Is Worth a Thousand Admonitions

Among the joint customer-supplier actions, the early involvement of the supplier in meeting a scientifically determined target cost (see Chapter 19) is the starting point. From these joint design efforts, clear and mutually acceptable specifications can be formulated and key parameters flagged using the discipline of classification of characteristics. The next step—even before product is shipped from the supplier—is to determine the compatibility of measurements made by instruments, gauges, and test equipment at both locations. Many a conflict between a supplier's outgoing tests and a customer's incoming tests can be resolved with this simple procedure. This is particularly true for complex, costly, and software-controlled products. Further, in the spirit of partnership, the supplier should be invited to review the use of his product in the customer's application and even to participate in systems testing and field checks with the customer and *his* customer to assure compatability of requirements. The supplier can often suggest alternatives that can improve field reliability or reduce costs and cycle time.

Not enough can be said about active, concrete help to the supplier. It is said that a picture is worth a thousand words. Similarly, a problem-solving demonstration is worth a thousand customer admonitions. Nothing convinces a supplier of the value of a customer or fires him up with respect and enthusiasm more than the customer's ability to roll up his sleeves and work alongside the supplier's people to solve chronic quality problems, using DOE or MEOST or *poka-yoke* sensors. Table 18-1 lists several of these joint actions.

Supplier Actions: Where the Buck Must Finally Stop

Only after these customer actions and joint actions have been taken can the supplier be expected to shoulder 100 percent responsibility for continual quality improvement. Table 18-1 lists these specific supplier actions, all of which have been explained in previous chapters. They are a distillation of those techniques that can achieve a quick and lasting breakthrough for quality. Now the pushbutton supplier excuses vanish. There is nowhere for him to hide. The buck stops there!

Parts Qualification: Proof of the Pudding

A supplier may pass a detailed quality system survey and other hurdles along the way. But the proof of the pudding will be his ability to deliver defect-free parts. This process begins with a physical qualification of the supplier's parts, generally by the components engineering department of the customer company. There are two sets of actions required.

Supplier Actions

- Provide physical samples, per customer-supplier agreed-upon specifications.
- Create SPC data ($^{C}p_k$ and precontrol).
- Supply reliability stress test data.

Customer Actions

- Conduct parametric tests (comparing customer-run data with data submitted by the supplier).
- Conduct reliability stress tests (comparing customer-run tests with data on tests conducted by the supplier under specified stress conditions).
- Run destructive physical analysis (DPA) (dissecting the samples to determine construction, process, and assembly defects that may not be detected in other tests).
- Give feedback to the supplier.

Often, the customer approval cycle takes weeks, time that can't be afforded when an early product launch into the market is projected. Most of the cycle time is expended in detailed reliability stress tests that consume up to 1,000 hours and more. This long cycle can be short-circuited through:

- Parallel testing by customer and partnership supplier.
- Joint testing by customer and partnership supplier at the supplier's facility.
- Multiple environment overstress tests that can compress time yet enhance reliability evaluations.

As a result, a qualification process that ordinarily takes six to twelve weeks can be shrunk to two weeks or less.

Sampling Plans: The Tired Quality Workhorse That Should Be Put to Pasture

For some time, until confidence in the supplier is fully established, customer incoming inspection with sampling plans is a necessary evil. When quality control "graduated" from brute force inspection in the 1950s, sampling plans became its shining symbol. A quality control program was considered useless unless it was peppered with sampling plans for every conceivable application, just as today many companies measure the worth of their quality programs by the amount of wall space covered with control charts! In fact, when I was asked to teach a course on quality in the graduate school of a prestigious university several years ago, I was horrified to discover that fourteen out of sixteen weeks of the curriculum had been devoted to sampling plans.

The most famous, and now notorious of these sampling plans, is the overworked, overblown, and underachieving Mil-Std-105D. Its earliest version, Mil-Std-105, was jointly developed in the 1940s by the United States, Great Britain, and Canada. Table 18-2 lists several traditional sampling plans, along with the applications and salient features of each plan. Conventional quality control textbooks are replete with the theory and methodology of these sampling plans. All of these sampling plans, with one exception, have outlived their usefulness, just as control charts have outlived theirs. Most sampling plans suffer from one or both of two diseases: inadequate protection, and high cost.

AQL Plans

Every sampling plan has its own unique operating characteristics (O-C) curve, relating percent defectives in a lot to the probability of the lot's acceptance. Figure 18-1 shows such an O-C curve for a particular sampling plan. A customer must first decide what quality level he desires, for instance, no more than 1 percent defective. The statistical definition of an acceptable quality level (AQL) of 1% is: If a lot with exactly 1 percent defects is received from a supplier, its probability of acceptance, using a sampling plan, would be exactly 95 percent, as shown in the figure. This is reasonable. However, if the quality in the supplier's lot is 2 percent defective, it would still be accepted 60 percent of the time. And if the quality is 3 percent defective, that is, three times worse than the desired quality level, it would still be accepted 25 percent of the time by the selected AQL sampling plan. In short, AQL sampling plans—with Mil-Std-105D as its best-known example—afford very poor protection against quality levels much worse than what the customer company has stipulated to the supplier.

LTPD Plans

The lack of protection to the customer inherent in AQL plans can be overcome through the use of Lot Tolerance Percent Defective (LTPD) sampling plans. As an example, for an LTPD of a 4 percent specified quality level, the

Table 18-2.   Salient features of traditional sampling plans.

Plan	Application	Salient Features
Mil-Std 105D (attributes)	In receiving inspection; end items; in-process inspection; supplies; paperwork and procedures.	Slanted toward AQLs and thus favors "producer"; reduces rejection risk of good lots; provides poor assurance against bad lots.
Dodge-Romig (attributes)	Useful where rejected lots can be 100% inspected.	Weighted toward LTPD and AOQL and thus favors "consumer"; inspection costs are high.
H-107 (attributes) Multi-level continuous	Suitable for high-volume continuous production.	Penalizes poor quality; rewards good quality.
H-106 (attributes) Multi-level continuous	Suitable for high-volume continuous production.	Same as H-107; it is the most economical of all plans if the quality level is better than specified.
Chain sampling (attributes)	When costly or destructive tests are called for.	Gives a second chance in C=0* plans by going back in history to include more units in sample if a single defect is found in present sample.
Discovery sampling (attributes)	Where probabilities of defective lots can be estimated.	Can be fitted into any other attributes plan with the object of reducing sample sizes based on estimated probabilities of lots being defective.
Mil-Std 414 (variables)	Specially useful when only a few characteristics need be controlled. Distribution, however, must be normal or quazi-normal.	Sample sizes much smaller than attributes plan with the same AQLs. Calculations are involved.

*C=0 refers to an acceptance number (of defects) of zero. With C=0, if the sample has 1 defect, the entire lot is rejected.

Figure 18-1. O-C curves for AQL and LTPD plans.

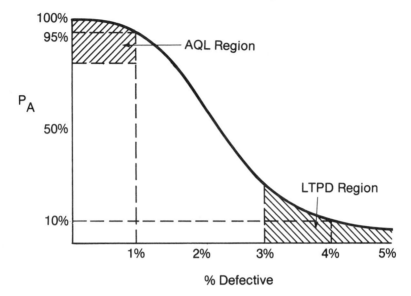

statistical interpretation is: If the supplier sent in a lot exactly 4 percent defective, its probability of acceptance, using the sampling plan and O-C curve of Figure 18-1, would be exactly 10 percent. In other words, such a quality level would be rejected 90 percent of the time. But the objective of incoming inspection is not to reject material masochistically. So the supplier and customer should mutually target a much lower percentage defective that has a higher probability of acceptance. The weakness, however, of LTPD sampling plans is that the sample size required is much larger than it is for AQL plans and thus more expensive.

AOQL Plans

Average Outgoing Quality Level (AOQL) plans use AQL plans to begin with, but revert to 100 percent inspection if the AQL sampling rejects the lot. The advantage of AOQL plans is that they put a ceiling on the percent defective allowed, such as 1 percent. The disadvantages are that: (1) this maximum defective is only an average figure, as individual lots can still be accepted at higher defect levels; (2) 100 percent inspection/screening is never 100 percent effective; and (3) 100 percent inspection is expensive.

The conclusion is inescapable, therefore, that AQL, LTPD, and AOQL plans all have fundamental and structural weaknesses. There is, however, an even more compelling weakness as customers increasingly demand higher and higher quality levels from suppliers, moving from percent defectives to parts per million (ppm) defectives. No sampling plan, except one, can discriminate between good quality and bad at levels below 500 ppm (that is, 0.05 percent defective) without recourse to 100 percent inspection. The more progressive customer companies are demanding of suppliers' defect levels below 100 ppm. That makes the whole sorry pack of sampling plans obsolete!

The Lot Plot Plan: Shainin to the Rescue

Dorian Shainin, who has devised the simplest and the best design of experiment tools for variation reduction, and the most economic and powerful tool of multiple environment overstress test for reliability breakthroughs, has also come up with the lot plot plan for sampling. In fact, this was Shainin's first claim to fame. Developed as early as the 1940s, it has languished in obscurity as new pretenders to sampling technology legitimacy have occupied the limelight. One reason why its light has been hidden under a bushel basket is that some of the calculations required by it, like average and standard deviation, have made application of the plan a bit tedious before the age of the handheld calculator and the computer. Another reason is the somewhat larger sample size of fifty pieces it requires. But as the drive for lower and lower defect levels progresses, the lot plot plan story could have a Cinderella finale.

Its methodology is simplicity itself. The sample size is always 50 regardless of whether a supplier lot is 100 parts or more than 100,000 parts. From the sample of 50, the average, $\bar{x}$, and the standard deviation (σ) of the sample are easily computed today. Next, the process limits, $\bar{x} \pm 3\sigma$, are calculated. If the specification limits for the parameter being checked are wider than the $\bar{x} \pm 3\sigma$ process limits, the lot quality (for a two-sided specification) is no worse than 2,600 ppm (that is 0.26 percent). This is shown in Figure 18-2, which depicts a normal curve* and the areas inside and outside various values of $\bar{x} \pm y\sigma$ where y ranges from 1 to 6. If quality levels tighter than 2,600 ppm are desired, the $\bar{x} \pm 4\sigma$ limits can be used. If the specification limits are wider than $\bar{x} + 4\sigma$, the quality level is no worse than 120 ppm. Similarly, if the specification limits are wider than $\bar{x} \pm 5\sigma$, the quality level is no worse than 0.57 ppm. Finally, if the specification limits are wider than $\bar{x} \pm 6\sigma$, the quality level will be no worse than 0.002 ppm, or 2,000 parts per billion (ppb)!

Like all other Shainin techniques, the lot plot sampling plan is simple to

---

*It may be argued that the percentages or ppm's calculated in this discussion apply only to normal curves and would not be valid for nonnormal distributions. However, if the *actual* process spread in the sample of 50 units, that is, the range, can be used instead of the $\bar{X} \pm y\sigma$ spread, the question of normality does not matter and the above ppm levels are still valid.

Figure 18-2. The Shainin lot plot sampling plan.

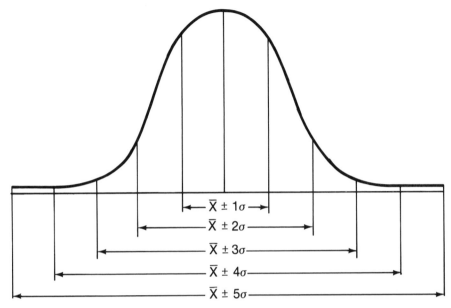

Limits	AREA		
	Within Limits	Outside Limits	
	2-Sided Specification	2-Sided Specification	1-Sided Specification
$\overline{X} \pm 1\sigma$	68.2%	31.8%	15.9%
$\overline{X} \pm 2\sigma$	95.44%	4.56%	2.28%
$\overline{X} \pm 3\sigma$	99.74%	0.26%	0.13%
$\overline{X} \pm 4\sigma$	99.998%	120 ppm	60 ppm
$\overline{X} \pm 5\sigma$	99.999943%	0.59 ppm	0.29 ppm
$\overline{X} \pm 6\sigma$	99.9999998%	0.002 ppm i.e., 2,000 ppb	0.001 ppm i.e., 1,000 ppb

understand, easy to administer, and statistically powerful. It is the only sampling plan that is effective below 500 ppm. The lot plot is a variables plan (requiring measurements) as opposed to an attributes plan (requiring go/no go, accept/reject decisions). The conversion from attributes to variables was discussed in Chapter 14 under precontrol, with the use of a linear scale (dubbed the Bo Derek scale) from 1 to 10, or by assigning weights to each attribute in terms of importance. The same techniques can be used with the lot plot plan, making it even more versatile.

Skip Lot Plans

Once several lots from a supplier, generally five to ten, have passed through incoming inspection without rejection, a skip lot plan can be introduced whereby only one out of three or five or ten lots is checked. Skip lot is a halfway house between traditional sampling plans and the total elimination of incoming inspection. It is generally used in the early stages of supplier partnership when confidence in his quality is still tentative. In some companies, however, one part from every lot is checked anyway just to make sure that the parts received are the same as those ordered. This technique is referred to as "identity inspection."

The IBM Story

In the final analysis, a reliance on any sampling plan, even the excellent lot plot, is a postmortem crutch. This is best illustrated by an experience IBM had with a new Japanese supplier. "Big Blue," with its reputation for quality, stipulated in its order that the maximum defect level allowable was 3 per 10,000 parts (that is, 300 ppm, a respectable quality level). When the shipment was received, the parts were found to be perfect; there were zero defects. But, along with the parts, a small box had also been shipped. Inside, IBM found this note:

> We do not understand your American specifications. However, here are the three defective parts we made specially, to conform to your requirements.

Certification and Self-Certification

Any inspection, whether on incoming lots, on the line, or on outgoing product, is too late. The quality is already built in by the supplier or in production. Inspection, then, is only a brute-force sorting function. One of the quality goals of the customer-supplier partnership is to rapidly graduate from incoming inspection and sampling plans to skip lot to certification (that is, no incoming inspection). But this should not be based on results at the customer's plant alone. Some suppliers in their eagerness to achieve certification status with their customers screen their products before shipment with two, three, and four successive final inspections. That is not quality. It is stupidity.

For certification to have meaning, the supplier should have done his homework, albeit with the help of the customer, in designing experiments to reduce his product, process, and material variations. He should then maintain statistical control through the use of precontrol. That is what is meant by self-certification. The final step is for the supplier to send precontrol data, not histograms, to the customer with each lot as hard evidence of complete control. (In some companies, even this requirement is eliminated, as complete trust in the supplier is built up.)

Figure 18-3 is an example of a certification policy formulated by a company that has been a pioneer in supply management. It clearly states the prerequisites, before certification can be initiated, along with the responsibilities of both supplier and customer as they move to the ultimate in certification. It is a tough policy, but when fulfilled, the supplier can easily claim the distinction of being world-class.

Figure 18-3.   Company M certification policy.

Prerequisities

1. Clear, complete, meaningful, and mutually acceptable specifications along with the classification of characteristics.
2. Correlation of Company M and supplier test methods, equipment, and measurements.
3. Minimum of five lots with no lot rejections. Failure to meet stipulated C_{p_k} levels for critical parameters will constitute a lot rejection even though the lot contains zero defects vis-à-vis specifications.
4. No line or field rejects on critical parameters. In the absence of field history, the results of multiple environment overstress tests will be used.
5. Feedback system in place to monitor line and field rejects, and to furnish data back to the supplier in a timely manner.

Supplier Requirements for Certification

1. Use of design of experiments to identify and reduce variations in product, process, and material.
2. Reliability stress tests, preferably multiple environment overstress tests (MEOST), to assure maximum field reliability.

(continued)

Figure 18-3. *Continued.*

3. Use of SPC (Positrol, process certification, and precontrol) to maintain stipulated $^{C}P_k$ levels and to transmit precontrol data to Company M.
4. Feed-forward information or early warning (before shipment) to Company M on: plant location change; any design/process/material change; any out-of-control products.

Company M Requirements for Certification

1. Periodic visits and help in DOE, SPC, and MEOST.
2. Periodic reliability stress tests (preferably MEOST).
3. Periodic destructive physical analysis (DPA) and tear-down audits.

Decertification

1. If line or stress test or field failures are found by Company M and determined, through failure analysis, to be the supplier's responsibility, the supplier's part is immediately decertified.
2. The penalty for decertification, depending upon severity, can range from reinstituting incoming inspection to sorting and purging at the supplier's expense, to financial penalties, to a termination of relations.

Recertification

To qualify for recertification, the supplier must:
1. Investigate, with company M personnel, the root cause of the reject or failure.
2. Investigate how the defect escaped the safety net of SPC maintenance controls.
3. Demonstrate how the SPC safety net has been tightened to prevent a recurrence.
4. Reestablish steps 3 and 4 of the prerequisites.

Interim Role for Incoming Inspection

As a result of certification, with a goal of 90 percent certified parts,* incoming inspection manpower can be reduced drastically. But it cannot be reduced to zero. There will always be new suppliers to "prove in" and occasionally, old suppliers who because of a temporary decertification may require a period of inspection "prop-up."

---

*Certification is mostly on the basis of part numbers. Only rarely, when *all* of the supplier's parts are certified, can certification by supplier be considered.

The most important task for incoming inspection, however, is to move from an evaluation of quality alone to an evaluation of reliability. This is not required for every lot received. It should be done periodically with:

1. Appropriate reliability stress tests (especially MEOST).
2. Tear-down audits of product assemblies, so that design and assembly weaknesses that may not be detected in routine tests can be found.
3. Destructive physical analysis (DPA), at the component level, where the part is physically dissected in an attempt to find construction flaws and anomalous "maverick" phenomena not detectable in tests. The technique of paired comparisons previously shown in Table 14-2 is a useful discipline in DPA work.

Two Case Studies of Quality Breakthroughs

The roadmap charted in this chapter will be illustrated with the success stories of two suppliers, each with his own unique problems, who were converted from disqualification to certified suppliers with near-perfect quality.

The Saving of a Metal Fabricator

The first case involves a metal fabricator who thought he had reason to be proud of the quality levels he delivered to his prime customer. These were in the range of 97 percent and 98 percent acceptance by the customer's sampling inspection. The supplier honestly believed that he was producing at a quality level that "even exceeded military requirements." (He was not far from wrong, considering the lack of real quality progress in that branch of government since the early 1970s!) But the customer, however, was disgusted with the supplier's quality. Fierce competition in the marketplace required this customer to improve his quality levels by a minimum of ten times, and unless his suppliers achieved a similar improvement he felt he would be competing with one hand tied behind his back. A new defect level of 0.1 percent or 1,000 ppm—twenty to thirty times lower than the 2 to 3 percent defects that the supplier was delivering—had been mandated. With tightened sampling plans, 8 to 10 percent of the lots were being rejected.

The situation created frustration all around. The customer's management, annoyed by the slow pace of progress and feeling hampered by "dull-witted" suppliers, leaned hard on its quality department to straighten things out. Quality, feeling the pressure, recommended that the supplier be terminated. Purchasing, for its part, faced a dilemma. On the one hand, the supplier handled a large volume of business, had much of the tooling "locked up," and had a history of extreme cooperation: "They have turned on a dime to accommodate our crazy schedules." On the other, Purchasing's buyers were being severely chastised for lack of attention to the new quality religion.

The supplier meanwhile was sitting on a time bomb. The harder he tried, the worse he fared in the customer's incoming inspection. He privately argued that at least 50 percent of the material rejected was the customer's responsibility. His rationale was as follows:

1. The customer's standards had been drastically tightened. What he had accepted yesterday, he rejected today.
2. The customer's incoming inspection was divided into "fiefdoms." One inspector would reject what another would pass. There was little consistency and little coordination.
3. Several specifications were needlessly tight—and costly.
4. The customer was making too many changes and the directions would come from his engineering and purchasing departments separately, and often orally.
5. The customer's schedules, in terms of delivery and quantity, fluctuated wildly and frequently.

Act I. Internal Customer Review: In desperation, Purchasing called on the assistance of a senior corporate consultant. His immediate task was to calm the waters and move the situation from confrontation to cooperation. (Partnership seemed out of reach.) He started with the customer rather than with the supplier.

The incoming history was reviewed to determine the part numbers with the highest rejects. The most frequent defect modes in these part numbers were pinpointed. He next reviewed specifications and drawings on these parts with Engineering, objectively challenging every dimension, tolerance, or finish required. Finally, the customer's incoming inspection disciplines and procedures were improved and made consistent.

Act 2. Customer-Supplier Interface: The next task was to get the customer's engineers and the supplier's technical people together to review all requirements. This resulted in:

- Firm, unambiguous, and mutually acceptable specifications.
- Classification of various parameters in terms of importance. (On the

truly important parameters, the supplier had to go beyond zero defects to achieve a minimum $^{C_{P_k}}$ of 2.0.)

- Recalibration of test equipment and gauges between customer and supplier to ensure accuracy and correlation.
- Insistence on all customer orders for changes being put in writing over a buyer's signature. A special form was devised to facilitate the transmission.
- Agreement for blanket orders, with schedules frozen for the first thirty days.

Act 3. Supplier Coaching: The main challenge was at the supplier's facility, which the consultant visited once a week on average with the object of offering active, concrete help. Meetings were held, first with the supplier's management and then with the entire supervisory staff, to point out the reasons for elevating quality: profitability for the company, job security and job enhancement for all employees. Additional "town meetings" elicited quality problems from the supervisory staff and key employees, and teams were formed to solve the supplier's top five problems. At subsequent meetings, proposed solutions were discussed and implemented.

Elementary quality costs—customer returns, scrap, repair, inspection, and test—were gathered and analyzed. Key product lines were flow charted and the defects and associated costs at each work station gathered. A cycle time profile—from customer order to shipment—was developed.

Training commenced for management, supervisory staff, and key employees in the design of experiments, SPC, and *poka-yoke.* Three experiments were conducted to reduce variability on key processes.

Positrol and process certification were established for key processes and work stations respectively. Pre-control was initiated throughout the plant on all key variables. *Poka-yoke* was designed to prevent "silly" operator-controllable errors. The practice of next operator as customer (NOAC) was introduced, as a further check on passed-through errors.

Supervisors were encouraged to be teachers and coaches, rather than parts chasers and expediters, and a pilot training program for the supplier's key suppliers was started. Finally, a small financial reward system was established for teams that met new standards on yields and cycle time.

Epilogue: The following results were achieved:

- At the end of the first month, the lot reject level at the customer's incoming inspection was still 8 percent.
- At the end of the second month, the lot reject level was down only to 7 percent.
- At the end of the third month, lot reject levels reached zero.

- For the next six months, lot reject levels continued at zero.
- Subsequently, the supplier was put on self-certification.
- The customer's commodity team elevated the supplier from near-disqualification to best-in-class status among the seven suppliers in that commodity.
- The supplier experienced dramatic reductions in his quality costs as well as in his cycle time.

Resolving a Finishing Operation Crisis

In a second case, a veritable three-ring circus was going on among a customer, his sheet-metal suppliers, and the subsuppliers who performed plating and painting operations for the suppliers. The customer blamed his suppliers for the poor appearance of the plated and painted parts he was receiving. To the suppliers' pleas that they were at the mercy of their plating and painting subsuppliers, the customer's response was that that was their problem: "Find better finishers. Your job is to give us quality parts."

The suppliers gave the crossed-arm salute, silently accusing the other two parties while considering themselves Simon-pure. They blamed the customer for inconsistent cosmetic standards, for "fly-specking," and for turning a deaf ear to suggestions for improvement. They faulted their finishing suppliers for shoddy quality, poor processes, an uncaring attitude, and high prices at every turn.

The finishers, for their part, put the blame squarely on the suppliers. They complained that the suppliers (1) did not control their metal thicknesses, thereby making a quality finish a hit-or-miss proposition; (2) did not pay sufficient attention to metal corrosion; (3) did not have a FIFO (first in, first out) stock rotation system; (4) did not have an adequate packaging system to prevent damage in handling and transportation; and (5) were always squeezing them for price reductions, threatening to take their business elsewhere if the finishers did not "play ball."

A Commodity Team to the Rescue: The customer's sheet-metal commodity team took on the responsibility for resolving these persistent problems once and for all. They had already begun to narrow the list of suppliers for that commodity. They went further and selected the five best suppliers. The team requested these suppliers to cooperate among themselves and to select no more than four finishing suppliers with whom, collectively, they would do business in the future.

The commodity team then convened a conference of suppliers and finishers at which mutual problems were frankly but constructively discussed. In response to one supplier's suggestion, it was decided to use plating only where the part was not visible to the end user. The primary purpose of plating would be protection against corrosion, not cosmetics. Painting would be used where cosmetics and end-user visibility were important. An evaluation of various painting approaches, based on value engineering techniques, led to the selection of two judged to be attractive to the user and in which blemishes would be the least noticeable and therefore the least objectionable.

All three parties agreed to the use of a "Bo Derek" linear scale for measuring product quality, and this agreement was captured in ten physical samples, ranging from the very poor, rating a 1, to the perfect, rating a 10. This removed subjectivity from the inspection process and thus did away with a major cause of controversy in the past.

Packaging issues, to protect the parts against damage, during handling and transportation, were resolved. The customer's commodity team was persuaded to accept slightly higher prices, but benefited by the overall savings that could be expected from eliminating 100 percent inspection—now no longer necessary—and from not having to contend with rejections at all four stages of raw metal supplier, finisher, stamping supplier, and customer, as well as appreciable reductions in cycle time.

The suppliers were persuaded to demand improved quality from the metal mills. Their plea that the steel mills were a law unto themselves, too big to influence, and had a "take it or leave it" attitude, was looked upon as a cop-out in today's competitive market. The commodity team* pointed out that the automotive companies, working closely with domestic suppliers, had improved the quality of U.S. steel beyond that used by their Japanese competitors. Several smaller steel companies, it was suggested, were aggressively pursuing quality and had surpassed the larger mills.

The most important actions were taken at the finishers' plants. If the suppliers were in the dark ages of quality, the finishers were in the stone age! In seminars and in individual visits, the finishers were coached in the importance of quality. Because they were more process-oriented, design of experiments were conducted to identify important process parameters and to control them through Positrol and precontrol. The concept of next operation as customer (NOAC) was also implemented.

The Bottom Line: It took several months of intensive effort to turn around the chaotic situation that had existed among squabbling customer, suppliers, and subsuppliers. The successful outcome can be measured by the tangible results in three areas:

- *Quality:* Reject levels from suppliers to finishers, finishers to suppliers, and suppliers to customer were reduced by 12 to 1. The 100 percent

---

* The commodity team offered to intercede with the metal mills on behalf of the suppliers, but this step did not occur.Another innovation that wasn't pursued was to have the customer buy metal directly from the mill suppliers. The large quantities as well as the reputation of the customer company could have resulted in lower costs and better quality for all.

inspections at each stage were reduced to sample inspections and even skip lot. The next milestone will be self-certification at each stage. (There was, however, a lack of progress in quality improvement from the mills.)

- Cost: Despite an increase in packaging costs, the overall cost reduction was estimated in the millions of dollars. The most dramatic break-through occurred in the value engineering of the plating versus painting requirements.

- Cycle time: Yield improvements at the finishers' plants, drastic reductions from 100 percent inspections, and elimination of endless arguments about product acceptability all contributed to appreciable reductions in cycle time. A chaotic hand-to-mouth delivery was transformed into a smoother just-in-time (JIT) process.

Part IV

COST REDUCTION AND CYCLE TIME MANAGEMENT: THE OTHER POWERFUL MEMBERS OF THE TROIKA

Chapter 19

Supplier Cost Reduction: Tapping the Gold Mine

If someone offered you an opportunity to improve your company's performance and productivity, increase profit, reduce costs, provide greater employee involvement, while developing in them positive habits and attitudes, wouldn't you want to know about such a process?

—Delco Electronics pamphlet on value engineering

Selling Prices Lower Than Our Bill of Material Costs

Some companies are flabbergasted to discover that their foreign competition's selling prices are actually lower than their own bill of material costs. In frustration, they attribute the cost differential to "cheap labor," "new plant equipment that we funded," "dumping," "foreign government subsidies," and a host of other causes that serve as convenient excuses. Only recently have U.S. companies begun to turn the searchlight on themselves.

As we have seen, arbitrary layoffs or fleeing overseas to reduce insignificant direct labor costs do not provide the answer to the cost reduction problem. Among the more positive approaches to cost reduction previously discussed, we know that:

313

- Quality improvement remains the fastest, easiest, and surest route to cost reduction. Among its many tools, the elimination of needless, burdensome specifications and classification of characteristics deserve special mention. And, of course, yield improvement and the drastic reductions in costs from poor quality are veritable gold mines.
- Supplier partnerships can achieve substantial savings in material costs through the larger volumes ordered from suppliers and longer-term contracts offered suppliers.
- The leverage provided by corporate negotiations is another battering ram in bringing down high cost walls.
- Electronic communications in several customer-supplier interfaces, from engineering to accounts payable, reduce costs through the elimination of paperwork and bureaucracy.
- A "lessons learned" log prevents repetition of the same mistakes in the next generation of designs.
- Training prevents job obsolescence and enhances the productivity of all employees.
- The team concept, especially the supply management team, which includes the supplier as an extension of the company, is the key to having people work together to achieve management's goals, instead of having guerrilla warfare waged across departmental boundaries.

This chapter will concentrate on methods that are even more directly associated with cost reduction, methods that can help to achieve reductions in supply costs of 10 percent and more, not on a one-time basis but each year.

Chapter 20 will discuss how cycle time reduction in both manufacturing and support services can drastically reduce inventories of product and people and improve cash flow.

Preventing Part Number Proliferation and Pollution

As with quality, so also with costs, the initiative must come from the customer company. Foremost among the actions the customer must take before reaching for supplier cost reductions is a reduction of his part numbers. This should precede reducing the number of suppliers. The cost leverage of a reduced supplier base can be checkmated if the part number base is allowed to expand indiscriminately by an uncaring, autonomous engineering department.

As a first step toward preventing this part number proliferation, a customer company must reassess its strategic business units (SBUs). Figure 19-1 is the well-known Boston Consulting Group (BCG) portfolio analysis that separates SBUs into four categories on the basis of their competency versus their industry attractiveness:

Figure 19-1. Boston Consulting Group portfolio analysis contrasting U.S. and foreign approaches to SBUs.

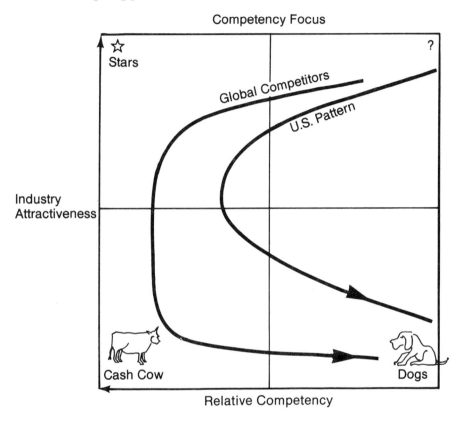

1. "Dog" SBUs, with low competency and low industry attractiveness, should be divested.
2. "Cash Cow" SBUs, with high competency but low industry attractiveness, should be "harvested." That is, no resources need be poured in, but they should be milked to provide cash for the question mark and star SBUs.
3. "Question mark" SBUs, with low competency but high industry attractiveness, should be nurtured with cash inflows to move them into the star category.
4. "Star" SBUs, with high competency and high industry attractiveness, should be a major company focus.

Figure 19-1 also shows the difference between U.S. companies and their more aggressive global competitors. The former stay in question mark businesses too long, barely advance to star businesses, and then stay there for too short a time. When industry attractiveness fades and these businesses become cash cows, U.S. companies do not harvest them to the fullest extent before they degenerate into dog businesses. Global competitors, on the other hand, rapidly increase their own competencies to move from question mark to star businesses, capitalize on that ideal situation longer, and then, when industry attractiveness is gone, milk the cash cows for all they are worth before they reach dog status.

The unprofitable, unattractive dog businesses form an ideal starting point on the long road to part number reduction. Divesting them is usually a wrenching decision for management. Emotions get in the way. What to do with the good, loyal people who will be affected is the most difficult aspect of divestiture. Nevertheless, as the dean of management, Peter F. Drucker, stresses, a company must make concentration decisions from time to time in order to survive. A single divestiture of an unprofitable business can reduce a large volume of part numbers in one stroke. As an example, when a medium-size company made the bold decision to get out of the consumer business with which it had started fifty years before, it instantly reduced its total part number base from 64,000 to 37,000

Next in line should be the systematic reduction of product lines that are unprofitable or relatively unimportant to customers. Pareto's law, which indicates a nonlinear relationship between cause and effect, can be applied here. Generally, 80 percent or more of the total number of product lines contribute 20 percent or less to profit. Some of these "80 percenters" are prime candidates for elimination.

Third, the same logic should apply to the vast array of models within a product line. Pareto's 80 to 20 law can again be applied to reduce those models that constitute 80 percent of the total number of models but contribute 20 percent or less to overall profitability. One manufacturer of entertainment products surveyed his entire line. He found that 76 percent of the models had a cumulative pack total of less than 5,000 units per year; 13 percent were between 5,000 and 10,000 units; and 11 percent were over 10,000 units. The obvious area in which to trim the number of models was the 76 percent group. A plan was drawn up to eliminate 60 percent of the models in this group. At first, the sales force resisted. Customers, they argued, wanted diversity, and one of the competitive advantages of this company was its broad line. The plan was redrawn. Through a combination of greater model commonality, selective price increases and appeals to the customer, a third of the models in the 76 percent group and a tenth of the models in the 13 percent group were eliminated.

A fourth technique in reducing part number counts is to reduce the number of product options offered by a company. Unchecked, models can multiply faster than rabbits. By grouping several options together and offering customers a limited grouping of such options, a measure of standardization can be introduced in production. For instance, a Ford LTD and a Honda

Accord can be considered, roughly, to be in the same price range of cars. If Ford were to build a separate car for each combination of its numerous options, 64,000 LTDs would be lined up—no two of them exactly alike! The same figure for Honda would be 464 separate cars.

Group Technology: The Rookie Likely to Become MVP

The latest addition to the list of cost reduction disciplines is group technology (GT). And this rookie may well vie for the honor of being most valuable player on the cost reduction team. The cost savings potential of group technology in ten areas can be seen from the following list.*

- 52 percent in new part design
- 10 percent in number of drawings
- 30 percent in new shop drawings
- 60 percent in industrial engineering time
- 20 percent in production floor space
- 42 percent in raw material stocks
- 69 percent in setup times
- 70 percent in through-put times
- 62 percent in WIP inventory
- 82 percent in overdue orders

Other research† enumerates the following additional benefits of GT:

- Expenditures for new machines reduced by up to 25 percent
- Tooling costs reduced by up to 35 percent
- Capacity of existing machinery increased by up to 40 percent
- Process planning reduced by up to 50 percent
- Rework and scrap reduced by up to 75 percent

An additional gold nugget, included in another GT study,§ is the cost of introducing a new part into manufacturing, which can range from $1,300 to $12,000, including expenses for design, planning and control, and tools and fixtures. Let us assume, for instance, that a company releases 1,000 new parts per year (not an untypical number for a medium- to large-size com-

---

*Reprinted by permission from "Group Technology: An Overview and Bibliography," 1976, Metcut Research Associates, Inc.
†Carried out by Erik Nebergall and Bill Santen, of Cincinnati Milacron, and presented in *Production Magazine*, December 1987.
§"Group Technology and Productivity" by Nancy L. Hyer and Urban Wemmerlov in the July–August 1984 issue of *Harvard Business Review*, an excellent reference work on GT.

Figure 19-2. The burgeoning costs of adding a new part.

One-Time Expenses

- Drafting the print; *$20 to $100*
- Securing a print number from specs: *$10*
- Loading the part in the bill of material in development: *$10*
- Print reviews by development, manufacturing, quality, purchasing: *$20 to $200*
- Release of the print through specs department: *$20 to $100*
- Copies made and distributed (to purchasing for quotes, etc.) *$100 to $200*
- Purchasing quote cycle (phone and mailing expenses): *$100 to $200*
- Vendor survey: *$50 to $1,000*
- Tooling costs if unique tool is required: *$200 to $200,000*
- Test equipment expenses if unique electrically: *$200 to $10,000*
- Qualification costs: *$500 to $800*

Continuing Expenses

- Inspection costs (new files, new lots to handle, new training, etc.)
- Stock costs (new bins, stock inventory, offshore pipe to fill, etc.)
- Pick to the line
- Bin addition on line
- Added material tracking and ordering for production
- Added purchasing tracking and buying
- Carrying costs

---

pany). If it could substitute current parts for only 10 percent of these new parts, the savings would range from $130,000 to $1.2 million! One company flow-charted the various steps involved in adding a new part and the associated costs for each step. These are listed in Figure 19-2, which shows how rapidly costs can pile up in the production of a new part, without mentioning the cost of maintaining it in the system in perpetuity.

Since GT is so good, what is it, and how does it work? The principle of GT is that parts that are similar in shape, size, tolerances, and other design characteristics can be consolidated into fewer parts, and that parts using similar manufacturing processes can be grouped together in smaller, dedicated processes called group technology cells. Its uses extend to:

- Parts design and design retrieval coding
- Manufacturing cells
- Computer-aided process planning (CAPP)
- Purchasing and tooling
- Substitution and cost estimation

Parts Design and Design Retrieval

How does part design proliferation occur? It happens when engineers, who are otherwise rational, do not have either a system to find or the patience to look for closely similar parts already in existence. Thus they keep designing new ones to meet every special need. Take the case of General Dynamics,* where a virtually identical nut and coupling unit had been designed on five separate occasions by five different design engineers and drawn by five draftsmen. To compound the irony, the parts were purchased from five different suppliers at prices ranging from 22 cents to $7.50 each!

Coding. Design retrieval is greatly facilitated today with the use of the computer. In the B.C. (before computer) era, a part could not be completely characterized by a part number. In a seven-digit part number, for instance, the first two digits would be significant in describing the part category or commodity, but the remaining digits would be chosen at random and thus nonsignificant. In the computer age, however, a code of twenty to thirty digits can be assigned to a part that would completely describe (or characterize) it. Each digit would be associated with a particular characteristic, such as shape, tolerance, and so forth. The code could pinpoint external and internal shapes, dimensions, tolerances, chemistry of the raw material, surface finish, and a series of manufacturing processes.

The aim of GT is not to standardize parts in any straitjacket fashion. Rather, it is to find the largest area of commonality. A GT coded parts population does away with the cumbersome engineering task of sifting through old drawings to find an already designed part. The designer can enter on a CRT a partial code describing the main characteristics of the needed part. The computer will then search the GT data base for all parts with the same partial code, that is, parts in the same family. The designer can then review the specifications of each of these parts and either select an existing part or modify it slightly.

The Harris Corporation used a novel method to convert to GT. It selected a random sample of 3,000 parts from a total of 21,000 fabricated parts. Each of these was photographed against a grid of 1-inch squares to show its configuration and approximate size. The photographs were then sorted into only eleven separate part families requiring a mere eighteen GT manufacturing cells!

Manufacturing Cells (GT Cells)

Another major feature of GT is its ability to create manufacturing cells (or group technology cells). A cell is a collection of machine tools and mate-

---

*Raymond J. Levulis, "Group Technology," K.W. Tunnell Consulting Company report.

rials-handling equipment grouped to process a family of parts. The allocation of dedicated equipment to a subset of parts may increase capital expenditures somewhat and may also reduce equipment utilization time. But those costs become insignificant when compared with the substantial gains in run time (cycle time), quality, and materials handling (transportation), as well as the reductions in setup time, inventories, and the all-important response time to customers made possible by group technology cells.

One U.S. manufacturer, EG&G Sealol,* converted 900 parts into GT cells. In one cell alone, 324 parts that had formerly been routed to twenty-two machines were now produced on seven machines. Total output rose 150 percent, while work in process (WIP) was reduced by 15 percent. Otis Engineering in Carrollton, Texas, estimated that its cost of $5 million a year on setups was reduced by 35 percent through the use of GT cells.

Another benefit of GT cells is job enrichment for the equipment operators through wider task variety, requiring higher skills and flexibility—all important motivation factors. The role of the foreman or supervisor also changes from managing just a single process to controlling the production of a part entirely through its several process steps.

Process Planning

Two important tasks in manufacturing planning and manufacturing engineering are scheduling and process planning. Job scheduling establishes the order in which parts should be processed and their expected completion times. Process planning is more detailed. It decides on the sequence of machines through which a part is routed and the number of operations required at each machine. It determines tool, jig, and fixture selection and time standards for each operation.

Before GT, process planners would develop different process plans for the same part. Furthermore, they would rarely update these plans when new equipment required that changes be made. With computer-aided process plans (CAPP) and GT, these process plans can be standardized, reduced in number, stored, retrieved, edited, and printed efficiently. One company, which used 477 separate process plans for 523 different gears, was able to eliminate 400 of them with GT. Another company, which had used 87 different process plans and 51 machine tools to produce 150 parts, reduced the task to 31 process plans and only 8 machines by using GT. At Otis Engineering, the time it took to produce a new NC tape dropped from between 4 and 8 hours to 30 minutes when GT was introduced.

* James Nolan, "Cellular Manufacturing at EG&G Sealol," Society of Manufacturing Engineering seminar, Dallas, 1983.

Purchasing and Tooling

A natural extension of GT is the use of the GT coding system to reduce the proliferation of purchases of different kinds of parts and tools that serve identical or similar functions. GT can now help Purchasing to act as a check on Engineering by obtaining a list of identical parts for which designers specified different brands.

Substitution and Cost Estimation

GT can also be used to find substitute parts more easily if a shortage should develop, and can be used to make cost estimates on new bids. Along with CAPP, GT can construct cost estimates more quickly and accurately than can traditional methods. Finally, GT can help to determine anticipated changes in raw material costs. With GT coding, a list of all parts that use a particular raw material can be obtained within minutes and new costs estimated.

Roadblocks to Implementing GT

If GT produces all these benefits, why have most companies not embraced it? First, most don't even know of its existence. Second, among those exposed to it, the complex coding system frightens the timid ones. It is true that devising a coding system to completely characterize a whole range of parts can be quite difficult. More than one coding system may be required. Off-the-shelf coding systems are available, but some customizing is inevitable within each company. Coding requires planning, resources, time—months, perhaps even years—but once in place, the payoff is one big bonanza.

Organizational and individual resistance to change also act as roadblocks. A part number culture so long ingrained in a company is hard to change. Engineers, who tend to be conservative by nature, may balk at GT, especially when the financial rewards they receive are based on the number of parts or drawings they churn out! Unions tend to look upon the multiskilled, flexible worker as yet another management trick to put them out of business. Finally, the GT cell requires greater attention to total preventive maintenance, more knowledgeable foremen, greater autonomy for the work force, and a breakup of the empires of large, bureaucratic and centralized support departments.

GT history indicates that starting is the hardest. But once the journey is begun, not a single company has looked back.

Alternatives to Group Technology

For companies that are afraid to commit to the heavy up-front investment in group technology and its coding, a few "poor man's GT" approaches are available. Some of these are old, others new.

Standardization

One of the oldest and most enduring techniques is standardization—not only of parts but also of subassemblies, modules, circuits, and even software. Along with simplification, standardization has proved to be a well-worn path to success for Japanese companies. It is seldom realized that whenever a company develops a drawing or a print, it automatically becomes a single, unique customer! It has been estimated that it costs an average of $3,000 to introduce a new drawing or print. So the more unique the parts a company develops for a product are, the greater will be the development costs and the recurring costs of procurement. In fact, one measure of a product's cost effectiveness is the percentage of standard, off-the-shelf parts used in the design. Some Japanese companies go one step further. They use as many of their competitors' parts as possible so that they can get lower prices from common suppliers.

Preferred Parts List

Having a preferred parts list can be described as a first, tentative step toward GT. A company's components engineering department searches through hundreds of components in each commodity and settles on a much narrower list of parts that are labeled preferred parts. The list is circulated to engineering, purchasing, and specifications departments along with management instructions that any new part not on the preferred parts list should be flagged and requires the approval of the chief engineer before procurement can begin. In addition, audits are conducted periodically on new designs to determine the number of preferred parts actually used as a percentage of the maximum number that should have been used. Using these techniques, one company selected 16,458 preferred parts from its sprawling list of 53,526 active part numbers. In its audits a year later, the number of preferred parts used as a percentage of a maximum total increased from less than 50 percent to 87 percent.

Description Data Base

A few companies have settled on a technique that is halfway between the preferred parts list approach and full-fledged GT. Called a description data base (DDB), it permits the translation of engineering characteristics to part numbers and vice versa. To take a simple example, when an engineer wants to know if a part number exists for a fixed carbon, 10,000 ohm, 5 percent, ¼ watt resistor, he or she accesses the DDB computer system and specifies the term "resistor." A menu appears on the screen that permits the parameters—fixed carbon, 10,000 ohms, 5 percent, and ¼ watt—to be entered. The DDB system then conducts a search and displays all the part numbers that satisfy the selected parameters.

The DDB system also keeps track of print issue, tracing location, cost, qualified part code, and facility usage. It bypasses the need for extensive recoding of part numbers in GT and may be useful for somewhat homogeneous part families, such as electronic parts. One company that was afflicted by having more than 9,000 separate semiconductor part numbers, 14,000 fixed capacity part numbers, and 13,000 resistor part numbers was able, first, to characterize these parts with DDB and, second, to reduce the parts pollution.

However, DDB is not as versatile as GT is in covering vastly different part families, especially in the mechanical areas; nor is it a useful tool in the construction of GT cells.

Reverse Engineering, Benchmarking, and Cost Targeting

Besides reducing its part number base and adopting group technology, a customer company must undertake three other disciplines before involving its partnership suppliers in its cost reduction drive.

Reverse engineering is a new name for an old technique—competitive analysis. It evaluates a competitor's physical product by examining its features, construction, and the materials used in it, by assessing its performance and reliability, and by estimating its cost. The latter is done by highly qualified cost estimators who have strong engineering, production, and financial backgrounds. They can estimate, within an amazing degree of accuracy, the cost of the competitor's product, subassembly, or key piece part. These costs then become a target for the company and its partnership supplier to meet or beat. Xerox, a prime innovator of this technique, has sixty professional cost estimators, and they are worth their weight in gold.

The objective of establishing a cost target for a part can also be approached through benchmarking. The commodity team has the responsibility for determining which among its several suppliers within that commodity offers the best price, quality, and delivery. It further attempts to translate that price into labor, material, and overhead costs. This process of benchmarking supplier costs is repeated each year. Such benchmarking is not a violation of the partnership process. Its purpose is to help the partnership supplier close the gap between himself and a best-in-class company.

Armed with this advance information on a target cost, either through reverse engineering, benchmarking, or both, the customer company approaches its selected partnership supplier for the part and specifies a cost that the supplier must meet or beat. But it is not an arbitrary figure that is imposed on the supplier. It starts with a print that is a blank sheet of paper! The customer's engineers and the supplier's technical people mutually develop requirements and specifications that can achieve the target cost.

This is a revolutionary departure from the old purchasing practice of sending out for three or more quotes from various suppliers, negotiating with them, and then whipsawing them for cost reductions. The old method is fatally flawed from the outset. When a print is sent out for quotes, it is already cast in concrete. At this stage, it is almost too late to get any valuable inputs from suppliers for cost reduction or quality improvement, even if they are willing to take the chance of being considered noncompliant. With cost targeting, there is no need to go to other suppliers. By virtue of benchmarking, the customer company has already chosen the best supplier. There is also no need to solicit prices from suppliers. The customer company, not the supplier, now determines the price. Old-fashioned negotiations become obsolete. Instead, the customer's and supplier's technical people take on the challenge of working in harness to achieve the cost target.

Early Supplier Involvement: Sashimi Style

Early supplier involvement (ESI) represents a symbolic continental divide between archaic, old-line procurement practices and modern supply management. ESI involves the pre-selection of a partnership supplier and a customer-determined price instead of bids and negotiations. Several benefits accrue to both parties:

- Shorter design cycle times
- Optimal designs, materials, and tolerances
- Minimal design changes
- Mutually determined specifications
- Utilization of the supplier's technology
- Optimal match between part design and supplier process technology
- Improved first-time quality
- Improved delivery
- Lower development and part cost
- Improved customer-supplier communications and trust

Most of these benefits are obvious. The first mentioned, shorter design cycle time, needs some explanation. In a pre-ESI era, a series approach was the norm. Engineers in the customer's company would work on a design, give it to drafting to draw up a print, then forward it to Purchasing, which would send out a request for quotes from several suppliers and select one of them. If there was time, the supplier would suggest design changes and another time cycle would be started all over again.

ESI, on the other hand, facilitates a parallel approach to design. The Japanese dish of sashimi consists of sushi (raw fish) arranged overlapping one another in an artistic, colorful display of culinary art. Similarly, in ESI, the customer's engineering efforts and the supplier's efforts overlap one another. They work iteratively and in parallel. In fact, sections of a product design are turned over to the supplier, which frees up the design engineer's time, and, above all, shortens the overall design cycle time. It is in this crucial area of design cycle time reduction that some of the fiercest battles today are being waged by competing companies.

A few administrative matters connected with ESI should be addressed. A customer who reveals a confidential design, no matter how sketchy it may be, to a supplier needs to be protected by means of a general confidential agreement signed by both parties. And the supplier, for his part, should be adequately compensated for any designs he may develop, experiments he may conduct, or samples he may build. Finally, the ESI process should not be a once only effort at product launch. It should continue over the life of the part. It is necessary, therefore, to establish mutually acceptable targets and timetables to achieve them. Companies that have launched ESI are emphatic that a full-time ESI "ambassador" be appointed in the customer company. He must have an excellent engineering background and be highly respected by the engineering community so that he can resolve technical differences between customer and supplier and champion worthwhile supplier ideas.

ESI Success Stories

Companies such as General Electric, 3M, Hewlett-Packard, Xerox, Motorola, and Tektronix have been pioneers in developing viable ESI processes. A few examples will illustrate their successes. (To preserve confidentiality, specific customer and supplier names are not used.)

- *Anchor Spin Weld:* A customer company had used a hand-applied adhesive-backed metal screw anchor for its plastic liner. Through ESI, the supplier introduced a new spin weld plastic fastener as a new technology. In addition, the supplier was totally involved in automating the assembly line for this application. While the piece part cost increased by 59 cents and a $280,000 robot was installed, the payback in reduced labor and space savings took less than two years and there was an appreciable quality improvement.

- *Fuser Roller:* To help a customer company improve imaging, its ESI supplier recommended a compounding and application of a silicone rubber coating on the fuser roll. The result: a 20 percent cost reduction on the part, along with a 300 percent improvement in cycle life.

- *Accumulator:* One ESI supplier helped to redesign an accumulator used in rotary compressors. In addition, the supplier was involved, from the start, in the manufacturing and testing. The result was a long-term agreement for high quality parts at a cost 15 percent below the Japanese cost. The total savings was $685,000 per year.

- *Microphone:* New technology enabled a customer company to reduce the subassembly size inside its microphone housing. Its engineers next wanted to miniaturize the housing for the subassembly. It invited its preselected ESI supplier to tackle the job and suggested a 20 percent size reduction. There were no drawings, not even sketches. The supplier accepted the challenge, made samples, and tested prototypes—all 20 percent smaller. The design was accepted; the cost was 12 percent less than that of the original housing; and the customer's engineers saved crucial design time. The supplier gained an exclusive, long-term contract.

Learning Curves and Experience Curves to Track Supplier Cost Reductions

Another simple but effective cost reduction tool in the customer/supplier interface is the learning curve. It has long been used in industry to track reduced costs resulting from volume increases. The "learning" or cost reductions can come from technology breakthroughs, improved process/equipment efficiencies, better methods, improved operator skills, and cycle time reductions. An 80 percent learning curve means that for every doubling of unit volume, the unit cost is reduced to 80 percent of the original cost (that is, a 20 percent cost reduction). A 100 percent learning curve signifies no improvement with doubled volumes, whereas a zero percent learning curve means infinite cost reduction.

Every single process in manufacturing has its own unique learning curve, just as every sampling plan has its own unique operating characteristic (O-C) curve. Information on these curves can be found in industrial literature. Learning curves apply mainly to direct labor, whereas experience curves, which are based on the same principle, apply to total costs and are therefore more appropriate to track supplier productivity improvements.

As an example, even today the experience curve for custom-integrated circuits (ICs) in the semiconductor industry is 70 percent. This translates to a 30 percent cost reduction that customers can expect for every doubling of custom-IC volumes. In a prepartnership era, a buyer can ask for three different price quotes at the desired volume, double the volume, and half the volume. With these three points, he can then plot the experience curves of each of the responding suppliers and match them against a norm or a standard for the particular process. A shallow experience curve, that is one higher than the standard, would indicate that a supplier's price is too high. The inference would be that the supplier is either inefficient or wants to keep the productivity gains for himself.

In a partnership relationship with a supplier, experience curves should not be used for bidding purposes or to detect a supplier's overcharging. But it is still a very useful tool for tracking cost reduction progress at the supplier's facility against a negotiated experience curve at the start of a contract. For instance, if a 75 percent experience curve is agreed upon at the initiation of an order, and the final result, with a doubling or quadrupling of the required quantity, is only an 85 percent experience curve, the customer company can discuss the slippage with the supplier and render concrete help to restore the 75 percent figure.

It should be pointed out, however, that a doubling of the supplier's volume refers to the supplier's total volume of a particular part or product and not just to a particular customer's volume unless it is a unique part produced only for that customer. Further, a doubling of a supplier's volume is not related to a yearly volume. On new products, there may be a doubling of volume every two or three months. On established, mature products, such doubling may not occur for the next ten years or more. Experience curves are not useful for such mature products.

Examples of the former abound in the dramatic way that prices of pocket calculators fell from more than $300 in the early 1970s to the $5 to $10 range in the 1980s. Similar experience curves now operate to reduce the prices of VCRs and computers. It is not inconceivable that in a few years the price of a PC computer will dip below $100! By contrast, a small signal plastic transistor (TO-92) that cost over 20 cents when first introduced in the 1960s and has come down the experience curve to 3 cents today is not likely to be reduced further because several hundred million have been made and the total quantity produced is not likely to double for several years to come.

Value Engineering (VE): A Forgotten Cost Reduction Champion

If quality improvement is the king of cost reduction, value engineering can be considered its Prince of Wales, the heir apparent. Its benefits are legendary:

- An average reduction of 25 percent in procurement costs. A minimum 10 percent reduction can be achieved "with eyes closed," and 75 percent reductions are not uncommon.
- A 10 to 1 return on investment is achievable, and 100 to 1 returns have

been registered frequently. Further, the amount of investment required up front for such returns is modest.

- Improved customer satisfaction: VE is not just a cost reduction tool. In its proper application, it enhances *all* elements of customer satisfaction previously shown in Figure 11-1 and improves the worth to cost ratio of a product or part.
- Serendipity: In exploring the byways of new technology and materials, it stumbles upon amazing discoveries that can reduce costs.
- Higher employee morale: The basic building block of value engineering is an interdisciplinary team. The pursuit of cost reduction using its methodology becomes a game. It is fun. It builds camaraderie among team members as no other technique is capable of doing. Years after a VE project is finished, team members look back upon the chase for dollars with affection and nostalgia.

VE History

Amazingly enough, the VE discipline originated in Purchasing. Larry Miles, the founder of value engineering, was the head of General Electric's purchasing research department in the early 1940s. During World War II, he was assigned the task of finding substitutes for scarce materials. He discovered, perhaps through serendipity, that the substitute materials were not only less expensive but better in quality as well. A new cost reduction star was born.

Value engineering's usefulness might have remained undetected had it not been for the powerful championship of the Department of Defense, especially under Secretary of Defense Robert McNamara. Prior to 1960, the Defense Department would ask its contractors and suppliers for cost reduction ideas. Many complied. But the government simply pocketed all the savings, leaving its suppliers high and dry. As a result, the ideas stopped coming until McNamara introduced value engineering clauses stating that savings would be shared equitably with suppliers. Savings on current contracts were generally shared 50-50 with the supplier. On follow-on contracts, the supplier would receive 10 percent of the savings even if he was not awarded the follow-on contract. Value engineering came into its own and enjoyed the spotlight for ten to fifteen years. Gradually, however, the Defense Department's bureaucracy torpedoed progress. Its contract administrators did not want to be bothered with evaluating value engineering ideas and negotiating payouts. They privately let it be known that if a contractor submitted a value engineering proposal, it would be his last! Many administrators unfairly accused contractors of submitting high bids and then using VE to squeeze money out of the government. Today, value engineering, although still on the books, seems to be headed for the Smithsonian Institution as a historic relic.

If its Department of Defense sponsorship died, VE never even had a proper birth in commercial industry. A few progressive companies have used it to advantage, but the great majority of U.S. companies have not even heard of VE, much less practice it. As one would expect, the Japanese have not hesitated to pick up, use, and milk to the fullest yet another technique invented in the United States. Larry Miles's authoritative textbook *Techniques of Value Analysis and Engineering* (1972)* has been translated into Japanese, and today in Japan VE is a way of life. The Japanese value-engineer their products to death before the start of production, because it is at the design stage where there is the greatest VE bang for the VE buck.

VE Methodology: A Distinct Departure From Cost Reduction

In traditional cost reduction techniques, the part or product design is kept essentially the same. The object is to make the item cheaper either through material or labor cost reductions. Often, however, "cheaper" is translated into lower quality, lower customer satisfaction.

In value engineering, the challenge is to look at the function, at what the part *does* rather than what it *is*. The next step is to research alternative ways of providing that function at lower cost but *with better quality*. Functions are divided into two categories: 1) basic functions that make the product work; and 2) supporting functions that make the product sell. In order to simplify the work and focus upon the improvement "process," a two-word approach (a verb and a noun) is used to describe each function. For instance, supporting functions are generally described as follows:

> assure dependability   satisfy user
> assure convenience   attract user

The highest-order basic function is called the "task."

The Tie-Clip Example: A simple example will illustrate the VE methodology. A tie-clip, which may sell for $10 in a store, generally costs $2 or less to manufacture. Traditional cost-reduction techniques would maintain the integrity of the original design of the tie-clip and concentrate on finding less expensive materials and/or manufacturing processes. Value engineering, by contrast, examines the clip's function and describes it in two words: "holds tie." It then brings an interdisciplinary team together to brainstorm alternative—and radically different—ways of performing the function of holding a tie. In the initial brainstorming, or creative, phase of VE, all ideas, no

---

*I have co-authored a book with John Fasal: *Practical Value Analysis Methods* (New York: Hayden Co., 1974), and have taught VE in the Graduate School of the Illinois Institute of Technology.

Table 19-1. The value engineering job plan.

Job Plan	Functional Analysis	Key Techniques	VE Questions	Supporting Techniques
1. Information	Identify function and separate specifications Determine cost per functional relationships Define function Determine basic function	Use good human relations Get all the facts Get information from the best sources Use accurate cost Employ cost visibility	What is it? What must it do? What does it cost?	To be used as the problem dictates throughout all phases of job plan: (1) Spend company money as you would your own (2) Record everything (3) Employ good human relations (4) Overcome roadblocks (5) Work on specifics, not generalities
2. Speculation		Creative thinking Use industrial standards Blast and refine	What else will accomplish the function?	
3. Evaluation	Evaluate function	Put $ on and develop the main idea Use company services Use specialty vendors' materials, products, and processes Put $ on each tolerance Evaluate by comparison Apply the "Value Control Design Guide" Use your judgment Overcome roadblocks	What will that cost?	
4. Planning		Work on specifics, not generalities		
5. Execution		DOE, MEOST ensure that quality/reliability are not compromised		
6. Report		Use VE proposal form Use good human relations		

matter how wild, are accepted as a starting point. In fact, it has been proven that the worth of the final idea, the final alternative, is directly proportional to the number of brainstorming ideas generated.

In the tie-clip example, a number of alternatives can surface in a brainstorming session:

• paper clip	• chewing	• no tie	• paint
• clothespin	gum	• bow tie	on shirt
• staple	• safety	• tuck in	• tie loop
• button	pin	shirt	• no tie-
	• velcro	• tuck in	clip
	• tape	pants	

Obviously, most of the alternatives are frivolous. But a few of them such as a paper clip, cost a fraction of a cent—a savings of more than 100 to 1. Of course, the poor ornamental and prestige value of a paper clip would preclude it as a viable alternative. However, a tie loop is not only almost as inexpensive as a paper clip but is also the fashion. Today the tie-clip has gone the way of the dodo bird! But the first and most important value engineering question should always be: "Can the function itself be eliminated altogether!"

Table 19-1 is a summary of the more formal methodology, called the value engineering job plan. It has six phases:

1. Information or Data Gathering.
2. Speculation or Brainstorming or Creativity.
3. Evaluation, in which viable alternatives to the original design are considered.
4. Planning, in which experiments to test the alternatives are formulated with the customer, with the customer's management, and with the supplier.
5. Execution or development, in which the alternatives are tested, especially to ensure that quality, reliability, and other aspects of customer satisfaction are not adversely affected, but are actually enhanced by the new design.
6. The concluding report, in which the savings and the investment are calculated and, where necessary, communicated to the customer.

The FAST Diagram

An important VE tool is the FAST (Function Analysis using a Systems Technique) diagram. It is a systematic way to go from higher-order functions of a product to lower-order functions and finally down to the parts in a systematic way. It can also uncover functions that are not needed. Figure 19-3

Figure 19-3. Function Analysis Systems Technique (FAST) diagram.

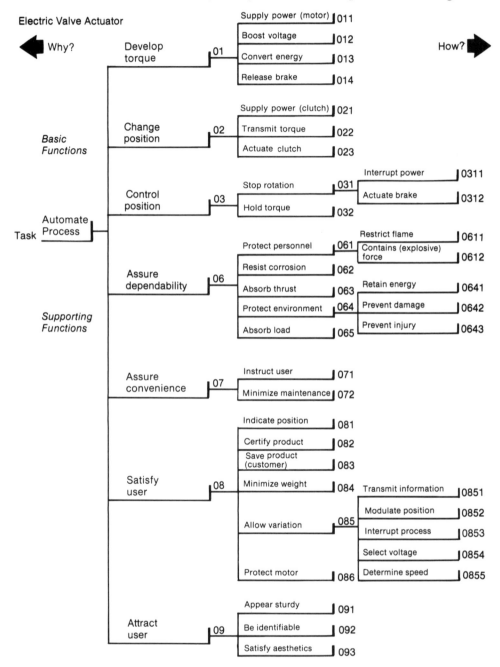

is an example of a FAST diagram applied to an electric value actuator. The figure starts with the task—the highest-order function—on the left. Then a series of "how" questions is asked to determine "how to perform the task." The questions address both the basic and the supporting functions, which are placed to the right of the task in the FAST diagram. Further "how" questions lead to the next order of detailed functions and so on until additional "how" questions can only be answered by the product's parts and/or manufacturing processes. A FAST diagram, being limited to a function chart, should not include these parts or processes. Similarly, "why" questions (that is, "why do we perform this particular function?") lead from right to left in the function tree until the task is reached. Asking "why" questions often reveals that a particular function (and its associated parts) is not necessary or that it can be combined with another function to reduce parts.

In fact, the "why" aspect of a FAST diagram can be applied to VE problem solving in white-collar, administrative work.* It starts on the left with a statement of the problem. The "why" question leads to one or more causes that are listed to the right. In the next sequence of a "why" question, the causes become problems and their underlying causes are listed further to the right. The why-why diagram finally ends when the root cause of a particular branch of the problem tree is pinpointed. Solutions to reach root cause are then developed by the VE team.

Cost Breakdown in a FAST Diagram: The next step is to break down product costs part by part, with each part further subdivided into material, labor, and overhead costs. Parts have costs and parts have functions. Therefore, functions have costs. Because a single part could perform multiple functions, a VE team systematically allocates the various detailed costs of each of the lowest-order functions on the right side of a FAST diagram. This gives a precise picture of how the total cost of a product is distributed among the various functions that a product performs.

Value Research: Once the cost of each function is known in detail, the worth of the functions is then determined through value research (see Chapter 11). Input from end users/customers is the most important part of the VE process. By means of surveys, meetings, or actual use, customers are asked to rate the product's features by importance and to give them a 1 to 10 rating in terms of the satisfaction, or dissatisfaction, or neutrality associated with each feature. Usually, an end-user sample of thirty is sufficient to obtain a reasonable profile of customer "likes," "dislikes," or indifference to each feature.

Value = Function Worth/Function Cost: These end-user ratings are then allocated to the furthest right functions in every branch of a FAST diagram,

---

*For further details, see Howard H. Bailie, "Organize Your Thinking with a Why-Why Diagram," *Quality Progress*, December 1985.

so that every function has a cost as well as an end-user worth or rating. Functions analyzed in this fashion fall into four categories, as shown in the following analysis of function worth and cost table. The required actions are now easy to segregate and implement.

Function Worth (End-User Rating)	Function Cost	Action Required
High	Low	None—advertise
High	High	Reduce cost
Low	Low	Attempt improvement of worth
Low	High	Attempt to eliminate function

Value Engineering and Creativity

Albert Einstein once said that "imagination is much more important than knowledge." This spirit is captured in the most important aspect of value engineering, its creativity. The task of the VE team is to conjure up alternative ideas—wild or sober—by which the basic and supporting functions of a product can be performed.

Creativity, which can also be called deferred judgment, is stimulated by a checklist of questions such as the following:

- Can the function itself be eliminated?
- Can the part be eliminated?
- Can it be simplified?
- Can it be altered to accommodate a faster method?
- Can standard parts or materials be used?
- Can *all* specifications be challenged and modified?
- Can lower-cost processes or materials be used?
- Can a higher-cost material be used that will simplify the design and/or production?
- Can tolerances, finishes, tests, or packaging be reduced in cost?
- Can quality/reliability be increased at no extra cost?
- Can other features important to customers, for example, service, delivery, human engineering, safety, be pursued?

From this creativity phase of VE the less practical ideas are dropped and a thorough evaluation of the truly feasible alternatives made, with sufficient testing to assure that quality and reliability are not degraded. One of the major setbacks in any VE work is when inadequate attention is paid to quality and reliability, while the almighty dollar is being chased. In the final analysis, customer satisfaction is the name of the game. Often, good value engineering will accommodate a price increase so long as customer satisfaction is advanced even more.

VE Organization: The Psychological Factor

Many a VE effort is stalled or even torpedoed when value engineering is organized as a separate department or if another group is assigned the VE task. VE sometimes requires a second look, but if an outside team determines the improvements, the original design group usually feels that it is being "shown up as incompetent," regardless of the urgency of the VE effort or the skills of the outside team. Good value engineering is as much psychological as it is technical. It stands to reason that the original design group be made part of the solution rather than part of the problem. A team approach is the essence of good value engineering. Team members are generally drawn from purchasing, manufacturing, quality, and other disciplines, as needed. But the team leader should always be drawn from the original engineering group so that the effort can be looked upon as an improvement in the product rather than as a slap at engineering.

Because of Japanese competition, one Motorola division found that it would be necessary to substantially reduce the cost of its radio. The cost reduction task was given to the research department, a collection of high-powered talent. Research made several recommendations for reducing costs. The proposal then went to the development engineering group that had produced the original design. For a variety of reasons, not a single idea was accepted. The project was stalled.

The division general manager then directed me to initiate a value engineering effort. My first action was to establish six interdisciplinary teams to tackle various aspects of the product. But I persuaded the chief engineer of the development group to serve as overall captain, and obtained the services of several of his engineering managers as team leaders. A goal of roughly $1 million in cost reduction was established for each team, with a grand total of $6 million, representing an 18 percent reduction, as the overall target. As an added incentive, each team member was promised a color television set if the team goal was achieved. The enthusiasm generated was more spectacular than anything previously seen. The teams labored long and hard, often working on their own time after regular hours and on Saturdays. At the end of six months, the total savings was $4.2 million, as verified by the accounting department. Four teams achieved their goals. Two did not. The cost reduction did not reach the goal of 18 percent, but the 12 percent actual reduction enabled the division to successfully block the Japanese challenge.

The Supplier's Role: A Key to Value Engineering

Early supplier involvement (ESI) provides the administrative and managerial framework for the supplier's role in reducing design cycle time and cost. Value engineering is the technical and operational arm of ESI. It is the catalyst that adds synergy to the engineering-purchasing-supplier link. Yet the supplier's role in VE savings has not been utilized to anywhere near its maximum potential.

What can happen when customer and supplier jointly pursue value engineering is illustrated by a case study in which I was personally involved.

A crystal filter supplier had quoted a 44 MHZ filter at a price of $73.50 per unit. The customer's specifications were:

- Insertion loss: 10db max. at room temp.: 11.5 db at 75°c.
- Bandwidth: (1) 40 KHZ min. at − 6db from center frequency (44MHZ).
  (2) 150 KHZ max. at − 60 db from center frequency (44 MHZ).
  (3) No spurs allowed.
- Weight: 10 oz.
- Packaging: potted and hermetically sealed.

The supplier, asked to identify the high cost areas, pointed to the insertion loss and spur requirements, where a relaxation of specifications could appreciably reduce the cost. Engineering's initial reaction was to reject the supplier's ideas, but it was persuaded to reevaluate the design. An intensive one-day marathon session, involving both the customer's and the supplier's technical people, made the following decisions:

- The insertion loss requirements were tightened even further to 8.5db.
- The bandwidth at the − 6db points was reduced to 36 KHZ.
- The bandwidth at the − 60 db points was relaxed to 152 KHZ.
- Spurs were allowed beyond ± 300 KHZ, as long as they were below − 60 db.

With these concessions, the supplier was able to redesign the eight-section filter using just five sections. He was also able to reduce crystal cost by plating the crystals slightly differently. Tests were run to make sure that the final product (of which the crystal filter was only one component) was not degraded in performance and reliability.

The results? Final cost per unit was reduced to $27, almost a 3 to 1 reduction in the cost of the product.

That customer companies sometimes prevent the playing out of such happy scenarios is revealed by a study conducted by the magazine *Purchasing* in 1987 on the reasons why suppliers do not respond sufficiently to value engineering. The results of this survey are depicted in Figure 19-4.

Figure 19-4. Reasons for low supplier involvement in VE.

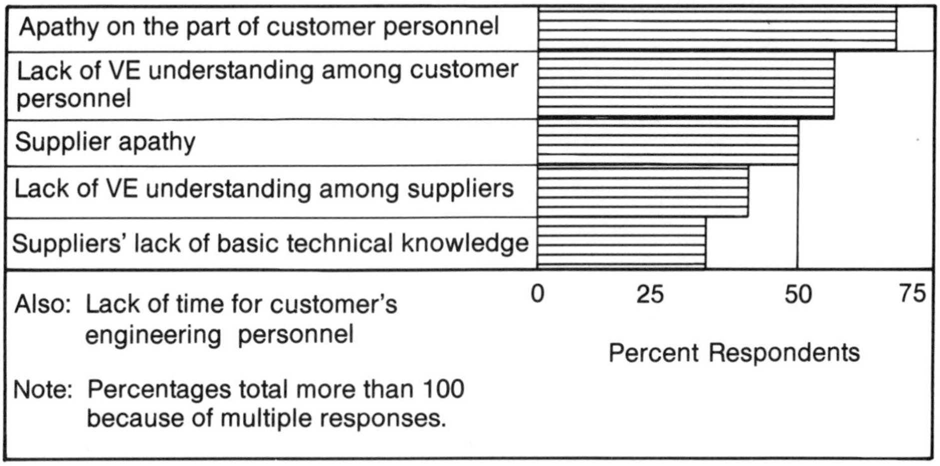

Source: Purchasing (February 1987).

The largest single reason is apathy among customer personnel. This is attributable not to the customer's purchasing people who—once they know about the enormous potential of VE—promote it, but to the customer's engineers, who do not want to be bothered with evaluating supplier ideas or who feel that such ideas only serve to point a finger at their own inadequacy.

The second largest reason is the lack of understanding of VE principles and practice among all customer personnel, especially engineering, quality, and purchasing—in short, the commodity teams. VE seminars are useful in remedying this situation, especially if less than 25 percent of the total time is spent in classroom instruction and more than 75 percent in actual project work (selected on the basis of the highest potential savings or beating the competition to the punch). Ideas generated in a two-week seminar of this type can save a company hundreds of thousands of dollars. It is instant success!

Customer Company VE Homework

Before a company reaches out to its suppliers, the optimum material and manufacturing process must be selected. Value Analysis, Inc., a reputable company with the longest history of consultations in VE, has a comprehensive VE guide to help the selection process. Table 19-2 is an example of a Value Analysis, Inc. guideline for a cone or cup concentric metallic part. It

(text continues on page 340)

Table 19-2. Value Analysis, Inc., guideline for choices in determining the optimum process for a cone or cup concentric metallic part.

Index	Process	Comments	Raw Material	Maximum Size	Minimum Size	General Tolerance
II -1 III-1	Sand Casting	Most economical process for low production—parts usually require machining.	Ingot	Limited in size only by the foundry capacity.	Less than one pound	± 1/16 to ± 1/8
II -1 III-2	Die Casting	Excellent for intricate—close tolerance—high production—alum., zinc, magnesium, copper alloys	Ingot	Up to 100 pounds 10# average	Less than one ounce	± 002 to ± 010
II -1 III-7	Centrifugal Casting	Basically a pressure method for long or large hollow shapes; produces sound castings	Ingot	1,000 pounds 54" O.D. x 342" length	2" I.D. x 1/4" wall thickness	± 1/16 to ± 1/8
II -1 III-6	Permanent Mold Casting	Widely used for high strength aluminum, gray iron and copper base alloys	Ingot	300 pounds	Less than one pound	± 010 to ± 030
II -1 III-5	Shell Molding	Close tolerance and excellent surface finish	Ingot	Maximum 200# 25# average	Less than one pound	± 005 to ± 015
II -1 III-3	Investment Casting	Best for intricate shapes—good for casting hard-to-machine metals	Ingot	Maximum 100# generally less than 10 pounds	Less than one pound	± 003 under 1" ± 005 over 1"
II -1 III-4	Plaster Mold Casting	Similar to permanent mold casting, except molds are plaster-base material	Ingot	Standard flask size 12"x18"x4" depth (about 15#)	Less than one pound	± 005 to ± 015
II -3 III-13	Die Forging	Increases steel strength; used for high stress parts	Bar, Rod	1,000 pounds	Less than one pound	± 008 to ± 1/8
II -9 III-44	Powder Metallurgy	Best for parts under 4" in diameter—larger parts can be made	Powder	8" dia. x 8" lg	Less than 1/16" dia.	± 001 to ± 005
II -3 III-17	Impact Extrusion	Aluminum, zinc, copper alloys and some steel parts	Bar, Rod	5" dia. x 12" length	.004 wall thickness, less than one pound	± 0005 wall thickness ± 002 general
II -3 III-16	Continuous Extrusion	Good for complex cross-section contours	Billet	12" dia.	.050 sections	± 003 to ± 020
II -3 III-19	Roll Forging	Good for long narrow parts—requires finish machining—a hot working process	Bar, Rod	23 sq. inch cross section 75" length	1 1/2" length	Avg. dia. + 1/32 − 1/64 lg. dia. + 3/32 − 1/32 lengths broad
II -3 III-14	Hot Upsetting	Complex, small parts, requires additional machining	Bar, Rod, Wire	10" dia. x 8" length	1/16" dia. up	± 003 to ± 1/32
II -2 III-9	Vertical Turret Lathe	For small quantity Large parts	Fabrications, plate, castings, forgings	4, 5, 6 ft. diameter tables common	4" dia. practical	± 001 to ± 015
II -2 III-9	Horizontal Turret Lathe	For general machining, small medium production	Bar, Rod, Tube, Preforms	3' dia. x 8' lengths	1/2" dia.	± 001 to ± 015
II -2 III-12	Automatic Screw Machine	Small high production parts	Rod, Bar	2" dia.	1/16 dia.	± 0005 to ± 003
II -2 III-12	Swiss Screw Machine	Small precision parts, excellent finish	Rod	1/2" dia.	1/32 dia.	± 0002 to ± 001
II -3 III-18	Rotary Swaging	Excellent for symmetrical parts	Rod, Tube	3 3/4" dia. rods 7" dia. tubing	1/16" dia. rod .005" dia. wire	± 001 to ± 010
II -5 III-31	Crush Grinder	High production, precision parts, excellent tolerance control	Rod, Wire, Bars	16" dia. x 80" length	1/16" dia.	0005 or less
II -3 III-15	Cold Heading	High production method, exacting tolerance, metal improvement	Bar, Rod, Wire	1" dia. x 9" length	.020 dia.	± 002 or better

Surface Finish (RMS)	Pieces Per/Hour	Tooling	Labor	Material Waste	1	10	100	1000	10,000	50,000	100,000	
250–1000	Up to 30											
32–125	Up to 550											
125–1000	Up to 50											
125–250	10–360											
32–250	10–75											
63–125	80–1500/day											
32–125	5–10											
125–500	10–400											
32–63	100–4,000											
8–250	200/hr & more on small parts											
63–125	2–700 FPM											
125–500	30–100											
125–250	Up to 2500											
125–250	1–10											
125–250	1–20											
63–125	20–100											
32–125	30–300											
16–125	100–600											
8–32	20–1200											
16–63	2,000–20,000											

Figure 19-5. Value improvement checklist for stampings.

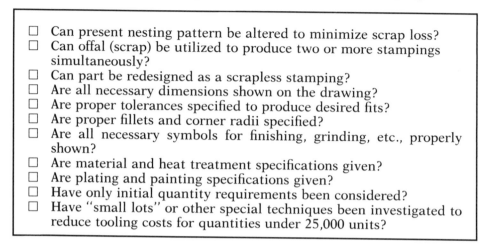

☐ Can present nesting pattern be altered to minimize scrap loss?
☐ Can offal (scrap) be utilized to produce two or more stampings simultaneously?
☐ Can part be redesigned as a scrapless stamping?
☐ Are all necessary dimensions shown on the drawing?
☐ Are proper tolerances specified to produce desired fits?
☐ Are proper fillets and corner radii specified?
☐ Are all necessary symbols for finishing, grinding, etc., properly shown?
☐ Are material and heat treatment specifications given?
☐ Are plating and painting specifications given?
☐ Have only initial quantity requirements been considered?
☐ Have "small lots" or other special techniques been investigated to reduce tooling costs for quantities under 25,000 units?

starts with the part shape. A number of alternative processes are then listed. Each process is described, along with the raw material used; the maximum and minimum sizes; the tolerances possible; the surface finish achievable; the production rate per hour; the tooling, labor, and material wastage costs; and the optimum production quantities. Today, there are CAE software programs that similarly assist engineers in selecting optimum processes.

There are also checklists, available to Engineering and Purchasing, for improving value for specific types of parts. Figure 19-5 is an example of such a checklist for stampings. Other sources where value engineering assistance can be obtained include:

- The Society of American Value Engineers (SAVE), Southfield, Michigan
- The National Association of Purchasing Management (NAPM), New York
- The American Management Association (AMA), New York
- VA Resource Center, Miami University Libraries, Oxford, Ohio
- University of Wisconsin Extension courses, Madison, Wisconsin

Companies that have not yet entered the world of early supplier involvement (ESI) can send out a guideline form along with a print or drawing to stimulate cost reduction/value engineering ideas from suppliers. Figure 19-6 is an example of such a guideline. The all-important task is to challenge every specification and to put a dollar sign on every parameter, every tolerance, every finish, every test, and then to determine value engineering alternatives to all high cost requirements.

Figure 19-6. Guideline form for stimulating supplier ideas.

GUIDELINES FOR SUPPLIER RECOMMENDATIONS TO REDUCE COSTS

Your expertise and suggestions are important to our company in our continuing efforts to improve our products and reduce costs. Please use this form to challenge any of our specifications and to indicate the operational and financial impacts. We want to review those requirements that contribute to costs but that may not be necessary for performance, quality, or reliability as well as those requirements that your company may have difficulty in meeting. Thank you.

Recommended Modifications

Our Company Part No. _____ Supplier Part No. _____

Specifications contributing to your highest costs:

Electrical specifications:

Mechanical specifications:

Tolerance increases:

Test procedures/parameters:

Material:

Packaging/delivery:

Finish/plating/appearance:

Standization/consolidation:

Quality/yield improvement:

Please return to Purchasing.   Date_____

Supplier Name_____

Value Engineering Financial Incentives

Some companies that have embraced supply management nevertheless feel that preselecting a single supplier during early supplier involvement (ESI) needlessly restricts competition.* An alternate route made possible by value engineering is to grant "consultant" status to a few chosen suppliers with track records for generating good value engineering ideas. These suppliers are called in by ESI specialists to brainstorm new approaches. They work on new ideas before drawings have been made.

The $64 question is how to reward such consulting efforts. One way is to split the contract among them. But the lower volume produced by each supplier under these conditions invariably raises costs. A preferred method is illustrated by a hypothetical example involving two suppliers, A and B, and four possible scenarios, shown in the accompanying table.

In the first scenario, both suppliers give a quote on a preestablished specification. Considering B's lower price and assuming that all other factors (quality, delivery, and so on) are the same, B gets the order.

In the second scenario, Supplier A submits a value engineering idea, X. It is accepted by the customer's engineers and A's price is reduced to 90 cents per part. B does not bother to come up with any cost reduction idea. By prearranged rules of idea incentives, A gets the order.

In the third scenario, A turns in idea X and B turns in idea Y, which differs from idea X. Both ideas are acceptable to the customer's engineers. If there is no time for further negotiations, B gets the order.

If, however, the print is more in the "sketch" stage and there is time and the ground rules for idea incentives have been defined in advance, both suppliers are requested to requote on both idea X and idea Y. In this fourth scenario, B's price is still lower than A's. This poses a dilemma. If B gets the order because of his lower price and A gets nothing, supplier A would feel that the rug has been pulled out from under him. From that point on, he would tell the customer to "get lost." If, on the other hand, the order is split between A and B, the price will be higher because of lower volumes for each. What, then, is the solution?

The answer is that the customer would give B the order but pay both A and B *a value engineering royalty*, limited to the order or to a year's contract, for the use of their ideas. In this particular case, the customer would save at least 20 cents per part and therefore can afford to give A and B each a 2- or 3-cent royalty payment. B is happy to get the order as well as a royalty bonus. A is happy to have parlayed his idea into cash, amounting to at least

---

*Partnership suppliers also complain that ESI permits the selection of only one supplier for a given part, with the others left out. These concerns are overcome if partnership suppliers are given consultant status.

50 percent of the profit he would have made had he received the order. This is a clear case of win-win-win for all!

Scenario		Supplier A	Supplier B
1	Unit price (per print)	$1.00	$0.95
2	Unit price (idea X from Supplier A)	$0.90	$0.95
3	Unit price (idea X from A, idea Y from B)	$0.90	$0.85
4	Unit price (ideas X and Y from A and B)	$0.80	$0.75

If there are more than two such "consultant suppliers," each receives a value engineering royalty or incentive award that represents a fraction of the savings that each has contributed to the customer company. The only stumbling blocks to this unique concept would be an unimaginative management and an antediluvian accounting department!

Financial Incentives and Penalties: The Carrot and the Stick

Once the mindset of giving suppliers "nothing beyond the order" is lifted, several win-win arrangements are possible between customer and supplier. The value engineering idea incentive is only one such arrangement. Others are based on quality, reliability, delivery, and performance.

In this area, as in the adoption of an equitable savings-sharing system in the 1960s, the Department of Defense has been a great teacher and innovator. It has developed incentive contracts for its suppliers, operating on the principle of the carrot and the stick. The financial carrot is for better than agreed-upon quality, reliability, delivery, or performance; and the financial stick, or penalty, for worse than agreed-upon levels for these parameters. Both incentives and penalties are percentages, usually in the range of ± 5 percent to 10 percent, of the contract price.

It is tragic that this excellent principle of incentive contracting is almost unknown to commercial industry except in the construction and housing sectors. In the very few cases where it has been applied, it has always been a one-way street, that is, penalties flowing from customer to supplier. Any talk of reverse traffic, of incentives to suppliers, is considered "subversive." In one case, an automotive company, concerned that its repairs per 100 cars during the warranty period of the car were almost twice that of its foreign benchmark competition, sought to impose financial penalties on one of its key suppliers for higher than targeted field failure rates. The supplier's

Figure 19-7. Supplier incentives/penalties for four parameters.

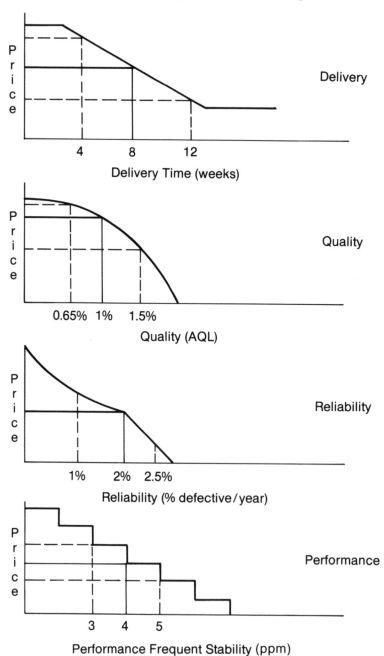

management was willing to accept such a penalty provided the automotive company also granted equivalent financial incentives for lower than targeted field failure rates. The automotive company refused this balanced offer, thereby setting back incentive contracting a few years. Fortunately, a few brave companies, even in the commercial field, have dared much and gained much for themselves and their suppliers.

Figure 19-7 represents various arrangements for incentives and penalties as applied to delivery, quality, reliability, and performance. The share line, which determines the rate of incentive or penalty, can be straight, curved, discontinuous, or a step function. In most applications, the share line is a straight line, with its slope determining in a linear manner the amount of incentive or penalty. The break-even point is at a parameter level where there is neither an incentive or penalty.

Incentive/penalty contracts should come into play only under special circumstances:

1. When there is a repetitive problem between a customer and a supplier, in one or more of the following areas: delivery, quality, reliability, or performance. (If the problem is delivery only, there is no need for the incentive/penalty contract to include other parameters).
2. When the repetitive problem is measurable in terms of dollars and is sufficiently large that an improvement could benefit both parties.
3. When the freedom to change suppliers is limited because:
   - The supplier has the best technology or price or quality, but is deficient in one of the other parameters.
   - The supplier is a sister division in a large company, and buying internally is mandated.
   - There is an early-stage, tentative partnership relationship with the supplier that needs nurturing.
   - The problem must be capable of correction, technically.

Examples of Financial Incentives/Penalties: The Westinghouse Corporation provides an early example of the use of financial incentives and penalties in contracting. On one very large contract, twenty-seven of its more than one hundred suppliers were not meeting one or more of the quality, reliability, or delivery requirements. The incentive/penalty system introduced by Westinghouse to deal with the problem is shown below.

Parameter	Percentage of Purchase Price	
	Incentive	*Penalty*
Delivery	+2	−2
Quality	+1	−1
Reliability	+4	−4

Figure 19-8. Reliability incentive penalty plan.

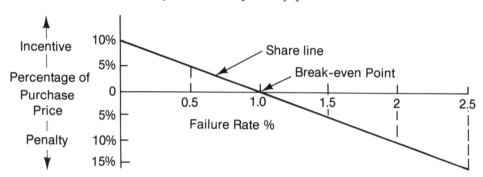

If a supplier's delivery was on time, he received an incentive of 2 percent of the purchase price. If delivery was more than one week later than the agreed-upon date, he received a 2 percent penalty. If the supplier's lot was accepted by incoming inspection, he was given a 1 percent incentive. If the lot was rejected, he was subjected to a 1 percent penalty. If the supplier's reliability, as measured in the customer's life-stress tests, was found acceptable, he was awarded a 4 percent incentive. If the lot was rejected in these life-stress tests, he was slapped with a 4 percent penalty.

As a result of the incentive/penalty system, twenty-one of the twenty-seven suppliers improved their performance in terms of delivery, quality, reliability, or all three. Six of the twenty-seven did not improve. Five of these six suppliers had such low volumes that the incentives or penalties were too small to influence their actions.

The Westinghouse system is not necessarily a good model. It combined delivery, quality, and reliability incentives in a single package even though each supplier was not necessarily deficient in all three parameters. Further, the incentives and penalties were relatively low.

In another example, a large multinational company was buying a family of semiconductors from a supplier that amounted to approximately $1 million. The supplier's history indicated that his price was excellent, his delivery always on time, and his quality, as measured by the customer's incoming inspection, acceptable. But his reliability was poor, causing the customer to experience a 2 percent failure rate in the field. That failure rate, when the cost of the field labor expended in removing and replacing the supplier's defective parts was added, amounted to an alarming $400,000 loss per year. The poor reliability had to do with wire-bond failures, and there was no easy way to screen for potential failures either at the supplier's or the customer's facility.

After much arm twisting, the supplier, whose excellent price was a major factor in his retention, was persuaded to accept an incentive/penalty contract devoted entirely to reliability improvement, as depicted in Figure 19-8. The share line was a simple straight line, with a break-even point at a 1 percent failure rate, where there would be no incentive or penalty payment. If the supplier achieved a 1 percent failure rate, the customer company's losses would be reduced to $200,000. If he did not improve, the original 2 percent failure rate would now cost the supplier a penalty of $100,000. If he achieved a 0.5 percent failure rate, the supplier would receive a $50,000 incentive payment and the customer would reduce his own warranty cost from $400,000 to $100,000.

At the end of one year, the supplier had reduced the failure rate to 0.38 percent. The supplier received an incentive payment of approximately $80,000. The customer saved approximately $350,000 minus the $80,000 payment (in other words, $270,000)—a win-win arrangement for both customer and supplier.

Chapter 20

Cycle Time Reduction: The Integrator

Just-in-time manufacturing is driving a revolution in automotive production. It's changing every aspect of automaking: production quality; scheduling and batch size; delivery of parts; and communications between automakers and suppliers. At its best, just-in-time (JIT) manufacturing is integrating the supplier's production with the automaker's, linking the two plants as if they were one.

—Detroit Editor, *Iron Age Magazine*

Inventory Is the Graveyard of Poor Management

Since the early 1980s, it has become fashionable to say that "inventory is evil," just as we now say in quality assurance that "variation is evil." The question arises as to why high levels of inventory were tolerated in the past. There are several reasons.

First of all, inventory was used as an insurance policy to make on-time deliveries to customers and to meet production schedules. It was the essential ingredient in "just-in case" systems:

- Just in case suppliers were delinquent or delivered poor quality.
- Just in case line problems or equipment breakdowns developed.

348

- Just in case absenteeism or turnover in personnel affected scheduling.
- Just in case forecasts proved unreliable.

Even more important, managers, and even top managers, were not measured on inventory or penalized for its excess. Nowhere does inventory appear in profit and loss statements. And in balance sheets, inventory is mentioned—but as an asset, not as a liability!

Today, along with its synonyms (such as short cycle manufacturing, just-in-time (JIT),* zero inventory, and stockless production), inventory reduction is rapidly becoming part of a new manufacturing culture. But why is inventory evil?

It drags down asset turns and return on investment (ROI). This can be stated in the equation:

$$\text{Asset turns} = \frac{\text{sales}}{\text{total assets}} = \frac{\text{sales}}{\substack{\text{inventory and receivables} \\ \text{and fixed assets}}}$$

Any decrease in inventory therefore increases asset turns, which multiply profit on sales into return on investment. Because inventory generally accounts for at least 20 to 40 percent of total assets, reducing it has the greatest single impact on asset turns and ROI.

Inventory consumes 30 to 40 percent of material costs, including the cost of interest (capital is tied up), obsolescence, shrinkage, utilities, and insurance.

Its hidden costs include *waste.*

- Waste of time, space, and manpower.
- Waste, through poor quality, of materials, labor, and equipment: Poor quality increases cycle time because of the dreary circle of rejection, rework, and reinspection.
- Waste of support personnel in paperwork, expediting, and transport.
- Waste of customer satisfaction and goodwill, because of delinquencies, broken promises, and poor forecasts.

Benefits of Inventory Reduction

The advantages of inventory reduction and JIT are so compelling that it is a wonder that corporate management was so dull-witted for so many years before recognizing their full potential. The benefits include:

---

*The term just-in-time conveys nothing more than on-time delivery. It hardly captures the enormous scope of cycle time reduction, which embraces the elimination of *waste*, including all nonvalue-added operations.

- Greater customer satisfaction. A supplier who through cycle time reduction can get a product to his customer with only two weeks of lead time, versus the more traditional eight-week lead time of competing suppliers, will have the inside track.*
- Reduced supplier lead-time. A minimum 10 to 1 reduction can be achieved.
- Improved cash flow. This could be one of the greatest advantages of reduced inventories.† The positive cash flow generated can serve a number of purposes: less need to borrow from banks, less dependency on public offerings of stock, and less concern about the volatility of the stock market.
- Reduced space requirements. With the institutionalization of cycle time reduction, a company can easily reduce its manufacturing space by 50 percent, thus eliminating the need for new plants or plant expansion in growth periods.
- Improved quality. The visibility that JIT affords to problems makes possible quick and massive corrective action, leading to better yields, less inspection and test, higher machine up time, and better supplier quality.
- Faster responses to customer demand for model variety and quantity changes.
- More manufacturable designs, more model commonality, less proliferation of parts, fewer design changes, greater ease of assembly, and less obsolescence.
- Less waiting (queue) time, less setup time, more level schedules.
- Smoother production flow through the "pull" system rather than "batch" production using the push system.
- Better cost accounting methods for today's needs.

Success at Hewlett-Packard

As a practical example of the benefits of inventory reduction, Hewlett-Packard, one of the pioneers in inventory reduction and cycle time management, recorded the following results after a four-year effort at its Vancouver (Washington) division:

---

*One enterprising Motorola plant reduced its internal production cycle time from fourteen weeks to three in just 4½ months of effort. Earlier its lead-time commitments to customers had been fourteen to sixteen weeks. It now guarantees four weeks, and stipulates that if actual delivery is over four weeks, the shipment will be made at no charge to the customer! In the meantime, it has continued to reduce the internal cycle time—down to one week.

†The Sheldahl Corporation was almost bankrupt. Under imaginative cycle time leadership, it reduced its inventory so drastically and generated such a positive cash flow that it has become the Cinderella of its industry!

1. Product volume shipped increased by 20 percent.
2. Work-in process (WIP) inventory decreased by 82 percent.
3. Space requirements decreased by 40 percent.
4. Labor productivity increased by 33 percent.
5. Scrap/rework decreased by 30 percent.

These can be considered modest results. But the division had no benchmark companies from which to learn and had to blaze its own JIT trail.

Figure 20-1. River flow analogy: Causes of inventory buildup.

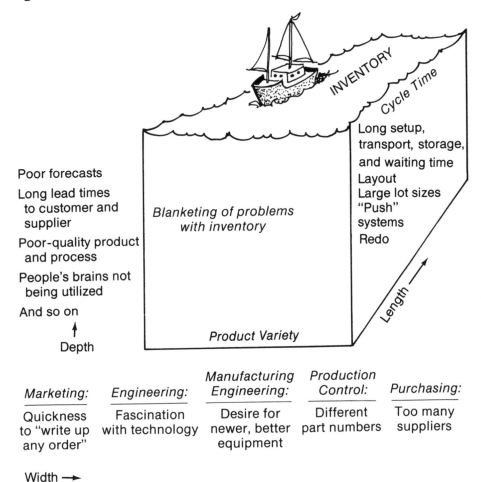

Poor forecasts

Long lead times
to customer and
supplier

Poor-quality product
and process

People's brains not
being utilized

And so on

Depth

*Blanketing of problems
with inventory*

Long setup,
transport, storage,
and waiting time
Layout
Large lot sizes
"Push"
systems
Redo

Length

Product Variety

Marketing:	Engineering:	Manufacturing Engineering:	Production Control:	Purchasing:
Quickness to "write up any order"	Fascination with technology	Desire for newer, better equipment	Different part numbers	Too many suppliers

Width →

Inventory: The River Analogy

Before tackling inventory reduction, it is helpful to a company to conceptualize inventory. A river analogy is useful. Figure 20-1 depicts a river, with the volume of water in the river representing inventory. A river has width, depth, and length—and so does inventory. Figure 21-1 lists the ostensible causes, as well as the underlying causes, for excesses in the width, depth, and length of inventory.

Width comes from product variety, from the proliferation of models and parts needed to support a full line for customers. This adds to inventory. Marketing, Engineering, Manufacturing, and Purchasing all contribute to needless product variety. If the underlying causes in this category can be corrected, product variety can be curbed. However, in today's explosion of customized products, variety is becoming a necessity. It has to be addressed, in the factory of the future, with computer integrated manufacturing (CIM), which permits many different models to be produced in small quantities almost as economically as a narrow line.

Inventory depth is illustrated by the well-known rocks in the river analogy, shown in Figure 20-2. This compares the old U.S. and the current Japanese approaches to inventory. The U.S. approach was to avoid the rocks by raising the level of the water, so that the production ship could experience smooth sailing. The rocks, of course, are quality problems, supplier delays, equipment down time, and so forth. The Japanese approach, by contrast, is to deliberately reduce the level of the water in order to expose the rocks. Lowering the level of inventory gives visibility to the several quality and delivery problem rocks, which they quickly proceed to break up with sledgehammer force!

Finally, inventory length is caused by long cycle times, the reduction of which is the main focus of this chapter.

Cycle Time: A Single Parameter to Integrate Quality, Cost, Delivery, and Effectiveness

Like profits, inventory is only a result, a measurement. Cycle time provides the means. Cycle time can be defined as the clock time spent from the start of a process to its completion, whether that process be production, a new design introduction, order processing, or any support function's operation. The beauty of cycle time is that it integrates, with a single measurement, quality, cost, delivery, and effectiveness. This can be expressed pseudo-mathematically as:

$$\text{Cycle time} = \int q, c, d, e$$

where q, c, d, and e are quality cost, delivery, and effectiveness, respectively. If quality is poor, the long checking, auditing, correcting, and re-

Figure 20-2. U.S. vs. Japanese approaches to inventory.

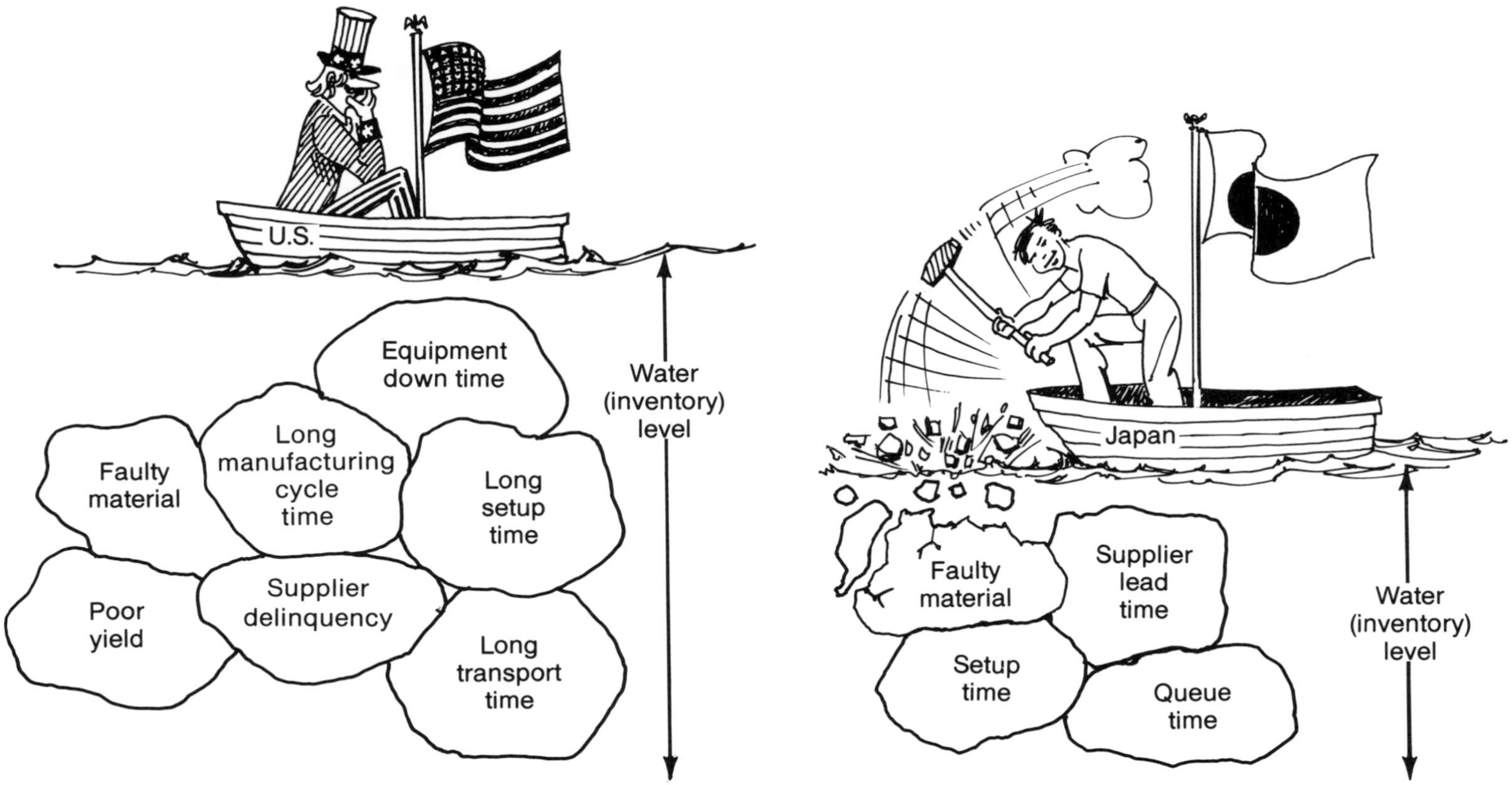

Figure 20-3. Cycle time to produce a Ford car, 1922.

	Cumulative Time (hours)
Iron ore boat docked	0
Molten iron cast into engine blocks	16
Casting cooled	20
Machining completed	28
Engine assembly completed	30
Engine taken to assembly plant	32
Final assembly completed	48

checking the loops add to cycle time. Cost (materials and manpower) is also a function of time. Poor deliveries results in long cycle times. Finally, ineffectiveness of a policy, procedure, or practice manifests itself in a long cycle time. Hence, if a company chooses to monitor only one parameter for each of its processes, it should be cycle time—the integrator.

Early History

Cycle time reduction, contrary to popular myth, did not start in Japan with *Kanban* in the 1960s. It started in the United States with Henry Ford in the 1920s. Figure 20-3 shows a total cycle time of 48 hours from the time iron ore landed on Ford's river docks to a finished Ford car on its way to the dealer! Even with today's cycle time progress, such speed is incredible. Alas, somewhere along the line, Henry Ford's successors lost the recipe for this amazing cycle time that was standard practice sixty years ago.

In the meantime, Henry Ford's book,* where his unique approach to manufacturing is spelled out in detail, has become a best seller in Japan. The concept was given further impetus when a Toyota executive visited a grocery chain store in the United States in the 1960s. He observed that while its profit on sales was very low, the fantastic inventory turns enabled the grocery chain to achieve a very respectable return on investment. The idea came to him that the same techniques could be applied to improving inventory turns in manufacturing. With this, the Toyota *Kanban* system was born. It is refreshing, however, to see how well cycle time reduction has caught on in the United States—at a speed equal to or even greater than quality improvement.

---

*_Today and Tomorrow_, originally published in 1926 by Doubleday Page & Company, was reprinted in 1988 by Productivity Press of Cambridge, Mass.

Figure 20-4. Nonvalue-added operations in production.

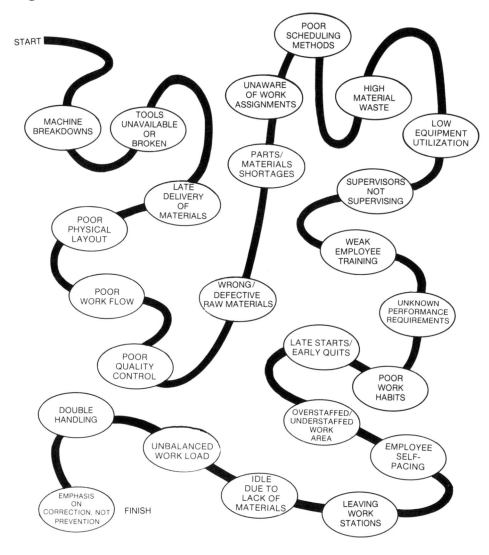

Cycle Time Reduction: The War on Waste

In any industrial process, whether it is in manufacturing or in white-collar work, there are many nonvalue-added operations. Figure 20-4 is an example of typical nonvalue-added operations in production, each of which lengthens the cycle time from start to finish. Cycle time management is, therefore, a war on waste. The elements of waste include poor quality, machine break-downs, poor space utilization, long setup time, long transport time, and the killer—waiting time.

Figure 20-5 is a graphic portrayal of cycle time and waste in various operations within a company. In A, the cycle time in production is made up of actual direct labor, setup time, transport time, and waiting time. Of these elements, only direct labor is value added. And just as direct labor consti-tutes only 5 percent or less of the sales dollar, so also in cycle time direct labor constitutes 5 percent or less of the total production cycle time. If the nonvalue-added operations of setup, transport, and waiting that consume 95 percent of the total cycle time can be drastically reduced, production cycle time can be compressed to a value no more than twice direct labor time. This is called theoretical cycle time, a target figure that can be and has been achieved.

Similarly, in the total manufacturing cycle time loop, shown in B, receiv-ing, incoming inspection, and the stockroom are at the front end of produc-tion and finished goods at the back end. Ninety percent of these support operations as well as 90 percent of the production operations (from A) are a waste. Therefore the total manufacturing cycle time can be reduced by 90 percent.

The in-plant cycle time loop, C, consists of planning, forecasting, sched-uling, and purchasing—ahead of the manufacturing cycle. In an ideal JIT plant, these preliminary activities can be eliminated or drastically reduced in time. As an example, with a pull system, small lots, and focused factories, forecasting is no longer necessary. Consider also the typical waste in the purchase cycle. Purchase order releases, acknowledgements, expediting, counting, inspection, sorting, scrap, rework, repackaging, and invoices add almost no value. The other functions can all be reduced to achieve a total in-plant cycle time reduction of 90 percent.

The last repetitive cycle time loop, D, is from the time the customer's order is booked to the time it is shipped to him. The longest single element in this loop is supplier lead time, which—as discussed later in this chap-ter—can also be reduced by 90 percent and more.

Finally, there are similar cycle time loops in all support services and white-collar work, of which the new product introduction cycle time, E, is the most important. The first cycle time element is the customer/marketing/sales/engineering interface. The second and largest element is design cycle time, which is so important that it can make or break a company. Proven ways to reduce design cycle time include:

- The team approach, in which Marketing, Engineering, and Production work together from the very inception of the project instead of sepa-rately and sequentially.
- Computer-aided engineering (CAE), which can replace clay models with mathematical models and short-circuit hours of development time.

Figure 20-5. The elements of cycle time and waste.

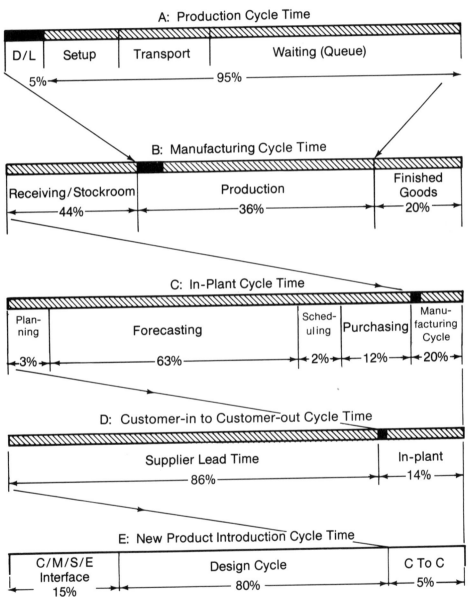

- Emphasis on quality so that the right things are done right the first time.
- Supplier links, in which the supplier develops part, model, and even higher-level assembly designs in parallel with and for the customer.

A Blueprint for Drastic Cycle Time Reduction

Several major characteristics of cycle time management must be present for a significant breakthrough in cycle time reduction: *

The Focused Factory

As opposed to the behemoth factories of yesterday that produced a wide variety of products, the focused factory is a plant within a plant that manufactures only a family of closely related products, and is managed by a dedicated, semiautonomous, interdisciplinary team.

To assure the transition from the all-purpose plant to the focused factory, the product designs should be scrubbed for best manufacturability, part number reduction, component standardization, modularization to accommodate some model variety, a simplified bill of material structure, and simplified routing.

Product Flow vs. Process Flow

Conventional thinking was premised on common processes being located in one area, generating "process islands" scattered throughout a plant. Backtracking and crossovers were common. As a result, the enemies of cycle time reduction—transport time and waiting time—escalated. In one factory, a part actually traveled nine miles within a plant area of 30,000 square feet before shipment. One wag said "it went round and round the plant until it developed enough kinetic energy to go out the door!"

Structured flow paths, by contrast, make for a smooth product flow that minimizes transport and waiting time. Preferably, the product flow is a U-shaped design that allows maximum operator flexibility and control. This does create some duplication of processes, but the advantages of substantially improved inventory turns and other cycle time benefits greatly out-

---

* The author is greatly indebted to Dr. Ed Heard, president of E. Heard Associates and one of the outstanding authorities on cycle time management, for the framework of cycle time reduction used in this chapter.

weigh the increased capital equipment costs. Further, even these capital costs can be minimized by the use of smaller, simpler, and more flexible processes and equipment. The old order believed that people and equipment must be kept busy at all times, no matter how much excess inventory they produced.* The new order believes that permitting workers and equipment to stand idle is not a crime, but that having idle material is a sin.

A simple way to assess product flow is to measure travel distances for all products and then to establish plans for their systematic reduction. Another method is to determine product flows between plants. There have been horror stories of product fabricated in the United States, assembled in Korea, tested in Hong Kong, quality audited in the U.S., and distributed abroad again—all in the name of chasing direct labor or getting around tariff barriers and other intergovernmental regulations. The damage caused by these practices to cycle time and return on investment is almost too painful to measure. In one company, there was actually a case of a part that crossed the oceans seven times during the total manufacturing cycle! Any departure from a single plant, even a feeder plant, for product movement should be considered only as a last resort.

The ideal focused factory layout is line-of-sight manufacturing, where the production status can be visually ascertained by all at a glance. Production rates, quality levels, maintenance charts, and so forth should be posted for all to see. Storage racks, the handmaiden of work-in-process inventory, should be banished.

Unified Teams

In the old, unfocused factory, line support operations reported to bosses who were detached from manufacturing except at the very top rung—the plant manager. Departments such as manufacturing engineering, industrial engineering, process engineering, plant quality, plant purchasing, and maintenance protected their own fiefdoms. Teamwork was difficult at best.

In the focused factory, these departmental walls come tumbling down. Its one focal point is a business manager or product manager to whom all support functions report, the only exception being a few specialists who serve as internal consultants covering several focused factories. In the ideal focused factory, this not only includes all manufacturing support functions but others such as purchasing, engineering, and sales as well.

The Goal, by Eliyahu Goldratt and Jeff Cox, is an excellent treatment of the principles of cycle time reduction, written in storybook fashion. Published by Creative Output, Milford, Conn., in 1984, a revised edition (1986) is also available in paperback from North River Press, Croton-on-Hudson, New York.

The Flat Pyramid

The organization in a focused factory resembles a shallow pyramid, with authority and accountability permeating down to the lowest levels. Cycle time training is given to all people in order to maximize understanding, commitment, and enthusiastic involvement in cycle time management. Through cross training, the number of job classifications are drastically reduced. A worker's flexibility and problem-solving ability now become the criteria for pay grade elevation and eventual promotion. In one of Motorola's divisions, the pay grades in one of its focused factories are based on the total number of machines and processes that an operator is certified to handle. Its focused factory, located in a high-wage area in the United States, has not only successfully challenged Japanese competition; it has knocked out several of its Japanese competitors.

Continuous Flow

Continuous flow as an attribute of cycle time management represents quality control at its best. The object is to ensure that poor designs, unstable processes, defective materials and marginal workmanship are not only corrected but prevented from happening again, so that there can be a continuous, uninterrupted, and one-way flow of product with zero defects, 100 percent yield, minimal variation within specification limits, and no inspection and test. This, of course, is an ideal, but the several chapters in this book devoted to quality improvement—especially the techniques of design of experiments, SPC, *poka-yoke*, and total preventive maintenance (TPM)—offer an excellent blueprint for the eventual attainment of this ideal.

Pull vs. Push System

The fame of the Japanese *Kanban* system has heightened interest in the "pull" system of product control as opposed to the old "push" system. In the latter, operators pile up product at a work station in adherence to a regimented schedule or to keep machines and people busy, regardless of the pile-up of inventory or the lack of need for product further down the line. In the pull system, the last work station in the line paces the entire line, with each previous work station producing only the exact amount needed by the next station.

In the push system, problems are hidden. The cushion of large work-in-process (WIP) inventories allows for a leisurely approach to problem solving. The best feature of the pull system is that it heightens the visibility of any problem. If there is a quality or delivery or other problem that shuts down a given work station, the previous work station, sensing that product is not needed at the next station, also shuts down. The ripple effect is fast, and soon the entire production line is down. There is nothing more visible than a whole line shut down. This accentuates the urgency of immediately solving the problem at the offending work station. Workers, technicians, and engineers swarm over the station like bees to rapidly restore it to health so that the whole line can start up again.

Small Lot Sizes

A central feature of the pull system is that lot sizes are drastically reduced. In batch production, prevalent in most companies, large runs are the norm. If a process produces a 1,000-part run, with 10 at the exact same time, 990 parts do nothing but wait and twiddle their thumbs. If now the lot size is reduced to 10, waiting time is reduced to zero. This is the crucial difference between batch production and short cycle manufacturing using continuous flows.

Setup Time Reduction

Small lots, however, require drastic reductions in setup time in order to facilitate a line changeover from one model to the next. It has been demonstrated that setup time can be reduced by factors of 60 to 1 and more, given the use of ingenious industrial engineering methods fueled by workers' ideas.* One such ingenious method is to videotape the changeover process to pinpoint where time and motion are wasted.

Another technique is readying the workplace so that all tools and materials will be instantly available and there will be no need for even first piece part quality evaluations through external audits. A classic example of this would be changing a tire in record-breaking time. The operation takes the average motorist at least 20 minutes. At the Indy 500, taking as much as 20 seconds to change four tires could mean losing the race. Granted that the manpower and expense involved in effecting such a rapid changeover, though necessary to car racing, is impractical in most industrial situations. Yet the sport's masterful organization of material and labor, honed to a fine science through practice and drill, can provide many useful tips to manufacturing. Another example is provided by Toyota. In the early 1970s, it took three hours to make a die change in its large stamping machines. Hearing that Volkswagen had perfected a method to make the change in 1½ hours, Toyota engineers went to study VW's techniques, installed these techniques at Toyota, and went on to shave another half hour off setup time. Proudly they announced to their general manager that they had beaten VW. The manager

---

*An excellent book on this subject is *A Revolution in Manufacturing: The SMED System* by Shigeo Shingo (Cambridge, Mass.: Productivity Press, 1985).

said: "Good. My congratulations to your team. Now change the dies in 3 minutes!" Unattainable as the new goal seemed, the Toyota engineers—by the late 1970s—achieved this industrial equivalent of the 4-minute mile by proceeding to shave setup time down to 1½ minutes.

Linear Output

The benefits of a pull system are limited if the total quantity required by master schedules is allowed to vary from day to day. Such schedules should have nearly constant rates—known as "fidelity" or "linearity"—over short periods of time, with quantities being ramped up or down slowly. There can be model mixes within this linearity, but the total output of the mix should be held to an ideal ± 0 deviation from the constant rate.

Material Control

The old "just-in-case" system was characterized by incomplete picks, partial builds, expediting, parts chasing, inventory auditing, and an antediluvian cost accounting system—a bloated superstructure built on the vanishing foundations of a direct labor base.

In cycle time management, with a steady and dependable stream of just-in-time parts from suppliers, incomplete picks and partial builds are no longer necessary. Neither are parts chasing and expediting by supervisors, who can now divert the 90 percent of time previously spent on these useless activities to helping and coaching their people. The burdensome chores of physical inventory audits conducted once a month now disappear. The line-of-sight layout, the pull system, and small lot sizes facilitate easy counting, at no extra cost, directly by the operators themselves on a daily, and even an hourly, basis. Cost accounting too is beginning to enter the twenty-first century—directly from the nineteenth—with cycle time rather than direct labor as the base for overhead cost allocations.

People Power

Granting workers a sense of "ownership" is probably the most important attribute of cycle time management. The concepts and techniques of "ownership" are detailed in the next chapter. As a prerequisite, managers must become more *involved* with their workers and tap the mother lode—the worker's minds! To enhance worker ownership:

- Workers must be given the training in multiple skills.
- They must be coached in the use of simple, but powerful, problem-solv-

ing tools. Once trained and encouraged, line workers more often than not perform better than engineers. Further, there are far more problems than managers and technical professionals can solve by themselves. The possibilities of what can happen when a whole factory is turned loose on problem solving is mind-boggling.

- Team building must be nurtured.
- The next operation should be treated as the customer, not as the enemy.
- Fear among workers must be stamped out. It is far more widespread and deep-rooted than even sensitive managers can gauge.
- Workers' jobs should be redesigned to make them less boring and more exciting—without adding costs.

Dependable Supply and Demand

It is only when a company has put its own house in order by slashing its work-in-process inventory that it has a right to approach its suppliers and customers as partners in cycle time reduction. The specific techniques of supplier lead time reduction are discussed later in this chapter. With the aid of these techniques, suppliers can be encouraged, especially within the framework of partnership, to deliver a linear output of their products in smaller, more frequent lots.

Customers may also become converts to cycle time management when a company can deliver their order with shorter and shorter lead times. They can then begin, with greater confidence, to order smaller quantities more frequently. In time, they can also be persuaded to give longer-term contracts, blanket orders, and more stable forecasts—in short, to be partnership customers.

Tracking Progress

Cycle time management in manufacturing requires only two macroscopic measurements to track progress: yield and cycle time. Figure 20-6 shows how a product line in a computer company's focused factory was tracked for yield and cycle time improvements. It also indicates the major techniques used to achieve these improvements both in quality and in cycle time.

Cycle Time Management: From Theory to Action

The most frequently asked question about cycle time management is: "Where do we begin implementation?" As with other "processes" (as opposed to

Figure 20-6. Manufacturing yield/cycle time progress.

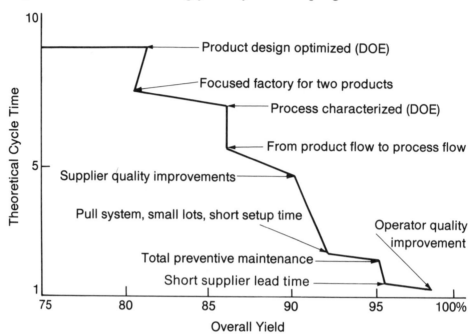

"programs") of importance, the start should be with top management exposure, education, and commitment. From that point forward, the following is a *suggested* sequence. It is not necessary, however, that these steps be taken in order. Parallel and iterative steps can be accommodated.

1. *Performance measurement parameters:* The focus must shift from profit to return on investment (ROI) for each strategic business unit (SBU); from direct labor to manufacturing cycle time; from single work station defect analysis to overall yield improvement; from manufacturing requirements planning (MRP) to just-in-time (JIT); from the vagaries of forecasting to build and ship to order with lightening speed.

2. *Pilot focused factory:* Rather than immediately breaking up a large plant into several focused factories, a single focused factory should be formed to act as a pilot, to manufacture a product family based on similar processing requirements and using similar parts.

3. *A focused factory management team:* Forming a focused factory management team may be the hardest step of all from the point of view of human relations because it disrupts traditional functional organizations and

breaks up "empires." A first step is to assign a task force role to a selected focused factory management team. As the task force begins to pull together and succeed, it can become a permanent focused factory organization, with an autonomous team consisting of a product manager and members from every function within manufacturing, followed soon after by all supporting functions, such as sales, engineering, supply management, and quality assurance.

4. *People power:* A focused factory, with its small size, natural work units, client relationships, quick feedback on performance, and sense of ownership, has a far greater chance than a traditional factory of welding its people into a family and unleashing full people power. The Hawthorne effect* may also come into play as its success becomes more widely recognized. Training of the work force in cycle time principles, multiple skills, and problem solving should begin with the creation of the focused factory.

5. *Poor quality—the first rock to blast:* In the "rocks in the river" analogy, there is no rock more formidable than poor quality. Tackling all quality problems must be the highest priority in the focused factory—from product yields to total preventive maintenance, from incoming inspection to supplier process control.

6. *Pull system:* To convert from a push to a pull system, lot sizes must be reduced gradually but systematically, with some inventory banks between stations at the start leading to an eventual elimination of such banks. Setup time reduction should be pursued and an attempt made at stabilizing the total model mix at a nearly constant rate.

7. *Dependable supply and demand:* The last steps involve influencing suppliers and customers. A demonstration of achievement in one's own plant is worth a thousand exhortations to suppliers and pleas to customers. Such achievement can then become the best sales tool for requesting blanket contracts and smaller, more frequent deliveries from suppliers and to customers.

Cycle Time Reduction in a High-Tech Company: A Case Study

The semiconductor business is characterized by rapid technological change, roller coaster demand, and intense competition. One company in this business decided that cycle time management would give it a distinct edge in meeting such competition. It took the following steps:

---

*Explained in Chapter 21.

Figure 20-7. The relentless march to quality/cycle time improvement.

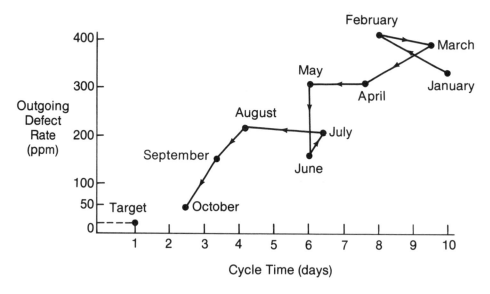

1. It elevated manufacturing to a strategic thrust.
2. It established two focused factories. One focused factory was dedicated to commodity (mature) products, with a focus on high volume, automation, and low cost. The second concentrated on customer products, with a focus on flexible manufacturing and fast design cycle time.
3. It trained all of its employees in quality and JIT and made this new culture pervasive throughout its plant.
4. It changed its plant layout from a process to a product flow. Its products used to move up and down between two floors, with long queues at staging points. Total production cycle time was ten days. The focused factories were consolidated, one on each floor. The number of racks required for lot staging was reduced by 80 percent. This WIP reduction alone achieved a space saving of over 25 percent, with better housekeeping and line-of-sight management. Cycle time was reduced to 2.5 days, with a new target of one day.
5. It gradually implemented the pull system with smaller and smaller lot sizes.
6. It emphasized quality from the very start, concentrating on yields, supplier quality, and outgoing quality. The latter improved from a defect rate of 300 parts per million (ppm) to 50 ppm, with a target of 10 ppm.

Figure 20-7 shows the progress the company made, as well as some minor backsliding, in cycle time reduction and quality improvement in just ten months.

Supplier Lead Time Reduction

When all is said and done, the greatest bang for the buck in cycle time reduction is supplier lead time reduction. Figure 20-8 shows a pie chart of a company's cycle time—from forecasting to shipping—for various functions. It is typical of most companies before cycle time management. The largest single element of cycle time, accounting for 85.9 percent of total cycle time, is supplier lead time. With the ten-point approach outlined here, a 20 to 1 reduction in supplier lead time is attainable. The customer company should:

1. Enter into *long-term contracts*.

2. Establish *stable forecasts*, with visibility for a year, updated monthly. As an example, the quantities for the first month could be frozen at ±0 deviation; for a three-month projection, at ±10% deviation; for a six-month projection, at ±20% deviation, and for a year's projection, at ±50% deviation.

Figure 20-8. Cycle time by function (actual = 4,749.8 hours).

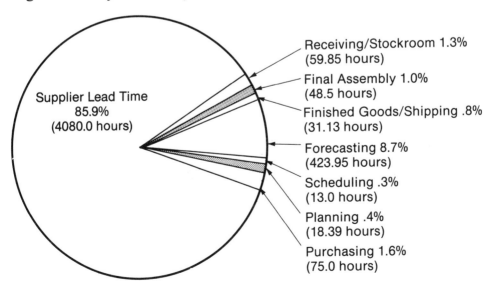

Table 20-1.   Traditional vs. effective A, B, C analysis.

	Traditional A, B, C Distribution			Effective A, B, C Distribution		
	A Items	*B Items*	*C Items*	*A Items*	*B Items**	*C Items*
Volume (%)	10	25	65	10	5	95
$ (%)	75	20	5	75	5	20
Receipt frequency	Weekly	Monthly	Quarterly	Daily	Daily	Quarterly
Strategy	EOQ**	EOQ	EOQ	Maximum Inventory Turns	Minimum Space	EOQ

*B items redefined as bulk items consuming space **EOQ = Economic order quantity based on inventory formulas

3. Use *blanket orders.* This is an old but still very useful technique in which the customer makes a firm commitment to buy a specified quantity, say, 10,000 units, from the supplier during the course of a year. If there is a degree of uncertainty about the quantity purchased, there could be a three-point blanket order, with an agreement to pay a slightly higher price for a lower than specified quantity and a slightly lower price for a higher than specified quantity. The new term for this type of agreement is volume-variable pricing, a technique increasingly used by the automotive companies with their key suppliers.

4. Authorize *a partial build* by the supplier, up to his longest cycle time, but with the least dollar expenditure. (For example, in semiconductors, the cycle time up to the wafer fabrication stage consumes almost 90 percent of the total cycle time, but only 40 percent of the total cost.) Even if such a partial build is too expensive for the customer company, an authorization to commit to the *supplier's raw material* should be a minimum.

5. Offer *financial incentives* for lead time reduction as discussed in Chapter 19.

6. Substitute a traditional A, B, C inventory analysis with a more *effective analysis*, as shown in Table 20-1. The main difference is the redefinition of B items as bulk items that consume space. In the revamped analysis, both A items and B items are received daily rather than weekly and monthly, respectively.

7. Use *local sourcing* to the greatest extent possible. The least important benefit of nearby sourcing is short transportation time. The largest benefit is the opportunity to visit suppliers and help them to reduce their cycle time. (Forcing suppliers to establish local warehouses simply to reduce customer inventory is, in the most charitable interpretation, a band-aid that

puts the entire burden of added inventory on the supplier, with the customer indirectly paying for the extra cost in the long run.)

8. Encourage the supplier to ship in *small quantities more frequently*. (Some factories in Japan have materials from their key suppliers shipped twenty-four times a day and delivered straight to production lines for maximum inventory turns and space reductions.)

9. *Ship by air* if the savings in lead time and inventory reduction exceed transportation costs.

10. In a strong demand market, negotiate *capacity reservations* with key suppliers. This is one of the benefits of partnership to customer companies.

In the final analysis, the supplier must be actively helped to systematically reduce his cycle time. Most suppliers are even further behind in the practice of cycle time than they are in quality progress. All the steps detailed under the heading Cycle Time Management should be repeated at the supplier's facility under the customer's guidance.

The supplier, in turn, should be encouraged to carry the cycle time message to his suppliers. Just as supplier lead time is the single longest element of cycle time for a customer company, so is the lead time of the supplier's supplier the single longest element of cycle time for the supplier company. If this practice were to be carried forward throughout the supply chain, imagine the inventory savings and positive cash flow that could accrue to American industry!

White-Collar Cycle Time Reduction

Important as reducing manufacturing cycle time is to any company customer or supplier, it pales by comparison with the problem posed by reducing cycle time in white-collar operations—that is, wherever a product, paper or information is moved from one "process" to the next. As mentioned in Chapter 17, direct labor productivity is well over 80 percent in most U.S. industries, but it is a dismal 40 percent or less in white-collar indirect labor operations. Further, if productivity is measured as the sales dollars or value added per employee, direct labor productivity has been rising by 2 to 3 percent per year, whereas indirect labor productivity has been declining by 1 percent per year—and that despite office automation. With the direct labor base shrinking fast and the indirect labor payroll bloating, American industry faces a formidable challenge in reversing these white-collar blues. The answer lies in marshaling an assault on all indirect labor, with cycle time as the tool par excellence.

Figure 20-9 shows how cost and cycle time accumulate in a factory. The customer purchases material at some cost from his suppliers. While it sits

Figure 20-9. Cost/cycle time profile in manufacturing.

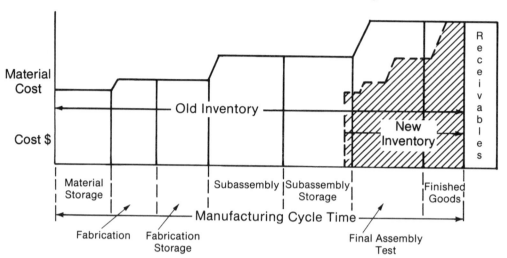

in storage, it does not add cost, but consumes cycle time. The next stage, fabrication, consumes both cost and time—and so on through the steps of fabrication, storage, subassembly, subassembly storage, and final assembly/ test to finished goods. Most of the time is wasted in setup time, transport time, and waiting time. The integral of this cost-time line, that is, the total area under the line, is inventory. None of this large inventory cost can be recovered until the product is sold and customer payments are collected through accounts receivable. Now, if cycle time is reduced by factors of 10 and more, the inventory costs are dramatically reduced (shown by the shaded area).

Manufacturing Cycle Time: A Small Fraction of Indirect Labor Cycle Time

Figure 20-10 portrays both indirect labor cycle time and manufacturing cycle time. Indirect labor starts with a large base of support services that consume people, money, and time even before a customer inquiry is processed. Then come marketing, sales, and engineering to obtain the customer's business. This is followed by the design and procurement cycles. Finally there is the manufacturing cycle of Figure 20-10, shown as a "pimple on the log" of indirect labor cycle time. The area under the curve in Figure 20-10 also represents inventory costs, although this is "invisible" inventory made up of indirect labor people rather than materials and labor. Not one penny of these invisible inventory costs is recovered until manufacturing ships the

Figure 20-10. Cost/cycle time profile for product development and manufacturing.

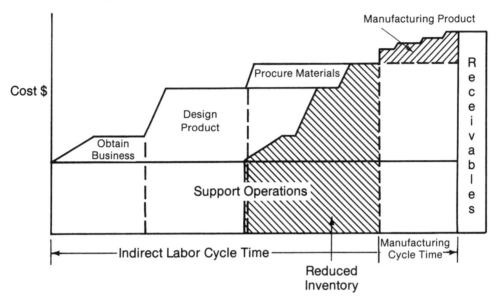

first product and receivables are collected. This makes for an astounding cash flow problem. It has been estimated that a typical company has a negative cash flow equivalent to almost one year of sales. Again, if indirect labor cycle time can be cut to a small fraction, the invisible inventory costs can be dramatically reduced (shaded area).

Total Company Cycle Time: A Small Fraction of Cycle Time in the Entire Supply Chain

Figures 20-9 and 20-10 can be equally applied to a supplier's manufacturing cycle time and inventory as well as to his indirect labor cycle time and invisible inventory. His material price, represented by the vertical line in Figure 20-9 is largely determined by his material cost and his total inventory (manufacturing plus indirect labor), in short, by his total cycle time. The same logic can be extended to the supplier's supplier and his supplier and so on through the supply chain. Now, if each supplier in the whole chain reduces not only his manufacturing inventory but also his invisible (people) inventory, the savings, in terms of reduced overall cycle times and reduced material costs, to the end customer can snowball. Even more important, the practice, if performed nationally, could make the United States cost-competitive with any nation!

NOAC Applied to Indirect Labor Cycle Time

While reducing indirect labor cycle time is still in its infancy when compared with the considerable progress made in reducing manufacturing cycle time, a systematic method utilizing the principle of the next operation as customer (NOAC) provides a powerful tool. NOAC is described in detail in Chapter 18. The emphasis there was quality improvement. But the same techniques can be used for cycle time improvement in indirect labor. The best way to follow the steps outlined in NOAC is to establish an ad hoc interdisciplinary team that will stay with the task full-time until the desired results are achieved. A high-level executive is selected as the team leader. He or she is called the "process owner," with a specific charge to break down organizational barriers and whatever standard operating policy (SOP) restrictions and other bureaucratic roadblocks stand in the way of team accomplishment.

Reducing Design Cycle Time: A Case Study

Nothing is more crucial to the survival of a company than reducing its design cycle time. This is the new battleground among competitors. One large computer company decided to attack its long design cycle time of twenty-six months. Table 20-2 is a Gantt chart showing the various elements associated with its typical design cycle time. As can be seen, many of these activities were in sequence with one another: one ending, the next beginning, with little or no overlap. The ground rules had been cast in concrete by means of standard operating practices (SOPs) established in a more leisurely era. To significantly reduce the cycle time to a little over ten months, the company made the changes shown as follows. The shortened design cycle time, far from reducing quality and reliability, enhanced them. Further results were seen in increased customer satisfaction, smoother production, higher company morale, and a big jump over the competition.

1. *Interface between customer, marketing, and engineering.* Instead of using time-consuming and ineffective market research techniques, the company held joint meetings with typical customers, marketing, and engineering. An analysis was made of features—by importance and cost. As a result, product descriptions and requirements were defined very early in the design cycle and not changed—contrary to past practices.

2. *Standardization.* Instead of engineers reinventing the wheel each time, they were encouraged to use standard modules for hardware; preferred parts

Table 20-2. Typical design cycle time based on SOP.

	1 Quarter	2 Quarter	3 Quarter	4 Quarter	1 Quarter	2 Quarter	3 Quarter	4 Quarter	1 Quarter	2 Quarter	3 Quarter
Design phase I		9 months									
Complete prints				2 months							
Get quotations (three vendors)					3 weeks						
Order tools					3 months						
Get first parts						1 month					
Correct tool						1 month					
Order final parts							3 weeks				
Build final proto-type							1 month				
Prototype: Accelerated life test								1.5 months			
Phase II											
Phase II evaluation											
Component approval											
Order all material									6 months		
Build pilot run											
Evaluation											
Final accelerated life test										1.5 months	
Ship acceptance											
Total Cycle Time 26 months											

(a simpler version of group technology), and standard modules for software—the last an effort in its infancy in the software industry.

3. *Print and tool development.* Instead of the old method of completing prints, sending out bids, selecting finalist suppliers, and entering into long negotiations with them, CAE/CAD systems were used to communicate electronically with parts and tool suppliers to finalize requirements much, much earlier.

4. *Ordering material.* Material, even for pilot runs, used to be ordered after completion and release of all process charts. The new system permitted the ordering of parts before designs were finalized, saving two to three months in cycle time, even though material costs went up slightly because of design changes.

5. *Part numbering.* The old systems policy required the company's part numbers on all parts. The new policy eliminated the necessity for issuing special prints, reducing the work load in the specifications department, and reduced supplier costs and delivery times.

6. *Component qualification.* The old system required an independent qualification of all parts by a components engineering group. By working closely with partnership suppliers, the qualification was done by the supplier under the guidance of a component engineer. This changed a series evaluation to a parallel evaluation, saving several weeks of cycle time.

7. *Accelerated life test.* By changing from single environment sequential test to multiple environment overstress tests, the cycle time was considerably shortened. Further, potential failures were found much earlier, and the designs made more robust even before production started.

8. *Design/manufacturing interface.* Instead of design development that was independent of production, manufacturing/engineering became involved in the design from Day 1, shortening the evaluation time in production.

9. *Manufacturing/equipment supplier interface.* Instead of the equipment supplier providing process equipment, followed by process engineering evaluating the equipment in the factory, joint supplier/process engineering experiments were conducted at the equipment supplier factory to "characterize the process," thus saving valuable evaluation time in pilot production.

10. *Design quality.* Instead of fitful starts and stops in design effort resulting from poor design quality, characterized by numerous engineering changes, the design/manufacturing team used all the quality tools to ensure right designs the first time.

Part V

CONTINUAL IMPROVEMENT

Chapter 21

Employees as Partners

If Just a Business Contract

Maybe our relationship is just a business contract.
You give me something and I give you something in turn.

You can try to get the most from me
And I can try to get the most from you.

When effort is thus called for on either's part
It becomes a sort of tug-of-war.
I try to give you the minimum
And you try to extract the maximum
And give me the minimum.

Of course, with unfortunate effects on business purpose,
Namely utilization of resources and creation of wealth. . . .

—Nagam Atthreya, *The You and I in Business*

Table 21-1. Needs of blue-collar workers listed in descending order of priority.

Management List	Worker List
1. Good wages	1. Full appreciation of work done
2. Job security	2. Feeling "in" on things
3. Promotion/growth	3. Sympathetic help for personal
4. Good working conditions	problems
5. Interesting work	4. Job security
6. Personal loyalty to workers	5. Good wages
7. Tactful disciplining	6. Interesting work
8. Full appreciation of work done	7. Promotion/growth
9. Sympathetic help for personal	8. Personal loyalty to workers
problems	9. Good working conditions
10. Feeling "in" on things	10. Tactful disciplining

Management Is Not "Tuned In" to Workers

In 1972, the U.S. Chamber of Commerce conducted a survey among both managers and workers in which both groups were asked to rank ten needs and interests felt by direct labor workers in descending order of importance. Table 21-1 shows the diametrically opposed assessments given by management and workers. This old survey has been replicated over the years many times by other institutions in large and small companies, for different industries, among both men and women, and in good times and bad. There is an uncanny consistency about the findings of such surveys. The three needs and interests listed at the top by the direct labor group—full appreciation of work done, sympathetic help for personal problems, and feeling "in" on things—are precisely those that appear at the bottom of management's list! How much more tuned out can management get!

Why is this so? Management believes that its direct labor workers have the same goals, aspirations, and drives that management has. But nonprofessional workers march to a different drummer. Their backgrounds, education, experiences and aspirations may have conditioned them to different needs. Management does not understand this. Workers yearn to be commended for a good job. This can range from a friendly pat on the back and a simple but direct "thank you," to bulletin board publicity, house organ mentions, and even monetary awards. Equally important, all employees like to be consulted, to feel needed, to participate.

The Hawthorne Effect

In the 1920s, Elton Mayo of Harvard University and his colleagues conducted their famous productivity studies at Western Electric's Hawthorne plant. They started by observing the effect of lighting on a group of six telephone assemblers. As the lighting increased, productivity went up. One of the researchers, who probably hailed from Missouri, questioned whether productivity would go down if the lighting was returned to its original condition. The research team members shared their approach with the assemblers. To their amazement, productivity increased when the original lighting conditions were restored. The team turned the lighting down until finally it had reached the level of bright moonlight. But productivity went on increasing! The reason for the increases was that the workers appreciated the attention showered on them by the researchers and felt special because they were chosen to participate in the experiment. The phenomenon, now universally known as the Hawthorne effect, embraces two very important motivation principles—worker recognition and worker participation. Both, in essence, appear at the top of the workers' list.

Motivation Theories

Motivation theory became a hot management topic during the 1970s. Motivation principles—from Abraham Maslow's hierarchy of human needs to Douglas McGregor's Theory X and Theory Y—were eagerly seized upon by managements anxious to build bridges to their workers. Two of the best examples were—and still are—Frederick Herzberg's monumental work on motivators and dissatisfiers and Scott Myers's on maintenance and motivational needs.

Herzberg's Motivators and Dissatisfiers

Herzberg drew a sharp distinction between worker needs that produce dissatisfaction when neglected and contentment at best when fulfilled and those that can be used to truly generate motivation. Factors affecting the former are company policy, supervision, salary, and working conditions. If poorly handled, they cause genuine dissatisfaction; but even if handled effectively, they produce only contentment—not motivation. By contrast, Herzberg's motivation factors—achievement, recognition, work itself, responsibility, and advancement—create the high worker attitudes that management seeks to nurture. Figure 21-1 is a graphic portrayal of Herzberg's motivators and dissatisfiers and of the extent of the negative and positive attitudes they engender.

Scott Myers's Motivation and Maintenance Needs

In an adaptation of Maslow's and Herzberg's theories, Scott Myers developed a "three-ring" concept of worker needs, as shown in Figure 21-2. Main-

Figure 21-1. Effects of motivators and dissatisfiers on worker's attitudes.

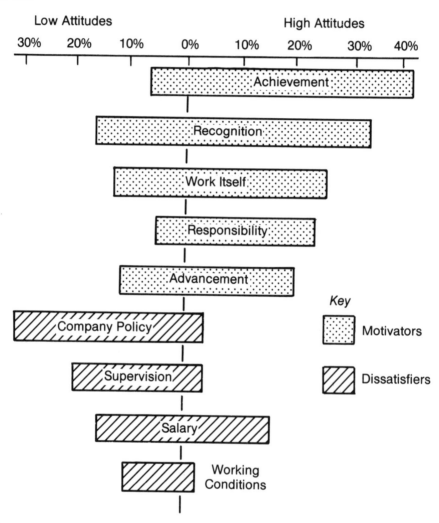

Source: Frederick Herzberg.

tenance needs, in the outer ring, include lower order needs such as: *physical*—food and shelter; *economic*—a paycheck; *security*—assurance of a job; *status*—dignity of the individual, and perks and prestige; and *social*—a person's need for interaction with fellow employees. These maintenance needs, similar to Herzberg's contentment factors, cause dissatisfaction when not met but do not, on the other hand, produce motivation when present. At best, they maintain the status quo and possibly prevent employees from

Figure 21-2. Employee needs: Maintenance and motivational.

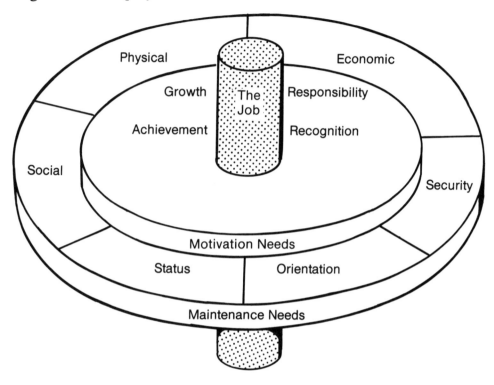

leaving the company. The inner ring contains the same motivation factors—growth, achievement, responsibility, and recognition—formulated by Herzberg. But the innermost ring, at the very core of motivation, is the job itself—its interest, its challenges, its excitement.

Management: From Boss to "Servant"

Most managers have some familiarity with motivation theory. It is almost impossible to be ignorant of it given the frequency and intensity with which the subject is covered in magazines, trade journals, books, and seminars. But the messages implicit in these articles and courses have fallen on deaf ears. Having heard, management has not listened. Having been exposed, management has not absorbed. And even when it has understood, management has not accepted.

Bossism

The cause of poor worker motivation is seldom the worker. It is management. And one of the main reasons is the manager's predilection to be a boss. To paraphrase an old saying, you can take the man out of the boss, but you can't take the boss out of the man! Most managers have risen to their positions of importance by their ability to get things done. They have succeeded in overcoming the bureaucratic inertia of their environments by the force of their personalities, by their hard-driving ways, and by their autocratic attitudes. They do not know that there is a better way—which is to release the creative and enthusiastic energies of all their employees, not just their own. They do not know that their employees often know more about what is going on and about what the problems are and how to solve them than they themselves do.

Management by Wandering Around

Management rehabilitation can start with what is now widely known as management by wandering around (MBWA). Worker attitude surveys invariably reveal that workers want to see their top bosses from time to time. But most top managers remain closeted in their ivory towers, too busy with "more important" issues to meet with their people. "It is too time-consuming and the pay-off is poor," they claim. The reform therefore, must start with top management. It must be convinced that there is a very rich and permanent payback in MBWA. Mr. Bill Weisz, vice-chairman of Motorola, urged his top managers to devote at least a half hour each day to MBWA.

The object is not just for top managers to see and be seen. It is to mingle with their people on a regular basis; to get to know them; to take a personal interest in them; to extend that interest beyond the workplace to their family situations, even to helping with personal problems if these are volunteered by the employees. At first, workers in such encounters will tend to be shy and cautious. Having been looked down upon for so long, they are not likely to open up immediately. They may even be suspicious of the manager's true motives. But once the door is opened, MBWA can replace fear with communication, trust, and enthusiasm. The good manager will listen. Having listened, he can turn gripes into constructive ideas. Having obtained constructive ideas, he can act on them. Having acted on them, he can give feedback, and in this way start an upward spiral of mutual confidence and respect.

Rap Sessions

Another way to bridge the manager-worker moat is for the top manager to conduct rap sessions with small groups of employees. Workers may be reluctant to speak up at large "communications" meetings. They may also be shy in one-on-one encounters. However, with the support of a few of their peers in small group meetings, they can enter into a meaningful dialogue with their top manager. It also provides the top manager with an opportunity for explaining in detail the pros and cons of an issue and why a certain decision, that may have puzzled employees, was reached.

The "Upside-Down" Organization

In the final analysis, a manager must not only meet with his people, rap with them, and listen to their ideas; he must also be a constant source of encouragement to them, cheer them on, provide vision and leadership. He must be able to provide them with active, concrete help. The word "help" should be tattooed across his chest. This spirit of help is captured in the concept of the "upside-down" organization, where the traditional pyramid organization chart is reversed and the top manager is at the bottom of the chart instead of at the top. His role is now to help the doers do their job— by removing roadblocks in their path and providing resources. He must be a facilitator, a consultant, a coach, a teacher.

The Manager as Servant

One CEO goes even further. In the March 1988 issue of *Metal Working News*, Gene Beaudet, its charismatic editor, asked his readers what American top management could do to overcome the mistrust and downright hostility that is said to exist in the lower ranks of American industry. The response from Robert M. Coombs, the CEO of ITS Industries in Kalamazoo, was a blockbuster. He wrote: "The chief executive must stop being the 'big boss' or the 'big wheel' and become a *servant* to his employees and stockholders! This change in attitude, or heart, would do wonders in changing the attitude of workers way down the line." Coombs closed his letter by referring to a group of 400 chief executives of a religious organization to which he belongs as backers of his views. He signed the letter with the title "CEO Servant."

The response to Mr. Coombs's letter was positive. One executive wrote: "It is marvelous to extend the possibilities that could be produced by a servant's heart to other activities in industry as well. . . . Imagine what could happen between the marketing department and the customers; or between the sheet metal shop and the production floor; or between the engineering department and the marketing department." Instead of building departmental walls and functional silos that only exacerbate battles over turf, genuine help from management, upside-down organizations, and the manager acting as servant could revolutionize industry.

Total Employee Involvement: Prerequisites

A fundamental change in management attitudes toward the worker, from one of bossism to partnership, is essential for expanding workers' motivation. To prepare a solid foundation for total employee involvement (TEI), three prerequisites must be present:

Job Security vs. the Damocles Sword of Layoffs

Foremost among these is the need to give workers at least minimal assurance of job security. Back in the 1940s, James Lincoln,* the president and founder of the phenomenally successful Lincoln Electric Company, expressed his view of management's responsibility respecting job security:

> The greatest fear of the worker, which is the same as the greatest fear of the industrialist in operating a company, is lack of income. . . . The worker's fear of no income is far more intense than the industrialist's, since his daily bread and that of his family depend on his job. . . .
>
> In spite of these facts, the industrialist will fire the worker any time he feels he can get along without him. The worker has no control over his future. Only management is responsible for the loss of the worker's job. Only management can follow and develop a program that will bring in orders. The worker can't. Management, which is responsible, keeps its job. The man who had no responsibility is thrown out. Management failed in its job and had no punishment. The wage earner did not fail in his job but was fired. . . . This fact has had more to do with production limitation than any other circumstances.

James Lincoln's words ring as true today as they did over forty years ago. Although several progressive companies have cushioned the shock of layoffs, much more can and should be done to cope with this problem. Attrition, early retirement, generous severance pay, the use of temporary workers and subcontracting as buffers, and a shortened work week are all measures far superior to the cyclical hiring and firing that characterizes American industry. However, the most important assurance that management can provide is that cost reductions, to which workers have voluntarily contributed, will not result in a loss of their jobs.

Training: A Passport to Total Employee Involvement

The higher managers travel up the corporate ladder, the more they believe that workers are capable of generating only low-grade ideas. "Better cafe-

---

* James F. Lincoln, *Incentive Management* (Cleveland: Lincoln Electric Co., 1951), p. 170.

teria food, cleaner washrooms, and improved parking are the only things workers are interested in," they claim. What these same managers do not realize is that by supporting workers, encouraging them, and, above all, training them they can greatly enhance the quality and quantity of their ideas.

Training workers is no longer a luxury. It is a necessity. It cannot be a once only effort or a spasmodic activity. It must be continual, never-ending, as we attempt to transform the single-skill worker of today into the flexible worker of tomorrow. Some of the progressive companies in the U.S., including mine, have mandated 1.5 to 5 percent of their payroll to training for all levels of their employees. In fact, U.S. companies today are training as many employees as U.S. universities are educating students and at less than two-thirds of the cost.

Training should start with a hardheaded assessment of the needs and challenges of each business, followed by a plan to develop a training curriculum that addresses those needs. For all levels, quality, cost, cycle time, and customer satisfaction are core subjects. For blue-collar workers, the needs are more basic. Functional illiteracy among them is far more widespread than is generally recognized. Basics such as reading, to enable workers to understand and follow simple instructions, and arithmetic, to permit them to perform elementary calculations, are a beginning. On-the-job training, involving multiple skills at multiple work stations, can be the next step. A few companies are beginning to encourage such horizontal job enlargement by granting differential pay for each additional skill mastered. Once the learning pump is primed, workers no longer need to be pushed into training. They will reach for it of their own accord, pursuing avenues of interest, such as computers, time and motion study, methods improvement, interpersonal skills, elementary SPC and problem-solving methods.

From Training to Testing to Implementation

Training is always good, but from a company viewpoint training without implementation is worse than useless. It adds cost without corresponding value. Yet the transition from training to results is an uncharted sea for many companies.

Xerox has developed a unique system to achieve this in its ongoing "Quality through Leadership" effort. The training starts at the very top, with the CEO and his direct "reports" being trained by professional quality consultants. Each person in the class is then asked to select one or two projects in which the techniques that were taught could be applied. Armed now with both theory and practice, these senior managers become the instructors— albeit with the professionals assisting—to the people who report to them. The cycle of instruction to projects to instruction at the next lower level is repeated throughout the entire organization. The central features of this innovative Xerox approach are: (1) Each manager is involved, committed to learn, and committed to teach; (2) projects, where classroom learning is applied, become mandatory.

Testing at the end of a training session is a controversial but worthwhile practice. Many training programs have the students rate the instructor. This is an excellent discipline to keep the instructor on his or her toes. But it should be reinforced by a serious attempt to determine how much of the material the student has really absorbed. The results of such testing can either be passed on to the student's manager, or a pass grade be made the prerequisite for more advanced, sequential training.

The workshop concept is probably one of the most productive methods in assuring implementation. Students, going through a training course that includes its practice, are required to select projects to work on—subject to the involvement and approval of their managers—and then to report back on progress in workshop sessions. The instructor in the original training session at this point becomes a facilitator and coach, guiding the students through each step of the implementation. It is implied, of course, that this workshop approach is fully supported by a top management that demands project selection, encourages action, follows progress, removes stumbling blocks, measures results, and rewards achievement.

Management by Objectives (MBO)

Only when management is participative and involved with its people, only when it assures job security, and only when it conducts effective training does it have a right to expect total employee involvement. Management by objectives, introduced to industry in the early 1950s by Peter F. Drucker, can be used as effectively for employees at all levels as it has been used by senior management. Yet only two ends of the industrial spectrum are truly measured for the on-the-job performance—the CEO and his senior management at the top, and the lowly direct labor worker at the bottom. The CEO and his staff have well defined MBO goals, with the financial analyst and the stock market as score-keepers of progress. John and Mary on the line are also measured for productivity, quality, and delivery. Even their tardiness and absenteeism are menacingly recorded.

But the vast crowds of middle managers, professionals, and white-collar workers escape measurement and accountability. True, some companies apply the MBO technique to this population too. But it often deteriorates into a ritual. Once a year, with one day's notice, the manager comes around asking for a set of goals from his employees. They respond with high-sounding statements that are difficult to quantify. The manager forwards these to higher levels. He then forgets about the goals, and the employee forgets about the goals till the next year's ritual. That is not management by objectives. That is management by New Year resolutions!

In companies where MBO is more than a game, the goals are carefully crafted, the measurement system finely tuned, and the progress against goals meticulously monitored. A list of important MBO principles that can transform a meaningless MBO facade into a hard-hitting participating process for all employees should include the following:

1. Employees, when given the opportunity and encouragement to truly participate and have "ownership" of their operations, will set higher goals than their management.
2. There should be goal congruence between the various levels of an organization, starting with the top down.
3. Employees must participate in goal setting, with agreement at three levels—the manager, his people, and his boss.
4. Goals, at least initially, should be reasonably simple to encourage a high success rate and generate employee confidence and self-esteem.
5. There should not be too many goals. Three or four vital goals that can be achieved are more productive than thirty or forty "cafeteria" type goals that dilute employee actions.
6. All departments can and must be measured.
7. Goal measurements should be meaningful, fair, easy to apply, nonsubjective, with little calibration error.
8. The cost of measurement should be at least an order of magnitude lower than the expected tangible benefits.
9. Each department should be measured against itself, using time comparisons, with the internal customer as scorekeeper.
10. The best measurements are a department's quality effectiveness, cost effectiveness, and cycle time effectiveness. Secondary measurements can be derived from these primary measurements.

Quality Circles: Good Strategy, Poor Tactics

In 1962, Japanese companies began to form quality circles among their employees, where small, homogeneous groups of workers with like functions formed teams to solve quality problems. With the exception of providing training and support, management was not directly involved. The quality circle movement became national in scope and widely credited as one of the factors that contributed to Japan's quality and cost success.

In the mid-1970s, American companies began importing Japanese-style quality circles as the cure for their quality malaise. It was part of the quick-fix, single-solution mentality. Quality circles mushroomed all over the industrial landscape, quality circle societies and seminars were spawned, and wild claims of their success were touted. Then, as happened with the zero defects movement of the 1970s, history repeated itself and disillusionment set in. Even in Japan, where they are an integral part of the industrial culture, quality circles account for only 10 percent of quality improvements. Today, in Japanese companies they are primarily used by direct labor to solve line problems with the elementary "seven QC tools," while the technical population has graduated to design of experiments.

Yet, quality circles have strategic value in marshaling the entire workforce to help solve simple problems, engender self-help, and improve morale. So there is no need to throw out the baby with the bath water. A list of the ten proven tactics—the critical factors or characteristics needed for quality circles to succeed—follows. By inference, the absence of these characteristics are the precise cause of past failures.

1. Top management commitment, support, involvement
2. Selling supervision and the work force
3. Elimination of fear and of the "we-they" mentality
4. High visibility
5. Continual training: (1) beyond the seven QC tools to simple DOE; (2) cycle time reduction; (3) goal setting; (4) creativity; (5) interpersonal relations; (6) conducting meetings
6. Small, short-term projects with high probability of success
7. Continuity in circle leadership: minimal transfers, no layoffs
8. Avoidance of stalemate and complacency after honeymoon period
9. Nourishment and renewal—beyond the company walls
10. Continual, never-ending improvement in goals and results

Gainsharing: The Acid Test of Management's Confidence in Its Workers

Quality circles go by many names: small group improvement activities; participative teams; *Kaizen* teams (after the Japanese word for continual improvement); and Quality of Work Life, where the focus is on reducing worker dissatisfaction. When well managed, they are one of the best ways of obtaining total employee involvement. They are certainly superior to suggestion systems, which are more individually focused than team-oriented.

The big debate concerns whether people who contribute ideas in quality circles or the equivalents should be paid for their tangible contributions to cost, quality, or cycle time improvement. On the one hand, certain management types feel that contributing ideas is part of the worker's job, that a bonus or reward for such ideas is, somehow, tainted money. They claim that workers will be deflected from their main mission of continuous improvement to concentrate on suboptimal ways of making a fast buck for themselves. By contrast, enlightened CEOs feel strongly that paying workers for their contributions over and above stipulated goals is the fair and proper thing to do, and that if bonuses and similar incentives are right for senior management, they are every bit as right for workers.

In the 1970s, the term gainsharing* entered the vocabulary of industrial relations. It can be broadly defined as an incentive process designed to involve employees in improving productivity. Both employees and the company share the financial gains according to a predetermined formula that reflects improved productivity and profitability. The emphasis is on group plans, not individual incentives. Gainsharing plans range from the company-wide Scanlon plan developed in the 1930s to the Rucker and Improshare plans of more recent vintage. Gainsharing is a powerful signal from management to the workers that it believes in the worth of people, in their creativity and ingenuity, and in converting mere brawn power into brain power to produce a win-win partnership.

"Our Workers Have Lost Their Pride of Workmanship!"

Unfortunately for industry, the so-called efficiency methods introduced by Frederick Taylor more than seventy years ago seem designed to make robots and idiots out of human beings. His technique of breaking up the work process into disconnected bits and pieces, in the name of the almighty assembly line, boils all the challenge, creativity, and excitement out of a job. Table 21-2 is a humorous but realistic portrayal of what would happen to a delightful, fun-filled sport like bowling if it were subjected to the rules and practices prevalent in industry today! Consider the worker who attaches six bolts to the wheel of a car as it goes by on an assembly line, day after day, week after week, month after month. What enthusiasm could a manager rustle up if he had to take this worker's place? Yet the same manager can be heard sorrowfully proclaiming that "workers today have lost their pride of workmanship"!

Job Redesign: The Centerpiece

Confirming the findings of the bowling analogy, behavioral scientists tell us that in order to inject fun into work, as well as in any sport, three psychological states must be present:

1. Meaningfulness: The worker must perceive his job as worthwhile or important.

---

*For an excellent treatment of the subject, see Carla S. O'Dell, *Gainsharing: Involvement, Incentives and Productivity,* an AMA Management Briefing published by the American Management Association in 1981.

Table 21-2. How bowling would be changed if played by industry rules.

Why Bowling Is Fun	*Bowling as Modified by Industry Rules*
1. Bowler has a visible target.	1. Eliminate the bowling pins so that no target is visible.
2. He has a challenging but attainable goal.	2. Drape bowling alley so as to prevent score keeping.
3. He is working according to his own personally accepted standards.	3. Under conditions 1 and 2, have a coach critique the bowler's performance, tell bowler he must do better—but not how.
4. He receives immediate feedback.	4. Change rules of game and standards of performance without involving the bowler in the change process or giving him reasons for the change.
5. He has an opportunity to satisfy social needs.	5. Prevent social interaction among bowlers; discourage team effort.
6. He is an accepted member of the group.	6. Give coach credit and recognition for the team's good performance; blame the team's "lack of pride in playing" for poor performance.
7. He can earn recognition.	7. Keep bowlers at play by threatening their expulsion from the facility.

Source: Adapted from M. Scott Myers, *Every Employee a Manager* (New York: McGraw-Hill, 1970).

2. Responsibility: The worker must believe that he is personally accountable for the results of his efforts.

3. Knowledge of Results: The worker must be able to determine, on a regular basis, whether the results of his efforts are satisfactory.

When these three psychological states are present, the worker feels good about himself when he performs well. It produces *internal motivation* rather than *external motivation*, such as pay or praise from the boss. If even one of these psychological states is missing from the job, the internal motivation is significantly reduced.

The Five "Core" Job Dimensions

Job characteristics that lead to the three psychological states necessary for internal motivation are:

1. *Skill variety:* A job calling for varied skills with the potential for appealing to the whole person.
2. *Task identity:* A job that is an identifiable "whole," for example, making a toaster as opposed to an electric cord assembly.
3. *Task significance:* A job that has an impact on others, for instance, making or assembling parts of an aircraft as opposed to *filling* paperclips into a box.
4. *Autonomy:* Freedom and discretion in planning, executing, and improving work.
5. *Feedback:* A job that permits measurement of results, especially feedback that comes directly from the worker himself.

A Full Model for Job Redesign

The concepts of psychological states and job dimensions essential to job satisfaction can be woven together to form a powerful model for redesigning jobs.* Scott Myers has indicated that at the very core of motivation is the job itself—the interest, challenge, and excitement it holds for the worker (see Figure 21-2). Figure 21-3 is a schematic representation of how a job can be redesigned so that it will produce true motivation in the worker.

At the right of Figure 21-3 are shown five goals that management and workers share: high internal motivation, high quality, high job satisfaction, low absenteeism, and low turnover. In order to achieve these goals, fun must be injected into the job through the three psychological states previously described. This, in turn, requires that the five core dimensions must be present in the job. Finally, there are powerful concepts, such as combining tasks, forming natural work units, establishing client relationships, vertical job enrichment, and opening feedback channels, that must be introduced into the core job dimensions for optimum results.

---

*I am grateful to Roy Walters of Roy Walters and Associates for his pioneering work on the exciting subject of job redesign.

Figure 21-3. The full model for job redesign.

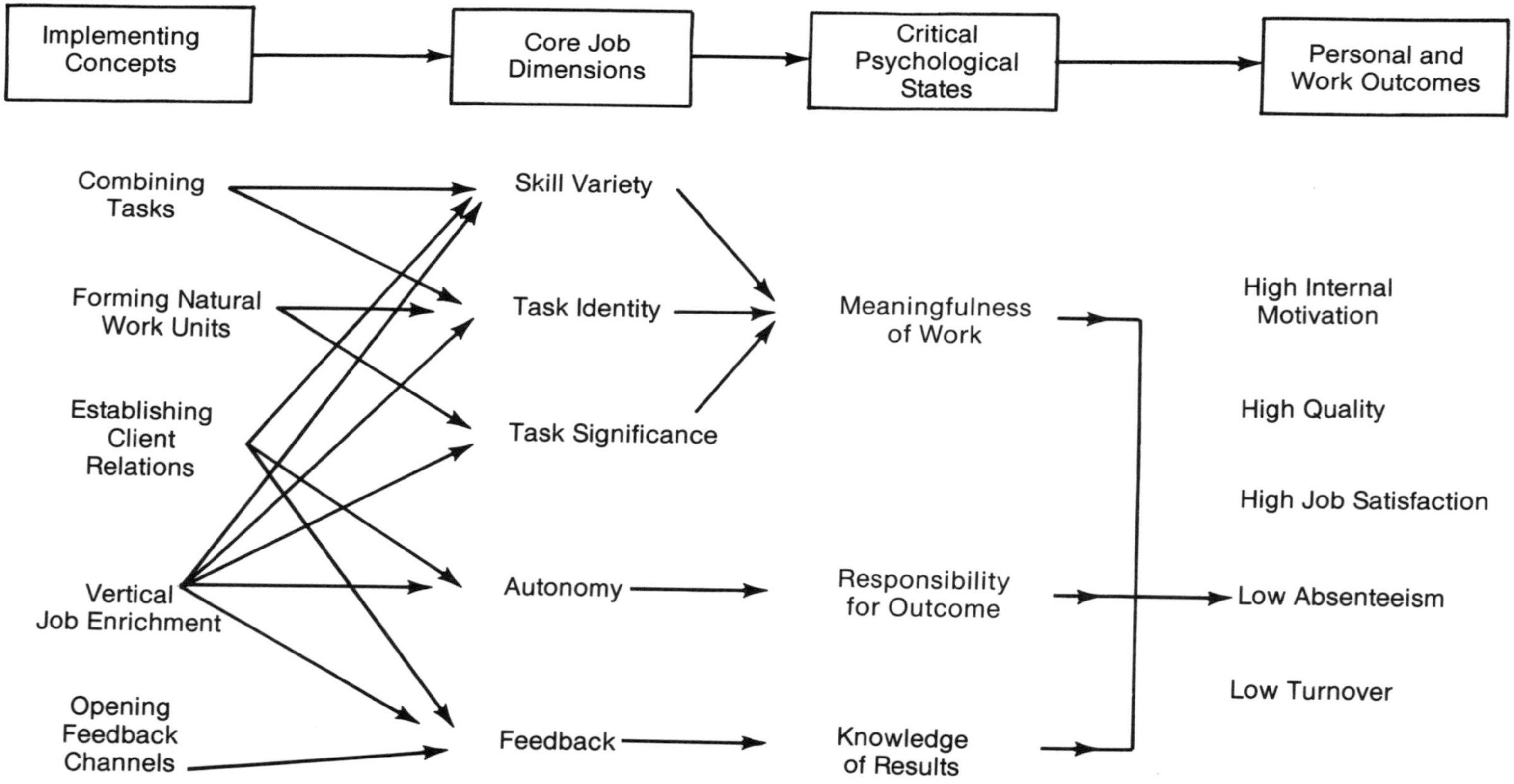

Injecting Excitement Into a Dull Assembly Line Job

For most professionals, the job itself provides adequate interest and challenge. But what about a dull, repetitive assembly line job? How can it be redesigned to inject some excitement into the worker's humdrum activities? By using the concepts outlined in Figure 21-3, we can apply the model's five implementing concepts to redesign a boring assembly line job into something much more challenging and exciting.

1. *Combining Tasks*
   - Obtain material.
   - Arrange/fill bins.
   - Check tools.
   - Learn multiple skills.
   - Help formulate instructions.
   - Administer self-inspection (aided by *poka-yoke*).
   - Self test.
   - Help in preventive maintenance.
2. *Natural Work Units*
   - Divide work by customer rather than by product line.
   - Work on all subassemblies of a product line instead of specific subassemblies of several product lines.
3. *Client Relationships*
   - Establish contact with external customer when possible.
   - Determine requirements of internal customer (next operation as customer) and measure progress against requirements.
   - Specify requirements to internal supplier (previous operation as supplier).
4. *Vertical Job Enrichment* (Most Important Aspect of Job Redesign)
   - Help formulate work hours, including flex time.
   - Help determine overtime and incentives.
   - Determine time standards line balancing/sequencing.
   - Work on methods improvement.
   - Determine work station layout.
   - Help reduce setup time through quicker model changes.
   - Help establish quality, productivity, cost reduction, and cycle time reduction goals and self-monitor progress.
   - Participate in problem-solving teams and meetings and make presentations to management.
   - Suggest simple sensors *(poke-yoke)* to prevent operator errors.
   - Assist in process certification.
   - Participate in ongoing training.
   - Design and conduct simple experiments (DOE).

5. *Feedback*
   - Get immediate, nonthreatening feedback through use of next operator as inspector.
   - Use self-inspection *(poke-yoke)*.
   - Get direct inputs from next department as customer.
   - Obtain inputs from external customer.
   - Visit customer sites and supplier sites where possible.

The measures specified may not remove all the tedium and drudgery from these types of jobs, but they do offer some measure of dignity and hope to the worker and move a long way toward making every employee a manager in his or her own area of work.

Employees as Partners: The Disney Example

The Walt Disney name is synonymous with the best in entertainment. What is less well known is how the Walt Disney World Company nurtures its employees as partners.

To begin with, Disney World stresses that it is totally dependent on its customers: "They are *guests* in our house. Our 'product' is being tested 10 million times a day." All Disney employees are called "cast members." There are 11,000 "cast members," but not a single job description! The Disney style has four distinct features.

1. Culture (Values)

- It stresses that its managers are not bosses, but rather coaches, quarterbacks, drumbeaters, nurturers, and, above all, cheerleaders.
- Its managers treat cast members (employees) the same way that cast members are expected to treat guests (customers)!
- The atmosphere is informal. It is taboo to say "that's not my job," whether referring to anything from picking up a gum wrapper dropped on the grounds to helping to man a ticket booth.
- Disney defines corporate culture as "nothing more than what your customers think of you and what your people think of its management."

2. Training

The first aspect of *training* instilled in cast members is *pride* in the organization. Once done, the technical stuff is easy. As an example, the down time on a Disney monorail is less than 1½ hours per year. The maintenance people live and die according to how well they maintain their machines.

3. Communications

Faced with the problem of sustaining employee motivation after two to five years of service, Disney is strong on *communications*—through the printed word, through audiovisual methods, and through a prevasive spirit of mutual help. But the strongest communication is through personal contact.

4. Management Attitude

Management's attitude is manifested by its listening to cast members in focus groups; by its open door policies; its "I have an idea" suggestion system; its exit interviews; and its opinion polls. But the most important concept that is nurtured is management caring for the people who do the work.

Chapter 22

Maintaining the
Momentum

This is not the beginning nor the end; nor is it the beginning of the end; it is only the end of the beginning.

—Winston Churchill

Winston Churchill's memorable words, expressed at a crucial turning point for the Allies in World War II, can be applied to supply management as well. In the preceding chapters we have discussed the infrastructure that is needed to build a viable partnership between customer and supplier; to move to world-class quality; to tap the gold mine of new cost reduction techniques and to cap these efforts with cycle time as the integrator. Formidable as these tasks may seem, they are the easy part of the endeavor. The newness of the techniques lend a certain excitement and the uncharted seas a sense of adventure.

The much more difficult part of the task is sustaining the entire process after the glamor has faded, after new priorities have diverted attention, and after stumbling blocks have dampened initial enthusiasm. Our concluding chapter, therefore, will concentrate on ways of maintaining the momentum.

Management: The Alpha and Omega of a Process

As with many other matters, top management plays a crucial role in determining the continuity and longevity of the process. Without its nurturing, no amount of enthusiasm at lower levels can bring success; with it, renewal and never-ending progress are assured.*

The continuity of top management's emphasis and direction is key. Many a process has been shipwrecked because the top manager supporting it moved on or out and his successor established his own priorities in different areas. Organizational change is always major surgery and should be undertaken only as a last resort.

Further, in developing five-year plans and in subsequent annual course corrections, supply management (which has become a key corporate strategy) must be reassessed to determine its strengths and weaknesses vis-à-vis the customer company's competition. This external view is best gained through benchmarking, which should not be a one-time effort, but should be reappraised each year to determine the gaps, which are never static, between the company and the best-in-class firm, be that a competitor or noncompetitor.

Voting for Supply Management With Your Feet

Some CEOs have now made it a practice to visit their key customers and personally determine the extent of customer satisfaction. Similarly, a smaller number of these CEOs have begun to visit their important suppliers to gain personal insight into the workings of partnership (without the filtering of information they would receive from their subordinates' reports). The visit encourages direct supplier feedback, promotes trust, and forms bonds. More important, it has an electrifying effect upon the supplier's entire organization, with incalculable benefits. As an extension of these practices, some CEOs have also begun to attend supplier council meetings, stressing, by their presence and participation, the importance of supply management.

The Steering Committee as Coach

The steering committee, as the extended arm of top management, also has an important role in maintaining the momentum. Its main job—the caring

---

*As an example, it was previously stated that Motorola won the prestigious Malcolm Baldrige Award for outstanding quality. At a supplier conference, Motorola Chairman Bob Galvin encouraged the company's partnership suppliers to apply for the award in future years. They did not have to win it, but the disciplines introduced in preparing for the award would help them greatly. Applying for the award would become a requirement for doing business with Motorola, whose resources would be available to help applying suppliers. That is statesmanship, par excellence!

and feeding of its commodity teams—has to be sustained. The greatest threat is a potential loss of funding for the commodity teams, especially during business downturns. The commodity team is a new concept and can fall prey to the ax of business managers, who tend to be short-term-oriented. The steering committee must guard against any measures that eat the seed-corn. However, it must prove to such business managers that funding commodity teams is an investment, with benefit to cost ratios of well over 10 to 1.

The steering committee must also guard against the political warfare that can ensue when a new organizational building block like the commodity team is introduced into a traditional, functional organization. It must encourage a win-win teamwork between the commodity teams and Engineering, Purchasing, and Quality Assurance and not a win-lose battle in the trenches.

Process Owner

The task of managing and directing several commodity teams can be difficult within a committee structure. It is advisable, therefore, to appoint one person within the steering committee, usually the director of Purchasing, as the overseer of the commodity teams. The new term is "process owner." As czar of the whole operation, such a person monitors the performance of each commodity team on a continuing basis; makes sure that partnership with suppliers is not just a one-way street; ascertains that the firm policy of buying on the basis of total cost rather than purchase price is not being subverted by unreformed buyers; smooths the way to establishing financial incentive and penalty contracts with suppliers; and last, but not least, visits partnership suppliers on a regular basis to set an example for continual contacts at lower levels.

Feeling the Pulse of the Supplier

Just as it is important for a supplier to be "close to the customer," the customer company must periodically—and earnestly—determine the supplier's attitudes towards it. The question "How can we become better customers to you?" should be asked, not just initially, but every year.

The steering committee is often faced with changes in the commodity teams because of promotions, transfers, and attrition. Team rotation, however, should be slow and deliberate so that team spirit and continuity are sustained and so that the team's links with partnership suppliers are preserved. Commodity team discontinuity can brake, stall, or even reverse the engine of supply management progress. Further, in the debate between part-time and full-time commodity teams, the steering committee should press for a full-time effort. The cost is higher, the resources scarcer, but the benefits are so great that a customer company cannot *not* afford such an investment.

The commodity teams should grow into reach-out tasks such as helping the partnership supplier with his supplier and consolidating material purchases for all partnership suppliers to mutually improve quality and reduce costs through the leverage of the customer company.

Professionalism Must Be Earned, Not Just Declared

A major, ongoing steering committee task is to constantly improve professionalism within the company so that it can convey a strong message to its suppliers: "Do as I do, not do as I say!" This means the buyers should become thoroughly familiar with the technology of the commodity and its associated manufacturing processes, and that they be knowledgeable about value engineering, group technology, experience curves, and especially cycle time reduction, so that they can truly help suppliers to reduce costs and cycle time. This means that quality personnel associated with procurement should be practitioners, not just preachers, of techniques such as design of experiments, *poka-yoke*, and multiple environment overstress testing so that they can solve supplier quality problems rather than engage in empty table pounding.

Fewer than 10 percent of customer companies have developed this degree of professionalism. It is no easy task, therefore, for a steering committee to turn the ship around. The committee must champion continual training, application of that training, and internal successes to sustain the effort.

Partnership Suppliers: Continuity, Communications, Caring

Customer companies, with their steering committees and commodity teams, can lead a horse to water, but they can't make him drink. Success, in the final analysis, can only be shaped and sustained by the partnership supplier. The same prescriptions apply to the supplier's management as apply to the customer company's management. These are the three Cs: continuity, communications, and caring—in reference to customers, employees, and suppliers.

Trust: The Hallmark of Partnership

To allow partnership to solidify and to permit the gradual fusing of two corporate entities into one, there should be as few discontinuities as possible in the supplier's organization. There must be free and open communications as the starting point of trust and loyalty. Trust, especially in the industrial environment, is a fragile plant. A change in management on either side, an overbearing buyer, an insensitive commodity team, an imperious engineer, an unreconstructed quality professional, or a supplier retrogressing to the old era of confrontation can set back months of progress in a matter of days. There are far more opportunities for dismantling trust than for building it up. Western culture, with its penchant for legal contracts and lawsuits, tends to institutionalize distrust rather than cultivating trust.

It becomes the responsibility of *all* people involved in supply management to build and nurture trust. Every action on both sides should be examined from this point of view: "Does this action advance trust or does it hurt trust?" And the question needs to be asked constantly, not just at the start of partnership. Trust is built on a series of small and iterative but concrete steps. It may take months, even years, to reach maturity. But it is the hallmark of partnership.

Total Customer Satisfaction

The supplier must also recognize that the change in emphasis from a profit orientation to total customer satisfaction is not a diminution of profit; rather, it is an enhancement. If the customer is truly and continually satisfied, profit will take care of itself. Customer satisfaction, therefore, cannot be a one-time thing. It takes constant vigilance to see that *all* aspects of customer satisfaction—not just quality—are met vis-à-vis the best of competition. This is especially important in that a customer's requirements and expectations are never static. They change frequently, requiring the supplier's finger on the customer's pulse constantly.

Further, the supplier must make sure that the newest customer culture—the next operation as customer (NOAC)—becomes firmly planted in his own organization. Like all industrial cultures, it takes years to root and be accepted by the rank and file. NOAC cannot be another program of the month. It has to become a way of life, with "customer" evaluation eventually replacing boss evaluation.

The Caring of Employees and the De-Bossing of Management

The Japanese assert that the main job of a CEO is the "caring and feeding" of his employees. The caring, however, should not be paternalistic but participative. One of the greatest challenges for top management, both on the customer side and the supplier side, is not just to make workers participative but to make managers participative. This requires constant prodding, perseverence, even fortitude. It is one of the hardest cultural adjustments to make in industry. Yet when finally achieved after years of persistence, it is the most rewarding.

Winning!

A decade ago, there was fear that American industry was becoming an "also ran" among the fleet foreign horses that seemed to be beating it to the finish line. There was fear of cheap foreign labor; of foreign government subsidies to their industries; of one-way trade; of a playing field that was not level. These push-button excuses created a national malaise in the United States that sapped its strength, dampened its natural buoyancy of spirit, and crippled its "can do" drive.

Fortunately, the country has now snapped out of that self-induced trance. The playing field is more level. Manufacturing is being restored to its importance as a key strategic thrust. The vanishing supplier base is being lured back to American shores. Quality is increasingly becoming a superordinate corporate value. And the maligned American workers are now considered, as they always should have been, among the very best in the world.

There is a growing realization that there is nothing cultural about foreign industrial successes. There is confidence that these successes can be replicated in the United States. This book has outlined many techniques, developed many specific tools to assure that success. It concentrates on areas where foreign competition is the most challenging—quality, cost, and cycle time. It emphasizes the crucial roles of the customer, the supplier, and employees. In short, it presents a game plan for winning!

Appendix 1.

Supplier Survey Questionnaire

As will be seen in the following questionnaire, the "ABC Company" asked its potential suppliers probing questions covering ten areas of supplier company performance. These can serve as a model for all such surveys (see Chapter 9 for an overview).

A. <u>Financial Strength, History, and Experience</u>

    1. How do you rate yourself financially? Provide documentation on Dunn & Bradstreet ratings, debt/equity ratios, stock market trends, price-to-earnings ratios, bank assessments, etc.

    2. What are your historic trends for profitability and return on investment?

    3. What is your market share for products supplied to ABC?

    4. Who are your top three competitors?

    5. Rank yourself vis-à-vis these competitors in terms of quality, technology, cost, delivery, service, and flexibility.

    6. What is/will be ABC'S percentage of your total sales?

    7. Where do the products supplied to ABC fall in the industry attractiveness* versus competitive position matrix?

---

*Detailed in Chapter 19.

8. Are you part of a larger company? If so, what is the degree of corporate support you receive in terms of resources, technology, plant capacity, etc.?

9. Would you be willing to enter into a system of financial incentives and penalties with ABC based upon delivery, quality, reliability, performance, and ideas?

10. Are you willing to share your costs, technology, and strategies with ABC on the basis of reciprocity?

B. Management Commitment to Excellence

1. Are you firmly committed to partnership with ABC—to provide high quality, low cost, and early delivery in return for longer-term agreements, larger dollar volume, technical and quality help and more stable forecasts?

2. Do you have a superordinate core value system? What are your company's superordinate values? How committed are your employees to them?

3. How do you facilitate the "process" of continual improvement in all operations?

4. What is your long-range strategic intent as a company? What are your strategic plans for technology, plant capacity and location, capital equipment, manpower, etc.? Are these strategies compatible with ABC's?

5. State the ways in which you are committed to technological innovation.

6. State the ways in which you are committed to quality, especially variation reduction and reliability growth.

7. State the ways in which you are committed to a systematic reduction in both manufacturing and indirect labor (white-collar work) cycle times.

8. How do you obtain meaningful employee participation? What concrete measures are you taking to assure that your managers are truly participative?

9. How do you support employee training? What percentage of your payroll is allocated to training? What are your core courses? How do you implement classroom training in the workplace?

10. How have you extended partnership to your suppliers?

C. Design Technology Expertise

1. Are you a leader in the technology of current parts/products required by ABC? How do you determine this, especially in terms of offshore competition?

2. Is your technology associated with ABC's products in danger of being made obsolete by new and substitute technology?

3. What percentage of your sales dollar is expended in research and development?
4. Is there an active program for patents and other proprietary projects that can give you a distinctive competence?
5. Do you promote intrapreneurship and "skunk works" to encourage innovation among your people? If so, how do you achieve this? What are the results?
6. Is there a systematic, disciplined process, including team work among marketing, engineering, production, and other departments, to assure that new products launched into production have shortened design cycle times, lower manpower requirements, greatly improved quality, and reduced costs? Do you use Quality Function Deployment (QFD) to facilitate the process?
7. Do you have a CAE/CAD/CAM/CIM system to improve engineering and manufacturing effectiveness? What guidelines do you have to design for maximum manufacturability and ease of service?
8. Can you link with ABC for electronic information and data transfer?
9. How do you determine your customers' future product needs and expectations and translate them into product specifications? How do you translate such product specifications into component specifications?
10. Do you establish applications reviews with your customers and conduct systems tests with them to analyze and reduce systems variations?

D. Quality Proficiency *

1. Describe your management philosophy on quality in terms of its economic importance, quality axioms, and the organizational infrastructure required.
2. Is quality one of your key strategies and do you formulate that strategy in quality plans that are updated annually?
3. Describe your overall quality system.
4. Do you use quality costs and quality audits to assure adherence to the quality system? If so, outline your methodology for these two disciplines.
5. How do you determine customer satisfaction for your products and services?
6. Do you use the concept of next operation as the customer? Give examples.

---

*Given the preeminence of quality, a comprehensive and detailed questionnaire applying only to quality is shown in Appendix 2. It is used not for an initial evaluation of a finalist supplier's capability but to audit a partnership supplier's quality system. An even more detailed questionnaire on a supplier's SPC and design of experiments performance is detailed in Appendix 3.

7. Describe the methods you use to assure that new product launches have a minimum of 90 percent overall yield at the start of production?
8. Do you use design of experiments to reduce product/process variation, and SPC to maintain variation reduction? Give examples.
9. What are the various reliability improvement tools you use? Give examples.
10. How do you evaluate, qualify, and rate your suppliers?

E. Cost Competitiveness

1. What is your pricing curve for the past three years compared against that of your best-in-class competitor? Are you a price leader against your competition?
2. Do you have long-term contracts/agreements with other customers? With whom? How long are such agreements for?
3. What is the maximum percentage of sales that you have with any one customer? Who is that customer?
4. How are you reducing your part number base? Do you use group technology and group technology coding?
5. Do you use cost targeting to establish a target price for your suppliers? Do you have professional cost estimators who can assess competitor costs with accuracy?
6. Do you accept experience curves as an approach to multi-year price reductions? What is your historic experience curve for ABC's products?
7. Do you use value engineering as a discipline to reduce costs while simultaneously improving quality?
8. Do you gather and analyze data on the costs of poor quality? Report on trends over the past three years. How do you attempt to identify and reduce the hidden costs of poor quality that are not tracked by accounting?
9. How do you measure overall (end-to-end) yield? What is your overall yield target and timetable to achieve it?
10. In your purchases, do you emphasize total costs, including the cost of poor quality and delivery, rather than just the purchase price?

F. Service/Flexibility/Dependability

1. Can you respond to fast-changing requirements in both quantity and performance that ABC may request on occasion?
2. How frequently are you in touch with your major customers to assess their changing expectations and to obtain feedback on their satisfaction with your company?

3. Are your tooling, sample delivery, and cost estimates timely and accurate? How long is your tooling cycle time?
4. Do you give early and honest notifications of quality, cost, or schedule concerns and problems that require ABC consultations or approvals? Before product shipment?
5. Is your manufacturing capacity capable of meeting upturns in ABC's quantity requirements?
6. Will you take on the responsibility for assuring accurate counts, thus relieving ABC of the necessity of verification?
7. Are there likely to be disruptions in your deliveries caused by such factors as labor strikes or unrest, nonavailability of critical materials, machine breakdowns, or transport problems?
8. What is your record on early and late shipments to your major customers and on over and under quantities in such shipments? Cite customer measurements on these parameters.
9. Will you guarantee a satisfactory lead time even in an economic upturn?
10. Do you have an effective after-sales service in terms of diagnosis, repair, parts availability, and training?

G. Manufacturing Capability

1. Do your line supervisors act more as consultants than as bosses? What percentage of their time is spent actually helping their workers, and what percentages in chasing parts or doing paperwork?
2. Are your line operators trained in multiple and multi-level skills to achieve maximum manufacturing flexibility? Does a system of job rotation and fewer job classifications facilitate this flexibility?
3. Is your cost accounting system based on traditional gathering of direct labor costs with overhead, or has it moved toward other systems such as direct costing or group/focused factory costing?
4. Are all levels of manufacturing trained in at least elementary quality improvement techniques, short cycle time, and basic time studies and methods improvement?
5. Do you have effective data integrity? What is your count accuracy? Do you have an effective change control system?
6. Do you use bar-coding and other techniques to achieve configuration control?
7. How much automation do you use in production? Is the focus of such automation on reducing direct labor, removing drudgery or safety?
8. Are you moving toward a paperless factory through the collection and analysis of data using computer-aided manufacturing or other methods?
9. Do you have a suggestion system or any other means of soliciting

ideas from your employees? Do you stimulate the generation of these ideas?
10. Do you break down departmental walls by encouraging team work and team problem solving? Give examples.

H. Cycle Time Concentration

1. What is your cycle time from order entry to shipment? What are the top five elements of lost time in this total?
2. What are your inventory turns, separately and collectively, for work in process (WIP), finished goods, and raw materials?
3. Do you have a major organizational thrust to reduce cycle time (steering committees, training, reorganization to reduce the size of support departments, and so on)?
4. Have you moved toward group technology cells and focused factories, with dedicated teams in each factory?
5. Is the factory layout process-oriented or is there a straight product line flow to minimize routing, transport, and waiting time?
6. Is there a *pull* system of material flow rather than a *push* system?
7. Is there a concentration on: reduced waiting time, reduced transport time, small lots, reduced setup time, and linear schedules?
8. Is there a total productive maintenance (TPM) program, measured in terms of factory overall effectiveness (FOE), to assure uninterrupted production and perfect quality?
9. Do you attempt to persuade your customers and your suppliers to accept/deliver small lots with greater frequency?
10. What techniques do you use to reduce cycle time in white-collar work, especially design cycle time, customer-marketing cycle time, and order processing cycle time?

I. Extension of Partnership to Subsuppliers

1. Are you actively attempting to reduce your supplier base? If so, what method are you using and what is the extent of the reduction achieved?
2. Do you have an active partnership relationship with your key suppliers? Describe your game plan.
3. What percentage of your total dollar purchases are you obtaining offshore? What criteria do you use to make this determination? What are your plans for reducing offshore purchases?
4. How important is the geographic proximity of your key suppliers?
5. What type of assistance do you render to your key suppliers? Quality? Cost? Cycle time? Training? Problem solving?
6. Do you encourage early supplier involvement in your initial designs, along with cost targeting?

7. Do you encourage value engineering ideas from your suppliers? Do you use financial incentives and penalties to effect quality, delivery, and performance improvements?

8. Do you classify important parameters for your suppliers and specify minimum $^{C}p_{k}s$ for them? What $^{C}p_{k}s$ do you specify?

9. What percentage of your total number of purchased parts is certified? What are your certification goals?

10. Do you encourage your suppliers to move toward partnership, so that the whole supply chain can be strengthened?

J. Employee Participative Climate

1. Do you attempt to stamp out fear among your employees so that they will feel free to speak out and contribute their ideas for improvement?

2. Do you actively encourage "management by wandering around" (MBWA) so that managers are visible, listen to their people, encourage them and act on their ideas? How do you monitor this?

3. Do you use your employee's brain rather than just his/her brawn to effect continual improvement?

4. Do you encourage your employees to participate in teams to formulate goals, pursue improvements, and measure results?

5. Are your workers treated with respect, dignity, and trust?

6. Are your workers given opportunities for both off-the-job and on-the-job training? Are they encouraged to implement that training?

7. Is performance appraisal done on a one-on-one basis, between the employee and the supervisor, or is it on the basis of the evaluations made by the employee's day-to-day internal customers?

8. Are your employees' achievements suitably recognized?

9. Are layoffs minimized to the greatest extent possible? Is help available to employees with personal problems, when they request such help?

10. Is there a gainsharing (financial) plan for employees in proportion to their team contribution to improvements in quality, cost, delivery, and profitability?

Appendix 2

Supplier Quality
Evaluation and Audit

Organization:	Subsystem Ratings				
	P o o r	*W e a k*	*M a r g i n a l*	*Q u a l i f i e d*	*O u t s t a n d i n g*
Date:					
Subsystems	*0 to 20*	*21 to 40*	*41 to 60*	*61 to 80*	*Over 80*
1. Management of the Quality System					
2. Customer Satisfaction					
3. Design Quality					
4. Supplier Quality					
5. Process Planning and Control					
6. Production Quality Control					
7. Field Reliability					
8. Support Services Quality					
9. Quality Awareness/Training					
10. Quality Motivation					

Total Score

Total system rating

0–200:	Poor
210–400:	Weak
401–600:	Marginal
601–800:	Qualified
Over 800:	Outstanding

Organization:

Date:

Subsystem: Management of the Quality System

	Weight (W)	Rating (R)					Score (W) × (R)
		Poor 2	Weak 4	Marginal 6	Qualified 8	Outstanding 10	

A. *Management of the quality system*
1. How much time (actual clock time) does top management devote to quality improvement?
2. How does top management *actively* encourage *all* departments to shoulder their quality responsibilities, instead of just quality departments?
3. How has top management driven out fear among its workers so that its managers can be involved with the workers, listen to them, and support their quality implementation ideas?
4. Is there a "Quality Breakthrough" management process for tackling chronic quality problems, *establishment of projects and teams for each project*, along with management guidance and progress follow-up?
5. What emphasis is there on design of experiments to solve and prevent chronic quality problems affecting products and processes?
6. How are the costs of poor quality gathered, analyzed, and reduced continuously?
7. Is there a comprehensive quality system whose elements are continually strengthened, and are quality system audits conducted periodically?
8. How is benchmarking conducted to determine performance gaps vis-à-vis the best-in-class companies?
9. Has top management instituted a partnership program with its key suppliers, with quality improvement as a major focus?
10. Is quality a key strategy for top management in its drive for profit improvement, market share and productivity. How is such a strategy developed?

Subsystem rating | 10

Organization:

Date:

Subsystem: Customer Satisfaction

Weight (W)	Rating (R)					Score (W) × (R)
	Poor	Weak	Marginal	Qualified	Outstanding	
	2	4	6	8	10	

B. Customer satisfaction

1. Are techniques such as Value Research, multi-attribute evaluation, QFD, and conjoint analysis, used to determine and prioritize customer needs?

2. How are the elements of customer dissatisfaction clearly identified and corrected?

3. Is quality a central marketing thrust, and is market share used as a measure of customer satisfaction?

4. What measurements are in place to assess customer satisfaction and to gain an overall customer perception of product and service?

5. How is continual contact maintained with the customer after a sale is consummated?

6. Is there an organization structure and focal point designated to identify potential product liability/safety hazards and prevent them?

7. Is there an effective systems testing with the customer and an evaluation of competitive products in terms of their performance, cost, and reliability?

8. Are customer/dealer/servicer councils established to obtain feedback from the field and guide policy?

9. What methods are used to promote and sustain the concept of next operation as customer (NOAC)?

10. What are the measurement systems and rewards/penalties associated with NOAC?

Subsystem rating | 10 |

Organization:

Date:

Subsystem: Design Quality

	Weight (W)	Rating (R)					Score (W) × (R)
		Poor	Weak	Marginal	Qualified	Outstanding	
		2	4	6	8	10	

C. Design quality

1. Are there goals, targeting (budgeting), prediction studies for reliability, FMEAs, and FTAs prepared to probe design, manufacturing, and supplier *weaknesses?*

2. Are *design reviews* held regularly? Are they timely, broad-based, procedur-ized, and effective? What topics are included in such design reviews?

3. What disciplines, such as value engineering, thermal analysis, de-rating guides, design for manufacturability, "human engineering," built-in diag-nostics, and ease of service, are used?

4. What systematic methods are used in designs to reduce models and part counts? Are group technology and standardization used?

5. Are comprehensive *multiple environment overstress tests to failure conducted?* How many series of tests? How long does each take?

6. What specific design of experiment tools are used to reduce variability in products, processes, and materials?

7. What product liability analysis disciplines are used to ensure safe products in the field?

8. Is there *early and meaningful involvement of Production, Quality, and Service* in the design cycle, with sign-off systems to assure minimum acceptable yields, uptime, and reliability?

9. Is there *adequate field testing* and selective market testing of product *ahead of full production?*

10. Is there a log of "lessons learnt," based on feedback from Production during the pilot run and early field history?

Subsystem rating | 10 | | | | | | |

Organization:

Date:

Subsystem: Supplier Quality Assurance

	Weight (W)	Poor 2	Weak 4	Marginal 6	Qualified 8	Outstanding 10	Score (W)×(R)

D. Supplier quality

1. Does the partnership program for key suppliers stress the supplier's responsibility to steadily improve quality, cost, delivery, and cycle time in return for the buyer's responsibility to grant larger and longer-term contracts, technical and quality assistance, and training?

2. Is there a policy of purchases based on lowest life-cycle costs rather than *lowest purchase price?*

3. Is cost-targeting and early supplier involvement (ESI) used in place of bidding and negotiations?

4. Are there *consultations with the supplier on design, specifications vs. cost trade-offs, classifications of parameters, and systematic reductions in cycle-time?*

5. Does the supplier use design of experiments to reduce variability, and reliability stress tests to achieve maximum reliability?

6. Does the supplier use Positrol, process certification, and precontrol to maintain variability at reduced levels. What are the minimum c_{p_k}'s used for important parameters?

7. Are there financial incentive/penalty programs to encourage *supplier ideas, delivery, and reliability?*

8. Is there a professional, timely, and effective supplier failure analysis capability?

9. Is there a systematic policy to reduce incoming inspection from 100 percent inspection to sampling to skip lot and *eventually to full certification, along with emphasis on reliability testing?*

10. Is there a financial recovery program from suppliers for line and field failures?

	10						

Subsystem rating

Organization:

Date:

Subsystem: Process Planning and Control

	Weight (W)	Rating (R) Poor 2	Weak 4	Marginal 6	Qualified 8	Outstanding 10	Score (W) × (R)

E. *Process planning and control*

1. Are process design reviews conducted well ahead of pilot runs, especially for test equipment development and software control?

2. Are design of experiments conducted a priori to define and characterize a process completely?

3. Are critical process parameters identified, measured, and controlled (via Positrol programs)?

4. Is there certification of the process (for example, environment, operator instructions, work layout, equipment calibration, fast feedback of reject information)?

5. Are statistical tools such as precontrol used for controlling important process and product parameters?

6. Are operators trained and *certified* for key processes and then periodically *recertified?*

7. Are neighbor inspection and *poka-yoke* (mistake-proof) methods used to eliminate operator-controllable defects?

8. Is total preventive maintenance (**TPM**) instituted, measured, and improved?

9. Is there a systematic program to reduce cycle time by reducing setup time, queueing time, transportation time, inspection and test time?

10. Is there a software quality "walk-through"?

Subsystem rating | 10 |

Organization:

Date:

Subsystem: Production Quality Control

	Weight (W)	Rating (R)					Score (W) × (R)
		Poor	Weak	Marginal	Qualified	Outstanding	
		2	4	6	8	10	

F. Production quality control

1. Are yield prediction and cycle time prediction studies conducted?
2. Is there a team approach to yield improvement, with measurements of over-all yield?
3. Are there systematic identifications of the top chronic problems, along with cost estimates, and *interdisciplinary teams to tackle and reduce them?*
4. Are significant quality data gathered, disseminated, analyzed, and acted upon in a timely, effective manner?
5. Is there a "field escape" control system to anticipate field failures?
6. Is there a truncated multiple environment overstress system to prevent field failures?
7. Is there an effective failure analysis system at the product and component levels?
8. Is there an effective gauge and equipment calibration system?
9. Is 100 percent external visual inspection being changed to neighbor inspec-tion and *poka-yoke* self checks with sensing devices?
10. Is there conformance to plant safety guidelines, Underwriters Laboratory guidelines, and electrostatic discharge protection guidelines?

Subsystem rating — 10

Organization:

Date:

Subsystem: Field Reliability

	Weight (W)	Rating (R)					Score (W) × (R)
		Poor	Weak	Marginal	Qualified	Outstanding	
		2	4	6	8	10	

G. *Field reliability*

1. Is there an effective early warning system (for example, customer plant returns and/or "zero time" failures) to detect, analyze, and correct failures very early in the customer's product life cycle?

2. Are packing/transportation practices and operating/installation instructions reviewed to ensure that product quality is not degraded?

3. Is there a systematic gathering of field reliability data (from service stations, parts traffic, sales, service, and customer inputs), and are reviews conducted to analyze and correct field problems?

4. How effective is the failure analysis capability in pinpointing the root cause of failures and preventing their recurrence?

5. Is there a partnership program with independent dealers/servicers to assure mutual benefit and maximize customer satisfaction?

6. Are special field services such as exchange programs, starter kits, and newsletters with key service stations (listening posts) in place to improve service to the customer?

7. Is there a company-owned network of service facilities to obtain an accurate profile of field failures and to enhance service to the customer?

8. Are customer surveys made to measure the timeliness and effectiveness of company-owned and independent services?

9. Is the parts service function meeting the needs of customers and servicers in terms of quality, delivery, and cost?

10. Is there feedback to Engineering for built-in diagnostics and reducing down time?

Subsystem rating | 10 |

Organization:

Date:

Subsystem: Support Services

	Weight (W)	Rating (R)					Score (W) × (R)
		Poor	Weak	Marginal	Qualified	Outstanding	
		2	4	6	8	10	

H. *Support services*
1. What percentage of all possible support services is selected for intensive quality measurement and improvement?
2. Are the requirements for each support service defined and translated into specifications?
3. Has a "process," similar to a manufacturing process, been charted for each support service?
4. Are firm goals, in terms of quality, delivery, and cost, established for each support service?
5. Is feedback from the external customer solicited and monitored?
6. What types of measurements and improvement tools are used to determine external customer satisfaction?
7. Has a system of next operation as customer (NOAC) been established?
8. How is (NOAC) used for measurement and improvement?
9. How are managers fully involved and employees fully participative in team efforts to improve support services?
10. Is there a climate for constant, never-ending improvement? How is it measured and nourished?

Subsystem rating 10

Organization:

Date:

Subsystem: Quality Awareness/Training

	Weight (W)	Rating (R)					Score (W) × (R)
		Poor 2	Weak 4	Marginal 6	Qualified 8	Outstanding 10	

I. *Quality awareness/training*

1. Are *longitudinal surveys* conducted periodically among employees to determine their perceptions of quality, and are the weaknesses acted upon by management?
2. Are quality system programs publicized to all personnel and are all personnel fully familiar with their quality systems roles?
3. Are there methods, such as *error cause removal (ECR) systems*, in place whereby employees can point to sources of defects that require quick correction?
4. How are training needs determined, prioritized, and focused on major issues?
5. Are there formal quality training programs for managers, technical personnel, and line workers *that emphasize problem solving* and problem prevention and use design of experiments?
6. Is quality training followed up with workshops and consultations to ensure implementation of classroom learning?
7. Are there formal, ongoing quality training programs and workshops for suppliers?
8. Are there product, installation, and application training programs for servicers, installers, and customers?
9. Is statistical problem solving, using design of experiments, encouraged through *project work*, and are *professional reviews of such projects* conducted?
10. How are the results of training evaluated and quantified?

Subsystem rating | 10

Organization:

Date:

Subsystem: Quality Motivation

	Weight (W)	Rating (R)					Score (W) × (R)
		Poor 2	Weak 4	Marginal 6	Qualified 8	Outstanding 10	

J. *Quality motivation*
1. What motivation theories are well understood by managers and workers?
2. How has top management driven out *fear* among its employees so that they feel they can speak out freely for their contributions to improvement?
3. How are managers at all levels involved with their people, and how do they support, encourage, and help them?
4. How much is the worker's brain, rather than just his brawn, utilized?
5. Are teams, such as quality circles and improvement teams, utilized to obtain synergistic solutions to problems?
6. Are presentations highlighting achievements made to top management by such teams?
7. Are workers trained in multiple skills so that they can feel "ownership" in focused factories?
8. Is there pursuit of *job redesign* to convert dull and boring jobs to more meaningful and exciting ones?
9. Is there holistic concern for the personal welfare of employees?
10. Is there a gainsharing system in place whereby employees gain financially in return for improvements exceeding stipulated goals?

Subsystem rating   10

Appendix 3

Survey of Supplier's DOE/SPC/Reliability

	Rating	Max. Rating
A. *Specifications*		
1. Have important specification values and tolerances been determined by design of experiments (DOE) conducted by the customer?	___	5
2. Are specifications unambiguous, firm, meaningful, fair, and mutually determined by customer and supplier?	___	4
3. Are the most important specifications highlighted for the supplier?	___	3
B. *Variation Measurement*		
1. Have the most important specifications been measured for process capability in terms of c_p and c_{pk}?	___	3
2. Have those important specifications below a c_{pk} of 2.0 been targeted for systematic variation reduction?	___	3
C. *Variation Reduction Using Design of Experiments*		
1. Have multi-vari experiments been conducted to identify the "family" of the "culprit" variable—the Red X?	___	5

	Rating	Max. Rating

2. Has a variables search or full factorial experiment been run to isolate the Red X, Pink X, etc.? _____ 10

3. Has a "B" vs. "C" run been conducted to validate earlier DOE tests? _____ 5

4. Has a scatter plot study been conducted to determine optimum values and realistic tolerances of the Red X, Pink X, versus specifications? _____ 7

D. *Maintenance Tools*

1. Is a Positrol discipline (plan and logs or precontrol) in place to monitor key *process* parameters? _____ 4

2. Is there a process certification discipline to assure that all peripherals affecting product quality, such as methods and environment, are in place? _____ 5

3. Is precontrol used on key product and process variables at each work station? _____ 3

4. Is there an operator certification and recertification program? _____ 5

5. Is there a *poka-yoke* (mistake-proof) system with *sensors* to *prevent* operator errors? _____ 6

6. Is there a total preventive maintenance (TPM) system in place to assure maximum up time, minimum setup time, and maximum yields? _____ 5

E. *Reliability Assurance*

1. Are reliability prediction studies, FMEAs, and FTAs conducted by the supplier? _____ 3

2. Are destructive physical analysis (DPA) and/or tear-down audits conducted by the supplier? _____ 4

3. Are reliability stress tests conducted periodically to assure the elimination of latent defects? _____ 5

4. Is there a move toward multiple environment overstress testing in the design cycle of the supplier's product? _____ 10

5. Is there a professional, independent failure analysis laboratory to analyze failures down to the root cause? _____ 5

Total rating   Maximum = 100

Results of Survey of Quality Perceptions of Employees: Plant D

Survey Statement	% of Responses		
	Negative/ Undesired	*Positive/ Desired*	*Neutral*
1. My Plant/General Management has a strong commitment to quality.	25	60	15
2. Quality is only "talked about" but not acted upon.	40	37	23
3. Activities affecting product quality are primarily the responsibility of the Quality Assurance Dept.	44	40	16
4. If quality results were posted, it would improve the quality of my work.	26	51	23
5. My management takes fast action on the quality problems I point out.	34	35	31
6. The emphasis on quality should be mainly through more rigid inspection and test.	6	80	14

7. Good quality costs more.	39	50	11
8. The quality of parts purchased from our suppliers is adequate.	65	10	25
9. The quality of design coming into production is good.	55	6	39
10. We can meet the Japanese challenge through improved quality.	24	65	11
11. I would like to be trained in simple quality control techniques.	26	50	24
12. I would like to participate in quality problem-solving on the job.	10	70	20

13. I know what my department's goals are.   Yes <u>64%</u>   No <u>35%</u>
14. The primary factors causing quality problems for the product or service I work on are:
(Enter 1 for the most important factor, No. 2 for the second most important factor, No. 3 for the third most important factor.)

Management Direction   <u>5</u>   Work Instructions   <u>6</u>
Product Design   <u>3</u>   Training   <u>8</u>
Purchased Parts   <u>1</u>   Inspection/Test   <u>9</u>
Processes/Equipment   <u>4</u>   Time to do a Good Job   <u>2</u>
Workers   <u>7</u>

Index